Advanced Metaprogramming in Classic C++

Davide Di Gennaro

Apress®

dvanced Metaprogramming in Classic C++

3N-13 (pbk): 978-1-4842-1011-6

3N-13 (electronic): 978-1-4842-1010-9

Managing Director: Welmoed Spahr
Lead Editor: Steve Anglin
Technical Reviewer: Sverrir Sigmundarson
Editorial Board: Steve Anglin, Louise Corrigan, Jonathan Gennick, Robert Hutchinson,
Michelle Lowman, James Markham, Susan McDermott, Matthew Moodie, Jeffrey Pepper,
Douglas Pundick, Ben Renow-Clarke, Gwenan Spearing, Steve Weiss
Coordinating Editor: Mark Powers
Copy Editor: Kezia Endsley
Compositor: SPi Global
Indexer: SPi Global
Artist: SPi Global
Cover Designer: Anna Ishchenko

ributed to the book trade worldwide by Springer Science+Business Media New York, Spring Street, 6th Floor, New York, NY 10013. Phone 1-800-SPRINGER, fax (201) 348-4505, e-mail rs-ny@springer-sbm.com, or visit www.springeronline.com. Apress Media, LLC is a California LLC the sole member (owner) is Springer Science + Business Media Finance Inc (SSBM Finance Inc). M Finance Inc is a Delaware corporation.

nformation on translations, please e-mail rights@apress.com, or visit www.apress.com.

ss and friends of ED books may be purchased in bulk for academic, corporate, or promotional use. k versions and licenses are also available for most titles. For more information, reference our Special Sales–eBook Licensing web page at www.apress.com/bulk-sales.

source code or other supplementary material referenced by the author in this text is available to readers v.apress.com/9781484210116. For detailed information about how to locate your book's source code, www.apress.com/source-code/.

Template metaprogramming and expression templates are not techniques for novice programmers, but an advanced practitioner can use them to good effect.

Technical Report on C++ Performance, ISO/IEC TR 18015:2006(I

Nothing described in this report involves magic.

Technical Report on C++ Performance, ISO/IEC TR 18015:2006(I

People should not be asked to do things "just because we say so". At least we can try to explain the reasons behind the rules.

An Interview with Bjarne Stroustrup - Dr. Dobb's Journ

I hope Tibet will find this book

as interesting as all the others he reads

Contents at a Glance

About the Author x

About the Technical Reviewer x

Acknowledgments xx

Preface xx

#include <prerequisites> ....

Chapter 1: Templates ....

Chapter 2: Small Object Toolkit ....

#include <techniques> 1

Chapter 3: Static Programming 1

Chapter 4: Overload Resolution 1

Chapter 5: Interfaces 2

Chapter 6: Algorithms 2

Chapter 7: Code Generators 3

Chapter 8: Functors 3

Chapter 9: The Opaque Type Principle 4

#include <applications> 4

Chapter 10: Refactoring ....

Chapter 11: Debugging Templates ....

Chapter 12: C++0x ....

Appendix A: Exercises **527**

Appendix B: Bibliography **533**

Index **535**

Contents

About the Author xi

About the Technical Reviewer x

Acknowledgments xx

Preface xx

#include <prerequisites> ....

Chapter 1: Templates ....

1.1. C++ Templates ....

1.1.1. Typename ....

1.1.2. Angle Brackets ....

1.1.3. Universal Constructors ....

1.1.4. Function Types and Function Pointers ....

1.1.5. Non-Template Base Classes ....

1.1.6. Template Position ....

1.2. Specialization and Argument Deduction ....

1.2.1. Deduction ....

1.2.2. Specializations ....

1.2.3. Inner Class Templates ....

1.3. Style Conventions ....

1.3.1. Comments ....

1.3.2. Macros ....

1.3.3. Symbols ....

1.3.4. Generality ....

1.3.5. Template Parameters..49
1.3.6. Metafunctions..50
1.3.7. Namespaces and Using Declarations..54
1.4. Classic Patterns..57
1.4.1. size_t and ptrdiff_t..57
1.4.2. void T::swap(T&)..58
1.4.3. bool T::empty() const; void T::clear()..62
1.4.4. X T::get() const; X T::base() const..62
1.4.5. X T::property() const; void T::property(X)..63
1.4.6. Action(Value); Action(Range)..63
1.4.7. Manipulators..63
1.4.8. Position of Operators..66
1.4.9. Secret Inheritance..67
1.4.10. Literal Zero..69
1.4.11. Boolean Type..69
1.4.12. Default and Value Initialization..71
1.5. Code Safety..72
1.6. Compiler Assumptions..74
1.6.1. Inline..76
1.6.2. Error Messages..79
1.6.3. Miscellaneous Tips..81
1.7. Preprocessor..85
1.7.1. Include Guards..85
1.7.2. Macro Expansion Rules..90
Chapter 2: Small Object Toolkit..**93**
2.1. Hollow Types..93
2.1.1. instance_of..93
2.1.2. Selector..94
2.1.3. Static Value..95
2.1.4. Size of Constraints..96

2.2. Static Assertions 9

2.2.1. Boolean Assertions 9

2.2.2. Assert Legal 10

2.2.3. Assertions with Overloaded Operators 10

2.2.4. Modeling Concepts with Function Pointers 1

2.2.5. Not Implemented 10

2.3. Tagging Techniques 10

2.3.1. Type Tags 1

2.3.2. Tagging with Functions 1

2.3.3. Tag Iteration 1

2.3.4. Tags and Inheritance 1

■#include <techniques> 11

■Chapter 3: Static Programming 1

3.1. Static Programming with the Preprocessor 1

3.2. Compilation Complexity 1

3.3. Classic Metaprogramming Idioms 1

3.3.1. Static Short Circuit ....

3.4. Hidden Template Parameters 1

3.4.1. Static Recursion on Hidden Parameters ....

3.4.2. Accessing the Primary Template ....

3.4.3. Disambiguation ....

3.5. Traits ....

3.5.1. Type Traits ....

3.5.2. Type Dismantling ....

3.6. Type Containers ....

3.6.1. typeat ....

3.6.2. Returning an Error ....

3.6.3. Depth ....

3.6.4. Front and Back ....

3.6.5. Find 154
3.6.6. Push and Pop 156
3.6.7. More on Template Rotation 158
3.6.8. Agglomerates 160
3.6.9. Conversions 164
3.6.10. Metafunctors 167
3.7. A Summary of Styles 171
Chapter 4: Overload Resolution 173
4.1. Groups 173
4.1.1. From Overload to Groups 174
4.1.2. Runtime Decay 181
4.2. More Traits 183
4.2.1. A Function Set for Strings 183
4.2.2. Concept Traits 186
4.2.3. Platform-Specific Traits 189
4.2.4. Merging Traits 194
4.3. SFINAE 199
4.3.1. SFINAE Metafunctions 200
4.3.2. Multiple Decisions 204
4.3.3. Only_If 206
4.3.4. SFINAE and Returned Functors 208
4.3.5. SFINAE and Software Updates 212
4.3.6. Limitations and Workarounds 215
4.3.7. SFINAE with Partial Specializations 220
4.4. Other Classic Metafunctions with Sizeof 221
4.5. Overload on Function Pointers 223
4.5.1. Erase 223
4.5.2. Swap 224
4.5.2. Argument Dominance 226

Chapter 5: Interfaces 22
5.1. Wrapping References 23
5.2. Static Interfaces 23
5.2.1. Static Interfaces 23
5.2.2. Common Errors 23
5.2.3. A Static_Interface Implementation 2
5.2.4. The Memberspace Problem 2
5.2.5. Member Selection 2
5.3. Type Hiding 25
5.3.1. Trampolines 2
5.3.2. Typeinfo Wrapper 2
5.3.3. Option_Map 2
5.3.4. Option_Parser 2
5.3.5. Final Additions 2
5.3.6. Boundary Crossing with Trampolines 2
5.4. Variant 2
5.4.1. Parameter Deletion with Virtual Calls 2
5.4.2. Variant with Visitors 2
5.5. Wrapping Containers 2
Chapter 6: Algorithms 2
6.1. Algorithm I/O 2
6.1.1. Swap-Based or Copy-Based ....
6.1.2. Classification of Algorithms ....
6.1.3. Iterator Requirements ....
6.1.4. An Example: Set Partitioning ....
6.1.5. Identifying Iterators ....
6.1.6. Selection by Iterator Value Type ....

6.2. Generalizations 293
6.2.1. Properties and Accessors 293
6.2.2. Mimesis 297
6.2.3. End of Range 301
6.3. Iterator Wrapping 304
6.3.1. Iterator Expander 305
6.3.2. Fake Pairs 311
6.4. Receipts 317
6.5. Algebraic Requirements 320
6.5.1. Less and NaN 320
6.6. The Barton-Nackman Trick 322
Chapter 7: Code Generators 327
7.1. Static Code Generators 327
7.2. Double checked Stop 331
7.3. Static and Dynamic Hashing 335
7.3.1. A Function Set for Characters 337
7.3.2. Changing Case 341
7.3.3. Mimesis Techniques 344
7.3.4. Ambiguous Overloads 345
7.3.5. Algorithm I/O 347
7.3.6. Mimesis Interface 349
.4. Nth Minimum 351
.5. The Template Factory Pattern 357
.6. Automatic Enumeration of Types 361
.7. If-Less Code 365
7.7.1. Smart Constants 365
7.7.2. Converting Enum to String 367
7.7.3. Self-Modifying Function Tables 369

■Chapter 8: Functors 37

8.1. Strong and Weak Functors 37

8.2. Functor Composition Tools 37

8.3. Inner Template Functors 38

8.3.1. Conversion of Functions to Functors 38

8.3.2. Conversion of Members to Functors 38

8.3.3. More on the Double Wrapper Technique 39

8.4. Accumulation 39

8.4.1. A Step-by-Step Implementation 3

8.5. Drivers 40

8.6. Algors 40

8.7. Forwarding and Reference Wrappers 4

■Chapter 9: The Opaque Type Principle 4

9.1. Polymorphic Results 4

9.2. Classic Lambda Expressions 4

9.2.1. Elementary Lambda Objects ....

9.2.2. Lambda Functions and Operators ....

9.2.3. Refinements ....

9.2.4. Argument and Result Deduction ....

9.2.5. Deducing Argument Type ....

9.2.6. Deducing Result Type ....

9.2.7. Static Cast ....

9.2.8. Arrays ....

9.3. Creative Syntax ....

9.3.1. Argument Chains with () and [] ....

9.4. The Growing Object Concept ....

9.4.1. String Concatenation ....

9.4.2. Mutable Growing Objects ....

9.4.3. More Growing Objects ....

9.4.4. Chain Destruction 460
9.4.5. Variations of the Growing Object 461
9.5. Streams 463
9.5.1. Custom Manipulators and Stream Insertion 463
9.5.2. Range Insertion with a Growing Object 466
9.6. Comma Chains 468
9.7. Simulating an Infix 473
#include <applications> 475
Chapter 10: Refactoring 477
10.1. Backward Compatibility 479
10.2. Refactoring Strategies 482
10.2.1. Refactoring with Interfaces 482
10.2.2. Refactoring with Trampolines 484
10.2.3. Refactoring with Accessors 486
10.3. Placeholders 489
10.3.1. Switch-Off 489
10.3.2. The Ghost 494
Chapter 11: Debugging Templates 501
1.1. Identify Types 501
11.1.1. Trapping Types 502
11.1.2. Incomplete Types 504
11.1.3. Tag Global Variables 507
1.2. Integer Computing 508
11.2.1. Signed and Unsigned Types 508
11.2.2. References to Numeric Constants 509
1.3. Common Workarounds 510
11.3.1. Debugging SFINAE 510
11.3.2. Trampolines 510
11.3.3. Compiler Bugs 511

Chapter 12: C++0x 51

12.1. Type Traits 51

12.2. Decltype 51

12.3. Auto 51

12.4. Lambdas 51

12.5. Initializers 52

12.6. Template Typedefs 52

12.7. Extern Template 52

12.7.1. Linking Templates 5

12.7.2. Extern Template 5

12.9. Variadic Templates 5

Appendix A: Exercises 5

A.1. Exercises 5

A.1.1. Extension 5

A.1.2. Integer 5

A.1.3. Date Format 5

A.1.4. Specialization 5

A.1.5. Bit Counting 5

A.1.6. Prime Numbers 5

A.1.7. Typeinfo without RTTI 5

A.1.8. Hints and Partial Solutions 5

Appendix B: Bibliography 5

Index 5

About the Author

I'm like a dog, when you whistle: yep, yep. Template? Good, good...

—Andrei Alexandrescu, build 20

Davide loves to introduce himself as a mathematician, but a better definition would be a philosopher. After studying history of art and functional analysis, he switched to algorithm design and C++. He has been showing the marvels of metaprogramming techniques since the late 90s. As nobody could really understan him, he was eventually nicknamed "the professor". He works for big companies, where his real identity is ignored, and he spends his free time as a photographer.

Someone said that, "he makes the impossible possible".

Tibet was born on September, 6th 1998, just close to the C++ standard. He immediately showed an unusual intelligence, learning more than 100 keywords in our natural language.

Active and proud of his C++-related work, during 2014 his health started to decline. Readers often ask when he will write another book. He knows, but he simply smiles.

About the Technical Reviewer

Sverrir Sigmundarson has over 15 years of industry experience building high performance, mission-critical software for the finance and software industries. He holds an MSc degree in Computer Science from Reykjavik University in Iceland. He is currently on a special assignment as a stay-at-home-dad living in Strasbourg, France with his wife and son. He can be contacted through his website `coruscantconsulting.co.uk` or via `linkedin.com/in/sverrirs`.

Acknowledgments

Learning C++ is a process that never ends. As someone wrote, C++ is the only language whose features get discovered as though they were unexplored lands.

While a book may be the work of a single person, discovery always comes from teamwork.

The author would like to thank all the teams that made possible his journey through C++. They all had something to teach, and their contributions—direct or indirect—led to this book. His family, Carla, Alberto Tibet and Asia; the people at Logikos, especially Max; the Natam core team, Alberto L., Alberto T., Bibo, Fabio, Graziano, Marco, Roberto, Rocco; the friends at Brainpower, in particular Alberto, Andrea, Davide, Fabio, Giacomo, Giancarlo, Luca, Marco D., Marco M., Matteo, Paolo, Pino, Vincenzo; and all the others.

I would like thank the many people at Apress who worked on the book, including Steve Anglin who talked me into it, Mark Powers for managing the project, Sverrir Sigmundarson for a fine job as technical reviewer, Jeff Pepper and Kezia Endsley for clarifying the words.

Many Googlers kindly reviewed the first chapters of the draft and provided suggestions, fixes, constructive criticism, exercises, or simply appreciation.

A very special thank goes to Attilio Meucci, who proved that writing a book is not impossible, and it's always worthwhile.

Preface

Template Metaprogramming (TMP from here on) is a new way of using C++:

- It has a *scope*: a known set of problems where it proves useful.
- It has a *philosophy*: a peculiar way of thinking about problems.
- It has a *language*: idioms and patterns.

This book, according to the 80-20 law, aims to be an introduction to the first 20% of metaprogramming—its philosophy, scope, and language—that can improve 80% of daily programming activities. All the chapters are driven by some simple ideas:

- With modern compilers, most practical benefits come from simple techniques, when correctly applied.
- TMP indeed produces better software. "Better" is simply a placeholder for faster, safer, more maintainable, more expressive, or a combination of these features.
- State-of-the-art TMP libraries usually offer a huge set of features. Unfortunately, documentation is either too large or too small. While reuse is a long-term winning strategy, mastering the basic principles may suffice.
- Getting gradually accustomed with elementary techniques, the reader will develop a deeper comprehension of the problems and eventually, if necessary, look for more advanced tools.

The reader is assumed at ease with classic C++ programming, including STL concepts and conventio

A systematic study of TMP exceeds the capacity (in C++ sense) of any single book. With over five year invested in creating this book, I hope you will find it more than a useful starting point. For comprehensive and robust training, the interested reader may want to see the bibliography.

Source Code

This book is not focused on results, but on the path—the steps and motivations that lead to a project's implementation. Many examples derive from production code. However, in a book, problems must look a easy and evident as possible, sometimes even more. In practice, they are never this way.

So for illustration purposes, the source code is unquestionably sub-optimal and oversimplified. Oversimplification means partial or full omission of implementation details, special cases, namespaces, system headers, compiler bugs, and so on. The most advanced programming technique is hardly an advantage if it crashes the company's official compiler.

In short, these details are important, as they make the difference between a curious prototype and a useful implementation.

In addition, code has been streamlined to satisfy visual constraints. In particular, indentation is systematically inconsistent, some function bodies have been removed, names may be shorter than necessary, and macros have been introduced for the sole purpose of shortening the text.

Readers are asked to be patient and review the Errata section that follows.

Finally, I admit that results are rarely supported with experimental data. TMP techniques give a compiler e opportunity to create optimized code, and as a rule, this book doesn't verify that it is indeed the case.

lassic and Modern C++

e C++ standard is being updated with lots of new features. The first edition of the document in 1998 had wer than 800 pages. A 200-page technical report was published in 2003 and revised in 2006. In March 2010, e committee released the FCD, a milestone draft more than 1,300 pages long. In August 2014, the vote approve the C++14 standard was completed. Some of the new language additions have already been plemented in compilers.

This book deals with a very small part of "C++0x" (yes, I use the familiar nickname of the new standard) d "C++14". More precisely, it discusses what has a serious impact on TMP code and is also available in the jor compilers. The focus of the book remains on classic C++, which can be utilized in any implementation C++. The so-called "modern C++" constituting the revisions incorporated in C++11 and C++14 is the topic discussion in Chapter 12 and is referenced accordingly in other parts of this book.

ook Structure

book is divided into three sections, and chapters are designed to be read in order. Each chapter starts h its own rationale, or a summary of the motivations for previous arguments.

The first section deals with the basics, and in particular Chapter 2 is a prerequisite for most of the rce code contained in the book. Chapter 2 contains a description of the basic class templates that will be stantly and silently reused without further comments.

The second part of the book develops some techniques for writing software, in the approximate order of reasing complexity.

The third part contains some practical advice for real-world issues, so it has been pretentiously labeled plications".

I refer to some compilers with abbreviations, followed by a version number: MSVC for Microsoft Visual - and GCC for GNU G++.

From time to time, I show the output of some compiler, without mentioning explicitly which one, to hasize what a "generic" compiler would emit.

This is a note. The following text contains a sample of the typographic conventions used in this book.

```
lename.cpp
->is(source*code);
```

This is the resulting compiler output.
The same format denotes an algorithm description in pseudo-code.

```
i = [[double square brackets denote
      a piece of pseudo-code inside valid code]];
```

Odd for a book that emphasizes readability, fragments of source code have no syntax highlighting, so will look scarier than they actually are.

Errata

Readers are encouraged to send their feedback to the book's page on Apress.com (www.apress.com/9781484210116).

Errata are published regularly on http://acppmp.blogspot.com.

Note to the Third Revision

This book was born in 2005, when C++11 was yet to come, and finished just before the new standard was published. On purpose, most of the new techniques on the way were ignored, simply because they were not widely available, not finalized, or just not completely understood. None of the revisions of this book changed this view, which is still essentially correct. So, while vendors are still releasing C++11 compilers, nc herculean attempt was made to upgrade the book contents.

Nonetheless, this should not be considered a limitation in any way. Starting TMP at a low level and wit simpler language tools means that your code will run on existing compilers, and is a powerful educational experience, and it will lead to a stronger appreciation of all the "syntactic sugar" that modern C++ offers.

PART 1

#include <prerequisites>
#include <techniques>
#include <applications>

CHAPTER 1

Templates

"C++ supports a variety of styles."

Bjarne Stroustrup, A Perspective on ISO C

Programming is the process of teaching something to a computer by talking to the machine in one of its common languages. The closer to the machine idiom you go, the less natural the words become.

Each language carries its own expressive power. For any given concept, there is a language where its description is simpler, more concise, and more detailed. In assembler, we have to give an extremely rich and precise description for any (possibly simple) algorithm, and this makes it very hard to read back. On the other hand, the beauty of C++ is that, while being close enough to the machine language, the language carries enough instruments to enrich itself.

C++ allows programmers to express the same concept with different *styles* and good C++ looks more natur

First you are going to see the connection between the templates and the style, and then you will dig ir the details of the C++ template system.

Given this C++ fragment:

```
double x = sq(3.14);
```

Can you guess what sq is? It could be a macro:

```
#define sq(x) ((x)*(x))
```

A function:

```
double sq(double x)
{
   return x*x;
}
```

A function template:

```
template <typename scalar_t>
inline scalar_t sq(const scalar_t& x)
{
   return x*x;
}
```

A type (an unnamed instance of a class that decays to a double):

```
lass sq

 double s_;

blic:

 sq(double x)
 : s_(x*x)
 {}

 operator double() const
 { return s_; }
```

A global object:

```
ass sq_t

lic:
 typedef double value_type;

 value_type operator()(double x) const
 {
    return x*x;
 }

st sq_t sq = sq_t();
```

Regardless of how sq(3.14) is implemented, most humans can guess what sq(3.14) does just looking . However, *visual equivalence* does not imply *interchangeableness*. If sq is a class, for example, passing a are to a function template will trigger an unexpected argument deduction:

```
plate <typename T> void f(T x);

s(3.14)); // instantiates f<double>
(3.14));  // instantiates f<sq>. counterintuitive?
```

Furthermore, you would expect every possible numeric type to be squared as efficiently as possible, but rent implementations may perform differently in different situations:

```
:vector<double> v;
:transform(v.begin(), v.end(), v.begin(), sq);
```

If you need to transform a sequence, most compilers will get a performance boost from the last ementation of sq (and an error if sq is a macro).

The purpose of TMP is to write code that is:

- Visually clear to human users so that nobody needs to look underneath.
- Efficient in most/all situations from the point of view of the compiler.
- Self-adapting to the rest of the program.[1]

Self-adapting means "portable" (independent of any particular compiler) and "not imposing constraints". An implementation of sq that requires its argument to derive from some abstract base class would not qualify as self-adapting.

The true power of C++ templates is *style*. Compare the following equivalent lines:

```
double x1 = (-b + sqrt(b*b-4*a*c))/(2*a);

double x2 = (-b + sqrt(sq(b)-4*a*c))/(2*a);
```

All template argument computations and deductions are performed at compile time, so they impose no runtime overhead. If the function sq is properly written, line 2 is at least as efficient as line 1 and easier t read at the same time.

Using sq is elegant:

- It makes code readable or self-evident
- It carries no speed penalty
- It leaves the program open to future optimizations

In fact, after the concept of squaring has been isolated from plain multiplication, you can easily plug i specializations:

```
template <typename scalar_t>
inline scalar_t sq(const scalar_t& x)
{
   return x*x;
}

template <>
inline double sq(const double& x)
{
   // here, use any special algorithm you have!
}
```

[1]Loosely speaking, that's the reason for the "meta" prefix in "metaprogramming".

.1. C++ Templates

ıe classic C++ language admits two basic types of templates—*function templates* and *class templates*[2]:

Here is a function template:

```
mplate <typename scalar_t>
alar_t sq(const scalar_t& x)

 return x*x;
```

Here is a class template:

```
nplate

 typename scalar_t,                // type parameter
 bool EXTRA_PRECISION = false,     // bool parameter with default value
 typename promotion_t = scalar_t // type parameter with default value

ıss sum

 // ...
```

When you supply suitable values to all its parameters, a template generates entities during compilation. ınction template will produce functions and a class template will produce classes. The most important as from the TMP viewpoint can be summarized as follows:

- You can exploit class templates to perform computations at compile time.
- Function templates can auto-deduce their parameters from arguments. If you call `sq(3.14)`, the compiler will automatically figure out that `scalar_t` is `double`, generate the function `sq<double>`, and insert it at the call site.

Both kinds of template entities start declaring a *parameter list* in angle brackets. Parameters can include *s* (declared with the keyword `typename` or `class`) and non-types: integers and pointers.[3]

Note that, when the parameter list is long or when you simply want to comment each parameter arately, you may want to indent it as if it were a block of code within curly brackets.

Parameters can in fact have a default value:

```
<double> S1;                   // template argument is 'double', EXTRA_PRECISION is false
<double, true> S2;
```

---

odern C++ there are more, but you can consider them extensions; the ones described here are metaprogramming class citizens. Chapter 12 has more details.

ally any integer type is accepted, including named/anonymous `enum`, `bool`, typedefs (like `ptrdiff_t` and `size_t`), ven compiler-specific types (for example, `__int64` in MSVC). Pointers to member/global functions are allowed no restriction; a pointer to a variable (having external linkage) is legal, but it cannot be dereferenced *at compile* so this has very limited use in practice. See Chapter 11.

A template can be seen as a metafunction that maps a tuple of parameters to a function or a class. For example, the sq template

```
template <typename scalar_t>
scalar_t sq(const scalar_t& x);
```

maps a type T to a function:

```
T → T (*)(const T&)
```

In other words, sq<double> is a function with signature double (*)(const double&). Note that doubl is the value of the parameter scalar_t.

Conversely, the class template

```
template <typename char_t = char>
class basic_string;
```

maps a type T to a class:

```
T → basic_string<T>
```

With classes, *explicit specialization* can limit the domain of the metafunction. You have a general template and then some specializations; each of these may or may not have a body.

```
// the following template can be instantiated
// only on char and wchar_t

template <typename char_t = char>
class basic_string;
// note: no body

template < >
class basic_string<char>
{ ... };

template < >
class basic_string<wchar_t>
{ ... };
```

char_t and scalar_t are called *template parameters*. When basic_string<char> and sq<double> ar used, char and double are called *template arguments*, even if there may be some confusion between doub (the template argument of sq) and x (the argument of the function sq<double>).

When you supply template arguments (both types and non-types) to the template, seen as a metafunction, the template is *instantiated*, so if necessary the compiler produces machine code for the entity that the template produces.

Note that different arguments yield different instances, even when instances themselves are identica sq<double> and sq<const double> are two unrelated functions.[4]

---

[4]The linker may eventually collapse them, as they will likely produce identical machine code, but from a language perspective they are different.

When using function templates, the compiler will usually figure out the parameters. We say that an gument *binds* to a template parameter.

```
mplate <typename scalar_t>
alar_t sq(const scalar_t& x) { return x*x; }

uble pi = 3.14;
(pi);                              // the compiler "binds" double to scalar_t

uble x = sq(3.14);                 // ok: the compiler deduces that scalar_t is double
uble x = sq<double>(3.14);         // this is legal, but less than ideal
```

All template arguments must be compile-time constants.

- Type parameters will accept everything known to be a type.
- Non-type parameters work according to the most automatic casting/promotion rule.[5]

Here are some typical errors:

```
plate <int N>
ss SomeClass


main()

int A = rand();
SomeClass<A> s;          // error: A is not a compile time constant

const int B = rand();
SomeClass<B> s;          // error: B is not a compile time constant

static const int C = 2;
SomeClass<C> s;          // OK
```

The best syntax for a compile-time constant in classic C++ is `static const [[integer type]]` `= value;`.

The static prefix could be omitted if the constant is local, in the body of a function, as shown previously. ever, it's both harmless and clear (you can find all the compile-time constants in a project by searching `static const`" rather than "`const`" alone).[6]

xception being that literal 0 may not be a valid pointer.

ections 1.3.6 and **11.2.2** for more complete discussions.

The arguments passed to the template can be the result of a (compile-time) computation. Every valid integer operation can be evaluated on compile-time constants:

- Division by zero causes a compiler error.
- Function calls are forbidden.[7]
- Code that produces an intermediate object of non-integer/non-pointer type is non-portable, except when inside `sizeof`: `(int)(N*1.2)`, which is illegal. Instead use `(N+N/5)`. `static_cast<void*>(0)` is fine too.[8]

```
SomeClass<(27+56*5) % 4> s1;
SomeClass<sizeof(void*)*CHAR_BIT> s1;
```

Division by zero will cause a compiler error only if the computation is entirely static. To see the difference, note that this program compiles (but it won't run).

```
template <int N>
struct tricky
{
   int f(int i = 0)
   {
      return i/N;             // i/N is not a constant
   }
};

int main()
{
   tricky<0> t;
   return t.f();
}

test.cpp(5) : warning C4723: potential divide by 0
```

On the other hand, compare the preceding listing with the following two, where the division by zero happens during compilation (in two different contexts):

```
int f()
{
   return N/N;             // N/N is a constant
}

test.cpp(5) : error C2124: divide or mod by zero
        .\test.cpp(5) : while compiling class template member function
                        'int tricky<N>::f(void)'
        with
        [
            N=0
        ]
```

[7]See the note in Section 1.3.2.

[8]You can cast a floating-point literal to integer, so strictly speaking, `(int)(1.2)` is allowed. Not all compilers are rigorous in regard to this rule.

And with:

```
icky<0/0> t;
```

```
st.cpp(12) : error C2975: 'N' : invalid template argument for 'tricky',
pected compile-time constant expression
```

More precisely, compile-time constants can be:

- Integer literals, for example, `27`, `CHAR_BIT`, and `0x05`
- `sizeof` and similar non-standard language operators with an integer result (for example, `__alignof__` where present)
- Non-type template parameters (in the context of an "outer" template)

```
template <int N>
class AnotherClass
{
   SomeClass<N> myMember_;
};
```

- Static constants of integer type

```
template <int N, int K>
struct MyTemplate
{
   static const int PRODUCT = N*K;
};

SomeClass< MyTemplate<10,12>::PRODUCT > s1;
```

- Some standard macros, such as `__LINE__` (There is actually some degree of freedom; as a rule they are constants with type `long`, except in implementation-dependent "edit and continue" debug builds, where the compiler must use references. In this case, using the macro will cause a compilation error.)[9]

```
SomeClass<__LINE__> s1;  // usually works...
```

A parameter can depend on a previous parameter:

```
plate
<
ypename T,
nt (*FUNC)(T)    // pointer to function taking T and returning int
>
s X
```

ıse of `__LINE__` as a parameter in practice occurs rarely; it's popular in automatic type enumerations (see Section 7.6) ı some implementation of custom assertions.

```
template
<
   typename T,      // here the compiler learns that 'T' is a type
   T VALUE          // may be ok or not... the compiler assumes the best
>
class Y
{
};

Y<int, 7> y1;       // fine
Y<double, 3> y2;    // error: the constant '3' cannot have type 'double'
```

Classes (and class templates) may also have *template member functions*:

```
// normal class with template member function

struct mathematics
{
   template <typename scalar_t>
   scalar_t sq(scalar_t x) const
   {
      return x*x;
   }
};

// class template with template member function

template <typename scalar_t>
struct more_mathematics
{
   template <typename other_t>10
   static scalar_t product(scalar_t x, other_t y)
   {
      return x*y;
   }
};

double A = mathematics().sq(3.14);
double B = more_mathematics<double>().product(3.14, 5);
```

1.1.1. Typename

The keyword typename is used:

- As a synonym of class, when declaring a type template parameter
- Whenever it's not evident to the compiler that an identifier is a type name

[10]We have to choose a different name, to avoid shadowing the outer template parameter scalar_t.

For an example of “not evident” think about `MyClass<T>::Y` in the following fragment:

```
mplate <typename T>
ruct MyClass

 typedef double Y;                          // Y may or may not be a type
 typedef T Type;                            // Type is always a type


mplate < >
ruct MyClass<int>

 static const int Y = 314;                  // Y may or may not be a type
 typedef int Type;                          // Type is always a type


t Q = 8;

nplate <typename T>
id SomeFunc()

MyClass<T>::Y * Q; // what is this line? it may be:
                   // the declaration of local pointer-to-double named Q;
                   // or the product of the constant 314, times the global variable Q
```

Y is a *dependent name*, since its meaning depends on T, which is an unknown parameter.

Everything that depends directly or indirectly on unknown template parameters is a dependent name. dependent name refers to a type, then it must be introduced with the typename keyword.

```
plate <typename X>
ss AnotherClass

MyClass<X>::Type t1_;            // error: 'Type' is a dependent name
typename MyClass<X>::Type t2_;   // ok

MyClass<double>::Type t3_;       // ok: 'Type' is independent of X
```

Note that typename is required in the first case and forbidden in the last:

```
late <typename X>
s AnotherClass

ypename MyClass<X>::Y member1_;        // ok, but it won't compile if X is 'int'.
ypename MyClass<double>::Y member2_; // error
```

typename may introduce a dependent type when declaring a non-type template parameter:

```
template <typename T, typename T::type N>
struct SomeClass
{
};

struct S1
{
   typedef int type;
};

SomeClass<S1, 3> x;    // ok: N=3 has type 'int'
```

As a curiosity, the classic C++ standard specifies that if the syntax typename T1::T2 yields a non-type during instantiation, then the program is ill-formed. However, it doesn't specify the converse: if T1::T2 has valid meaning as a non-type, then it could be re-interpreted later as a type, if necessary. For example:

```
template <typename T>
struct B
{
   static const int N = sizeof(A<T>::X);
   // should be: sizeof(typename A...)
};
```

Until instantiation, B "thinks" it's going to call sizeof on a non-type; in particular, sizeof is a valid operator on non-types, so the code is legal. However, X could later resolve to a type, and the code would be legal anyway:

```
template <typename T>
struct A
{
   static const int X = 7;
};

template <>
struct A<char>
{
   typedef double X;
};
```

Although the intent of typename is to forbid all such ambiguities, it may not cover all corner cases.[11]

[11]See also http://www.open-std.org/jtc1/sc22/wg21/docs/cwg_defects.html#666.

1.2. Angle Brackets

en if all parameters have a default value, you cannot entirely omit the angle brackets:

```
nplate <typename T = double>
ass sum {};

n<> S1;      // ok, using double
n S2;        // error
```

Template parameters may carry different meanings:

- Sometimes they are really meant to be generic, for example, `std::vector<T>` or `std::set<T>`. There may be some conceptual assumptions about T—say constructible, comparable...—that do not compromise the generality.
- Sometimes parameters are assumed to belong to a fixed set. In this case, the class template is simply the common implementation for two or more similar classes.[12]

In the latter case, you may want to provide a set of regular classes that are used without angle brackets, ou can either derive them from a template base or just use `typedef`[13]:

```
plate <typename char_t = char>
ss basic_string

 // this code compiles only when char_t is either 'char' or 'wchar_t'
 // ...


ss my_string : public basic_string<>

// empty or minimal body
// note: no virtual destructor!


edef basic_string<wchar_t> your_string;
```

A popular compiler extension (officially part of C++0x) is that two or more adjacent "close angle kets" will be parsed as "end of template," not as an "extraction operator". Anyway, with older compilers, ood practice to add extra spaces:

```
:vector<std::list<double>> v1;
                         ^^
ay be parsed as "operator>>"

:vector<std::list<double> > v2;
                         ^^^
lways ok
```

---

n if it's not a correct example, an open-minded reader may want to consider the relationship between `std::string`, `:wstring`, and `std::basic_string<T>`.
1.4.9.

1.1.3. Universal Constructors

A template copy constructor and an assignment are not called when dealing with two objects of the very same kind:

```
template <typename T>
class something
{
public:
   // not called when S == T
   template <typename S>
   something(const something<S>& that)
   {
   }

   // not called when S == T
   template <typename S>
   something& operator=(const something<S>& that)
   {
      return *this;
   }
};

   something<int> s0;
   something<double> s1, s2;

   s0 = s1;    // calls user defined operator=
   s1 = s2;    // calls the compiler generated assignment
```

The user-defined template members are sometimes called *universal copy constructors* and *universal assignments*. Note that universal operators take `something<X>`, not `X`.

The C++ Standard 12.8 says:

- "Because a template constructor is never a copy constructor, the presence of such a template does not suppress the implicit declaration of a copy constructor."
- "Template constructors participate in overload resolution with other constructors, including copy constructors, and a template constructor may be used to copy an object if it provides a better match than other constructors."

In fact, having very generic template operators in base classes can introduce bugs, as this example shows:

```
struct base
{
   base() {}

   template <typename T>
   base(T x) {}
};
```

```
:ruct derived : base

 derived() {}

 derived(const derived& that)
 : base(that) {}


 derived d1;
 derived d2 = d1;
```

The assignment d2 = d1 causes a stack overflow.

An implicit copy constructor must invoke the copy constructor of the base class, so by 12.8 above it can ver call the universal constructor. Had the compiler generated a copy constructor for derived, it would ve called the base copy constructor (which is implicit). Unfortunately, a copy constructor for derived given, and it contains an explicit function call, namely base(that). Hence, following the usual overload olution rules, it matches the universal constructor with T=derived. Since this function takes x by value, eeds to perform a copy of that, and hence the call is recursive.[14]

1.4. Function Types and Function Pointers

nd the difference between a function type and a pointer-to-function type:

```
plate <double F(int)>
uct A



plate <double (*F)(int)>
uct B
```

They are mostly equivalent:

```
ole f(int)

return 3.14;


<f> t1;    // ok
<f> t2;    // ok
```

side note, this shows once more that in TMP, the less code you write, the better.

Usually a function decays to a function pointer exactly as an array decays to a pointer. But a function type cannot be constructed, so it will cause failures in code that look harmless:

```
template <typename T>
struct X
{
   T member_;

   X(T value)
   : member_(value)
   {
   }
};

X<double (int)> t1(f);          // error: cannot construct 'member_'
X<double (*)(int)> t2(f);       // ok: 'member_' is a pointer
```

This problem is mostly evident in functions that return a functor (the reader can think about std::not or see Section **4.3.4**). In C++, function templates that get parameters by reference prevent the decay:

```
template <typename T>
X<T> identify_by_val(T x)
{
   return X<T>(x);
}

template <typename T>
X<T> identify_by_ref(const T& x)
{
   return X<T>(x);
}

double f(int)
{
   return 3.14;
}

identify_by_val(f);  // function decays to pointer-to-function:
                     // template instantiated with T = double (*)(int)

identify_by_ref(f);  // no decay:
                     // template instantiated with T = double (int)
```

For what concerns pointers, function templates with explicit parameters behave like ordinary functio

```
double f(double x)
{
   return x+1;
}
```

```
emplate <typename T>
 g(T x)

  return x+1;


pedef double (*FUNC_T)(double);

NC_T f1 = f;
NC_T f2 = g<double>;
```

However, if they are members of class templates and their context depends on a yet unspecified
rameter, they require an extra template keyword before their name[15]:

```
nplate <typename X>
ruct outer

 template <typename T>
 static T g(T x)
 {
    return x+1;
 }


plate <typename X>
d do_it()

 FUNC_T f1 = outer<X>::g<double>;                 // error!
 FUNC_T f2 = outer<X>::template g<double>;        // correct
```

Both typename and template are required for inner template classes:

```
plate <typename X>
uct outer

template <typename T>
struct inner {};


late <typename X>
 do_it()

ypename outer<X>::template inner<double> I;
```

Some compilers are not rigorous at this.

---

npare with the use of typename described in Section1.1.1.

1.1.5. Non-Template Base Classes

If a class template has members that do not depend on its parameters, it may be convenient to move them into a plain class:

```
template <typename T>
class MyClass
{
   double value_;
   std::string name_;
   std::vector<T> data_;

public:
   std::string getName() const;
};
```

should become:

```
class MyBaseClass
{
protected:
   ~MyBaseClass() {}

   double value_;
   std::string name_;

public:
   std::string getName() const;
};

template <typename T>
class MyClass : MyBaseClass
{
   std::vector<T> data_;

public:
   using MyBaseClass::getName;
};
```

The derivation may be public, private, or even protected.[16] This will reduce the compilation complexity and potentially the size of the binary code. Of course, this optimization is most effective if the template is instantiated many times.

[16]See the "brittle base class problem" mentioned by Bjarne Stroustrup in his "C++ Style and Technique FAQ" at `http://www.research.att.com/~bs/`.

.1.6. Template Position

ne body of a class/function template must be available to the compiler at every point of instantiation, the usual header/cpp file separation does not hold, and everything is packaged in a single file, with the p extension.

If only a declaration is available, the compiler will use it, but the linker will return errors:

```
 sq.h

mplate <typename T>
sq(const T& x);

 sq.cpp

mplate <typename T>
sq(const T& x)

 return x*x;


 main.cpp

clude "sq.h"                    // note: function body not visible

 main()

double x = sq(3.14);      // compiles but does not link
```

A separate header file is useful if you want to publish only some instantiations of the template. For example, author of sq might want to distribute binary files with the code for sq<int> and sq<double>, so that they the only valid types.

In C++, it's possible to explicitly force the instantiation of a template entity in a translation unit without r using it. This is accomplished with the special syntax:

```
plate class X<double>;

plate double sq<double>(const double&);
```

Adding this line to sq.cpp will "export" sq<double> as if it were an ordinary function, and the plain usion of sq.h will suffice to build the program.

This feature is often used with algorithm tags. Suppose you have a function template, say encrypt or ress, whose algorithmic details must be kept confidential. Template parameter T represents an option a small set (say T=fast, normal, best); obviously, users of the algorithm are not supposed to add own options, so you can force the instantiation of a small number of instances—encrypt<fast>, ypt<normal>, and encrypt<best>—and distribute just a header and a binary file.

---

ote C++0x adds to the language the external instantiation of templates. If the keyword extern is used e template, the compiler will skip instantiation and the linker will borrow the template body from another lation unit.

See also Section 1.6.1 below.

1.2. Specialization and Argument Deduction

By definition, we say that a name is *at namespace level*, at *class level*, or *at body level* when the name appea between the curly brackets of a namespace, class, or function body, as the following example shows:

```
class X                               // here, X is at namespace level
{
public:
   typedef double value_type;         // value_type is at class level

   X(const X& y)                      // both X and y are at class level
   {
   }

   void f()                           // f is at class level
   {
      int z = 0;                      //    body level
      struct LOCAL {};                //    LOCAL is a local class
   }
};
```

Function templates—member or non-member—can automatically deduce the template argument looking at their argument list. Roughly speaking,[17] the compiler will pick the most specialized function th matches the arguments. An exact match, if feasible, is always preferred, but a conversion can occur.

A function F is more specialized than G if you can replace any call to F with a call to G (on the same arguments), but not vice versa. In addition, a non-template function is considered more specialized than template with the same name.

Sometimes *overload* and *specialization* look very similar:

```
template <typename scalar_t>
inline scalar_t sq(const scalar_t& x);  // (1) function template

inline double sq(const double& x);      // (2) overload

template <>
inline int sq(const int& x);            // (3) specialization of 1
```

But they are not identical; consider the following counter-example:

```
inline double sq(float x);              // ok, overloaded sq may
                                        // have different signature

template <>                             // error: invalid specialization
inline int sq(const int x);             // it must have the same signature
```

[17]The exact rules are documented and explained in **[2]**. You're invited to refer to this book for a detailed explanation what's summarized here in a few paragraphs.

The basic difference between overload and specialization is that a function template acts as a single ity, regardless of how many specializations it has. For example, the call sq(y) just after (3) would force compiler to select between entities (1) and (2). If y is double, then (2) is preferred, because it's a normal ction; otherwise, (1) is instantiated based on the type of y: only at this point, if y happens to be int, the npiler notices that sq has a specialization and picks (3).

Note that two different templates may overload:

```
plate <typename T>
d f(const T& x)

std::cout << "I am f(reference)";




plate <typename T>
d f(const T* x)

std::cout << "I am f(pointer)";
```

On the other hand, writing a specialization when overloaded templates are present may require you to cify explicitly the parameters:

```
plate <typename T> void f(T) {}
plate <typename T> void f(T*) {}

plate <>
d f(int*)          // ambiguous: may be the first f with T=int*
                   // or the second with T=int

plate <>
d f<int>(int*)  // ok
```

Remember that template specialization is legal only at the namespace level (even if most compilers will ate it anyway):

```
s mathematics

emplate <typename scalar_t>
nline scalar_t sq(const scalar_t& x) { ... }; // template member function

emplate <>
nline int sq(const int& x) { ... };            // illegal specialization!
```

The standard way is to call a global function template from inside the class:

```
lobal function template: outside
late <typename scalar_t>
ne scalar_t gsq(const scalar_t& x) { ... };
```

```
// specialization: outside
template <>
inline int gsq(const int& x) { ... };

class mathematics
{
   // template member function
   template <typename scalar_t>
   inline scalar_t sq(const scalar_t& x)
   {
      return gsq(x);
   }
};
```

Sometimes you may need to specify explicitly the template parameters because they are unrelated to function arguments (in fact, they are called *non-deducible*):

```
class crc32 { ... };
class adler { ... };

template <typename algorithm_t>
size_t hash_using(const char* x)
{
   // ...
}

size_t j = hash_using<crc32>("this is the string to be hashed");
```

In this case, you must put non-deducible types and arguments first, so the compiler can work out all t remaining:

```
template <typename algorithm_t, typename string_t>
int hash_using(const string_t& x);

std::string arg("hash me, please");
int j = hash_using<crc32>(arg);          // ok: algorithm_t is crc32
                                         // and string_t is std::string
```

Argument deduction obviously holds only for function templates, not for class templates.

It's generally a bad idea to supply an argument explicitly, instead of relying on deduction, except in some special cases, described next.

- When necessary for disambiguation:

```
template <typename T>
T max(const T& a, const T& b)
{ ... }

int a = 7;
long b = 6;
```

```
long m1 = max(a, b);          // error: ambiguous, T can be int or long
long m2 = max<long>(a, b); // ok: T is long
```

- When a type is non-deducible[18]:

```
template <typename T>
T get_random()
{ ... }

double r = get_random<double>();
```

- When you want a function template to look similar to a built-in C++ cast operator:

```
template <typename X, typename T>
X sabotage_cast(T* p)
{
   return reinterpret_cast<X>(p+1);
}

std::string s = "don't try this at home";
double* p = sabotage_cast<double*>(&s);
```

- To perform simultaneously a cast and a function template invocation:

```
double y = sq<int>(6.28)   // casts 6.28 to int, then squares the value
```

- When an algorithm has an argument whose default value is template-dependent (usually a functor)[19]:

```
template <typename LESS_T>
void nonstd_sort (..., LESS_T cmp = LESS_T())
{
   // ...
}

// call function with functor passed as template argument
nonstd_sort< std::less<...> > (...);

// call function with functor passed as value argument
nonstd_sort (..., std::less<...>());
```

A template name (such as std::vector) is different from the name of the class it generates (such as :vector<int>). At the class level, they are equivalent:

```
late <typename T>
s something
```

---

the next section.

s example is taken from [2].

```
public:
   something() // ok: don't write something<T>
   {
      // at local level, 'something' alone is illegal
   }

   something(const something& that); // ok: 'something&' stands for
                                     // 'something<T>&'

   template <typename other_t>
   something(const something<other_t>& that)
   {
   }
};
```

As a rule, the word something alone, without angle brackets, represents a template, which is a well-defined entity of its own. In C++, there are *template-template parameters*. You can declare a template whose parameters are not just types, but are class templates that match a given pattern:

```
template <template <typename T> class X>
class example
{
   X<int> x1_;
   X<double> x2_;
};

typedef example<something> some_example; // ok: 'something' matches
```

Note that class and typename are not equivalent here:

```
template <template <typename T> typename X>     // error
```

Class templates can be fully or partially *specialized*. After the general template, we list specialized versions:

```
// in general T is not a pointer
template <typename T>
struct is_a_pointer_type
{
   static const int value = 1;
};

// 2: full specialization for void*
template <>
struct is_a_pointer_type<void*>
{
   static const int value = 2;
};
```

```
' 3: partial specialization for all pointers
mplate <typename X>
ruct is_a_pointer_type<X*>

 static const int value = 3;


t b1 = is_a_pointer_type<int*>::value;  // uses 3 with X=int
t b2 = is_a_pointer_type<void*>::value; // uses 2
t b3 = is_a_pointer_type<float>::value; // uses the general template
```

Partial specialization can be recursive:

```
nplate <typename X>
ruct is_a_pointer_type<const X>

static const int value = is_a_pointer_type<X>::value;
```

The following example is known as *the pointer paradox*:

```
clude <iostream>

plate <typename T>
d f(const T& x)

std::cout << "My arg is a reference";


plate <typename T>
d f(const T* x)

std::cout << " My arg is a pointer";
```

In fact, the following code prints as expected:

```
st char* s = "text";
;
14);

rg is a pointer
rg is a reference
```

Now write instead:

```
le p = 0;
);
```

You would expect to read `pointer`; instead you get a call to the *first* overload. The compiler is correct, type `double*` matches `const T*` with one trivial implicit conversion (namely, adding const-ness), but it hes `const T&` perfectly, setting `T=double*`.

1.2.1. Deduction

Function templates can deduce their parameters, matching argument types with their signature:

```
template <typename T>
struct arg;

template <typename T>
void f(arg<T>);

template <typename X>
void g(arg<const X>);

arg<int*> a;
f(a);                 // will deduce T = int*

arg<const int> b;
f(b);                 // will deduce T = const int
g(b);                 // will deduce X = int
```

Deduction also covers non-type arguments:

```
template < int I>
struct arg;

template <int I>
arg<I+1> f(arg<I>);

arg<3> a;
f(a);                 // will deduce I=3 and thus return arg<4>
```

However, remember that deduction is done via "pattern matching" and the compiler is not required to perform any kind of algebra[20]:

```
// this template is formally valid, but deduction will never succeed...
template <int I>
arg<I> f(arg<I+1>)
{
   // ...
}

arg<3> a;
f(a);                 // ...the compiler will not solve the equation I+1==3
arg<2+1> b;
f(b);                 // ...error again
```

```
No matching function for call to 'f'
Candidate template ignored: couldn't infer template argument 'I'
```

[20]In particular, the compiler is not required to notice that `void f(arg<2*N>)` and `void f(arg<N+N>)` are the same template function, and such a double definition would make a program ill-formed. In practice, however, most compilers will recognize an ambiguity and emit an appropriate error.

On the other hand, if a type is contained in a class template, then its context (the parameters of the iter class) cannot be deduced:

```
mplate <typename T>
id f(typename std::vector<T>::iterator);

d::vector<double> v;
v.begin());                // error: cannot deduce T
```

Note that this error does *not* depend on the particular invocation. This kind of deduction is logically not ssible; T may not be unique.

```
mplate <typename T>
ruct A
typedef double type; };

 if A<X>::type is double, X could be anything
```

A dummy argument can be added to enforce consistency:

```
plate <typename T>
d f(std::vector<T>&, typename std::vector<T>::iterator);
```

The compiler will deduce T from the first argument and then verify that the second argument has the rect type.

You could also supply explicitly a value for T when calling the function:

```
plate <typename T>
d f(typename std::vector<T>::iterator);

::vector<double> w;
ouble>(w.begin());
```

Experience shows that it's better to minimize the use of function templates with non-deduced ameters. Automatic deduction usually gives better error messages and easier function lookup; the owing section lists some common cases.

First, when a function is invoked with template syntax, the compiler does not necessarily look for a plate. This can produce obscure error messages.

```
ct base

emplate <int I, typename X>     // template, where I is non-deduced
oid foo(X, X)
```

```
struct derived : public base
{
   void foo(int i)                    // not a template
   {
      foo<314>(i, i);                 // line #13
   }
};
```

```
1>error: 'derived::foo': function call missing argument list; use '&derived::foo' to create
a pointer to member
1>error: '<' : no conversion from 'int' to 'void (__cdecl derived::* )(int)'
1>    There are no conversions from integral values to pointer-to-member values
1>error: '<' : illegal, left operand has type 'void (__cdecl derived::* )(int)'
1>warning: '>' : unsafe use of type 'bool' in operation
1>warning: '>' : operator has no effect; expected operator with side-effect
```

When the compiler meets `foo<314>`, it looks for any `foo`. The first match, within `derived`, is `void foo(int)` and lookup stops. Hence, `foo<314>` is misinterpreted as (ordinary function name) (less) (314) (greater). The code should explicitly specify `base::foo`.

Second, if name lookup succeeds with multiple results, the explicit parameters constrain the overload resolution:

```
template <typename T>
void f();

template <int N>
void f();

f<double>(); // invokes the first f, as "double" does not match "int N"
f<7>();      // invokes the second f
```

However, this can cause unexpected trouble, because some overloads[21] may be silently ignored:

```
template <typename T>
void g(T x);

double pi = 3.14;
g<double>(pi);        // ok, calls g<double>

template <typename T>
void h(T x);

void h(double x);

double pi = 3.14;
h<double>(pi);        // unexpected: still calls the first h
```

[21] Template functions cannot be partially specialized, but only overloaded.

Here's another example:

```
mplate <int I>
ass X {};

mplate <int I, typename T>
id g(X<I>, T x);

mplate <typename T>              // a special 'g' for X<0>
id g(X<0>, T x);                 // however, this is g<T>, not g<0,T>

uble pi = 3.14;
0> x;

0>(x, pi);                       // calls the first g
x, pi);                          // calls the second g
```

Last but not least, old compilers used to introduce subtle linker errors (such as calling the wrong action).

2.2. Specializations

nplate specializations are valid only at the namespace level[22]:

```
uct X

template <typename T>
class Y
{};

template <>              // illegal, but usually tolerated by compilers
class Y<double>
{};


plate <>                 // legal
ss X::Y<double>
```

The compiler will start using the specialized version only after it has compiled it:

```
late <typename scalar_t>
ar_t sq(const scalar_t& x)
. }
```

ortunately, some popular compilers tolerate this.

```
struct A
{
   A(int i = 3)
   {
      int j = sq(i);  // the compiler will pick the generic template
   }
};

template <>
int sq(const int& x)  // this specialization comes too late, compiler gives error
{ ... }
```

However, the compiler will give an error in such a situation (stating that *specialization comes after instantiation*). Incidentally, it can happen that a generic class template explicitly "mentions" a special case, a a parameter in some member function. The following code in fact causes the aforementioned compiler erro

```
template <typename T>
struct C
{
   C(C<void>)
   {
   }
};

template <>
struct C<void>
{
};
```

The correct version uses a *forward declaration*:

```
template <typename T>
struct C;

template <>
struct C<void>
{
};

template <typename T>
struct C
{
   C(C<void>)
   {
   }
};
```

Note that you can partially specialize (and you'll do it often) using integer template parameters:

```
' general template
emplate <typename T, int N>
ass MyClass
... };

 partial specialization (1) for any T with N=0
mplate <typename T>
ass MyClass<T, 0>
... };

 partial specialization (2) for pointers, any N
mplate <typename T, int N>
ass MyClass<T*, N>
... };
```

However, this approach can introduce ambiguities:

```
lass<void*, 0> m;        // compiler error:
                         // should it use specialization (1) or (2)?
```

Usually you must explicitly list all the "combinations". If you specialize X<T1, T2> for all T1 ∈ A and for T2 ∈ B, then you must also specialize explicitly X<T1,T2> ∈ A×B.

```
partial specialization (3) for pointers with N=0
plate <typename T>
ss MyClass<T*, 0>
.. };
```

It's illegal to write a *partial* specialization when there are dependencies between template parameters he general template.

```
parameters (1) and (2) are dependent in the general template

plate <typename int_t, int_t N>
ss AnotherClass


late <typename T>
ss AnotherClass<T, 0>


r: type 'int_t' of template argument '0' depends on template parameter(s)
```

Only a full specialization is allowed:

```
late <>
s AnotherClass<int, 0>
```

A class template specialization may be completely unrelated to the general template. It need not have the same members, and member functions can have different signatures.

While a gratuitous interface change is a symptom of bad style (as it inhibits any generic manipulation o the objects), the freedom can be usually exploited:

```
template <typename T, int N>
struct base_with_array
{
   T data_[N];

   void fill(const T& x)
   {
      std::fill_n(data_, N, x);
   }
};

template <typename T>
struct base_with_array<T, 0>
{
   void fill(const T& x)
   {
   }
};

template <typename T, size_t N>
class cached_vector : private base_with_array<T, N>
{
   // ...

public:
   cached_vector()
   {
      this->fill(T());
   }
};
```

1.2.3. Inner Class Templates

A class template can be a member of another template. One of the key points is syntax; the inner class has own set of parameters, but it knows all the parameters of the outer class.

```
template <typename T>
class outer
{
public:
   template <typename X>
   class inner
   {
      // use freely both X and T
   };
};
```

The syntax for accessing inner is outer<T>::inner<X> if T is a well-defined type; if T is a template arameter, you have to write outer<T>::template inner<X>:

```
ter<int>::inner<double> a;                 // correct

mplate <typename Y>
id f()

  outer<Y>::inner<double> x1;              // error
  outer<Y>::template inner<double> x1;     // correct
```

It's usually difficult or impossible to specialize inner class templates. Specializations should be listed tside of outer, so as a rule they require two template <...> clauses, the former for T (outer), the latter for inner).

---

mary template: it defines an inner<X> which we'll l informally inner_1.

```
template <typename T>
class outer
{
    template <typename X>
    class inner
    {
    };
};
```

l specializations of outer may contain an inner<X>, ich to the compiler is completely unrelated to er_1; we'll call this inner_2.

```
template <>
class outer<int>
{
    template <typename X>
    class inner
    {
        // ok
    };
};
```

r_2 can be specialized:

```
template <>
class outer<int>::inner<float>
{
    // ok
};
```

(*continued*)

specialization of inner_1 for fixed T (=double) and generic X.

```
template <>
template <typename X>
class outer<double>::inner
{
   // ok
};
```

specialization of inner_1 for fixed T (=double) and fixed X (=char).

```
template <>
template <>
class outer<double>::inner<char>
{
   // ok
};
```

It's *illegal* to specialize inner_1 for fixed X with any T.

```
template <typename T>
template <>
class outer<T>::inner<float>
{
   // error!
};
```

Note that, even if X is the same, inner_1<X> and inner_2<X> are completely different types:

```
template <typename T>
struct outer
{
   template <typename X> struct inner {};
};

template <>
struct outer<int>
{
   template <typename X> struct inner {};
};

int main()
{
   outer<double>::inner<void> I1;
   outer<int>::inner<void> I2;

   I1 = I2;
}
```

```
error: binary '=' : no operator found which takes a right-hand operand of type
'outer<int>::inner<X>' (or there is no acceptable conversion)
```

It's impossible to write a function that, say, tests any two "inner"s for equality, because given an tance of inner<X>, the compiler will not deduce its outer<T>.

```
nplate <typename T, typename X>
l f(outer<T>::inner<X>);    // error: T cannot be deduced?
```

The actual type of variable I1 is not simply inner<void>, but outer<double>::inner<void>. If for any X, inner<X> should have the same type, then inner must be promoted to a global template. If it were a plain ss, it would yield simply:

```
uct basic_inner



plate <typename T>
uct outer

typedef basic_inner inner;


plate <>
uct outer<int>

typedef basic_inner inner;
```

If inner does not depend on T, you could write[23]:

```
plate <typename X>
ict basic_inner



plate <typename T>
ict outer

emplate <typename X>
truct inner : public basic_inner<X>

   inner& operator=(const basic_inner<X>& that)
   {
      static_cast<basic_inner<X>&>(*this) = that;
      return *this;
   }
;
```

sider the simpler case when outer<T> is a container, inner1 is an "iterator," inner2 is "const_iterator," and both derive from an external common base, basic_outer_iterator.

```
template <>
struct outer<int>
{
   template <typename X>
   struct inner : public basic_inner<X>
   {
      inner& operator=(const basic_inner<X>& that)
      {
         static_cast<basic_inner<X>&>(*this) = that;
         return *this;
      }
   };
};
```

Otherwise, you have to design basic_inner's template operators that support mixed operations:

```
template <typename X, typename T>
struct basic_inner
{
   template <typename T2>
   basic_inner& operator=(const basic_inner<X, T2>&)
   { /* ... */ }
};

template <typename T>
struct outer
{
   template <typename X>
   struct inner : public basic_inner<X, T>
   {
      template <typename ANOTHER_T>
      inner& operator=(const basic_inner<X, ANOTHER_T>& that)
      {
         static_cast<basic_inner<X, T>&>(*this) = that;
         return *this;
      }
   };
};

template <>
struct outer<int>
{
   template <typename X>
   struct inner : public basic_inner<X, int>
   {
      template <typename ANOTHER_T>
      inner& operator=(const basic_inner<X, ANOTHER_T>& that)
      {
         static_cast<basic_inner<X, int>&>(*this) = that;
         return *this;
      }
   };
};
```

```
it main()

 outer<double>::inner<void> I1;
 outer<int>::inner<void> I2;

 I1 = I2;    // ok: it ends up calling basic_inner::operator=
```

This is known in the C++ community as the SCARY initialization.[24]

SCARY stands for *"Seemingly erroneous (constrained by conflicting template parameters), but actually rk with the right implementation"*. Put simply, two inner types that should be different (specifically, ter<T1>::inner and outer<T2>::inner) actually share the implementation, which means it's possible to at them uniformly as "two inners".

As you've seen for function templates, you should never instantiate the master template before the mpiler has met all the specializations. If you use only full specializations, the compiler will recognize a blem and stop. *Partial* specializations that come too late will be just ignored:

```
ruct A

 template <typename X, typename Y>
 struct B
 {
    void do_it() {}  // line #1
 };

 void f()
 {
    B<int,int> b;     // line #2: the compiler instantiates B<int,int>
    b.do_it();
 }


plate <typename X>
uct A::B<X, X>        // this should be a specialization of B<X,X>
                      // but it comes too late for B<int,int>

void do_it() {}       // line #3



);                    // calls do_it on line #1
```

extra "Y" is little more than poetic license. Refer to the excellent article from Danny Kalev at ://www.informit.com/guides/content.aspx?g=cplusplus&seqNum=454.

Furthermore, adding a full specialization of B will trigger a compiler error:

```
template <>
struct A::B<int, int>
{
   void do_it() {}
};

error: explicit specialization; 'A::B<X,Y>' has already been instantiated
        with
        [
            X=int,
            Y=int
        ]
```

The obvious solution is to move the function bodies after the specializations of `A::B`.

1.3. Style Conventions

Style is the way code is written; this definition is so vague that it includes many different aspects of programming, from language techniques to the position of curly braces.

All the C++ objects in namespace `std` exhibit a common style, which makes the library more coherent. For example, all names are lowercase[25] and multi-word names use underscores. Containers have a member function `bool T::empty() const` that tests if the object is empty and a `void T::clear()` that makes the container empty. These are elements of style.

A fictional STL written in pure C would possibly have a global function `clear`, overloaded for all possible containers. Writing code such as `cont.clear()` or `clear(&cont)` has the same net effect on `cont`, and might even generate the same binary file, but granted, it has a very different style.

All these aspects are important during code reviews. If style agrees with the reader forma mentis, the code will look natural and clear, and maintenance will be easier.

Some aspects of style are indeed less important, because they can be easily adjusted. For example, using beautifiers—each worker in a team might have a pre-configured beautifier on his machine, integrated with the code editor, which reformats braces, spaces, and newlines at a glance.

■ **Note** JEdit (see `http://www.jedit.org`) is a free multiplatform code editor that supports plugins.

AStyle (Artistic Style) is a command-line open source code beautifier (see `http://astyle.sourceforge.net`) whose preferences include the most common formatting option (see Figure 1-1).

---

[25]Except `std::numeric_limits<T>::quiet_NaN()`.

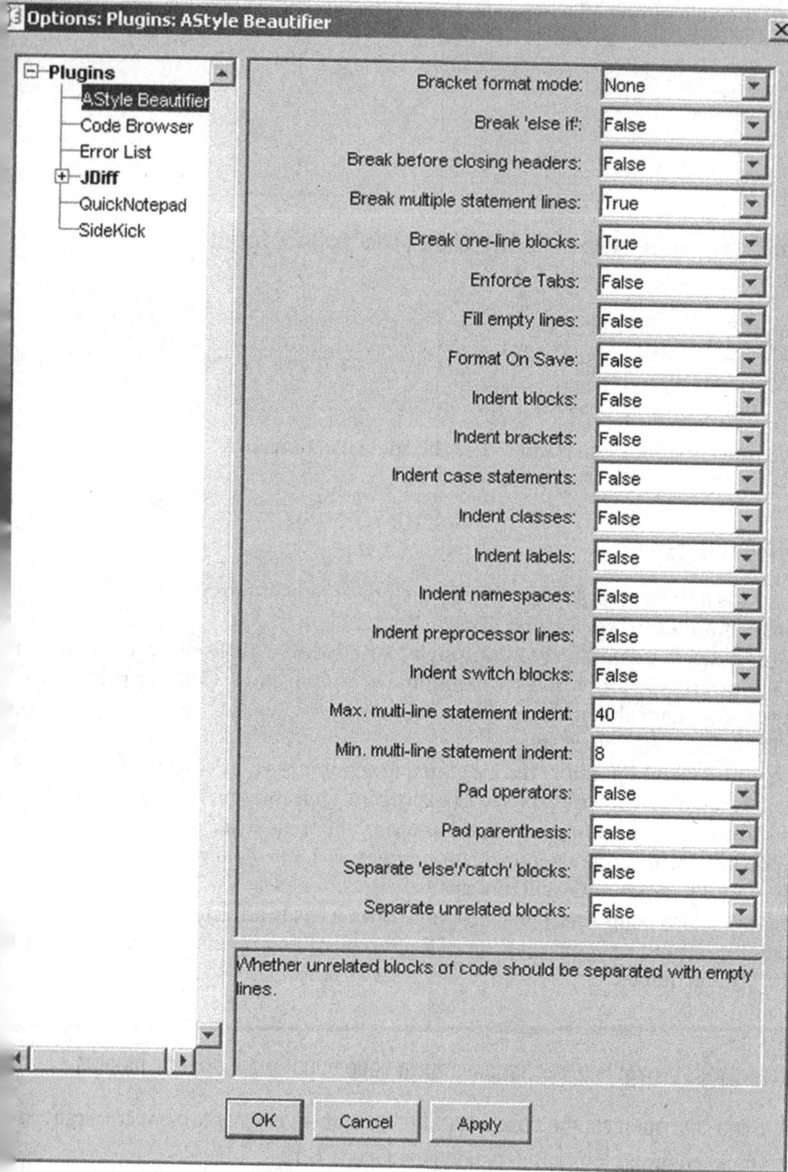

re 1-1. *The AStyle plugin for JEdit*

Most reasonable style conventions are equivalent; it's important to pick one and try to be consistent for e time.[26]

Ideally, if code is written according to some *common behavior conventions*, a reader may deduce how it s based on the style, without looking into the details.

---

n source code has a lifecycle and eventually it's going to "die," i.e., it will be rewritten from scratch. However the robust the design, the longer its life will be, and style is part of the design. See also [5].

For example:

```
void unknown_f(multidimensional_vector<double, 3, 4>& M)
{
   if (!M.empty())
      throw std::runtime_error("failure");
}
```

Most readers will describe this fragment as, "If the multidimensional vector is not empty, then throw a exception". However, nothing in the code states that this is the intended behavior except style.

In fact, `multidimensional_vector::empty` could in principle make the container empty and return a non-zero error code if it does not succeed.[27]

The naming convention is a big component of style.

The following example lists some ideas for how to convey extra meaning when building the name of a object. It is not intended as a set of axioms, and in particular no item is worse/better than its opposite, but it's a detailed example of how to assemble a style that can help you diagnose and solve problems.

Remember that the C++ standard prescribes that some identifiers are "reserved to the implementatio for any use" and some are reserved for names in the global or `std` namespace. That means user names should never:

- Begin with an underscore (in particular, followed by a capital letter)
- Contain a double underscore
- Contain a dollar sign (it's tolerated by some compilers, but it's not portable)

1.3.1. Comments

"Many good programming practices boil down to preparing for change or expressing intent. Novices emphasize the former, experts the latter."

—John D. Cc

Remember to add lots of comments to your code. If this is valid for any programming language, it is especially true for TMP techniques, which can easily be misunderstood. The correct behavior of TMP is based on bizarre entities, like empty classes, void functions, and strange language constructs that look lik errors. It's really hard for the author of the code to remember why and how these techniques work, and ev harder for other people who have to maintain the code.

1.3.2. Macros

Macros play a special role in TMP. Some programmers consider them a necessary evil and indeed they a necessary, but it's not obvious they are also evil.

Macros must:

- Allow the reader to recognize them
- Prevent name collisions

[27]As discussed in **[5]**, usually member function names should be actions. Thus `empty` should be a synonym for `make_empty` and not for `is_empty`. However, STL convention is established and universally understood. When in dc do as `std::vector` does.

The easiest way to satisfy both requirements is to choose a unique and sufficiently ugly common prefix r all macros and play with lower/uppercase to give extra meaning to the name.

As an example, you could agree that all macros begin with MXT_. If the macro is persistent, i.e. never ıdefined, the prefix will be MXT. If the macro's scope is limited (it's defined and undefined later in the me file), the prefix will be mXT_.

```
fndef MXT_filename_
efine MXT_filename_              // this is "exported" - let's name it MXT_*

efine mXT_MYVALUE 3              // this macro has limited "scope"
nst int VALUE = mXT_MYVALUE;     // let's name it mXT_*
ndef mXT_MYVALUE                 //

ndif //MXT_filename_
```

A lowercase prefix mxt is reserved to remap standard/system function names in different platforms:

```
fdef _WIN32
efine mxt_native_dbl_isfinite       _finite
lse
efine mxt_native_dbl_isfinite       isfinite
ndif
```

For better code appearance, you could decide to replace some keywords with a macro:

```
fine MXT_NAMESPACE_BEGIN(x)           namespace x {
fine MXT_NAMESPACE_END(x)             }

fine MXT_NAMESPACE_NULL_BEGIN()       namespace {
fine MXT_NAMESPACE_NULL_END()         }
```

And/or enclose the namespace directives in an ASCII-art comment box:

```
///////////////////////////////////////////////////////////////
_NAMESPACE_BEGIN(XT)
///////////////////////////////////////////////////////////////
```

It's useful to have some (integer) functions as a set of macros:

```
ine MXT_M_MAX(a,b)        ((a)<(b) ? (b) : (a))
ine MXT_M_MIN(a,b)        ((a)<(b) ? (a) : (b))
ine MXT_M_ABS(a)          ((a)<0 ? -(a) : (a))
ine MXT_M_SQ(a)           ((a)*(a))
```

The infix _M_ stands for "macro" and these will be useful when working with templates:

```
late <int N>
ct SomeClass

tatic const int value = MXT_M_SQ(N)/MXT_M_MAX(N, 1);
```

■ **Note** The C++11 Standard introduced a new keyword: constexpr.[28]

A function-declared constexpr has no side effects and it always returns the same result, deterministically, fro the same arguments. In particular, when such a function is called with compile-time constant arguments, its result will also be a compile-time constant:

```
constexpr int sq(int n) { return n*n; }
constexpr int max(int a, int b)
{ return a<b ? b : a; }

template <int N>
struct SomeClass
{
        static const int value = sq(N)/max(N, 1);
```

Finally, consider a special class of macros. A ***macro directive*** is a macro whose usage logically takes a entire line of code.

In other words, the difference between an ordinary macro and a directive is that the latter cannot coexist with anything on the same line (except possibly its arguments):

```
// directive
MXT_NULL_NAMESPACE_BEGIN()

#define MXT_PI          3.1415926535897932384626433832795029

// the use of MXT_PI does not take the whole line
// so it is not a directive.
const double x = std::cos(MXT_PI);

// directive
MXT_NULL_NAMESPACE_END()
```

The definition of a macro directive, in general, should not end with a semicolon, so the user is forced close the line manually (when appropriate), as if it were a standard function call.

```
// note: no trailing ';'
#define MXT_INT_I(k)        int i = (k)

int main()
{
   MXT_INT_I(0);        // put ';' here
   return 0;
}
```

[28]See http://en.cppreference.com/w/cpp/language/constexpr for the exact requirements and specifications.

Here is a more complex example. Note that the trailing semicolon is a very strong style point, so it's used
'en in places where, in ordinary code, a semicolon would be unnatural.

```
lefine mXT_C(NAME,VALUE)                              \
atic scalar_t NAME()                                  \
                                                      \
 static const scalar_t NAME##_ = (VALUE);             \
 return NAME##_;                                      \


mplate <typename scalar_t>
ruct constant

 // the final ';' at class level is legal, though uncommon
 mXT_C(Pi, acos(scalar_t(-1)));
 mXT_C(TwoPi, 2*acos(scalar_t(-1)));
 mXT_C(PiHalf, acos(scalar_t(0)));
 mXT_C(PiQrtr, atan(scalar_t(1)));
 mXT_C(Log2, log(scalar_t(2)));


def mXT_C

ble x = constant<double>::TwoPi();
```

However, special care is required when invoking macro directives, which expand to a sequence of
ructions:

```
fine MXT_SORT2(a,b)   if ((b)<(a)) swap((a),(b))

fine MXT_SORT3(a,b,c) \
MXT_SORT2((a),(b)); MXT_SORT2((a),(c)); MXT_SORT2((b),(c))

 a = 5, b = 2, c = 3;
_SORT3(a,b,c);                  // apparently ok: now a=2, b=3, c=5
```

Nevertheless, this code is broken:

```
 a = 5, b = 2, c = 3;

 a>10)
XT_SORT3(a,b,c);                // problem here!
```

Since it expands to:

```
a>10)
XT_SORT2(a,b);

SORT2(a,c);
SORT2(b,c);
```

More surprising is that the following fragment is clear, but incorrect:

```
if (a>10)
   MXT_SORT2(a,b);
else
   MXT_SORT2(c,d);
```

Because of the way if-then-else associates in C++, the macro expands as

```
if (a>10)
   if (a<b)
      swap(a,b);
else
   if (c<d)
      swap(c,d);
```

The indentation does not resemble the way code is executed; the block actually groups as

```
if (a>10)
{
   if (a<b)
      swap(a,b);
   else if (c<d)
      swap(c,d);
}
```

To solve the problem, you can use the do {...} while (false) idiom:

```
#define MXT_SORT3(a,b,c)    \
  do { MXT_SORT2((a),(b)); MXT_SORT2((a),(c)); MXT_SORT2((b),(c)); } \
  while (false)
```

This allows both to put "local code" inside a block and to terminate the directive with a semicolon. Remember that this will not save you from an error like:

```
MXT_SORT3(a, b++, c); // error: b will be incremented more than once
```

This is why we insist that macros are immediately recognizable by a "sufficiently ugly" prefix. To tackle the "if" macro problem, write a do-nothing else branch:

```
#define MXT_SORT2(a,b)    if ((b)<(a)) swap((a),(b)); else
```

Now MXT_SORT2(a,b); expands to if (...) swap(...); else; where the last semicolon is the emp statement. Even better[29]:

```
#define MXT_SORT2(a,b)    if (!((b)<(a))) {} else swap((a),(b))
```

---

[29]The difference between the last two implementations is largely how they react to an invalid syntax. As an exercise, consider some malicious code like MXT_SORT2(x, y) if (true) throw an_exception;.

As a final remark, never make a direct use of types that come from macros. Always introduce a typedef. the macro is not carefully written, the association between * and const may give unexpected results. onsider:

```
x = 0;
nst T* p = &x; // looks correct
```

Unless:

```
efine T     char*
```

Instead, consider intercepting the macro:

```
pedef T MyType;      // ok, even if T is a macro.
 #undef T if you like
Type x = 0;          //
nst MyType* p = &x;  // now it works.
```

3.3. Symbols

st C++ projects contain several kinds of symbols (classes, functions, constants, and so on). A rough ision line can be drawn between system/framework utilities, which are completely abstract and generic, l project specific entities, which contain specific logic and are not expected to be reused elsewhere.

This simple classification may turn out important for (human) debuggers. If any piece of code is isidered a "system utility," then it's implicitly trusted and it may usually be "stepped over" during debug. the other hand, project-specific code is possibly less tested and should be "stepped in".

We can agree that stable symbols should follow the STL naming conventions (lowercase, underscores, h as stable_sort, hash_map, and so on). This often will be the case for class templates.

The rest should be camel case (the Java convention is fine).

```
amework header) sq.hpp

plate <typename scalar_t>
lar_t sq(const scalar_t& x) { return x*x; }; // 'system-level' function - lowercase

oject file) custom_scalar.h

uct MySpecialScalarType      // 'project-level' class - mixed case

'/ ...


ject file) main.cpp

main()

ySpecialScalarType x = 3.14;
ySpecialScalarType y = sq(x);

eturn 0;
```

A *functor* is an instance of an object that implements at least one operator(), so the name of the instance behaves like a function.[30]

A functor is said to be *modifying* if it takes arguments by non-const references.

A *predicate* is a non-modifying functor that takes all arguments of the same type and returns a boolean. For example, less is a binary predicate:

```
template <typename T>
struct less
{
   bool operator()(const T&, const T&) const;
};
```

Most functors contain a typedef for the return type of operator(), usually named result_type or value_type.[31]

Functors are usually stateless or they carry few data members, so they are built on the fly. Occasionally you may need a meaningful name for an instance, and this may not be so easy, because if the functor has a limited "scope," the only meaningful name has already been given to the class.

```
calendar myCal;
std::find_if(year.begin(), year.end(), is_holiday(myCal));

// is_holiday is a class
// how do we name an instance?
```

You can use one of the following:

- Use a lowercase functor name and convert it to uppercase for the instance:

```
calendar myCal;
is_holiday IS_HOLIDAY(myCal);
std::find_if(year.begin(), year.end(), IS_HOLIDAY);
```

- Use a lowercase functor name with a prefix/postfix and remove it in the instance:

```
calendar myCal;
is_holiday_t is_holiday(myCal);
std::find_if(year.begin(), year.end(), is_holiday);
```

[30] The reader might want to review the simple example early in this chapter.

[31] See Section **6.2.1**.

.3.4. Generality

ne best way to improve generality is to reuse standard classes, such as `std::pair`.

This brings in well-tested code and increases interoperability; however, it may often hide some specific gic, for example the meaning of `pair::first` and `pair::second` may not be obvious at first sight. See the llowing paradigmatic example:

```
ruct id_value

 int id;
 double value;


_value FindIDAndValue(...);
```

This may be replaced by:

```
d::pair<int, double> FindIDAndValue(...)
```

However, the caller of the first function can write `p.id` and `p.value`, which is easier to read than `first` and `p.second`. You may want to provide a *less generic* way to access `pair` members:

- Macros

```
#define id              first       // bad idea?
#define value           second      // bad idea?

#define id(P)           P.first     // slightly better
#define value(P)        P.second    // slightly better
```

- Global functions (these are called *accessors*; see Section **6.2.1**)

```
inline int& id(std::pair<int, double>& P)
{ return P.first; }

inline int id(const std::pair<int, double>& P)
{ return P.first; }
```

- Global pointer-to-members

```
typedef std::pair<int, double> id_value;

int id_value::*ID = &id_value::first;
double id_value::*VALUE = &id_value::second;

// later
std::pair<int, double> p;
p.*ID = -5;
p.*VALUE = 3.14;
```

To make ID and VALUE constants, the syntax is:

```
int id_value::* const ID = &id_value::first;
```

1.3.5. Template Parameters

A fairly universally accepted convention is to reserve UPPERCASE names for non-type template parameters. This could cause some name conflict with macros. It's not always necessary to give a name to template parameters (as with function arguments), so when it's feasible, you'd better remove the name entirely:

```
// the following line is likely to give strange errors
// since some compilers define BIGENDIAN as a macro!

template <typename T, bool BIGENDIAN = false>
class SomeClass
{
};

template <typename T>
class SomeClass<T, true>
{
};
```

A safer declaration would be[32]:

```
template <typename T, bool = false>
class SomeClass
```

Type parameters are usually denoted by a single uppercase letter—usually T (or T1, T2...) if type can b indeed anything.[33] A and R are also traditionally used for parameters that match arguments and results:

```
int foo(double x) { return 5+x; }
template <typename R, typename A>
inline R apply(R (*F)(A), A arg)
{
   return F(arg);
}

template <typename R, typename A1, typename A2>
inline R apply(R (*F)(A1, A2), A1 arg1, A2 arg2)
{
   return F(arg1, arg2);
}

double x = apply(&foo 3.14);
```

[32]Some compilers, such as MSVC71, used to have problems with unnamed parameters; refer to paragraph 11.3.3 for detailed example.

[33]Some authors reserve the keyword typename for this purpose. In other words, they declare template <typename to mean that T is "any type" and template <class T> to suggest that T is indeed a class as opposed to a native type However, this distinction is rather artificial.

Otherwise, you might want to use a (meaningful) lowercase name ending with _t (for example, int_t, :alar_t, object_t, any_t, or that_t).

```
emplate <typename T, int N>
.ass do_nothing
```

```
mplate <typename int_t>   // int_t should behave as an integer type[34]
ruct is_unsigned

 static const bool value = ...;
```

The suffix _t, which in C originally means typedef, is also widely used for (private) typedefs standing template instances:

```
nplate <typename scalar_t>
ass SomeContainer

 // informally means:
 // within this class, a pair always denotes a pair of scalars

 private:
    typedef std::pair<scalar_t, scalar_t> pair_t;
```

On the other hand, a public typedef name usually is composed of lowercase regular English words ch as iterator_category). In that case, _type is preferred:

```
plate <typename scalar_t>
ss SomeContainer

public:
   typedef scalar_t result_type;
```

.6. Metafunctions

often meet stateless class templates whose members are only enumerations (as a rule, anonymous), c constants, types (typedefs or nested classes), and static member functions.

Generalizing Section 1.1, we consider this template a *metafunction* that maps its tuple of parameters to ss, which is seen as a *set of results* (namely, its members).

---

e that this is not a formal requirement; it's just a name! The name reflects how we think the type should be; later we nforce this, if necessary.

```
template <typename T, int N>
struct F
{
   typedef T* pointer_type;
   typedef T& reference_type;

   static const size_t value = sizeof(T)*N;
};
```

The metafunction F maps a pair of arguments to a triple of results:

```
(T,N)          →    (pointer_type, reference_type, value)
{type}×{int}   →    {type}×{type}×{size_t}
```

Most metafunctions return either a single type, conventionally named type, or a single numeric constant (an integer or an enumeration), conventionally named value.[35]

```
template <typename T>
struct largest_precision_type;

template <>
struct largest_precision_type<float>
{
   typedef double type;
};

template <>
struct largest_precision_type<double>
{
   typedef double type;
};

template <>
struct largest_precision_type<int>
{
   typedef long type;
};
```

Similarly:

```
template <unsigned int N>
struct two_to
{
   static const unsigned int value = (1<<N);
};
```

[35]The mathematically inclined reader should consider the latter as a special case of the former. The constant 5' can be replaced by a type named `five` or `static_value<int, 5>`. This leads to greater generality. See **[3]** for more informati

```
emplate <unsigned int N>
truct another_two_to

 enum { value = (1<<N) };


signed int i = two_to<5>::value;            // invocation
rgest_precision<int>::type j = i + 100; // invocation
```

Historically, the first metafunctions were written using enums:

```
mplate <size_t A>
ruct is_prime

 enum { value = 0 };

mplate <>
ruct is_prime<2>

 enum { value = 1 };

nplate <>
uct is_prime<3>

 enum { value = 1 };

...
```

The main reason was that compilers were unable to deal with static `const` integers (including `bool`).
advantage of using an `enum` over a static constant is that the compiler will *never* reserve storage space for constant, as the computation is either static or it fails.

Conversely, a static constant integer could be "misused" as a normal integer, for example, taking its ress (an operation that the compiler will disallow on `enums`).

---

ote According to the classic C++ standard, the use of a static constant as a normal integer is illegal ess the constant is re-declared in the `.cpp` file, as any other static data member of a class). ever, most compilers allow it, as long as the code does not try to take the address of the constant or bind it `const` reference. The requirement was removed in modern C++.

Furthermore, the language allows declaring a static integer constant (at function scope, not at class scope) is *dynamically* initialized, and so *not* a compile-time constant:

```
ic const int x = INT_MAX;                               // static
ic const int y = std::numeric_limits<int>::max();  // dynamic
ic const int z = rand();                                // dynamic

le data[y];                                             // error
```

In practice, an enum is usually equivalent to a *small* integer. enums are in general implemented as signed int, unless their value is too large. The most important difference is that you cannot bind an unnamed enum to a template parameter without an explicit cast:

```
double data[10];
std::fill_n(data, is_prime<3>::value, 3.14);    // may give error!
```

The previous code is non-portable, because std::fill_n may be defined.

```
template <..., typename integer_t, ...>
void fill_n(..., integer_t I, ...)
{
  ++I; // whatever...
  --I; // whatever...
}
```

```
error C2675: unary '--' : "does not define this operator or a conversion to a type
acceptable to the predefined operator
see reference to function template instantiation
'void std::_Fill_n<double*,_Diff,_Ty>(_OutIt,_Diff,const _Ty &,std::_Range_checked_iterator_tag
being compiled
        with
        [
            _Diff=,
            _Ty=double *,
            _OutIt=double **
        ]
```

In practice, an enum is fine to store a small integer (for example, the logarithm of an integer in base 2). Because its type is not explicit, it should be avoided when dealing with potentially large or unsigned constants. As a workaround for the std::fill_n call, just cast the enumeration to an appropriate integer:

```
std::fill_n(..., int(is_prime<3>::value), ...);    // now ok!
```

Frequently, metafunctions invoke helper classes (you'll see less trivial examples later):

```
template <int N>
struct ttnp1_helper
{
   static const int value = (1<<N);
};

template <int N>
struct two_to_plus_one
{
   static const int value = ttnp1_helper<N>::value + 1;
};
```

The moral equivalent of auxiliary variables are private members. From a TMP perspective, numeric onstants and type(def)s are equivalent compile-time entities.

```
emplate <int N>
ruct two_to_plus_one

ivate:
 static const int aux = (1<<N);

blic:
 static const int value = aux + 1;
```

The helper class is not private and not hidden,[36] but it should not be used, so its name is "uglified" with elper or _t (or both).

3.7. Namespaces and Using Declarations

ually all "public" framework objects are grouped in a common namespace and "private" objects reside in ecial nested namespaces.

```
nespace framework

 namespace undocumented_private
 {
    void handle_with_care()
    {
       // ...
    };
 }

 inline void public_documented_function()
 {
    undocumented_private::handle_with_care();
 }
```

It's not a good idea to multiply the number of namespaces unnecessarily, since argument-dependent e lookup may introduce subtle problems, and friend declarations between objects in different espaces are problematic or even impossible.

Usually, the core of a general-purpose metaprogramming framework is a set of headers (the extension p is in fact used for pure C++ headers). *Using-namespace declarations* in header files are generally sidered bad practice:

```
ramework.hpp

g namespace std;
```

ould reside in an anonymous namespace, but this does not make it inaccessible.

```
main.cpp
#include "my_framework.hpp"

// main.cpp doesn't know, but it's now using namespace std
```

However, *using-function declarations* in header files are usually okay and even desirable (see the do_something example later in the paragraph).

A special use for using-namespace declarations is header versioning.[37]

This is a very short example:

```
namespace X
{
   namespace version_1_0
   {
      void func1();
      void func2();
   }

   namespace version_2_0
   {
      void func1();
      void func2();
   }

#ifdef USE_1_0
   using namespace version_1_0;
#else
   using namespace version_2_0;
#endif
}
```

Thus the clients using the header always refer to X::func1.

Now we are going to describe in detail another case where using declarations can make a difference.

Function templates are often used to provide an "external interface," which is a set of global functions that allow algorithms to perform generic manipulations of objects[38]:

The author of a fictitious framework1 provides a function is_empty that works on a broad class of containers and on C strings:

```
// framework1.hpp
MXT_NAMESPACE_BEGIN(framework1)

template <typename T>
inline bool is_empty(T const& x)
{
   return x.empty();                        // line #1
}
```

[37]The advantages are described extensively in Apple Technical Note TN2185; refer to the following page: http://developer.apple.com/technotes/tn2007/tn2185.html.

[38]Such functions are denoted shims in [5].

```
emplate <>
nline bool is_empty(const char* const& x)

 return x==0 || *x==0;


T_NAMESPACE_END(framework1)
```

One of the good properties of this approach is the ease of extensibility. For any new type X, you can
ovide a specialized is_empty that will have priority over the default implementation. However, consider
at happens if the function is explicitly qualified:

```
 framework2.hpp
nclude "framework1.hpp"

T_NAMESPACE_BEGIN(framework2)

nplate <typename string_t>
id do_something(string_t const& x)

 if (!framework1::is_empty(x))          // line #2
 {
    // ...
 }


_NAMESPACE_END(framework2)

clude "framework2.hpp"

espace framework3

class EmptyString
{
};

bool is_empty(const EmptyString& x)
{
   return true;
}



 main()

ramework3::EmptyString s;
ramework2::do_something(s);             // compiler error in line #1
```

The user-supplied is_empty is ignored in line #2, since do_something explicitly takes is_empty from namespace framework1. To fix this, you can either reopen namespace framework1 and specialize is_empty there or modify do_something like this:

```
framework2.hpp
MXT_NAMESPACE_BEGIN(framework2)

using framework1::is_empty;

template <typename string_t>
void do_something(string_t const& x)
{
   if (!is_empty(x))
   {
      //...
   }
};
```

Thus, you let argument-dependent lookup pick an available is_empty but ensure that framework1 cal always supply a default candidate (see also the discussion in Section 1.4.2).

1.4. Classic Patterns

When coding a framework/library, it's typical to use and reuse a small set of names. For example, contain can be expected to have a member function [[integer type]] size() const that returns the number of elements.

Adopting a uniform style increases interoperability of objects; for more details, see Chapter 6.All the following paragraphs will try to describe the traditional meaning connected to a few common C++ names

1.4.1. size_t and ptrdiff_t

In C++ there's no unique standard and portable way to name large integers. Modern compilers will in general pick the largest integers available for long and unsigned long. When you need a large and fast integer quickly, the preferred choices are size_t (unsigned) and ptrdiff_t (signed).

size_t, being the result of sizeof and the argument of operator new, is large enough to store any amount of memory; ptrdiff_t represents the difference of two pointers. Since the length of an array of chars is end-begin, as a rule of thumb they will have the same size.

Furthermore, in the flat C++ memory model, sizeof(size_t) also will be the size of pointers, and th integers will likely have the natural size in an architecture—say, 32 bits on a 32-bit processor and 64 bits c a 64-bit processor. They will also be fast (the processor bus will perform atomic transport from registers t memory).

Given this class:

```
emplate <int N>
truct A

 char data[N];
```

sizeof(A<N>) is at least N, so it also follows that size_t is not smaller than int.[39]

.4.2. void T::swap(T&)

is function is expected to swap *this and the argument in constant time, without throwing an exception. practical definition of *constant* is "an amount of time depending only on T".[40]

If T has a swap member function, the user expects it to be not worse than the traditional three-copy ap (that is, X=A; A=B; B=X). Indeed, this is always possible, because a member function can invoke each ember's own swap:

```
ass TheClass

 std::vector<double> theVector_;
 std::string theString_;
 double theDouble_;

lic:
 void swap(TheClass& that);
 {
    theString_.swap(that.theString_);
    theVector_.swap(that.theVector_);
    std::swap(theDouble_, that.theDouble_);
 }
```

The only step that could take non-fixed time is swapping dynamic arrays element by element, but this be avoided by swapping the arrays as a whole.

The class std::tr1::array<T,N> has a swap that calls std::swap_range on an array of length N, s taking time proportional to N and depending on T. However, N is part of the type, so according to this nition, it is constant time. Furthermore, if T is a swappable type (e.g., std::string), swap_range will orm much better than the three copy procedure, so the member swap is definitely an advantage.

---

 is an array of T of length 2, then (char*)(&a[1])-(char*)(&a[0]) is a ptrdiff_t, which is at least as large as of(T). That means ptrdiff_t is at least as large as int as well. This argument actually shows that every result of of can be stored in a ptrdiff_t. A generic size_t may not be stored in a ptrdiff_t, because sizeof is not ssarily surjective—there may be a size_t value that is larger than every possible sizeof.

 example, to create a copy of std::string takes time proportional to the length of the string itself, so this depends nly on the type, but also on the *instance*; alternatively, copying a double is a constant-time operation. Mathematically king, the notion of "constant time" is not well defined in C++; the issue is too complex for a footnote, but we'll sketch dea. An algorithm is O(1) if its execution time is bounded by a constant K, for any possible input. If the number ssible inputs is finite, even if it's huge, the algorithm is automatically O(1). For example, in C++ the sum of two s O(1). In general, the C++ memory model has a finite addressable space (because all objects have a fixed size, n "address" is an object) and this implies that the number of possible inputs to some algorithms is finite. Quicksort lexity is O(N*log(N)), but std::sort may be formally considered O(1), where—loosely speaking—the constant e time required to sort the largest possible array.

The first problem to address is how to swap objects of unspecified type T:

```
template <typename T>
class TheClass
{
   T theObj_;        // how do you swap two objects of type T?

   void swap(TheClass<T>& that)
   {
      std::swap(theObj_, that.theObj_);
   }
};
```

The explicit qualification std:: is an unnecessary constraint. You'd better introduce a using declaratic as seen in Section 1.3.7:

```
using std::swap;

template <typename T>
class TheClass
{
   T theObj_;

public:
   void swap(TheClass<T>& that)          // line #1
   {
      swap(theObj_, that.theObj_);       // line #2
   }
};
```

However, this results in a compiler error, because by the usual C++ name resolution rules, swap in lin is the swap defined in line 1, which does not take two arguments.

The solution, an idiom known as *swap with ADL*, is to introduce a global function with a different na

```
using std::swap;

template <typename T>
inline void swap_with_ADL(T& a, T& b)
{
   swap(a, b);
}

template <typename T>
class TheClass
{
   T theObj_;
```

```
ublic:
  void swap(TheClass<T>& that)
  {
     swap_with_ADL(theObj_, that.theObj_);
  }
```

Due to lookup rules, swap_with_ADL forwards the call to either a swap function defined in the same amespace as T (which hopefully is T's own version), or to std::swap if nothing else exists. Since there's no cal member function with a similar name, lookup escapes class level.

The traditional argument for swap is T&; however, it may make sense to provide more overloads. If an ject internally holds its data in a standard container of type X, it might be useful to provide void swap(X&), th relaxed time-complexity expectations:

```
mplate <typename T>
ass sorted_vector

 std::vector<T> data_;

blic:
 void swap(sorted_vector<T>& that)
 {
    data_.swap(that.data_);
 }

 void swap(std::vector<T>& that)
 {
    data_.swap(that);
    std::sort(data_.begin(), data_.end());
 }
```

And even more[41]:

```
uct unchecked_type_t {};
ine unchecked_type_t unchecked() { return unchecked_type_t(); }

plate <typename T>
ss sorted_vector

// ...

void swap(std::vector<T>& that, unchecked_type_t (*)())

   assert(is_sorted(that.begin(), that.end()));
   data_.swap(that);
```

---

npare with Section **2.3.1**.

```
sorted_vector<double> x;
std::vector<double> t;

load_numbers_into(x);
x.swap(t);

// now x is empty and t is sorted
// later...

x.swap(t, unchecked);    // very fast
```

To sum up:

- Explicitly qualify `std::swap` with parameters of fixed native type (integers, pointers, and so on) and standard containers (including string).
- Write a using declaration for `std::swap` and call an unqualified `swap` when parameters have undefined type T in global functions.
- Call `swap_with_ADL` inside classes having a `swap` member function.

`std::swap` grants the best implementation for swapping both native and `std` types.

`swap` is used in algorithms with move semantics:

```
void doSomething(X& result)
{
   X temp;
   // perform some operation on temp, then...
   swap(temp, result);
}
```

and in implementing an exception-safe assignment operator in terms of the copy constructor:

```
class X
{
public:
   X(const X&);
   void swap(X&);
   ~X();

   X& operator=(const X& that)
   {
      X temp(that);        // if an exception occurs here, *this is unchanged
      temp.swap(*this);    // no exception can occur here
      return *this;        // now temp is destroyed and releases resources
   }
};
```

If you perform an unconditional swap, the most efficient solution is to take the argument by value:

```
 operator=(X that)

 that.swap(*this);
 return *this;
```

On the other hand, you might want to perform additional checks before invoking the copy constructor hand, even if it's less efficient[42]:

```
operator=(const X& that)

if (this != &that)
{
   X temp(that);
   temp.swap(*this);
}
return *this;
```

The drawback is that at some point, both that and temp are alive, so you may need more free resources ;., more memory).

4.3. bool T::empty() const; void T::clear()

e former function tests whether an object is empty; the latter makes it empty. If an object has a member ction size(), then a call to empty() is expected to be no slower than size()==0.

Note that an object may be empty but still control resources. For example, an empty vector might hold w block of memory, where in fact no element has yet been constructed.

In particular, it's unspecified if a clear function will or won't release object resources; clear is a onym of reset.

To enforce resource cleanup of an auto variable, the usual technique is to swap the instance with a porary:

```
;
now x holds some resources...
.swap(x);
```

.4. X T::get() const; X T::base() const

name get is used when type T wraps a simpler type X. A smart pointer's get would thus return the rnal plain pointer.

The function base instead is used to return a copy of the wrapped object, when the wrapper is just a rent interface. Since a smart pointer typically adds some complexity (for example, a reference count), name base would not be as appropriate as get. On the other hand, std::reverse_iterator is an face that swaps ++ and -- of an underlying iterator, so it has a base().

---

ne objects may want to check in advance if overwrite is feasible. For example, if T is std::string whose ()==that.size() then it might be able to perform a safe memcpy.

1.4.5. X T::property() const; void T::property(X)

In this section, "property" is a symbolic name. A class can expose two overloaded member functions called "property" with two different intents.

The first form returns the current value of the property for the current instance; the second sets the property to some new value. The property-set function can also have the form:

```
X T::property(X newval)
{
   const X oldval = property();
   set_new_val(newval);
   return oldval;
}
```

This convention is elegant but not universally used; it is present in `std::iostream`.

1.4.6. Action(Value); Action(Range)

In this section, "action" is again a symbolic name for an overloaded function or member function.

If an object's own action—for example `container.insert(value)`—is likely to be invoked sequentiall an object may provide one or more range equivalents. In other words, it can provide member functions wi two or more parameters that identify a series of elements at a time. Some familiar examples are:

- An element and a repeat counter
- Two iterators pointing to (begin...end)
- An array and two indexes

It's up to the implementation to take advantage of the range being known in advance. As usual, the range-equivalent function should never be worse than the trivial implementation `action(range) := for (x in range) { action(x); }`.

1.4.7. Manipulators

Manipulators are one of the least known and more expressive pieces of the C++ standard. They are simply functions that take a stream as an argument. Since their signature is fixed, streams have a special insertio operator that runs them:

```
class ostream
{
public:
   ostream& operator<<(ostream& (*F)(ostream&))
   {
      return F(*this);
   }

   inline ostream& endl(ostream& os)
   {
      os << '\n';
      return os.flush();
   }
};
```

```
nt main()

 // actually execute endl(cout << "Hello world")
 std::cout << "Hello world" << std::endl;
```

Some manipulators have an argument. The implementation may use a template proxy object to ansport this argument to the stream:

```
ruct precision_proxy_t

 int prec;

line ostream& operator<<(ostream& o, precision_proxy_t p)

 o.precision(p.prec);
 return o;

ecision_proxy_t setprecision(int p)

 precision_proxy_t result = { p };
 return result;

t << setprecision(12) << 3.14;
```

Note that a more realistic implementation may want to *embed* a function pointer in the proxy, so as to e only one insertion operator:

```
ss ostream;

plate <typename T, ostream& (*FUNC)(ostream&, T)>
uct proxy

T arg;

proxy(const T& a)
   : arg(a)
{
}

s ostream

ic:
emplate <typename T, ostream& (*FUNC)(ostream&, T)>
stream& operator<<(proxy<T, FUNC> p)
```

```
   {
      return FUNC(*this, p.arg);
   }
};

ostream& global_setpr(ostream& o, int prec)
{
   o.precision(prec);
   return o;
}

proxy<int, global_setpr> setprecision(int p)
{
   return p;
}

cout << setprecision(12) << 3.14;
```

■ **Note** Observe that in classic C++ FUNC would just be a member:

```
template <typename T>
struct proxy
{
   T arg;
   ostream& (*FUNC)(ostream&, T);
};

class ostream
{
public:
   template <typename T>
   ostream& operator<<(proxy<T> p)
   {
      return p.FUNC(*this, p.arg);
   }
};
```

In principle, a function template could be used as a manipulator, such as:

```
stream << manip1;
stream << manip2(argument);
stream << manip3<N>;
stream << manip4<N>(argument);
```

But in practice this is discouraged, as many compilers won't accept `manip3`.

.4.8. Position of Operators

's important to understand the difference between member and non-member operators.

When member operators are invoked, the left side has already been statically determined, so if any ljustment is necessary, it's performed only on the right side. Alternatively, non-member operators will only atch exactly or give errors.

Suppose you are rewriting std::pair:

```
mplate <typename T1, typename T2>
ruct pair

 T1 first;
 T2 second;

 template <typename S1, typename S2>
 pair(const pair<S1, S2>& that)
 : first(that.first), second(that.second)
 {
 }
```

Now add operator==. First as a member:

```
nplate <typename T1, typename T2>
uct pair

// ...

inline bool operator== (const pair<T1,T2>& that) const
{
   return (first == that.first) && (second == that.second);
}
```

Then you compile the following code:

```
pair<int, std::string> P(1,"abcdefghijklmnop");
pair<const int, std::string> Q(1,"qrstuvwxyz");
if (P == Q)
{ ... }
```

This will work and will call pair<int, string>::operator==. This function requires a constant rence to pair<int, string> and instead it was given pair<const int, string>. It will silently invoke emplate copy constructor and make a copy of the object on the right, which is undesirable, as it will e a temporary copy of the string.

It is slightly better to put the operator outside the class:

```
late <typename T1, typename T2>
 operator== (const pair<T1,T2>& x, const pair<T1,T2>& y)

return (x.first == y.first) && (x.second == y.second);
```

At least, this code will now fail to compile, since equality now requires identical pairs. Explicit failure is always more desirable than a subtle problem.

Analogous to the classic C++ rule, "if you write a custom copy constructor, then you'll need a custom assignment operator," we could say that if you write a universal copy constructor, you'll *likely* need universa operators, to avoid the cost of temporary conversions. In this case, use either a template member function with two parameters or a global operator with four. Some programmers prefer global operators when it's possible to implement them using only the public interface of the class (as previously shown).

```
template <typename T1, typename T2 >
struct pair
{
   // ...

   template <typename S1, typename S2>
   inline bool operator== (const pair<S1, S2>& that) const
   {
      return (first == that.first) && (second == that.second);
   }
};
```

This will work if `this->first` and `that.first` are comparable (for example, `int` and `const int`). Note that you may still have temporary conversions, because you are delegating to an unspecified `T1::operator==`.[43]

1.4.9. Secret Inheritance

Public derivation from a concrete class can be used as a sort of "strong typedef":

```
class A
{
   // concrete class
   // ...
};

class B : public A
{
};

// now B works "almost" as A, but it's a different type
```

You may need to implement one or more "forwarding constructors" in B.

[43]Note that the best option is to demand that the paired objects provide suitable operators, so we delegate the compari For example, `pair<const char*, int>` and `pair<std::string, int>` are unlikely to trigger the construction of temporary strings, because we expect the STL to supply an `operator==(const char*, const std::string&)`.

This is one of the strategies to simulate template typedefs (which do not exist yet in C++; see ection 12.6):

```
emplate <typename T1, typename T2>
.ass A

 // ...


mplate <typename T>
ass B : public A<T, T>
```

However, this is acceptable only if A is a private class whose existence is unknown or undocumented:

```
mplate <typename T>
ass B : public std::map<T, T>   // bad idea

nespace std

nplate <...>
ass map : public _Tree<...>        // ok: class _Tree is invisible to the user
```

A secret base class is often a good container of operators that does not depend on some template ameters. For example, it may be reasonable to test equality between two objects, ignoring all the ameters that are purely cosmetic:

```
plate <typename T, int INITIAL_CAPACITY = 16>
ss C;

plate <typename T>
ss H

lic:
H& operator==(const H&) const;


plate <typename T, int INITIAL_CAPACITY>
ss C : public H<T>
```

Comparisons between two containers C with a different INITIAL_CAPACITY will succeed and call their mon base H::operator==.

1.4.10. Literal Zero

Sometimes you need to write a function or an operator that behaves differently when a literal zero is passed. This is often the case with smart pointers:

```
template <typename T>
class shared_ptr
{
   //...
};

shared_ptr<T> P;
T* Q;

P == 7; // should not compile
P == 0; // should compile
P == Q; // should compile
```

You can distinguish 0 from a generic int by writing an overload that accepts a pointer to member of a class that has no members:

```
class dummy {};

typedef int dummy::*literal_zero_t;

template <typename T>
class shared_ptr
{
   // ...

   bool operator==(literal_zero_t) const
   {
```

The user has no way of creating a literal_zero_t, because dummy has no members of type int, so the only valid argument is an implicit cast of a literal zero (unless a more specialized overload exists).

1.4.11. Boolean Type

Some types, such as std::stream, have a cast-to-boolean operator. If implemented naively, this can lead inconsistencies:

```
class stream
{
   // ...

   operator bool() const
   {
      // ...
   }
};

stream s;
```

```
f (s)                  // ok, that's what we want

 int i = s + 2;        // unfortunately, this compiles
```

A classic workaround was to implement cast to void*:

```
ass stream

 // ...

 operator void*() const
 {
    // return 'this' when true or '0' when false
 }


ream s;

 (s)                   // ok, that's what we want

 int i = s + 2;        // good, this does not compile...
 free(s);              // ...but this goes on
```

A better solution is again a pointer to member:

```
uct boolean_type_t

int true_;


edef int boolean_type_t::*boolean_type;

fine mxt_boolean_true     &boolean_type_t::true_
fine mxt_boolean_false    0

ss stream

// ...

perator boolean_type() const

  // return mxt_boolean_true or mxt_boolean_false
```

1.4.12. Default and Value Initialization

If T is a type, then the construction of a default instance does not imply anything about the initialization of the object itself. The exact effect of

```
T x;
```

depends heavily on T. If T is a fundamental type or a POD, then its initial value is undefined. If T is a class, it's possible that some of its members are still undefined:

```
class A
{
   std::string s_;
   int i_;

public:
   A() {}  // this will default-construct s_ but leave i_ uninitialized
};
```

On the other hand, the line

```
T x = T();
```

will initialize T to 0, say for all fundamental types, but it may crash if T is A, because it's illegal to copy the uninitialized member i_ from the temporary on the right into x.

So to sum up:

```
T a();             // error:
                   // a is a function taking no argument and returning T
                   // equivalent to T (*a)()

T b;               // ok only if T is a class with default constructor
                   // otherwise T is uninitialized

T c(T());          // error: c is a function taking a function and returning T
                   // equivalent to T (*c)(T (*)())

T d = {};          // ok only if T is a simple aggregate44 (e.g. a struct
                   // without user-defined constructors)

T e = T();         // requires a non-explicit copy constructor
                   // and may yield undefined behaviour at runtime
```

[44]The definition of "aggregate" changed in C++11, where uniform initialization was introduced. As the issue is quite complex and detailed, readers may want to see the bibliography.

Value initialization (see paragraphs 8.5.1-7 of the standard) is a way to work around this problem. Since works only for class members, you have to write:

```
emplate <typename T>
ruct initialized_value

 T result;

 initialized_value()
 : result()
 {
 }
```

If T is a class with a default constructor, that will be used; otherwise, the storage for T will be set to 0. If T an array, each element will be recursively initialized:

```
itialized_value<double> x;          // x.result is 0.0
itialized_value<double [5]> y;      // y.result is {0.0, ..., 0.0}
itialized_value<std::string> z;     // z.result is std::string()
```

5. Code Safety

e spirit of TMP is "elegance first". In theory, some techniques can open vulnerabilities in source code, ich a malicious programmer could exploit to crash a program.[45]

Consider the following situations:

```
clude <functional>

ss unary_F : public std::unary_function<int,float>

lic:
// ...


 main()

unary_F u;

std::unary_function<int,float>* ptr = &u;   // ok, legal!
delete ptr;                                  // undefined behaviour!

return 0;
```

re may be a huge cost in increased complexity that comes from writing code "totally bulletproof". Sometimes this lexity will also inhibit some compiler optimizations. As a rule, programmers should always reason pragmatically ccept the fact that code will not handle every possible corner case.

The system header `<functional>` could make the counter-example fail by defining a protected destructor in the unary_function:

```
template<class _Arg, class _Result>
struct unary_function
{
   typedef _Arg argument_type;
   typedef _Result result_type;

protected:
   ~unary_function()
   {
   }
};
```

But this in general does not happen.[46]

The following idea is due to Sutter ([4]):

```
myclass.h
class MyClass
{
   private:
      double x_;
      int z_;

   public:
      template <typename stream_t>
      void write_x_to(stream_t& y)
      {
         y << x_;
      }
};
```

Is it possible to legally read/modify the private member MyClass::z_? Just add a specialization somewhere after including myclass.h:

```
struct MyClassHACK
{
};

template <>
void MyClass::write_x_to(MyClassHACK&)
{
   // as a member of MyClass, you can do anything...
   z_ = 3;
}
```

[46]See Section 1.6.

Finally, there are problems when declaring template friendship. First, there's no standard and portable ay to declare friendship with a template parameter (refer to **[5]** for more details).

```
emplate <typename T, int N>
.ass test

 friend class T; //uhm...
```

Second, there is no way to make `test<T,N>` a friend of `test<T,J>` (there is nothing like partial template endship). A common workaround is to declare `test<T,N>` a friend of `test<X,J>` for any other type `X`.

```
mplate <typename T, int N>
ass test

 template <typename X, int J>
    friend class test;        //ok, but every test<X,J> has access
```

The same malicious user, who wrote `MyClassHACK`, can add:

```
nplate <>
ass test<MyClassHACK, 0>

 public:
    template <typename T, int N>
    void manipulate(test<T,N>& x)
    {
        // a friend can do anything!
    }
```

You'll see that TMP sometimes makes use of techniques that are correctly labeled bad practice in ventional C++, including (but not limiting to):

- Lack of non-virtual protected destructor in (empty) base class
- Implementing cast operators `operator T() const`
- Declaring a non-explicit constructor with a single argument

5. Compiler Assumptions

vy usage of templates implies massive work for the compiler. Not all standard-conforming techniques ave identically on every *platform*.[47]

You denote by *language-neutral idioms* all the language features that don't have a standard-prescribed avior but only a reasonable expected behavior. In other words, when you use language-neutral n, you can expect that most compilers will converge on some (optimal) behavior, even if they are not anded by the standard to do so.

---

platform, usually we mean the set { processor, operating system, compiler, linker }.

■ **Note** For example, the C++ standard prescribes that `sizeof(T)>0` for any type `T`, but does not require the size of a compound type to be minimal. An empty `struct` could have size 64, but we expect it to have size 1 (or at worst, a size not larger than a pointer).

A standard-conforming compiler can legally violate the optimality condition, but in practice, such a situation is rare. In other words, a language-neutral idiom is a language construction that does not make a program worse, but gives a nice opportunity of optimization to a good compiler.

Several possible problems can arise from a perfect standard-conforming code fragment:

- Unexpected compiler errors
- Failures at runtime (access violations, core dumps, blue screens, and panic reactions)
- Huge compilation/link time
- Suboptimal runtime speed

The first two issues are due to compiler bugs and involve finding a language workaround (but the second one is usually met when it's too late).

The third problem mostly depends on poorly written template code.

The fourth problem involves finding language-neutral idioms that are not recognized by the optimizer and therefore unnecessarily slow down the program execution.

An example of expected behavior we do care about is the addition of an empty destructor to a base class.

```
class base
{
   public:
      void do_something() {}

   protected:
      ~base() {}
};

class derived : public base
{
};
```

Since the empty destructor adds no code, we expect the executable to be identical both with and without it.[48]

The compiler will be assumed able to understand and deal optimally with the situations listed in the next paragraphs.

---

[48]From empirical analysis, it looks like sometimes a protected empty destructor inhibits optimizations. Some measurements have been published in [3].

.6.1. Inline

ne compiler must be able to manage function inlining by itself, ignoring the inline directives and the code ositioning (where the body of the member functions is written).

The all-inline style places definitions and declarations inside the body of the class; every member nction is implicitly inline:

```
mplate <typename T>
ass vector

blic:
 bool empty() const
 {
    // definition and declaration
 }
```

The merged header style splits definitions and declarations of non-inline member functions, but keeps em in the same file:

```
plate <typename T>
ss vector

lic:
bool empty() const;   // declaration, non inline


plate <typename T>
l vector <T>::empty() const

// definition
```

In any case, whether you explicitly write it or not, the inline directive is just more than a hint. Some ular compilers indeed have an option to inline any function at the compiler's discretion.

Specifically, we assume that

- A sequence of inline functions is always "optimal" if the functions are simple enough, no matter how long the sequence is:

  ```
  template <typename T, int N>
  class recursive
  {
     recursive<T,N-1> r_;

  public:
     int size() const
     {
        return 1 + r_.size();
     }
  };
  ```

```
template <typename T>
class recursive<T, 0>
{
public:
   int size() const
   {
      return 0;
   }
};
```

In the previous construction, recursive<T,N>::size() will be inlined and the optimizer will simplify the call down to return N.[49]

- The compiler can optimize a call to a (const) member function of a stateless object, the typical case being binary relation's operator().

It's a common STL idiom to let a class hold a copy of a functor as a private member:

```
template <typename T>
struct less
{
   bool operator()(const T& x, const T& y) const
   {
      return x<y;
   }
};

template < typename T, typename less_t = std::less<T> >
class set
{
   less_t less_;                    // the less functor is a member

public:
   set(const less_t& less = less_t())
   : less_(less)
   {
   }

   void insert(const T& x)
   {
      // ...
      if (less_(x,y))            // invoking less_t::operator()
      // ...
   }

};
```

[49]Note that recursive<T, -1> will not compile.

If the functor is indeed stateless and operator() is const, the previous code should be equivalent to:

```
emplate <typename T>
truct less

 static bool apply(const T& x, const T& y)
 {
    return x<y;
 }
```

```
mplate < typename T, typename less_t = std::less<T> >
ass set

blic:
 void insert(const T& x)
 {
    // ...
    if (less_t::apply(x,y))
    {}
 }
```

However, you pay for the greater generality since the less_ member will consume at least one byte of ce. You can solve both issues if the compiler implements the EBO (*empty base optimization*).

```
ss stateless_base
```

```
ss derived : public stateless_base

// ...
```

In other words, any derivation from a stateless base will not make the derived class larger.[50] If less is ally a stateless structure, the EBO will not add extra bytes to the layout of set.

```
plate <typename T>
ct less

ool operator()(const T& x, const T& y) const

  return x<y;
```

---

st compilers implement this optimization, at least in the case of single inheritance.

```
template < typename T, typename less_t = std::less<T> >
class set : private less_t
{
   inline bool less(const T& x, const T& y) const
   {
      return static_cast<const less_t&>(*this)(x,y);
   }

public:
   set(const less_t& l = less_t())
   : less_t(l)
   {
   }

   void insert(const T& x)
   {
      // ...
      if (less(x,y))       // invoking less_t::operator() through *this
      {}
   }
};
```

Note the auxiliary member function less, which is intended to prevent conflicts with any other set::operator().

1.6.2. Error Messages

You would like a compiler to give precise and useful error diagnostics, especially when dealing with template Unfortunately, the meaning of "precise" and "useful" may not be the same for a human and a compiler.

Sometimes TMP techniques specifically induce the compiler to output a hint in the error message. Th user, on the other hand, should be ready to figure out the exact error from some keywords contained in the compiler log, ignoring all the noise. Here's an example of noise:

```
\include\algorithm(21) : error 'void DivideBy10<T>::operator ()(T &) const' : cannot conv
parameter 1 from 'const int' to 'int &'
        with
        [
            T=int
        ]
        Conversion loses qualifiers
        iterator.cpp(41) : see reference to function template instantiation '_Fn1
        std::for_each<XT::pair_iterator<iterator_t,N>,DivideBy10<T>>(_InIt,_InIt,_Fn1)'
        being compiled
        with
        [
            _Fn1= DivideBy10<int>,
            iterator_t=std::_Tree<std::_Tmap_traits<int,double,std::less<int>,std::alloca
            <std::pair<const int,double>>,false>>::iterator,
            N=1,
            T=int,
            _InIt=XT::pair_iterator<std::_Tree<std::_Tmap_traits<int,double,std::less<int
            std::allocator<std::pair<const int,double>>,false>>::iterator,1>
        ]
```

Here's what the user should see:

```
:erator.cpp(41) : error in 'std::for_each (iterator, iterator, DivideBy10<int>)'
    with
        iterator = XT::pair_iterator<std::map<int, double>::const_iterator, 1>

void DivideBy10<T>::operator ()(T &) const' : cannot convert parameter 1 from 'const int'
 'int &'
```

This means that the caller of `for_each` wants to alter (maybe divide by 10?) the (constant) keys of a `d::map`, which is illegal. While the original error points to `<header>`, the true problem is in `iterator.cpp`.

Unfriendly entries in error messages happen because the "bare bones error" that the compiler sees may "distant" from the semantic error.

ong Template Stack

shown previously, a function template can report an error, due to a parameter passed from its callers. odern compilers will list the whole chain of template instantiations. Since function templates usually rely template frameworks, these errors are often several levels deep in the stack of function calls.

plementation Details

the previous example, the compiler shows `std::_Tree` instead of `std::map` because `map::iterator` opens to be defined in a separate base class (named `_Tree`). `std::map` has a public `typedef` that borrows iterator from its base class:

```
edef typename _Tree<...>::iterator iterator;
```

These implementation details, which are usually hidden from the user of `std::map`, may leak in the or log.

panded Typedefs

error with `std::string` may show up as `std::basic_string<char, ...>` because some compilers will ace typedefs with their definition. The substitution may introduce a type that's unknown to the user.

However, it is truly impossible for the compiler to decide whether it's convenient or not to perform e substitutions.

Suppose there are two metafunctions called `F<T1>::type` and `G<T2>::type`:

```
edef typename G<T>::type GT;
edef typename F<GT>::type FGT;
```

An error may occur

- When `T` is not a valid argument for `G`, and in this case you'd like to read:

  ```
  error "F<GT> [where GT=G<int>::type]...".
  ```

- Because `G<T>::type` (which is defined but unknown to the user) is rejected by F, so it may be more useful:

  ```
  error "F<GT> [where GT=double]...".
  ```

However, if you don't know the result of G, a log entry such as `F<X> [where X=double]...` can be misleading (you may not even be aware that you are invoking `F<double>`).

Incomplete Types

If wisely used, an incomplete type can cause a specific error (see Section 2.2). However, there are situations where a type is *not yet* complete and this may cause bizarre errors. A long, instructive example is in Appendix A.

As a rule, when a compiler says that "a constant is not a constant" or that "a type is not a type," this usually means that you are either defining a constant recursively or are using a not-yet-complete class template.

1.6.3. Miscellaneous Tips

Regardless of assumptions, real compilers can do any sort of things, so this section outlines a few generic tips.

Don't Blame the Compiler

Bugs can lie:

- In the code, with probability (100-ε)%
- In the optimizer, with probability slightly greater than (ε/2)%
- In the compiler, with probability less than (ε/2)%

Even problems that show up only in release builds are rarely due to optimizer bugs. There are some natural differences between debug and release builds, and this may hide some errors in the program. Common factors are `#ifdef` sections, uninitialized variables, zero-filled heap memory returned by debug allocators, and so on.

Compilers do have bugs, but a common misconception is that they show up only in release builds. The following code, compiled by MSVC7.1, produces the right values in release and not in debug:

```
#include <iostream>

int main()
{
   unsigned __int64 x = 47;
   int y = -1;
   bool test1 = (x+y)<0;
   x += y;
   bool test2 = (x<0);
   bool test3 = (x<0);

   std::cout << test1 << test2 << test3;    // it should print 000

   return 0;
}
```

GCC4 in Mac OSX in debug builds does not warn the user that there are multiple `main` functions in a nsole program and it silently produces a do-nothing executable.[51]

eep Warnings at the Default Level

warning is just a guess. All compilers can recognize "idioms" that can be, with some probability, a mptom of human errors. The higher the probability is, the lower the warning level. Displaying top-level arnings is very unlikely to reveal an error, but it will flood the compiler log with innocuous messages.[52]

o Not Silence Warnings with "Dirty" Code Modifications

ome particular warning is annoying, legitimate, and probably not an error, don't modify the code. Place ompiler-specific `#pragma` disable-warning directive around the line. This will be useful to future code iewers.

However, this solution should be used with care (a warning in a deeply-nested function template might nerate many long, spurious entries in the compiler log).

One of the most dangerous warnings that should *not* be fixed is the "signed/unsigned comparison".

Many binary operations between mixed operands involve the promotion of both to unsigned, and gative numbers become positive and very large.[53] Compilers will warn in some—not all—of these ations.

```
ol f(int a)

unsigned int c = 10;
return ((a+5)<c);
```

```
t01.cpp(4) : warning C4018: '<' : signed/unsigned mismatch
```

The function returns `true` for a ∈ {-5,-4,...,4}. If you change `c` to `int`, the warning disappears, but the ction will behave differently.

The same code in a metafunction produces no warning at all:

```
plate <int A>
ss BizarreMF

static const int B = 5;
static const unsigned int C = 10;

lic:
static const bool value = ((A+B)<C);


 t = BizarreMF<-10>::value;          // returns false
```

OS X 10.4.8, XCode 2.4.1, GCC 4.01.

warnings at maximum level only once, in the very last development phase or when hunting for mysterious bugs.

3.7.2 in the standard.

In real code, two situations are likely vulnerable to "signedness bugs":

- Updating a metafunction return type from enum to a static unsigned constant:

```
static const bool value = (A+5) < OtherMF<B>::value;
// unpredictable result: the type of OtherMF is unknown / may vary
```

- Changing a container:

  The C++ standard does not define univocally an integer type for array indices. If p has type T*, then p[i] == *(p+i), so i should have type ptrdiff_t, which is signed. vector<T>::operator[] however takes an unsigned index.

To sum up, warnings are:

- Compiler specific
- Not related to code correctness (there exist both correct code that produces warnings and incorrect code that compiles cleanly)

Write code that produces the least warnings possible, but not less.

Maintain a Catalog of Compiler Bugs

This will be most useful when upgrading the compiler.

Avoid Non-Standard Behavior

This advice is in every book about C++, but we repeat it here. Programmers[54] tend to use their favorite compiler as the main tool to decide if a program is correct, instead of the C++ standard. A reasonable empirical criterion is to use two or more compilers, and if they disagree, check the standard.

Don't Be Afraid of Language Features

Whenever there's a native C++ keyword, function, or std:: object, you can assume that it's impossible to d better, unless by trading some features.[55]

It's usually true that serious bottlenecks in C++ programs are related to a *misuse* of language features (and some features are more easily misused than others; candidates are virtual functions and dynamic memory allocation), but this does not imply that these features should be avoided.

Any operating system can allocate heap memory fast enough that a reasonable number of calls to operator new will go unnoticed.[56]

Some compilers allow you to take a little memory from the stack via a function named alloca; in principle, alloca followed by a placement new (and an explicit destructor call) is roughly equivalent to ne but it incurs alignment problems. While the standard grants that heap memory is suitably aligned for any type, this does not hold for a stack. Even worse, building objects on unaligned memory may work by chan on some platforms and, totally unobserved, may slow down all data operations.[57]

---

[54]Including the author of this book.
[55]Of course, there are known exceptions to this rule: some C runtime functions (sprintf, floor) and even a few STL functions (string::operator+).
[56]Releasing memory may be a totally different matter, anyway.
[57]On AMD processors, double should be aligned to an 8-byte boundary; otherwise, the CPU will perform multiple unnecessary load operations. On different processors, accessing an unaligned double may instantly crash the prograr

The opposite case is trading features. It is sometimes possible to do better than new under strong extra ypotheses; for example, in a single threaded program where the allocation/deallocation pattern is known:

```
' assume T1 and T2 are unspecified concrete types, not template parameters

.d::multimap<T1, T2> m;

ile (m.size()>1)

  std::multimap<T1, T2>::iterator one = ...; // pick an element.
  std::multimap<T1, T2>::iterator two = ...; // pick another one.

  std::pair<T1, T2> new_element = merge_elements(*one, *two);

  m.erase(one);               // line #1
  m.erase(two);               // line #2

  m.insert(new_element);      // line #3
```

Here you may hope to outperform the default new-based allocator, since two deletions are always owed by a single allocation. Roughly speaking, when this is handled by system new/delete, the operating tem has to be notified that more memory is available in line #2, but line #3 immediately reclaims the ne amount of memory back.[58]

ink About What Users of Your Code Would Do

man memory is not as durable as computer memory. Some things that may look obvious or easily ucible in classic C++ may be more difficult in TMP.

Consider a simple function such as:

```
e_t find_number_in_string(std::string s, int t);
```

You can easily guess that the function looks for an occurrence of the second argument within the first. v consider:

```
plate <typename T, typename S>
e_t find_number_in_string(S s, T t);
```

---

n empirical test on a similar algorithm, a map with a custom allocator improved the whole program by 25%. A general gy is to reserve memory in chunks and free them with some degree of laziness.

While this may look natural to the author (S stands for string, after all), we should consider some memory-helping tricks.

- Any IDE with code completion will show the argument names:

```
template <typename T, typename S>
size_t find_number_in_string(S str, T number);

template <typename NUMBER_T, typename STRING_T>
size_t find_number_in_string(STRING_T str, NUMBER_T number);
```

- Insert one line of comment in the code before the function; an IDE could pick it up and show a tooltip.
- Adopt some convention for the order of arguments, or the result type (like C's `memcpy`).

1.7. Preprocessor

1.7.1. Include Guards

As already mentioned, a project is usually spread across many source files. Each file must be organized suc that all dependencies and prerequisites are checked by the included file, not by the caller. In particular, header inclusion should never depend on the order of `#include` statements.

```
file "container.hpp"

#include <vector>                   // dependency is resolved here, not outside

#ifdef _WIN32                       // preconditions are checked here
#error This file requires a 128-bit operating system. Please, upgrade.
#endif

template <typename T>
class very_large_container
{
   // internally uses std::vector...
};
```

Most frameworks end up having a sort of *root file* that takes care of preparing the environment:

- Detection of the current platform
- Translation of compiler-specific macros to framework macros
- Definition of general macros (such as `MXT_NAMESPACE_BEGIN`)
- Inclusion of STL headers
- Definition of lightweight structures, typedefs, and constants

All other headers begin by including the root file, which is rarely modified. This will often decrease compilation time, since compilers can be instructed to distill a pre-compiled header from the root file.

An example follows:

```
'//////////////////////////////////////////////////////////////////
' platform detection

.f defined(_MSC_VER)
lefine MXT_INT64    __int64
:lif defined(__GNUC__)
lefine MXT_INT64   long long
lse
 ...
ndif

//////////////////////////////////////////////////////////////////
 macro translation
 the framework will rely on MXT_DEBUG and MXT_RELEASE

f defined(DEBUG) || defined(_DEBUG) || !defined(NDEBUG)
efine MXT_DEBUG
lse
efine MXT_RELEASE
ndif

'//////////////////////////////////////////////////////////////////
 general framework macros

efine MXT_NAMESPACE_BEGIN(x)    namespace x {
efine MXT_NAMESPACE_END(x)      }

//////////////////////////////////////////////////////////////////
STL

clude <complex>
clude <vector>
clude <map>
clude <utility>

'//////////////////////////////////////////////////////////////////

ng std::swap;
ng std::size_t;

edef std::complex<double> dcmplx;
edef unsigned int uint;

//////////////////////////////////////////////////////////////////

ct empty
```

According to the basic *include guard* idiom, you should enclose each header in preprocessor directives, which will prevent multiple inclusions in the same translation unit:

```
#ifndef MXT_filename_
#define MXT_filename_

// put code here

#endif //MXT_filename_
```

As a small variation of this technique, you can assign a value to `MXT_filename_`. After all, the whole point of this book is storing information in unusual places:

```
#ifndef MXT_filename_
#define MXT_filename_ 0x1020   // version number

// put code here

#endif //MXT_filename_

#include "filename.hpp"

#if MXT_filename_ < 0x1010
#error You are including an old version!
#endif
```

Anyway, such a protection is ineffective against inclusion loops. Loops happen more frequently in TM where there are only headers and no `*.cpp` file, so declarations and definitions either coincide or lie in the same file.

Suppose `A.hpp` is self-contained, `B.hpp` includes `A.hpp`, and `C.hpp` includes `B.hpp`.

```
// file "A.hpp"

#ifndef MXT_A_
#define MXT_A_ 0x1010

template <typename T>   class A {};

#endif

// file "B.hpp"

#ifndef MXT_B_
#define MXT_B _ 0x2020

#include "A.hpp"
template <typename T>   class B {};        // B uses A

#endif
```

Later, a developer modifies A.hpp so that it includes C.hpp.

```
' file "A.hpp"

.fndef MXT_A_
lefine MXT_A_ 0x1020
nclude "C.hpp"
.
```

Now unfortunately, the preprocessor will produce a file that contains a copy of B before A:

```
 MXT_A_ is not defined, enter the #ifdef
efine MXT_A_ 0x1020

 A.hpp requires including "C.hpp"

 // MXT_C_ is not defined, enter the #ifdef
 #define MXT_C_ 0x3030

 // C.hpp requires including "B.hpp"

    // MXT_B_ is not defined, enter the #ifdef

    #define MXT_B _ 0x2020
    // B.hpp requires including A.hpp
    // however MXT_A_ is already defined, so do nothing!

    template <typename T> class B {};

    // end of include "B.hpp"

template <typename T>    class C {};

// end of include "C.hpp"

plate <typename T> class A {};
```

This usually gives bizarre error messages.

To sum up, you should detect circular inclusion problems where a file includes (indirectly) a copy of f before it has been fully compiled.

The following skeleton header helps (indentation is for illustration purposes only).

```
def MXT_filename_
'ine MXT_filename_ 0x0000      // first, set version to "null"

include "other_header.hpp"

'//////////////////////////////////////////////////////////////
XT_NAMESPACE_BEGIN(framework)
///////////////////////////////////////////////////////////////

/ write code here
```

```
//////////////////////////////////////////////////////////////////////
MXT_NAMESPACE_END(framework)
//////////////////////////////////////////////////////////////////////

// finished! remove the null guard
#undef MXT_filename_
// define actual version number and quit
#define MXT_filename_ 0x1000

#else                                   // if guard is defined...

   #if MXT_filename_ == 0x0000          // ...but version is null
   #error Circular Inclusion            // ...then something is wrong!
   #endif

#endif //MXT_filename_
```

Such a header won't *solve* circular inclusion (which is a design problem), but the compiler will *diagno* it as soon as possible. Anyway, sometimes it might suffice to replace the #error statement with some forward declarations:

```
#ifndef MXT_my_vector_
#define MXT_my_vector_ 0x0000

   template <typename T>
   class my_vector
   {
      public:

         // ...

   };

   #undef MXT_my_vector_
   #define MXT_my_vector_ 0x1000

#else

   #if MXT_my_vector_ == 0x0000

   template <typename T>
   class my_vector;

   #endif

#endif //MXT_my_vector_
```

.7.2. Macro Expansion Rules

smart use of macros can simplify metaprogramming tasks, such as automation of member function eneration. We briefly mention the non-obvious preprocessor rules here[59]:

- The token-concatenation operator ## produces one single token from the concatenation of two strings. It's not just a "whitespace elimination" operator. If the result is not a single C++ token, it's illegal:

```
#define M(a,b,c)  a ##b ## c

int I = M(3,+,2); // error, illegal: 3+2 is not a single token
int J = M(0,x,2); // ok, gives 0x2
```

- The stringizer prefix # converts text[60] into a *valid* corresponding C++ string, thus it will insert the right backslashes, and so on.

- Generally macro expansion is recursive. First, arguments are completely expanded, then they are substituted in the macro definition, then the final result is again checked and possibly expanded again:

```
#define A1        100
#define A2        200
#define Z(a,b)    a ## b

Z(A, 1);  // expands to A1, which expands to 100
Z(A, 3);  // expands to A3
```

- The two operators # and ##, however, *inhibit macro expansion* on their arguments, so:

```
Z(B, A1); // expands to BA1, not to B100
```

- To make sure everything is expanded, you can add an additional level of indirection that apparently does nothing:

```
#define Y(a,b)   a ## b
#define Z(a,b)   Y(a,b)

Z(B,A1);
// expands first to Y(B,A1). Since neither B nor A1 is an operand
// of #or ##, they are expanded, so we get Y(B,100),
// which in turn becomes B100
```

---

a complete reference, consider the GNU manual http://gcc.gnu.org/onlinedocs/cpp.pdf.
an be applied only to a macro argument, not to arbitrary text.

- Macros cannot be recursive, so while expanding Z, any direct or indirect reference to Z is not considered:

```
#define X  Z
#define Z  X+Z

Z;
// expands first as X+Z. The second Z is ignored; then the first X
// is replaced by Z, and the process stops,
// so the final result is "Z+Z"
```

- A popular trick is to define a macro as itself. This is practically equivalent to an #undef, except that the macro is still defined (so #ifdef and similar directives don't change behavior).

```
#define A  A
```

As a final recap:

```
#define A  1

#define X2(a, b)    const char* c##a = b
#define X(x)        X2(x, #x)
#define Y(x)        X(x)

X2(A, "A"); // → const char* c##A = "A" → const char* cA = "A";
X(A);       // → X2(A, #A) → X2(1, "A") → const char* c1 = "A";
Y(A);       // → X(A) → X(1) → X2(1, "1") → const char* c1 = "1";
```

Observe that, in this code, X may look just as a convenience shortcut for X2, but *it's not*. Normally you cannot observe the difference, but before X expands to X2, argument expansion occurs, something that dir invocation of X2 could have prevented.

How safe is it to replace a macro that defines an integer with a constant (either enum or static const int)? The answer is in the previous code snippet. After the change, preprocessor tricks will break:

```
//#define A  1
static const int A = 1;

// ...

X(A); // const char* cA = "A";
Y(A); // const char* cA = "A";
```

But if A is not *guaranteed* to be a macro, the replacement should be transparent.[61]

[61]Some C libraries, for example, list all the possible error codes without specifying the exact nature of these constants In this case, they should be used as enums. In particular, it should be safe to undefine them, if they happen to be macr and to replace them with real enumerations.

One more rule that is worth mentioning is that the preprocessor respects the distinction between acros with and without arguments. In particular it will not try to expand A followed by an open bracket, ad similarly for X not followed by a bracket. This rule is exploited in a popular idiom that prevents onstruction of unnamed instances of a type C[62]:

```
emplate <typename T>
lass C

blic:
 explicit C([[one argument here]]);


efine C(a)  sizeof(sorry_anonymous_instance_not_allowed_from_ ## a)

x("argument");         // ok: C not followed by bracket is not expanded
turn C("temporary"); // error: the sizeof statement does not compile
```

Finally, since many template types contain a comma, it's not generally possible to pass them safely ough macros:

```
efine DECLARE_x_OF_TYPE(T) T x

LARE_x_OF_TYPE(std::map<int, double>);  /* error:
                ^^^^^^^^^^^^  ^^^^^^^        two arguments */
```

There are several workarounds for this:

- Extra brackets (as a rule, this is *unlikely* to work, as in C++ there's not much use for a type in brackets):

```
DECLARE_x_OF_TYPE((std::map<int, double>));
// → (std::map<int, double>) x; → error
```

- A typedef will work, unless the type depends on other macro arguments:

```
typedef std::map<int, double> map_int_double;
DECLARE_x_OF_TYPE(map_int_double);
```

- Another macro:

```
#define mxt_APPLY2(T, T1, T2)          T< T1, T2 >

DECLARE_x_OF_TYPE(mxt_APPLY2(std::map,int,double));
```

---

s example will actually be clear only after reading Section 2,2.

CHAPTER 2

Small Object Toolkit

The previous chapter focused on the connection between template programming and style. In short, templates are elegant, as they allow you to write efficient code that looks simple because they hide the underlying complexity.

If you recall the introductory example of sq from Chapter 1, it's clear that the first problem of TMP is choosing the best C++ entity that models a concept and makes the code look clear at the point of instantiation.

Most classic functions use internally temporary variables and return a result. Temporary variables are cheap, so you must give the intermediate results a name to increase the readability of the algorithm:

```
int n_dogs = GetNumberOfDogs();
int n_cats = GetNumberOfCats();

int n_food_portions = n_dogs + n_cats;

BuyFood(n_food_portions);
```

In TMP, the equivalent of a temporary variable is an auxiliary type.

To model a concept, we will freely use lots of different types. Most of them do nothing except "carry a meaning in their name," as in `n_food_portions` in the previous example.

This is the main topic of Section 2.3.

The following paragraphs list some extremely simple objects that naturally come up as building blocks of complex patterns. These are called "hollow," because they carry no data (they may have no members at all). The code presented in this chapter is freely reused in the rest of the book.

2.1. Hollow Types

2.1.1. instance_of

One of the most versatile tools in metaprogramming is `instance_of`:

```
template <typename T>
struct instance_of
{
    typedef T type;

    instance_of(int = 0)
    {
    }
};
```

The constructor allows you to declare global constants and quickly initialize them.

```
onst instance_of<int> I_INT = instance_of<int>(); // ok but cumbersome
onst instance_of<double> I_DOUBLE = 0;             // also fine.
```

Note Remember that a `const` object must either be explicitly initialized or have a user-defined default nstructor. If you simply write

```
ruct empty

 empty() {}

nst empty EMPTY;
```

compiler may warn that EMPTY is unused. A nice workaround to suppress the warning is in fact:

```
ruct empty

 empty(int = 0) {}

st empty EMPTY = 0;
```

1.2. Selector

aditional code in classic C++ stores information in variables. For example, a `bool` can store two different ies. In metaprogramming, all the information is contained in the type itself, so the equivalent of a `bool` is emplate) type that can be instantiated in two different ways. This is called a `selector`:

```
plate <bool PARAMETER>
uct selector



edef selector<true> true_type[1];
edef selector<false> false_type;
```

Note that all instances of `selector<true>` convey the same information. Since their construction is pensive, `instance_of` and `selector` are both useful to replace explicit template parameter invocation:

```
late <bool B, typename T>
 f(const T& x)
```

---

lers who are familiar with modern C++ will recognize that such a typedef already exists in namespace `std`. I will say on this argument in Section 12.1.

```
int main()
{
   double d = 3.14;
   f<true>(d);                        // force B=true and deduce T=double
};
```

Or equivalently:

```
template <typename T, bool B>
void f(const T& x, selector<B>)
{
}

int main()
{
   double d = 3.14;
   f(d, selector<true>());            // deduce B=true and T=double
};
```

One of the advantages of the latter implementation is that you can give a meaningful name to the second parameter, using a (cheap) constant:

```
const selector<true> TURN_ON_DEBUG_LOGGING;
// ...
double d = 3.14;
f(d, TURN_ON_DEBUG_LOGGING);       // deduce B=true and T=double
```

2.1.3. Static Value

The generalization of a selector is a static value:

```
template <typename T, T VALUE>
struct static_parameter
{
};

template <typename T, T VALUE>
struct static_value : static_parameter<T, VALUE>
{
   static const T value = VALUE;
};
```

Note that you could replace `selector<B>` with `static_value<bool, B>`. In fact from now on, you car assume that the implementation of the latter is the same.[2]

In a `static_value`, T must be an integer type; otherwise, the static const initialization becomes illega Instead, in `static_parameter`, T can be a pointer (and VALUE can be a literal zero).

---

[2]You could let `selector` derive from the other, but you can't assume explicitly that they are convertible. Under C++0x, could also write a template typedef with the new `using` notation (see Section 12.6).

A member cast operator may be added to allow switching from a static constant to a runtime integer[3]:

```
emplate <typename T, T VALUE>
truct static_value : static_parameter<T, VALUE>

  static const T value = VALUE;

  operator T () const
  {
     return VALUE;
  }

  static_value(int = 0)
  {
  }
```

So you can pass an instance of `static_value<int, 3>` to a function that requires `int`. However, it's ually safer to write an external function:

```
nplate <typename T, T VALUE>
line T static_value_cast(static_value<T, VALUE>)

 return VALUE;
```

1.4. Size of Constraints

C++ standard does not impose strict requirements on the size of elementary types[4] and compound types have internal padding anywhere between members.

Given a type `T`, say you want to obtain another type, `T2`, whose `sizeof` is different.

A very simple solution is:

```
plate <typename T>
ss larger_than

T body_[2];   // private, not meant to be used
```

It must hold that `sizeof(T)<2*sizeof(T)£sizeof(larger_than<T>)`. However, the second inequality be indeed strict, if the compiler adds padding (suppose `T` is `char` and any struct has a minimum size of bytes).

The most important use of this class is to define two types (see Section 4.2.1):

```
def char no_type;
def larger_than<no_type> yes_type;
```

---

also Section 4.12.

weak ordering is granted: `1=sizeof(char)≤sizeof(short)≤sizeof(int)≤sizeof(long)`.

■ **Warning** These definitions are not compatible with C++0x `std::false_type` and `std::true_type`, which instead are equivalent to `static_value<bool, false>` and `static_value<bool, true>`.

In practice, you can safely use `char`, whose size is 1 by definition, and `ptrdiff_t` (in most platforms a pointer is larger than one byte).

It is possible to declare a type having exactly size `N` (with `N>0`):

```
template <size_t N>
struct fixed_size
{
   typedef char type[N];
};
```

So that `sizeof(fixed_size<N>::type) == N.`

Note that `fixed_size<N>` itself can have any size (at least `N`, but possibly larger).

Remember that it's illegal to declare a function that returns an array, but a *reference* to an array is fine and has the same size[5]:

```
fixed_size<3>::type f();    // error: illegal

int three = sizeof(f());

fixed_size<3>::type& f();   // ok

int three = sizeof(f());    // ok, three == 3
```

2.2. Static Assertions

Static assertions are simple statements whose purpose is to induce a (compiler) error when a template parameter does not meet some specification.

I illustrate here only the most elementary variations on the theme.

The simplest form of assertion just *tries to use* what you require. If you need to ensure that a type `T` indeed contains a constant named `value` or a type named `type`, you can simply write:

```
template <typename T>
void myfunc()
{
   typedef typename T::type ERROR_T_DOES_NOT_CONTAIN_type;

   const int ASSERT_T_MUST_HAVE_STATIC_CONSTANT_value(T::value);
};
```

If `T` is not conformant, you will get an error pointing to a sort of "descriptive" line.

For more complex assertions, you can exploit the fact that an incomplete type cannot be constructed that `sizeof(T)` causes a compiler error if `T` is incomplete.

[5]This remark will be clear in view of the material presented in Section 4.2.1.

.2.1. Boolean Assertions

he easiest way to verify a statement is to use a selector-like class whose body is not present if the condition false:

```
mplate <bool STATEMENT>
ruct static_assertion



mplate <>
ruct static_assertion<false>;

t main()

 static_assertion<sizeof(int)==314> ASSERT_LARGE_INT;
 return 0;


ror C2079: 'ASSERT_LARGE_INT' uses undefined struct 'static_assertion<false>'
```

All variations on the idiom try to trick the compiler into emitting more user-friendly error messages. drei Alexandrescu has proposed some enhancements. Here's an example.

```
nplate <bool STATEMENT>
uct static_assertion;

plate <>
uct static_assertion<true>

static_assertion()
{}

template <typename T>
static_assertion(T)
{}


plate <> struct static_assertion<false>;

ict error_CHAR_IS_UNSIGNED {};

 main()

nst static_assertion<sizeof(double)!=8> ASSERT1("invalid double");
nst static_assertion<(char(255)>0)> ASSERT2(error_CHAR_IS_UNSIGNED());
```

If the condition is false, the compiler will report something like, "cannot build `static_assertion<false>` `error_CHAR_IS_UNSIGNED`".

Each assertion wastes some bytes on the stack, but it can be wrapped in a macro directive using sizeof:

```
#define MXT_ASSERT(statement)     sizeof(static_assertion<(statement)>)
```

The invocation

```
MXT_ASSERT(sizeof(double)!=8);
```

will translate to [[some integer]] if successful and to an error otherwise. Since a statement like 1 is a no-op, the optimizer will ignore it.

The very problem with macro assertions is the *comma*:

```
MXT_ASSERT(is_well_defined< std::map<int, double> >::value);
//                                       ^
//                                   comma here
//
// warning or error! MXT_ASSERT does not take 2 parameters
```

The argument of the macro in this case is probably the string up to the first comma (is_well_defined< std::map<int), so even if the code compiles, it won't behave as intended.

Two workarounds are possible—you can either typedef away the comma or put extra brackets around the argument:

```
typedef std::map<int, double> map_type;
MXT_ASSERT( is_well_defined<map_type>::value );
```

or:

```
MXT_ASSERT(( is_well_defined< std::map<int, double> >::value ));
```

The C++ preprocessor will be confused only by commas that are at the same level[6] as the argument of the macro:

```
assert( f(x,y)==4 ); // comma at level 2: ok
assert( f(x),y==4 ); // comma at level 1: error
```

static_assertion can be used to make assertions in classes using private inheritance:

```
template <typename T>
class small_object_allocator : static_assertion<(sizeof(T)<64)>
{
};
```

[6]The level of a character is the number of open brackets minus the number of closed brackets in the string from the beginning of the line up to the character itself.

Note static_assert is a keyword in the modern C++ Standard. Here, I use a similar name for a class for ustration purposes. C++0x static_assert behaves like a function that takes a constant Boolean expression d a string literal (an error message that the compiler will print):

```
.atic_assert(sizeof(T)<64, "T is too large");
```

nilarly to the private inheritance described previously, C++0x static_assert can also be a class member.

2.2. Assert Legal

different way of making assertions is to require that some C++ expression represents valid code for type T, urning non-void (most often, to state that a constructor or an assignment is possible).

```
efine MXT_ASSERT_LEGAL(statement)        sizeof(statement)
```

If void is allowed instead, just put a comma operator inside sizeof:

```
efine MXT_ASSERT_LEGAL(statement)        sizeof((statement), 0)
```

For example:

```
nplate <typename T>
.d do_something(T& x)

MXT_ASSERT_LEGAL(static_cast<bool>(x.empty()));

If (x.empty())
{
   // ...
}
```

This example will compile, and thus it will not reject T if x.empty(), whatever it means, returns ything convertible to) bool. T could have a member function named empty that returns int or a member ned empty whose operator() takes no argument and returns bool.

Here's another application:

```
fine MXT_CONST_REF_TO(T)        (*static_cast<const T*>(0))
fine MXT_REF_TO(T)              (*static_cast<T*>(0))

late <typename obj_t, typename iter_t>
ss assert_iterator

um

 verify_construction =
    MXT_ASSERT_LEGAL(obj_t(*MXT_CONST_REF_TO(iter_t))),

 verify_assignment =
   MXT_ASSERT_LEGAL(MXT_REF_TO(obj_t) = *MXT_CONST_REF_TO(iter_t)),
```

```
        verify_preincr =
            MXT_ASSERT_LEGAL(++MXT_REF_TO(iter_t)),

        verify_postincr =
            MXT_ASSERT_LEGAL(MXT_REF_TO(iter_t)++)
    };
};
```

A human programmer should read, "I assert it's legal to construct an instance of obj_t from the result of dereferencing a (const) instance of iter_t" and similarly for the remaining constants.

■ **Note** Observe that some standard iterators may fail the first test. For example, a back_insert_iterator may return itself when dereferenced (a special assignment operator will take care of making *i = x equivalent to i = x)

The assert_iterator<T,I> will compile only if I acts like an iterator having a value type (convertible to) For example, if I does not support post-increment, the compiler will stop and report an error in assert_iterator<T,I>::verify_postincr.

Remember that, with the usual restrictions on comma characters in macros, MXT_ASSERT_LEGAL never instantiates objects. This is because sizeof performs only a dimensional check on its arguments[7].

Also, note the special use of a macro directive. MXT_ASSERT_LEGAL should take the whole line, but since it resolves to a compile-time integer constant, you can use enums to "label" all the different assertions abo a class (as in assert_iterator) and make the code more friendly.

The compiler might also emit useful warnings pointing to these assertions. If obj_t is int and iter_t double*, the compiler will refer to the verify_assignment enumerator and emit a message similar to:

```
warning: '=' : conversion from 'double' to 'int', possible loss of data
        : see reference to class template instantiation 'XT::assert_iterator<obj_t,iter_t>
        being compiled
        with
        [
            obj_t=int,
            iter_t=double *
        ]
```

Using the very same technique, you can mix static assertions of different kinds:

```
#define MXT_ASSERT(statement)         sizeof(static_assertion<(statement)>)

template <typename obj_t, typename iter_t>
class assert_iterator
{   enum
    {
```

[7]However, a few compilers will generate a warning on MXT_INSTANCE_OF anyway, reporting that a null reference i not allowed.

```
    //...
    construction =
       MXT_ASSERT_LEGAL(obj_t(*MXT_CONST_REF_TO(iter_t))),
    size =
       MXT_ASSERT(sizeof(int)==4)
 };
```

As an exercise, I list some more heuristic assertions on iterators.

As is, class assert_iterator validates forward const_iterators. We can remove the const-ness:

```
mplate <typename obj_t, typename iter_t>
ass assert_nonconst_iterator : public assert_iterator<obj_t, iter_t>

 enum
 {
    write =
      MXT_ASSERT_LEGAL(*MXT_REF_TO(iter_t) = MXT_CONST_REF_TO(obj_t))
 };
```

Sometimes, an algorithm that works on iterators does not need to know the actual type of the derlying objects, which makes the code even more general. For example, std::count could look like this:

```
nplate <typename iter_t, typename object_t>
 count(iter_t begin, const iter_t end, const object_t& x)

int result = 0;
while (begin != end)
{
   if (*begin == x)
      ++result;
}
return result;
```

You don't need to know if *begin has the same type as x. Regardless of what exactly *begin is, you can ıme that it defines an operator== suitable for comparing against an object_t.

Suppose instead you have to store the result of *begin before comparison.

You may require the iterator type to follow the STL conventions, which means that object_t and rator::value_type must somehow be compatible[8]:

```
plate <typename obj_t, typename iter_t>
s assert_stl_iterator

edef typename std::iterator_traits<iter_t>::value_type value_type;

m
```

ally, dereferencing the iterator returns std::iterator_traits<iterator_t>::reference, but value_type e constructed from a reference.

```
    assign1 =
     MXT_ASSERT_LEGAL(MXT_REF_TO(obj_t) = MXT_CONST_REF_TO(value_type)),

    assign2 =
     MXT_ASSERT_LEGAL(MXT_REF_TO(value_type) = MXT_CONST_REF_TO(obj_t))
  };
};
```

Finally, you can perform a rough check on the iterator type, using `indicator_traits` to get its tag or writing operations with `MXT_ASSERT_LEGAL`:

```
enum
{
   random_access =
     MXT_ASSERT_LEGAL(
       MXT_CONST_REF_TO(iter_t) + int() == MXT_CONST_REF_TO(iter_t))
};
```

2.2.3. Assertions with Overloaded Operators

`sizeof` can evaluate the size of an arbitrary expression. You can thus create assertions of the form `sizeof(f(x))`, where `f` is an overloaded function, which may return an incomplete type.

Here, I just present an example, but the technique is explained in Section 4.2.1.

Suppose you want to put some checks on the length of an array:

```
T arr[] = { ... };

// later, assert that length_of(arr) is some constant
```

Since static assertions need a compile-time constant, you cannot define `length_of` as a function.

```
template <typename T, size_t N>
size_t length_of(T (&)[N])
{
   return N;
}

MXT_ASSERT(length_of(arr) == 7);   // error: not a compile-time constant
```

A macro would work:

```
#define length_of(a)     sizeof(a)/sizeof(a[0])
```

But it's risky, because it can be invoked on an unrelated type that supports `operator[]` (such as `std::vector` or a pointer), with nasty implications.

However, you can write:

```
class incomplete_type;
class complete_type {};

template <size_t N>
```

```
:ruct compile_time_const

  complete_type& operator==(compile_time_const<N>) const;

  template <size_t K>
  incomplete_type& operator==(compile_time_const<K>) const;


mplate <typename T>
mpile_time_const<0> length_of(T)

 return compile_time_const<0>();


mplate <typename T, size_t N>
mpile_time_const<N> length_of(T (&)[N])

 return compile_time_const<N>();
```

This works, but unfortunately the syntax of the assertion is not completely natural:

```
_ASSERT_LEGAL(length_of(arr) == compile_time_const<7>());
```

You can combine these techniques and the use of `fixed_size<N>::type` from Section 2.1.4, wrapping n additional macro:

```
plate <typename T, size_t N>
ename fixed_size<N>::type& not_an_array(T (&)[N]);   // note: no body

fine length_of(X) sizeof(not_an_array(X))
```

Now `length_of` is again a compile-time constant, with some additional type-safety checks. The name `_an_array` was chosen on purpose; it is usually hidden from the user, but it will usually be printed when argument is incorrect:

```
ss AA {};

 a[5];
 b = length_of(a);

aa;
 c = length_of(aa);

r: no matching function for call to 'not_an_array(AA&)'
```

.4. Modeling Concepts with Function Pointers

following idea has been documented by Bjarne Stroustrup.
A *concept* is a set of logical requirements on a type that can be translated to syntactic requirements.

For example, a "less-than comparable" type must implement operator < in some form. The exact signature of a<b doesn't matter as long as it can be used as a Boolean.

Complex concepts may require several syntactic constraints at once. To impose a complex constraint on a tuple of template parameters, you simply write a static member function, where all code lines together model the concept (in other words, if all the lines compile successfully, the constraint is satisfied). Then, you induce the compiler to emit the corresponding code simply by initializing a dummy function pointer in the constructor of a dedicated assertion class (the concept function never runs):

```
template <typename T1, typename T2>
struct static_assert_can_copy_T1_to_T2
{
    static void concept_check(T1 x, T2 y)
    {
        T2 z(x);          // T2 must be constructable from T1
        y = x;            // T2 must be assignable from T1
    }

    static_assert_can_copy_T1_to_T2()
    {
        void (*f)(T1, T2) = concept_check;
    }
};
```

The concept check can be triggered when you're either building an instance on the stack or deriving from it:

```
template <typename T>
T sqrt(T x)
{
    static_assert_can_copy_T1_to_T2<T, double> CHECK1;
}

template <typename T>
class math_operations : static_assert_can_copy_T1_to_T2<T, double>
{};
```

2.2.5. Not Implemented

While C++0x allows you to "delete" member functions from a class, in classic C++, you'll sometimes want express the fact that an operator should not be provided:

```
template <typename T>
class X
{
    // ...

    X<T>& operator= (X<T>& that) { NOT_IMPLEMENTED; }
};
```

here the last statement is a macro for a static assertion that fails. For example:

```
efine NOT_IMPLEMENTED     MXT_ASSERT(false)
```

The rationale for this idiom is that the member operator will be compiler-only on first use, which is actly what you want to prevent.

However, this technique is risky and non-portable. The amount of diagnostics that a compiler can nit on unused template member function varies. In particular, if an expression does not depend on T, the mpiler may legitimately try to instantiate it, so MXT_ASSERT(false) may trigger anytime.

At least, the return type should be correct:

```
X<T>& operator= (X<T>& that) { NOT_IMPLEMENTED; return *this; }
```

A second choice is to make the assertion dependent on T:

```
efine NOT_IMPLEMENTED     MXT_ASSERT(sizeof(T)==0)
```

Finally, a portable technique is to cause a *linker* error with a fake annotation. This is less desirable than ompiler error, because linker errors usually do not point back to a line in source code. This means they not easy to trace back.

```
fine NOT_IMPLEMENTED

X<T>& operator= (X<T>& that) NOT_IMPLEMENTED;
```

3. Tagging Techniques

ume you have a class with a member function called swap and you need to add a similar one called afe_swap. In other words, you are adding a function that's a variation of an existing one. You can:

- Write a different function with a similar name and (hopefully) a similar signature:

```
public:
   void swap(T& that);
   void unsafe_swap(T& that);
```

- Add (one or more) overloads of the original function with an extra runtime argument:

```
private:
   void unsafe_swap(T& that);

public:
   void swap(T& that);

   enum swap_style { SWAP_SAFE, SWAP_UNSAFE };

   void swap(T& that, swap_style s)
   {
      if (s == SWAP_SAFE)
         this->swap(that);
      else
         this->unsafe_swap(that);
   }
```

- Add an overload of the original function with an extra static *useless* argument:

```
public:
    void swap(T& that);
    void swap(T& that, int);    // unsafe swap: call as x.swap(y, 0)
```

None of these options is completely satisfactory. The first is clear but does not scale well, as the interface could grow too much. The second may pay a penalty at runtime. The last is not intuitive and shoul be documented.

Instead, TMP makes heavy use of *language-neutral idioms*, which are language constructs that have no impact on code generation.

A basic technique for this issue is overload resolution via *tag objects*. Each member of the overload set has a formal unnamed parameter of a different static type.

```
struct unsafe {};

class X
{
public:
   void swap(T& that);
   void swap(T& that, unsafe);
};
```

Here's a different example:

```
struct naive_algorithm_tag {};
struct precise_algorithm_tag {};

template <typename T>
inline T log1p(T x, naive_algorithm_tag)
{
   return log(x+1);
}

template <typename T>
inline T log1p(T x, precise_algorithm_tag)
{
   const T xp1 = x+1;
   return xp1==1 ? x : x*log(xp1)/(xp1-1);
}

// later...

double t1 = log1p(3.14, naive_algorithm_tag());
double t2 = log1p(0.00000000314, precise_algorithm_tag());
```

Building a temporary tag is inexpensive (most optimizing compilers will do nothing and behave as if you had two functions named log1p_naive and log1p_precise, with one parameter each).

So, let's dig a bit further into the mechanisms of overload selection.

Recall that you are facing the problem of picking the right function at compile time, supplying an ext parameter that's human-readable.

The extra parameter is usually an unnamed instance of an empty class:

```
emplate <typename T>
nline T log1p(T x, selector<true>);

emplate <typename T>
nline T log1p(T x, selector<false>);

 code #1
eturn log1p(x, selector<PRECISE_ALGORITHM>());
```

You might wonder why a type is necessary, when the same effect can be achieved with simpler syntax:

```
 code #2
 (USE_PRECISE_ALGORITHM)
 return log1p_precise(x);
se
 return log1p_standard(x);
```

The key principle in tag dispatching is that the program compiles only the functions that are strictly cessary. In code #1, the compiler sees one function call, but in the second fragment, there are two. The `if` cision is fixed, but is irrelevant (as is the fact that the optimizer may simplify the redundant code later).

In fact, tag dispatching allows the code to select between a function that works and one that would not en compile (see the following paragraph about iterators).

This does not imply that *every* `if` with a static decision variable must be turned into a function call. pically, in the middle of a complex algorithm, an explicit statement is cleaner:

```
it();
it_again();

(my_options<T>::need_to_clean_up)

std::fill(begin, end, T());
```

3.1. Type Tags

simplest tags are just empty structures:

```
uct naive_algorithm_tag {};
uct precise_algorithm_tag {};

plate <typename T>
ne T log1p(T x, naive_algorithm_tag);

plate <typename T>
ne T log1p(T x, precise_algorithm_tag);
```

You can use template tags to transport extra parameters to the function:

```
late <int N>
ct algorithm_precision_level {};
```

```
template <typename T, int N>
inline T log1p(T x, algorithm_precision_level<N>);

// ...

double x = log1p(3.14, algorithm_precision_level<4>());
```

You can use derivation to build a tag hierarchy.

This example sketches what actual STL implementations do (observe that inheritance is public by default):

```
struct input_iterator_tag {};
struct output_iterator_tag {};
struct forward_iterator_tag : input_iterator_tag {};
struct bidirectional_iterator_tag : forward_iterator_tag {};
struct random_access_iterator_tag : bidirectional_iterator_tag {};

template <typename iter_t>
void somefunc(iter_t begin, iter_t end)
{
   return somefunc(begin, end,
      typename std::iterator_traits<iter_t>::iterator_category());
}

template <typename iter_t>
void somefunc(iter_t begin, iter_t end, bidirectional_iterator_tag)
{
   // do the work here
}
```

In this case, the bidirectional and random_access iterators will use the last overload of somefunc. Alternatively, if somefunc is invoked on any other iterator, the compiler will produce an error.

A generic implementation will process all the tags that do not have an exact match[9]:

```
template <typename iter_t, typename tag_t>
void somefunc(iter_t begin, iter_t end, tag_t)
{
   // generic implementation:
   // any tag for which there's no *exact* match, will fall here
}
```

This generic implementation can be made compatible with the tag hierarchy using pointers:

```
template <typename iter_t>
void somefunc(iter_t begin, iter_t end)
{
  typedef
    typename std::iterator_traits<iter_t>::iterator_category cat_t;
  return somefunc(begin, end, static_cast<cat_t*>(0));
}
```

---

[9]In particular, this will process random_access iterators as well. That is, it blindly ignores the base/derived tag hierarc

```
emplate <typename iter_t>
oid somefunc(iter_t begin, iter_t end,
             std::bidirectional_iterator_tag*)

 // do the work here


mplate <typename iter_t>
id somefunc(iter_t begin, iter_t end,
             void*)

 // generic
```

The overload resolution rules will try to select the match that loses less information. Thus, the cast rived*-to-base* is a better match than a cast to void*. So, whenever possible (whenever the iterator tegory is at least bidirectional), the second function will be taken.

Another valuable option is:

```
nplate <typename iter_t>
id somefunc(iter_t begin, iter_t end, ...)

 // generic
```

The ellipsis operator is the worst match of all, but it cannot be used when the tag is a class (and this is ctly why you had to switch to pointers and tags).

3.2. Tagging with Functions

ightly more sophisticated option is to use function pointers as tags:

```
m algorithm_tag_t

NAIVE,
PRECISE


ine static_value<algorithm_tag_t, NAIVE> naive_algorithm_tag()

return 0; // dummy function body: calls static_value<...>(int)


ine static_value<algorithm_tag_t, PRECISE> precise_algorithm_tag()

eturn 0; // dummy function body: calls static_value<...>(int)
```

The tag is not the return type, but the function itself. The idea comes somehow from STL stream manipulators (that have a common signature).

```
typedef
   static_value<algorithm_tag_t, NAIVE> (*naive_algorithm_tag_t)();

typedef
   static_value<algorithm_tag_t, PRECISE> (*precise_algorithm_tag_t)();

template <typename T>
inline T log1p(T x, naive_algorithm_tag_t);

// later
// line 4: pass a function as a tag

double y = log1p(3.14, naive_algorithm_tag);
```

Since each function has a different unique signature, you can use the function name (equivalent to a function pointer) as a global constant. Inline functions are the only "constants" that can be written in head files without causing linker errors.

You can then omit brackets from the tags (compare line 4 above with its equivalent in the previous example). Function tags can be grouped in a namespace or be static members of a struct:

```
namespace algorithm_tag
{
   inline static_value<algorithm_tag_t, NAIVE> naive()
   { return 0; }

   inline static_value<algorithm_tag_t, PRECISE> precise()
   { return 0; }
}
```

or:

```
struct algorithm_tag
{
   static static_value<algorithm_tag_t, NAIVE> naive()
   { return 0; }

   static static_value<algorithm_tag_t, PRECISE> precise()
   { return 0; }
};

double y = log1p(3.14, algorithm_tag::naive);
```

Another dramatic advantage of function pointers is that you can adopt a uniform syntax for the same runtime and compile-time algorithms:

```
enum binary_operation
{
   sum,   difference,   product,   division
```

```
;

lefine mxt_SUM     x+y
lefine mxt_DIFF    x-y
lefine mxt_PROD    x*y
lefine mxt_DIV     x/y

 define both the tag and the worker function with a single macro

efine mxt_DEFINE(OPCODE, FORMULA)                                      \
                                                                       \
line static_value<binary_operation, OPCODE> static_tag_##OPCODE()      \
                                                                       \
 return 0;                                                             \
                                                                       \
                                                                       \
mplate <typename T>                                                    \
binary(T x, T y, static_value<binary_operation, OPCODE>)               \
                                                                       \
 return (FORMULA);                                                     \

:_DEFINE(sum, mxt_SUM);
:_DEFINE(difference, mxt_DIFF);
_DEFINE(product, mxt_PROD);
_DEFINE(division, mxt_DIV);

plate <typename T, binary_operation OP>
ine T binary(T x, T y, static_value<binary_operation, OP> (*)())

return binary(x, y, static_value<binary_operation, OP>());
```

This is the usual machinery needed for the static selection of the function. Due to the way you defined rloads, the following calls produce identical results (otherwise, it would be quite surprising for the user), n if they are not identical. The first is preferred:

```
ble a1 = binary(8.0, 9.0, static_tag_product);
ble a2 = binary(8.0, 9.0, static_tag_product());
```

However, with the same tools, you can further refine the function and add a similar runtime algorithm[10]:

```
late <typename T>
inary(T x, T y, const binary_operation op)

witch (op)

ase sum:         return mxt_SUM;
ase difference:  return mxt_DIFF;
```

s example anticipates ideas from Section 7.3.

```
    case product:      return mxt_PROD;
    case division:     return mxt_DIV;
    default:
       throw std::runtime_error("invalid operation");
    }
}
```

The latter would be invoked as:

```
double a3 = binary(8.0, 9.0, product);
```

This may look similar, but it's a completely different function. It shares some implementation (in this case, the four kernel macros), but it selects the right one *at runtime*.

- Manipulators (see Section 1.4.7 are similar to functions used as compile-time constants. However, they differ in a few ways too:
- Manipulators are more generic. All operations have a similar signature (which must be supported by the stream object) and any user can supply more of them, but they involve some runtime dispatch.
- Function constants are a fixed set, but since there's a one-to-one match between signatures and overloaded operators, there is no runtime work.

2.3.3. Tag Iteration

A useful feature of functions tagged with static values is that, by playing with bits and compile-time computations, it's possible to write functions that automatically unroll some "iterative calls".

For example, the following function fills a C array with zeroes:

```
template <typename T, int N>
void zeroize_helper(T* const data, static_value<int, N>)
{
   zeroize_helper(data, static_value<int, N-1>());
   data[N-1] = T();
}

template <typename T>
void zeroize_helper(T* const data, static_value<int, 1>)
{
   data[0] = T();
}

template <typename T, int N>
void zeroize(T (&data)[N])
{
   zeroize_helper(data, static_value<int, N>());
}
```

You can swap two lines and iterate backward:

```
emplate <typename T, int N>
oid zeroize_helper(T* const data, static_value<int, N>)

  data[N-1] = T();
  zeroize_helper(data, static_value<int, N-1>());
```

This unrolling is called *linear* and with two indices, you can have *exponential* unrolling. Assume for nplicity that N is a power of two:

```
mplate <int N, int M>
ruct index



nplate <typename T, int N, int M>
id zeroize_helper(T* const data, index<N, M>)

 zeroize_helper(data, index<N/2, M>());
 zeroize_helper(data, index<N/2, M+N/2>());


nplate <typename T, int M>
.d zeroize_helper(T* const data, index<1, M>)

data[M] = T();


plate <typename T, int N>
d zeroize(T (&data)[N])

zeroize_helper(data, index<N, 0>());


ble test[8];
oize(test);
```

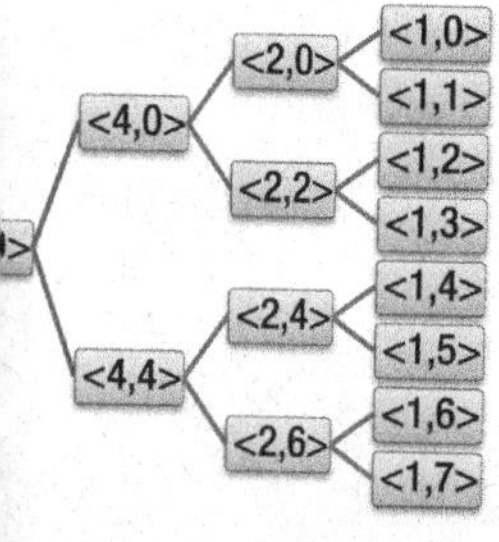

re 2-1. *Exponential unrolling for N=8*

As a more complex case, you can iterate over a set of *bits*.

Assume an enumeration describes some heuristic algorithms in increasing order of complexity:

```
enum
{
    ALGORITHM_1,
    ALGORITHM_2,
    ALGORITHM_3,
    ALGORITHM_4,
    // ...
};
```

For each value in the enumeration, you are given a function that performs a check. The function returns true when everything is okay or false if it detects a problem:

```
bool heuristic([[args]], static_value<size_t, ALGORITHM_1>);
bool heuristic([[args]], static_value<size_t, ALGORITHM_2>);

// ...
```

What if you wanted to run some or all of the checks, in increasing order, with a single function call?

First, you modify the enumeration using powers of two:

```
enum
{
    ALGORITHM_1 = 1,
    ALGORITHM_2 = 2,
    ALGORITHM_3 = 4,
    ALGORITHM_4 = 8,
    // ...
};
```

The user will use a static value as a tag, and algorithms will be combined with “bitwise or” (or +).

```
typedef static_value<size_t, ALGORITHM_1 | ALGORITHM_4> mytag_t;

// this is the public function
```

```
emplate <size_t K>
ool run_heuristics([[args]], static_value<size_t, K>)

 return heuristic([[args]],
                  static_value<size_t, K>(),
                  static_value<size_t, 0>());
```

Here are the “private” implementation details:

```
efine VALUE(K)     static_value<size_t, K>

mplate <size_t K, size_t J>
ol heuristic([[args]], VALUE(K), VALUE(J))

 static const size_t JTH_BIT = K & (size_t(1) << J);

 // JTH_BIT is either 0 or a power of 2.
 // try running the corresponding algorithm, first.
 // if it succeeds, the && will continue with new tags,
 // with the J-th bit turned off in K and J incremented by 1

 return
    heuristic([[args]], VALUE(JTH_BIT)()) &&
    heuristic([[args]], VALUE(K-JTH_BIT)(), VALUE(J+1)());


plate <size_t J>
l heuristic([[args]], VALUE(0), VALUE(J))

// finished: all bits have been removed from K
return true;


plate <size_t K>
l heuristic([[args]], VALUE(K))

// this is invoked for all bits in K that do not have
// a corresponding algorithm, and when K=0
// i.e. when a bit in K is off

return true;
```

.4. Tags and Inheritance

e classes inherit additional overloads from their bases. So an object that dispatches a tagged call might
now which of the bases will answer.

Suppose you are given a simple allocator class, which, given a fixed size, will allocate one block of memory of that length.

```
template <size_t SIZE>
struct fixed_size_allocator
{
   void* get_block();
};
```

You now wrap it up in a larger allocator. Assuming for simplicity that most memory requests have a size equal to a power of two, you can assemble a compound_pool<N> that will contain a fixed_size_allocator<J> for J=1,2,4,8. It will also resort to ::operator new when no suitable J exists (all at compile-time).

The syntax for this allocation is[11]:

```
compound_pool<64> A;
double* p = A.allocate<double>();
```

The sketch of the idea is this. compound_pool<N> contains a fixed_size_allocator<N> and derives from compound_pool<N/2>. So, it can directly honor the allocation requests of N bytes and dispatch all other tags to base classes. If the last base, compound_pool<0>, takes the call, no better match exists, so it will call operator new.

More precisely, every class has a pick function that returns either an allocator reference or a pointer. The call tag is static_value<size_t, N>, where N is the size of the requested memory block.

```
template <size_t SIZE>
class compound_pool;

template < >
class compound_pool<0>
{
protected:

   template <size_t N>
   void* pick(static_value<size_t, N>)
   {
      return ::operator new(N);
   }
};

template <size_t SIZE>
class compound_pool : compound_pool<SIZE/2>
{
   fixed_size_allocator<SIZE> p_;
```

[11]Deallocation has been omitted on purpose.

```
rotected:
  using compound_pool<SIZE/2>::pick;

  fixed_size_allocator<SIZE>& pick(static_value<SIZE>)
  {
     return p_;
  }

blic:
 template <typename object_t>
 object_t* allocate()
 {
    typedef static_value<size_t, sizeof(object_t)> selector_t;
    return static_cast<object_t*>(get_pointer(this->pick(selector_t())));
 }

ivate:
 template <size_t N>
 void* get_pointer(fixed_size_allocator<N>& p)
 {
    return p.get_block();
 }

 void* get_pointer(void* p)
 {
    return p;
 }
```

Note the using declaration, which makes all the overloaded pick functions in every class visible. Here, pound_pool<0>::pick has a lower priority because it's a function template, but it always succeeds. thermore, since it returns a different object, it ends up selecting a different get_pointer.

PART 2

#include <prerequisites>

#include <techniques>

#include <applications>

CHAPTER 3

Static Programming

Templates are exceptionally good at forcing the compiler and optimizer to perform some work only when the executable program is generated. By definition, this is called *static* work. This is as opposed to dynamic work, which refers to what is done when the program runs.

Some activities must be completed before runtime (computing integer constants) and some activities have an impact on runtime (generating machine code for a function template, which is later executed).

TMP can produce two types of code—metafunctions, which are entirely static (for example, a metafunction `unsigned_integer<N>::type` that returns an integer holding at least `N` bits) and mixed algorithms, which are part static and part runtime. (STL algorithms rely on `iterator_category` or on the `zeroize` function explained in Section 4.1.2.

This section deals with techniques for writing efficient metafunctions.

3.1. Static Programming with the Preprocessor

The classic way to write a program that takes decisions about itself is through preprocessor directives. The C++ preprocessor can perform some integer computation tests and *cut off* portions of code that are nc appropriate.

Consider the following example. You want to define fixed-length unsigned integer types, such as `uint32_t`, to be exactly 32-bits wide, and do the same for any bit length that's a power of two.

Define

```
template <size_t S>
struct uint_n;

#define mXT_UINT_N(T,N) \
   template <> struct uint_n<N> { typedef T type; }
```

and specialize `uint_n` for all sizes that are indeed supported on the current platform.

If the user tries `uint_n<16>::type` and there's no suitable type, she will get a proper and intelligible compiler error (about a missing template specialization).

So you have to ask the preprocessor to work out the sizes by trial and error[1]:

```
include <climits>

lefine MXT_I32BIT          0xffffffffU
lefine MXT_I16BIT          0xffffU
lefine MXT_I8BIT           0xffU

f (UCHAR_MAX == MXT_I8BIT)
T_UINT_N(unsigned char,8);
ndif

f (USHRT_MAX == MXT_I16BIT)
T_UINT_N(unsigned short,16);
lif UINT_MAX == MXT_I16BIT
T_UINT_N(unsigned int,16);
ndif

f (UINT_MAX == MXT_I32BIT)
T_UINT_N(unsigned int,32);
lif (ULONG_MAX == MXT_I32BIT)
T_UINT_N(unsigned long,32);
ndif
```

This code works, but it's rather fragile because interaction between the preprocessor and the compiler imited.[2]

Note that this is not merely a generic style debate (macro versus templates), but a matter of correctness. ne preprocessor removes portions of the source file, the compiler does not have a chance to diagnose errors until macro definitions change. On the other hand, if the TMP decisions rely on the fact that the npiler sees a whole set of templates, then it instantiates only some of them.

---

lote The preprocessor is not "evil".

processor-based "metaprogramming," like the previous example, usually compiles much faster and—if it's ple—it's highly portable. Many high-end servers still ship with old or custom compilers that do not support uage-based (template) metaprogramming. On the other hand, I should mention that, while compilers tend onform 100% to the standard, this is not true for preprocessors. Therefore, obscure preprocessor tricks may to produce the desired results, and bugs caused by misusing the preprocessor are quite hard to detect.[3]

An implementation of `uint_n` that does not rely on the preprocessor is shown and explained in ion 3.6.10.

---

ember that the preprocessor runs *before* the compiler so it cannot rely on `sizeof`.
d the previous note again ☺.
also `http://www.boost.org/doc/libs/1_46_0/libs/wave/doc/preface.html`.

3.2. Compilation Complexity

When a class template is instantiated, the compiler generates:

- Every member signature at class level
- All static constants and typedefs
- Only strictly necessary function bodies

If the same instance is needed again in the same compilation unit, it's found via lookup (which need n be particularly efficient, but it's still faster than instantiation).

For example, given the following code:

```
template <size_t N>
struct sum_of_integers_up_to
{
   static const size_t value = N + sum_of_integers_up_to<N-1>::value;
};

template <>
struct sum_of_integers_up_to<0>
{
   static const size_t value = 0;
};

   int n9 = sum_of_integers_up_to<9>::value;            // mov dword ptr [n9],2Dh
   int n8 = sum_of_integers_up_to<8>::value;            // mov dword ptr [n8],24h
```

The initialization of n9 has a cost of 10 template instantiations, but the subsequent initialization of n8 has a cost of *one* lookup (not 9). Both instructions have zero runtime impact, as the assembly code shows.

As a rule, most metafunctions are implemented using recursion. The compilation complexity is the number of template instances recursively required by the metafunction itself.

This example has linear complexity, because the instantiation of X<N> needs X<N-1>... X<0>. While you'll usually want to look for the implementation with the lowest complexity (to reduce compilation tim not execution times), you can skip this optimization if there's a large amount of code reuse. Because of lookups, the first instantiation of X<N> will be costly, but it allows instantiation of X<M> for free in the sam translation unit if M<N.

Consider this example of an optimized low-complexity implementation:

```
template <size_t N, size_t K>
struct static_raise
{
   static const size_t value = /* N raised to K */;
};
```

The trivial implementation has linear complexity:

```
template <size_t N, size_t K>
struct static_raise
{
   static const size_t value = N * static_raise<N, K-1>::value;
};
```

```
emplate <size_t N>
truct static_raise<N, 0>

  static const size_t value = 1;
;
```

To obtain static_raise<N,K>::value, the compiler needs to produce K instances: static_raise<N,K-1>, atic_raise<N,K-2>,...

Eventually static_raise<N,1> needs static_raise<N,0>, which is already known (because there's an plicit specialization). This stops the recursion.

However, there's a formula that needs only about log(K) intermediate types:

Note If the exponent is a power of two, you can save a lot of multiplications via repeated squaring. To mpute X^8, only three multiplications are needed if you can store only the intermediate results. Since $= ((X^2)^2)^2$, you need to execute

```
= x*x; t = t*t; t = t*t; return t;
```

general, you can use recursively the identity:

$$X^N = X^{N \bmod 2} \cdot \left(X^{\lfloor N/2 \rfloor}\right)^2$$

```
efine MXT_M_SQ(a)          ((a)*(a))

plate <size_t N, size_t K>
uct static_raise;

plate <size_t N>
uct static_raise<N, 0>

static const size_t value = 1;


plate <size_t N, size_t K>
uct static_raise

vate:
static const size_t v0 = static_raise<N, K/2>::value;

lic:
static const size_t value = MXT_M_SQ(v0)*(K % 2 ? N : 1);
```

Note the use of MXT_M_SQ (see Section 1.3.2).

A final remark: Just because the natural implementation of metafunctions involves recursion, does not mean that *any* recursive implementation is equally optimal.[4]

Suppose N is an integer in base 10 and you want to extract the i-th digit (let's agree that digit 0 is the right-most) as digit<I,N>::value:

```
template <int I, int N>
struct digit;
```

Clearly, you have two choices. One is a "full" recursion on the main class itself

```
template <int I, int N>
struct digit
{
   static const int value = digit<i-1, N/10>::value;
};

template <int N>
struct digit<0, N>
{
   static const int value = (N % 10);
};
```

Or you can introduce an auxiliary class main class:

```
template <int I>
struct power_of_10
{
   static const int value = 10 * power_of_10<I-1>::value;
};

template <>
struct power_of_10<0>
{
   static const int value = 1;
};

template <int I, int N>
struct digit
{
   static const int value = (N / power_of_10<I>::value) % 10;
};
```

While the first implementation is clearly simpler, the second scales better. If you need to extract the 8th di from 100 different random numbers, the former is going to produce 800 different specializations because chances of reuse are very low. Starting with digit<8,12345678>, the compiler has to produce the sequen digit<7,1234567>, digit<6,123456>..., and each of these classes is likely to appear only once in the entire program.

On the other hand, the latter version produces eight different specialized powers of 10 that are reuse every time, so the compiler workload is just 100+10 types.

---

[4]This example was taken from a private conversation with Marco Marcello.

.3. Classic Metaprogramming Idioms

letafunctions can be seen as functions that take one or more types and return types or constants. You'll see this section how to implement some basic operations.

Binary operators are replaced by metafunctions of two variables. The concept `T1==T2` becomes `ypeequal<T1, T2>::value`:

```
emplate <typename T1, typename T2>
ruct typeequal

 static const bool value = false;


mplate <typename T>
ruct typeequal<T, T>

 static const bool value = true;
```

Whenever possible, you should derive from an elementary class that holds the result, rather than roduce a new type/constant. Remember that `public` inheritance is implied by `struct`

```
nplate <typename T1, typename T2>
ruct typeequal : public selector<false>        // redundant


plate <typename T>
uct typeequal<T, T> : selector<true>           // public
```

The ternary operator `TEST ? T1 : T2` becomes `typeif<TEST, T1, T2>::type`:

```
plate <bool STATEMENT, typename T1, typename T2>
uct typeif

typedef T1 type;


plate <typename T1, typename T2>
ict typeif<false, T1, T2>

ypedef T2 type;
```

Or, according to the previous guideline:

```
late <bool STATEMENT, typename T1, typename T2>
ct typeif : instance_of<T1>
```

```
template <typename T1, typename T2>
struct typeif<false, T1, T2> : instance_of<T2>
{
};
```

The strong motivation for derivation is an easier use of tagging techniques. Since you will often "embed the metafunction result in a selector, it will be easier to use the metafunction itself as a selector. Suppose you have two functions that fill a range with random elements:

```
template <typename iterator_t>
void random_fill(iterator_t begin, iterator_t end, selector<false>)
{
   for (; begin != end; ++begin)
      *begin = rand();
}

template <typename iterator_t>
void random_fill(iterator_t begin, iterator_t end, selector<true>)
{
   for (; begin != end; ++begin)
      *begin = 'A' + (rand() % 26);
}
```

Compare the invocation:

```
random_fill(begin, end, selector<typeequal<T, char*>::value>());
```

with the simpler[5]:

```
random_fill(begin, end, typeequal<T, char*>());
```

■ Note Note as a curiosity, that header files that store a version number in their guard macro can be used a `typeif`. Compare the following snippets

```
#include "myheader.hpp"

typedef
typename typeif<MXT_MYHEADER_==0x1000, double, float>::type float_t;

#if MXT_MYHEADER_ == 0x1000
typedef double float_t;
#else
typedef float float_t;
#endif
```

The first snippet will not compile if `MXT_MYHEADER_` is undefined. The preprocessor instead would behave as if the variable were `0`.

---

[5] I do not always use the derivation notation in the book, mainly for sake of clarity. However, I strongly encourage ado it in production code, as it boosts code reuse.

.3.1. Static Short Circuit

s a case study of template recursion, let's compare the pseudo-code of a static and dynamic operator:

```
emplate <typename T>
ruct F : typeif<[[CONDITION]], T, typename G<T>::type>


t F(int x)

 return [[CONDITION]] ? x : G(x);
```

These statements are *not* analogous:

- The runtime statement is short-circuited. It will not *execute* code unless necessary, so G(x) might never run.
- The static operator will always *compile* all the mentioned entities, as soon as one of their members is mentioned. So the first F will trigger the compilation of `G<T>::type`, regardless of the fact that the result is used (that is, even when the condition is true).

There is no automatic static short-circuit. If underestimated, this may increase the build times without ra benefits, and it may not be noticed, because results would be correct anyway.

The expression may be rewritten using an extra "indirection":

```
nplate <typename T>
uct F

typedef
   typename typeif<[[CONDITION]], instance_of<T>, G<T> >::type
   aux_t;
typedef typename aux_t::type type;
```

Here, only `G<T>` is mentioned, not `G<T>::type`. When the compiler is processing typeif, it needs only now that the second and third parameters are valid types; that is, that they have been declared. If the dition is false, aux_t is set to `G<T>`. Otherwise, it is set to `instance_of<T>`. Since no member has been iested yet, nothing else has been compiled. Finally, the last line triggers compilation of either `tance_of<T>` or `G<T>`.

So, if CONDITION is true, `G<T>::type` is never used. `G<T>` may even lack a definition or it may not contain ember named type.

To summarize:

- Delay accessing members as long as possible
- Wrap items to leverage the interface

An identical optimization applies to constants:

```
static const size_t value = [[CONDITION]] ? 4 : alignment_of<T>::value;

typedef typename
  typeif<[[CONDITION]], static_value<size_t, 4>, alignment_of<T>>::type
  aux_t;

static const size_t value = aux_t::value;
```

At first, it may look like there's no need for some special logic operator, since all default operators on integers are allowed inside of templates[6]:

```
template <typename T1, typename T2>
struct naive_OR
{
   static const bool value = (T1::value || T2::value);   // ok, valid
};
```

The classic logical operators in C++ are short-circuited; that is, they don't *evaluate* the second operato if the first one is enough to return a result. Similarly, you can write a static OR that does not *compile* its seco argument unnecessarily. If T1::value is true, T2::value is never accessed and it might not even exist (AND obtained similarly).

```
// if (T1::value is true)
//    return true;
// else
//    return T2::value;

template <bool B, typename T2>
struct static_OR_helper;

template <typename T2>
struct static_OR_helper<false, T2> : selector<T2::value>
{
};

template <typename T2>
struct static_OR_helper<true, T2> : selector<true>
{
};

template <typename T1, typename T2>
struct static_OR : static_OR_helper<T1::value, T2>
{
};
```

[6]Except casts to non-integer types. For example, N*1.2 is illegal, but N+N/5 is fine.

.4. Hidden Template Parameters

ome class templates may have undocumented template parameters, generally auto-deduced, that silently elect the right specialization. This is a companion technique to tag dispatching, and an example follows:

```
mplate <typename T, bool IS_SMALL_OBJ = (sizeof(T)<sizeof(void*))>
ass A;

mplate <typename T>
ass A<T, true>

 // implementation follows


mplate <typename T>
ass A<T, false>

 // implementation follows
```

The user of A will accept the default, as a rule:

```
har> c1;
har, true> c2;    // exceptional case. do at own risk
```

The following is a variation of an example that appeared in[3].

```
plate <size_t N>
uct fibonacci

static const size_t value =
    fibonacci<N-1>::value + fibonacci<N-2>::value;


plate <>
uct fibonacci<0>

static const size_t value = 0;


plate <>
ct fibonacci<1>

static const size_t value = 1;
```

It can be rewritten using a hidden template parameter:

```
template <size_t N, bool TINY_NUMBER = (N<2)>
struct fibonacci
{
   static const size_t value =
      fibonacci<N-1>::value + fibonacci<N-2>::value;
};

template <size_t N>
struct fibonacci<N, true>
{
   static const size_t value = N;
};
```

To prevent the default from being changed, you can rename the original class by appending the suffix _helper and thus introducing a layer in the middle:

```
template <size_t N, bool TINY_NUMBER>
struct fibonacci_helper
{
   // all as above
};

template <size_t N>
class fibonacci : fibonacci_helper<N, (N<2)>
{
};
```

3.4.1. Static Recursion on Hidden Parameters

Let's compute the highest bit of an unsigned integer x. Assume that x has type size_t and, if x==0, it will conventionally return -1.

A non-recursive algorithm would be: set N = the number of bits of size_t; test bit N-1, then N-2..., and so on, until a non-zero bit is found.

First, as usual, a naive implementation:

```
template <size_t X, size_t K>
struct highest_bit_helper
{
   static const int value =
      ((X >> K) % 2) ? K : highest_bit_helper<X, K-1>::value;
};

template <size_t X>
struct highest_bit_helper<X, 0>
{
   static const int value = (X % 2) ? 0 : -1;
};
```

```
emplate <size_t X>
truct static_highest_bit
 highest_bit_helper<X, CHAR_BIT*sizeof(size_t)-1>

;
```

As written, it works, but the compiler might need to generate a large number of different classes per atic computation (that is, for any X, you pass to `static_highest_bit`).

First, you can rework the algorithm using bisection. Assume X has N bits, divide it in an upper and a wer half (U and L) having (N-N/2) and (N/2) bits, respectively. If U is 0, replace X with L; otherwise, replace X th U and remember to increment the result by (N/2)[7]:

In pseudo-code:

```
ze_t hibit(size_t x, size_t N = CHAR_BIT*sizeof(size_t))

 size_t u = (x>>(N/2));
 if (u>0)
    return hibit(u, N-N/2) + (N/2);
 else
    return hibit(x, N/2);
```

This means:

```
nplate <size_t X, int N>
:uct helper

static const size_t U = (X >> (N/2));

static const int value =
   U ? (N/2)+helper<U, N-N/2>::value : helper<X, N/2>::value;
```

As written, each `helper<X, N>` induces the compiler to instantiate the template again *twice*—namely `per<U, N-N/2>` and `helper<X, N/2>`—even if only one will be used.

Compilation time may be reduced either with the static short circuit, or even better, by moving all the hmetic inside the type.[8]

```
plate <size_t X, int N>
uct helper

static const size_t U = (X >> (N/2));

static const int value = (U ? N/2 : 0) +
         helper<(U ? U : X), (U ? N-N/2 : N/2)>::value;
```

ractice, N is always even, so N-N/2 == N/2.

also the double-check stop in Section 7.2.

This is definitely less clear, but more convenient for the compiler.

Since N is the number of bits of X, N>0 initially.

You can terminate the static recursion when N==1:

```
template <size_t X>
struct helper<X, 1>
{
   static const int value = X ? 0 : -1;
};
```

Finally, you can use derivation from static_value to store the result:

```
template <size_t X>
struct static_highest_bit
: static_value<int, helper<X, CHAR_BIT*sizeof(size_t)>::value>
{
};
```

The recursion depth is fixed and logarithmic. static_highest_bit<X> instantiates at most five or six classes for every value of X.

3.4.2. Accessing the Primary Template

A dummy parameter can allow specializations to call back the primary template.

Suppose you have two algorithms, one for computing cos(x) and another for sin(x), where x is any floating-point type. Initially, the code is organized as follows:

```
template <typename float_t>
struct trigonometry
{
   static float_t cos(const float_t x)
   {
      // ...
   }

   static float_t sin(const float_t x)
   {
      // ...
   }
};

template <typename float_t>
inline float_t fast_cos(const float_t x)
{
   return trigonometry<float_t>::cos(x);
}

template <typename float_t>
inline float_t fast_sin(const float_t x)
{
   return trigonometry<float_t>::sin(x);
}
```

Later, someone writes another algorithm for cos<float>, but not for sin<float>.

You can either specialize/overload fast_cos for float or use a hidden template parameter, as shown:

```
emplate <typename float_t, bool = false>
truct trigonometry

  static float_t cos(const float_t x)
  {
     // ...
  }

  static float_t sin(const float_t x)
  {
     // ...
  }


mplate <>
ruct trigonometry<float, false>

 static float_t cos(const float_t x)
 {
    // specialized algorithm here
 }

 static float_t sin(const float_t x)
 {
    // calls the general template
    return trigonometry<float, true>::sin(x);
 }
```

Note that in specializing the class, it's not required that you write <float, false>. You can simply enter:

```
plate <>
uct trigonometry<float>
```

ause the default value for the second parameter is known from the declaration.

Any specialization can access the corresponding general function by setting the Boolean to true icitly.

This technique will appear again in Section 7.1.

A similar trick comes in handy to make partial specializations unambiguous.

C++ does not allow specializing a template twice, even if the specializations are identical. In particular, u mix cases for standard typedefs and integers, the code becomes subtly non-portable:

```
late <typename T>
ct is_integer

tatic const bool value = false;
```

```
template < > struct is_integer<short>
{ static const bool value = true; };

template < > struct is_integer<int>
{ static const bool value = true; };

template < > struct is_integer<long>
{ static const bool value = true; };

template < > struct is_integer<ptrdiff_t>      // problem:
{ static const bool value = true; };           // may or may not compile
```

If `ptrdiff_t` is a fourth type, say `long long`, then all the specializations are different. Alternatively, if `ptrdiff_t` is simply a `typedef` for `long`, the code is incorrect. Instead, this works:

```
template <typename T, int = 0>
struct is_integer
{
   static const bool value = false;
};

template <int N> struct is_integer<short, N>
{ static const bool value = true; };
template <int N> struct is_integer<int  , N>
{ static const bool value = true; };
template <int N> struct is_integer<long , N>
{ static const bool value = true; };

template <>
struct is_integer<ptrdiff_t>
{
   static const bool value = true;
};
```

Since `is_integer<ptrdiff_t, 0>` is more specialized than `is_integer<long, N>`, it will be used unambiguously.[9]

This technique does not scale well,[10] but it might be extended to a small number of `typedefs`, by addi more unnamed parameters. This example uses `int`, but anything would do, such as `bool = false` or `typename = void`.

```
template <typename T, int = 0, int = 0>
struct is_integer
{
   static const bool value = false;
};
```

[9] I insist that the problem is solvable because the implementations of `is_integer<long>` and `is_integer<ptrdiff_t` identical; otherwise, it is ill-formed. For a counterexample, consider the problem of converting a `time_t` and `long` string; even if `time_t` is `long`, the strings need to be different. Therefore, this issue cannot be solved by TMP technic

[10] This is a good thing, because a well-built template class shouldn't need it.

```
emplate <int N1, int N2>
truct is_integer<long, N1, N2>
 static const bool value = true; };

emplate <int N1>
truct is_integer<ptrdiff_t, N1>
 static const bool value = true; };

emplate < >
ruct is_integer<time_t>
static const bool value = true; };
```

.4.3. Disambiguation

TMP it's common to generate classes that derive several times from the same base (indirectly). It's not yet ne to list a full example, so here's a simple one:

```
mplate <int N>
ruct A {};

mplate <int N>
ruct B : A<N % 2>, B<N / 2> {};

nplate <>
uct B<0> {};
```

For example, the inheritance chain for B<9> is illustrated in Figure 3-1.

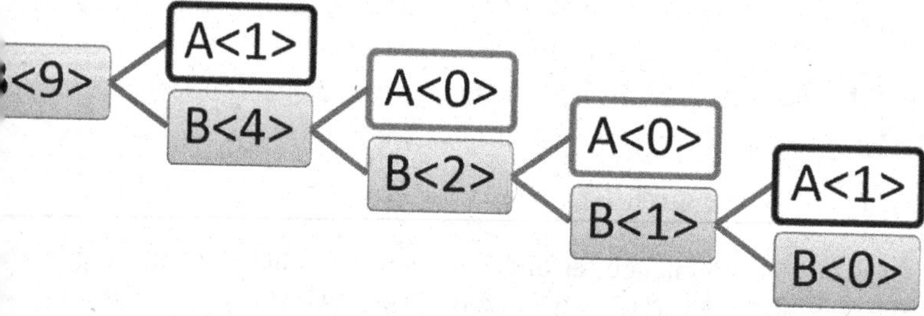

ure 3-1. The inheritance chain for B<9>

Note that A<0> and A<1> occur several times. This is allowed, except that you cannot cast, explicitly or licitly, B<9> to A<0> or A<1>:

```
late <int N>
ct A

nt getN() { return N; }
```

```
template <int N>
struct B : A<N % 2>, B<N / 2>
{
   int doIt() { return A<N % 2>::getN(); }     // error: ambiguous
};
```

What you can do is add a hidden template parameter so that different levels of inheritance correspond to physically different types.

The most popular disambiguation parameters are counters:

```
template <int N, int FAKE = 0>
struct A {};

template <int N, int FAKE = 0>
struct B : A<N % 2, FAKE11>, B<N / 2, FAKE+1> {};

template <int FAKE>
struct B<0, FAKE> {};
```

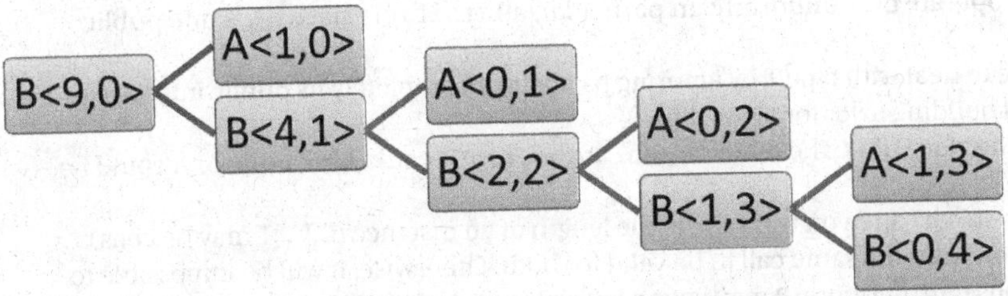

***Figure 3-2.** The modified inheritance chain for B<9> using a counter*

Another commonly used disambiguator tag is the type this:

```
template <int N, typename T>
struct A {};

template <int N>
struct B : A<N % 2, B<N> >, B<N/2> {};

template <>
struct B<0> {};
```

[11]Here, FAKE and FAKE+1 both work.

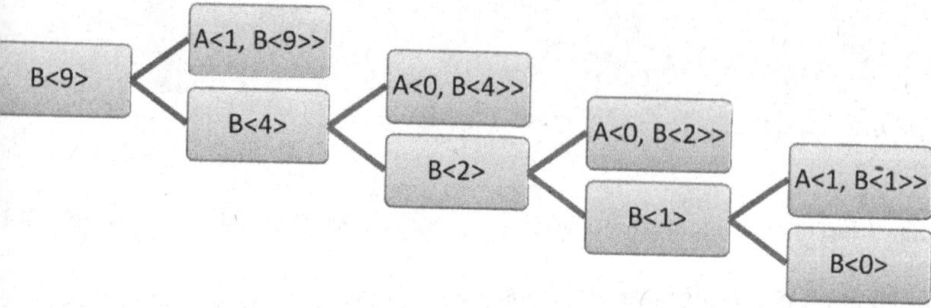

gure 3-3. *The modified inheritance chain for* `B<9>` *using a tag-type*

This idea is used extensively in Section 5.2

.5. Traits

aits classes (or simply, traits) are a collection of static functions, types, and constants that abstract the blic interface of a type `T`. More precisely, for all `T` representing the same concept, `traits<T>` is a class nplate that allows you to operate on `T` uniformly. In particular, all `traits<T>` have the same public erface.[12]

Using traits, it's possible to deal with type `T` by ignoring partially or completely its public interface. is makes traits an optimal building layer for algorithms.

Why ignore the public interface of `T`? The main reasons are because it could have none or it could be ppropriate.

Suppose `T` represents a "string" and you want to get the length of an instance of `T`. `T` may be `const r*` or `std::string`, but you want the same call to be valid for both. Otherwise, it will be impossible to te template string functions. Furthermore, `0` may have a special meaning as a "character" for some `T`, but for all.

The first rigorous definition of traits is an article by Nathan Myers,[13] dated 1995.

The motivation for the technique is that, when writing a class template or a function, you'll realize that ne types, constants, or atomic actions are parameters of the "main" template argument.

So you could put in additional template parameters, but that's usually impractical. You could also up the parameters in a traits class. Both the next example and the following sentences are quotes from ers' article[14]:

---

ne does not imply that all functions must be identical, as some differences may have a limited impact on "uniform use". trivial example, arguments may be passed by value or by const reference.

ilable at: cantrip.org/trails.html. The article cites as previous bibliography [10], [11] and [12].

sentences have been slightly rearranged.

Because the user never mentions it, the [traits class] name can be long and descriptive.

```
template <typename char_t>
struct ios_char_traits
{
};

template <>
struct ios_char_traits<char>
{
    typedef char char_type;
    typedef int  int_type;
    static inline int_type eof() { return EOF; }
};

template <>
struct ios_char_traits<wchar_t>
{
    typedef wchar_t char_type;
    typedef wint_t  int_type;
    static inline int_type eof() { return WEOF; }
};
```

The default traits class template is empty. What can anyone say about an unknown character type? However, for real character types, you can specialize the template and provide useful semantics.

To put a new character type on a stream, you need only specialize `ios_char_traits` *for the new type.*

Notice that `ios_char_traits` *has no data members; it only provides public definitions. Now you can define the* `streambuf` *template:*

```
template <typename char_t>
class basic_streambuf
```

Notice that it has only one template parameter, the one that interests users.

In fact, Myers concludes his article with a formal definition and an interesting observation:

Traits class:

A class used in place of template parameters. As a class, it aggregates useful types and constants. As a template, it provides an avenue for that "extra level of indirection" that solves all software problems.

This technique turns out to be useful anywhere that a template must be applied to native types, or to any type for which you cannot add members as required for the template's operations.

Traits classes may be "global" or "local". Global traits are simply available in the system and they can e freely used anywhere. In particular, all specializations of a global traits class have system-wide scope (so ecializations are automatically used everywhere). This approach is in fact preferred when traits express operties of the platform.

```
mplate <typename char_t>
ass basic_streambuf

 typedef typename ios_char_traits<char_t>::int_type int_type;
 ...
```

Note For example, you could access the largest unsigned integer, of `float`, available. Consider the lowing pseudo-code:

```
nplate <typename T>
ruct largest;

nplate <>
ruct largest<int>

typedef long long type;


nplate <>
uct largest<float>

typedef long double type;


plate <>
uct largest<unsigned>

typedef unsigned long long type;
```

ently, a call such as `largest<unsigned>::type` is expected to return a result that's constant in the form, so all customizations—if any—should be global to keep the client code coherent.

A more flexible approach is to use local traits, passing the appropriate type to each template instance n additional parameter (which defaults to the global value).

```
late <typename char_t, typename traits_t = ios_char_traits<char_t> >
s basic_streambuf

ypedef typename traits_t::int_type int_type;
..
```

The following sections focus on a special kind of traits—pure static traits, which do not contain functions but only types and constants. You will come back to this argument in Section 4.2.

3.5.1. Type Traits

Some traits classes provide `typedef`s only, so they are indeed multi-value metafunctions. As an example, consider again `std::iterator_traits`.

Type traits[15] are a collection of metafunctions that provide information about qualifiers of a given type and/or alter such qualifiers. Information can be deduced by a static mechanism inside traits, can be explicitl supplied with a full/partial specialization of the traits class, or can be supplied by the compiler itself.[16]

```
template <typename T>
struct is_const : selector<false>
{
};

template <typename T>
struct is_const<const T> : selector<true>
{
};
```

■ **Note** Today, type traits are split to reduce compile times, but historically they were large monolithic class with many static constants.

```
template <typename T>
struct all_info_together
{
   static const bool is_class = true;

   static const bool is_pointer = false;
   static const bool is_integer = false;
   static const bool is_floating = false;
   static const bool is_unsigned = false;

   static const bool is_const = false;
   static const bool is_reference = false;
   static const bool is_volatile = false;
};
```

---

[15]The term *type traits,* introduced by John Maddock and Steve Cleary, is used here as a common name, but it is also po as a proper name, denoting a particular library implementation. See `http://cppreference.com/header/type_tr` or `http://www.boost.org/doc/libs/1_57_0/libs/type_traits/doc/html/index.html`.

[16]In modern C++, there's a dedicated `<type_traits>` header that contains most of the metafunctions described here, many more that cannot be replicated in classic C++. For example, `has_trivial_destructor<T>` is indeducible wi the cooperation of the compiler, and current implementations always return `false`, except for built-in types.

As a rule, traits have a general implementation with conservative defaults, including partial specializations ith meaningful values for classes of types and full specializations customized on individual types.

```
emplate <typename T>
truct add_reference

 typedef T& type;


mplate <typename T>
ruct add_reference<T&>

 typedef T& type;


mplate < >
ruct add_reference<void>

 // reference to void is illegal. don't put anything here[17]
```

Traits are often recursive:

```
nplate <typename T>
ruct is_unsigned_integer : selector<false>


plate <typename T>
uct is_unsigned_integer<const T> : is_unsigned_integer<T>


plate <typename T>
uct is_unsigned_integer<volatile T> : is_unsigned_integer<T>


plate < >
uct is_unsigned_integer<unsigned int> : selector<true>


late < >
ct is_unsigned_integer<unsigned long> : selector<true>


dd more specializations...
```

possible to define add_reference<void>::type to be void.

Traits can use inheritance and then selectively hide some members:

```
template <typename T>
struct integer_traits;

template <>
struct integer_traits<int>
{
   typedef long long largest_type;
   typedef unsigned int unsigned_type;
};

template <>
struct integer_traits<long> : integer_traits<int>
{
   // keeps integer_traits<int>::largest_type
   typedef unsigned long unsigned_type;
};
```

■ **Note** In C++, a template base class is not in scope of name resolution:

```
template <typename T>
struct BASE
{
   typedef T type;
};

template <typename T>
struct DER : public BASE<T>
{
   type t;   // error: 'type' is not in scope
};
```

However, from a static point of view, `DER` *does* contain a `type` member:

```
template <typename T>
struct typeof
{
   typedef typename T::type type;
};

typeof< DER<int> >::type i = 0;      // ok: int i = 0
```

Type traits, if not carefully designed, are vulnerable to hard conceptual problems, as the C++ type ystem is a lot more complex than it seems:

```
emplate <typename T>
truct is_const : selector<false>



emplate <typename T>
ruct is_const<const T> : selector<true>



mplate <typename T>
ruct add_const : instance_of<const T>



mplate <typename T>
ruct add_const<const T> : instance_of<const T>
```

Here are some oddities:

- If `N` is a compile-time constant and `T` is a type, you can form two distinct array types: `T [N]` and `T []`.[18]
- Qualifiers such as `const` applied to array types behave a bit oddly. If `T` is an array, for example, `double [4]`, `const T` is an "array of four `const double`," not "`const` array of four `double`". In particular, `const T` is *not* `const`:

```
typedef double T1;
typedef add_const<T1>::type T2;
T2 x = 3.14;                          // x has type const double
bool b1 = is_const<T2>::value;        // b1 is true

typedef double T3[4];
typedef add_const<T3>::type T4;       // T4 is "array of 4 const double"...
T4 a = { 1,2,3,4 };
bool b2 = is_const<T4>::value;        // ...which does not match "const T"
                                      // so b2 is false
```

So, you should add more specializations:

```
plate <typename T, size_t N>
ct is_const<const T [N]>

tatic const bool value = true;
```

---

s is actually used. Some smart pointers, including `std::unique_ptr`, use `operator delete []` when the type hes `T[]` and single deletion in any other case.

```
template <typename T >
struct is_const<const T []>
{
   static const bool value = true;
};
```

There are two possible criteria you can verify on types:

- A match is satisfied; for example, `const int` matches `const T` with `T==int`.
- A logical test is satisfied; for example, you could say that `T` is `const` if `const T` and `T` are the same type.

The C++ type system is complex enough that criteria may look equivalent in the majority of cases, but still not be identical. As a rule, whenever such a logical problem arises, the solution will come from more precise reasoning about your requirements. For any `T`, `is_const<T&>::value` is `false` because `T&` does not satisfy a match with a `const` type. However, `add_const<T&>::type` is again `T&` (any qualifiers applied to a reference are ignored). Does this mean that references are `const`?

Should you add a specialization of `is_const<T&>` that returns `true`? Or do you really want `add_const<T&>::type` to be `const T&`?

In C++, objects can have different degrees of `const`-ness. More specifically, they can be

- Assignable
- Immutable
- `const`

Being *assignable* is a syntactic property. An assignable object can live on the left side of `operator=`. A `const` reference is not assignable. In fact, however, `T&` is assignable whenever `T` is. (Incidentally, an assignment would change the referenced object, not the reference, but this is irrelevant.)

Being *immutable* is a logical property. An immutable object cannot be changed after construction, either because it is not assignable or because its assignment does not alter the state of the instance. Since you cannot make a reference "point" to another object, a reference is immutable.

Being `const` is a pure language property. An object is `const` if its type matches `const T` for some `T`. A `const` object may have a reduced interface and `operator=` is *likely* one of the restricted member functions.

References are not the only entities that are both immutable and assignable. Such a situation can be reproduced with a custom `operator=`.

```
template <typename T>
class fake_ref
{
   T* const ptr_;

public:

   // ...

   const fake_ref& operator=(const T& x) const
   {
      *ptr_ = x;         // ok, does not alter the state of this instance
      return *this;
   }
};
```

This also shows that const objects may be assignable,[19] but it does not imply that references are const, nly that they can be simulated with const objects.

So the standard approach is to provide type traits that operate atomically, with minimal logic and just a atch. is_const<T&>::value should be false.

However, type traits are also easy to extend in user code. If an application requires it, you can introduce ore concepts, such as "intrusive const-ness"

```
mplate <typename T>
ruct is_const_intrusive : selector<false>


mplate <typename T>
ruct is_const_intrusive<const T> : selector<true>


mplate <typename T>
ruct is_const_intrusive<const volatile T> : selector<true>


nplate <typename T>
ruct is_const_intrusive<T&> : is_const_intrusive<T>
```

Type traits have infinite applications; this example uses the simplest. Assume that C<T> is a class plate that holds a member of type T, initialized by the constructor. However, T has no restriction, and in ticular it may be a reference.

```
plate <typename T>
ss C

T member_;

lic:

explicit C(argument_type x)
: member_(x)
{
}
```

You need to define argument_type. If T is a value type, it's best to pass it by reference-to-const. But if T is erence, writing const T& is illegal. So you'd write:

```
def typename add_reference<const T>::type argument_type;
```

---

ernatively, std::pair<const int, double> is neither const nor assignable.

Here, add_reference<T> returns const T&, as desired.

If T is a reference or reference-to-const, const T is T and add_reference returns T. That means the argument type is again T.

3.5.2. Type Dismantling

A type in C++ can generate infinitely many "variations" by adding qualifiers, considering references, pointers, and arrays, and so on. But it can happen that you have to recursively remove all the additional attributes, one at a time. This recursive process is usually called *dismantling*.[20]

This section shows a metafunction, named copy_q, that shifts all the "qualifiers" from type T1 to type T2, so copy_q<const double&, int>::type will be const int&.

Type deduction is entirely recursive. You dismantle one attribute at a time and move the same attribute to the result. To continue with the previous example, const double& matches T& where T is const double, so the result is "reference to the result of copy_q<const double, int>," which in turn is "const result of copy_q<double, int>". Since this does not match any specialization, it gives int.

```
template <typename T1, typename T2>
struct copy_q
{
   typedef T2 type;
};

template <typename T1, typename T2>
struct copy_q<T1&, T2>
{
   typedef typename copy_q<T1, T2>::type& type;
};

template <typename T1, typename T2>
struct copy_q<const T1, T2>
{
   typedef const typename copy_q<T1, T2>::type type;
};

template <typename T1, typename T2>
struct copy_q<volatile T1, T2>
{
   typedef volatile typename copy_q<T1, T2>::type type;
};

template <typename T1, typename T2>
struct copy_q<T1*, T2>
{
   typedef typename copy_q<T1, T2>::type* type;
};
```

[20]The expression "type dismantling" was introduced by Stephen C. Dewhurst.

```
emplate <typename T1, typename T2, int N>
truct copy_q<T1 [N], T2>

  typedef typename copy_q<T1, T2>::type type[N];
;
```

A more complete implementation could address the problems caused by T2 being a reference:

```
py_q<double&, int&>::type err1;     // error: reference to reference
py_q<double [3], int&>::type err2; // error: array of 'int&'
```

However, it's questionable if such classes should silently resolve the error or stop compilation. Let's just te that declaring a `std::vector<int&>` is illegal, but the compiler error is not "trapped":

```
sr/include/gcc/darwin/4.0/c++/ext/new_allocator.h: In instantiation of
_gnu_cxx::new_allocator<int&>':
sr/include/gcc/darwin/4.0/c++/bits/allocator.h:83:   instantiated from
td::allocator<int&>'
sr/include/gcc/darwin/4.0/c++/bits/stl_vector.h:80:   instantiated from
td::_Vector_base<int&, std::allocator<int&> >::_Vector_impl'
sr/include/gcc/darwin/4.0/c++/bits/stl_vector.h:113:   instantiated from
td::_Vector_base<int&, std::allocator<int&> >'
sr/include/gcc/darwin/4.0/c++/bits/stl_vector.h:149:   instantiated from
td::vector<int&, std::allocator<int&> >'
in.cpp:94:   instantiated from here
sr/include/gcc/darwin/4.0/c++/ext/new_allocator.h:55: error: forming pointer to
ference type 'int&'
```

6. Type Containers

So what is a typelist? It's got to be one of those weird template beasts, right?

—Andrei Alexandrescu

maximum number of template parameters is implementation-defined, but it's usually large enough to a class template as *a container of types*.[21]

This section shows how some elementary *static algorithms* work, because you'll reuse the same niques many times in the future. Actually, it's possible to implement most STL concepts in TMP, uding containers, algorithms, iterators, and functors, where complexity requirements are translated at npilation time.[22]

This section shows the ideas of the elementary techniques; you'll see some applications later.

The simplest type containers are *pairs* (the static equivalent of linked lists) and *arrays* (resemble C-style ys of a fixed length).

C++ Standard contains an informative section, called "Implementation Quantities," where a recommended minimum ggested for the number of template arguments (1024) and for nested template instantiations (1024), but compilers do eed to respect these numbers.

reference on the argument is [3].

```
template <typename T1, typename T2>
struct typepair
{
   typedef T1 head_t;
   typedef T2 tail_t;
};

struct empty
{
};
```

In fact, you can easily store a list of arbitrary (subject to reasonable limitations) length using pairs of pairs. In principle, you could form a complete binary tree, but for simplicity's sake, a list of types (T1, T2... Tn) is represented as typepair<T1, typepair<T2, ...> >. In other words, you'll allow the second component to be a pair. Actually, it forces the second component to be a typepair or an empty, which is the list terminator. In pseudo-code:

```
P0 = empty
P1 = typepair<T1, empty >
P2 = typepair<T2, typepair<T1, empty> >
// ...
Pn = typepair<Tn, Pn-1>
```

This incidentally shows that the easiest operation with typepair-sequences is push_front.

Following Alexandrescu's notation (see [1]), I call such an encoding a *typelist*. You say that the first accessible type Tn is the *head* of the list and Pn-1 is the *tail*.

Alternatively, if you fix the maximum length to a reasonable number, you can store all the types in a ro Due to the default value (which can be empty or void), you can declare any number of parameters on the same line:

```
#define MXT_GENERIC_TL_MAX          32
// the code "publishes" this value for the benefit of clients

template
<
   typename T1  = empty,
   typename T2  = empty,
   // ...
   typename T32 = empty
>
struct typearray
{
};

typedef typearray<int, double, std::string> array_1;  // 3 items
typedef typearray<int, int, char, array_1> array_2;   // 4 items
```

The properties of these containers are different. A typelist with J elements requires the compiler to produce J different types. On the other hand, arrays are direct-access, so writing algorithms for type array involves writing many (say 32) specializations. Typelists are shorter and recursive but take more time to compile.

Note Before the theoretical establishment made by Abrahams in [3], there was some naming confusion. ne original idea of type pairs was fully developed by Alexandrescu (in [1] and subsequently in CUJ), and he troduced the name *typelist*.

pparently, Alexandrescu was also the first to use type arrays as wrappers for declaring long typelists in an sy way:

```
mplate <typename T1, typename T2, ..., typename Tn>
ruct cons

 typedef typepair<T1, typepair<T2, ...> > type;
```

wever, the name *typelist* is still widely used as a synonym of a more generic type container.

6.1. typeat

peat is a metafunction that extracts the Nth type from a container.

```
ruct Error_UNDEFINED_TYPE;       // no definition!

mplate <size_t N, typename CONTAINER, typename ERR = Error_UNDEFINED_TYPE>
ruct typeat;
```

If the Nth type does not exist, the result is ERR.

The same metafunction can process type arrays and typelists. As anticipated, arrays require all the ssible specializations. The generic template simply returns an error, then the metafunction is specialized t on type arrays, and then on typelists.

```
plate <size_t N, typename CONTAINER, typename ERR = Error_UNDEFINED_TYPE>
uct typeat

typedef ERR type;


plate <typename T1, ... typename T32, typename ERR>
uct typeat<0, typearray<T1, ..., T32>, ERR>

typedef T1 type;


late <typename T1, ... typename T32, typename ERR>
ct typeat<1, typearray<T1, ..., T32>, ERR>

ypedef T2 type;

rite all 32 specializations
```

The same code for typelists is more concise. The Nth type of the list is declared equal to the (N-1)th type in the tail of the list. If N is 0, the result is the head type. However, if you meet an empty list, the result is ERR.

```
template <size_t N, typename T1, typename T2, typename ERR>
struct typeat<N, typepair<T1, T2>, ERR>
{
   typedef typename typeat<N-1, T2, ERR>::type type;
};

template <typename T1, typename T2, typename ERR>
struct typeat<0, typepair<T1, T2>, ERR>
{
   typedef T1 type;
};

template <size_t N, typename ERR>
struct typeat<N, empty, ERR>
{
   typedef ERR type;
};
```

Observe that, whatever index you use, typeat<N, typearray<...>> requires just one template instantiation. typeat<N, typepair<...>> may require N different instantiations.

Note also the shorter implementation:

```
template <size_t N, typename T1, typename T2, typename ERR>
struct typeat<N, typepair<T1, T2>, ERR> : typeat<N-1, T2, ERR>
{
};
```

3.6.2. Returning an Error

When a metafunction F<T> is undefined, such as with typeat<N, empty, ERR>, common options for returning an error include:

- Removing the body of F<T> entirely.
- Giving F<T> an empty body, with no result (type or value).
- Defining F<T>::type so that it will cause compilation errors, if used (void or a class that has no definition).
- Defining F<T>::type using an user-supplied error type (as shown previously).

Remember that forcing a compiler error is quite drastic; it's analogous to throwing exceptions. It's ha to ignore, but a bogus type is more like a return false. A false can be easily converted to a throw and a bogus type can be converted to a compiler error (a static assertion would suffice).

.6.3. Depth

ealing with type arrays can be easier with the help of some simple macros[23]:

```
lefine MXT_LIST_0(T)
lefine MXT_LIST_1(T)    T##1
lefine MXT_LIST_2(T)    MXT_LIST_1(T), T##2
lefine MXT_LIST_3(T)    MXT_LIST_2(T), T##3
 ...
lefine MXT_LIST_32(T)  MXT_LIST_31(T), T##32
```

Surprisingly, you can write class declarations that look extremely simple and concise. Here is an ample (before and after preprocessing).

```
mplate <MXT_LIST_32(typename T)>
ruct depth< typelist<MXT_LIST_32(T)> >

mplate <typename T1, ... , typename T32>
ruct depth< typelist<T1, ... T32> >
```

The metafunction called depth returns the length of the typelists:

```
nplate <typename CONTAINER>
ruct depth;

nplate <>
ruct depth< empty > : static_value<size_t, 0>


plate <typename T1, typename T2>
uct depth< typepair<T1, T2> > : static_value<size_t, depth<T2>::value+1>
```

- The primary template is undefined, so depth<int> is unusable.
- If the depth of a typelist is K, the compiler must generate K different intermediate types (namely depth<P1>... depth<Pn> where Pj is the jth tail of the list).

For type arrays, you use macros again. The depth of typearray<> is 0; the depth of typearray<T1> is 1; in fact the depth of typearray<MXT_LIST_N(T)> is N.

```
plate <MXT_LIST_0(typename T)>
ict depth< typearray<MXT_LIST_0(T)> >
tatic_value<size_t, 0> {};
```

boost preprocessor library would be more suitable, anyway, but its description would require another chapter. the focus is on the word *simple*: a strategic hand-written macro can improve the esthetics of code noticeably.

```
template <MXT_LIST_1(typename T)>
struct depth< typearray<MXT_LIST_1(T)> >
: static_value<size_t, 1> {};

// ...

template <MXT_LIST_32(typename T)>
struct depth< typearray<MXT_LIST_32(T)> >
: static_value<size_t, 32> {};
```

Note that even if a malicious user inserts a fake empty delimiter in the middle, depth returns the position of the last non-empty type:

```
typedef typearray<int, double, empty, char> t4;
depth<t4>::value; // returns 4
```

In fact, this call will match depth<T1, T2, T3, T4>, where it happens that T3 = empty. In any case, empty should be confined to an inaccessible namespace.

3.6.4. Front and Back

This section shows you how to extract the first and the last type from both type containers.

```
template <typename CONTAINER>
struct front;

template <typename CONTAINER>
struct back;
```

First, when the container is empty, you cause an error:

```
template <>
struct back<empty>;

template <>
struct front<empty>
{
};
```

While front is trivial, back iterates all over the list:

```
template <typename T1, typename T2>
struct front< typepair<T1, T2> >
{
    typedef T1 type;
};

template <typename T1>
struct back< typepair<T1, empty> >
{
    typedef T1 type;
};
```

```
emplate <typename T1, typename T2>
truct back< typepair<T1, T2> >

  typedef typename back<T2>::type type;
;
```

simply:

```
mplate <typename T1, typename T2>
ruct back< typepair<T1, T2> > : back<T2>
```

For type arrays, you exploit the fact that depth and typeat are very fast and you simply do what is tural with, say, a vector. The back element is the one at size-1. In principle, this would work for typelists o, but it would "iterate" several times over the whole list (where each "iteration" causes the instantiation of new type).

```
mplate <MXT_LIST_32(typename T)>
ruct back< typearray<MXT_LIST_32(T)> >

 typedef typelist<MXT_LIST_32(T)> aux_t;
 typedef typename typeat<depth<aux_t>::value - 1, aux_t>::type type;


nplate <>
uct back< typearray<> >



plate <MXT_LIST_32(typename T)>
uct front< typearray<MXT_LIST_32(T)> >

typedef T1 type;


plate <>
uct front< typearray<> >
```

.5. Find

can perform a sequential search and return the index of the (first) type that matches a given T. If T does appear in CONTAINER, you return a conventional number (say -1), as opposed to causing a compiler error. The code for the recursive version basically reads:

- Nothing belongs to an empty container.
- The first element of a pair has index 0.
- The index is one plus the index of T in the tail, unless this latter index is undefined.

```
template <typename T, typename CONTAINER>
struct typeindex;

template <typename T>
struct typeindex<T, empty>
{
   static const int value = (-1);
};

template <typename T1, typename T2>
struct typeindex< T1, typepair<T1, T2> >
{
   static const int value = 0;
};

template <typename T, typename T1, typename T2>
struct typeindex< T, typepair<T1, T2> >
{
   static const int aux_v = typeindex<T, T2>::value;
   static const int value = (aux_v==-1 ? -1 : aux_v+1);
};
```

The first implementation for type arrays is:

```
/* tentative version */

template <MXT_LIST_32(typename T)>
struct typeindex< T1, typearray<MXT_LIST_32(T)> >
{
   static const int value = 0;
};

template <MXT_LIST_32(typename T)>
struct typeindex< T2, typearray<MXT_LIST_32(T)> >
{
   static const int value = 1;
};

// ...
```

If the type you are looking for is identical to the first type in the array, the value is 0; if it is equal to the second type in the array, the value is 1, and so on. Unfortunately the following is *incorrect*:

```
typedef typearray<int, int, double> t3;

int i = typeindex<int, t3>::value;
```

There's more than one match (namely, the first two), and this gives a compilation error. I defer the solution of this problem until after the next section.

.6.6. Push and Pop

was already mentioned that the easiest operation with type pairs is push_front. It is simply a matter of rapping the new head type in a pair with the old container:

```
mplate <typename CONTAINER, typename T>
ruct push_front;

mplate <typename T>
ruct push_front<empty, T>

 typedef typepair<T, empty> type;


mplate <typename T1, typename T2, typename T>
ruct push_front<typepair<T1, T2>, T>

 typedef typepair< T, typepair<T1, T2> > type;
```

Quite naturally, pop_front is also straightforward:

```
nplate <typename CONTAINER>
ruct pop_front;

nplate <>
uct pop_front<empty>;

nplate <typename T1, typename T2>
uct pop_front< typepair<T1, T2> >

typedef T2 type;
```

To implement the same algorithm for type arrays, you must adopt a very important technique named *plate rotation*. This rotation shifts all template parameters by one position to the left (or to the right).

```
plate <P1, P2 = some_default, ..., P_N = some_default>
uct container

typedef container<P2, P3, ..., P_N, some_default> tail_t;[24]
```

The type resulting from a pop_front is called the *tail* of the container (that's why the source code atedly refers to tail_t).

Parameters need not be types. The following class computes the maximum in a list of positive integers.

---

rinciple, some_default should not be explicitly specified. All forms of code duplication can lead to maintenance s. Here, I show it to emphasize the rotation.

```
#define MXT_M_MAX(a,b)          ((a)<(b) ? (b) : (a))

template <size_t S1, size_t S2=0, ... , size_t S32=0>
struct typemax : typemax<MXT_M_MAX(S1, S2), S3, ..., S32>
{
};

template <size_t S1>
struct typemax<S1,0,0,...,0> : static_value<size_t, S1>
{
};
```

As a side note, whenever it's feasible, it's convenient to *accelerate* the rotation. In the previous example you would write

```
template <size_t S1, size_t S2=0, ... , size_t S32=0>
struct typemax
: typemax<MXT_M_MAX(S1, S2), MXT_M_MAX(S3, S4), ..., MXT_M_MAX(S31, S32)>
{
};
```

To compute the maximum of N constants, you need only log2(N) instances of typemax, instead of N. It's easy to combine rotations and macros with elegance[25]:

```
template <typename T0, MXT_LIST_31(typename T)>
struct pop_front< typearray<T0, MXT_LIST_31(T)> >
{
   typedef typearray<MXT_LIST_31(T)> type;
};

template <MXT_LIST_32(typename T), typename T>
struct push_front<typearray<MXT_LIST_32(T)>, T>
{
   typedef typearray<T, MXT_LIST_31(T)> type;
};
```

Using pop_front, you can implement a generic sequential find. Note that for clarity, you want to add some intermediate typedefs. As in metaprogramming, types are the equivalent of variables in classic C++ You can consider typedefs as equivalent to (named) temporary variables. Additionally, private and publ sections help separate "temporary" variables from the results:

The procedure you'll follow here is:

- The index of T in an empty container is -1.
- The index of T1 in array<T1, ...> is 0 (this unambiguously holds, even if T1 appears more than once).

[25]See Section 3.6.3.

- To obtain the index of T in `array<T1, T2, T3, ...>`, you compute its index in a rotated array and add 1 to the result.

```
template <typename T>
struct typeindex<T, typearray<> >
{
   static const int value = (-1);
};

template <MXT_LIST_32(typename T)>
struct typeindex< T1, typearray<MXT_LIST_32(T)> >
{
   static const int value = 0;
};


template <typename T, MXT_LIST_32(typename T)>
struct typeindex< T, typearray<MXT_LIST_32(T)> >
{
private:
   typedef typearray<MXT_LIST_32(T)> argument_t;
   typedef typename pop_front<argument_t>::type tail_t;

   static const int aux_v = typeindex<T, tail_t>::value;

public:
   static const int value = (aux_v<0) ? aux_v : aux_v+1;
};
```

6.7. More on Template Rotation

nplate arguments can be easily rotated; however, it's usually simpler to consume them left to right. pose you want to compose an integer by entering all its digits in base 10. Here's some pseudo-code.

```
plate <int D1, int D2 = 0, ... , int D_N = 0>
uct join_digits

static const int value = join_digits<D2, ..., D_N>::value * 10 + D1;


plate <int D1>
uct join_digits<D1>

static const int value = D1;


_digits<3,2,1>::value;      // compiles, but yields 123, not 321
```

Observe instead that it's not so easy to consume DN in the rotation. This will not compile, because whenever DN is equal to its default (zero), value is defined in terms of itself:

```
template <int D1, int D2 = 0, ..., int D_N-1 = 0, int D_N = 0>
struct join_digits
{
  static const int value = join_digits<D1,D2, ...,D_N-1>::value * 10 + D_N;
};
```

Rotation to the right won't produce the correct result:

```
template <int D1, int D2 = 0, ..., int D_N-1 = 0, int D_N = 0>
struct join_digits
{
  static const int value = join_digits<0,D1,D2, ...,D_N-1>::value * 10 + D_N;
};
```

The solution is simply to store auxiliary constants and borrow them from the tail:

```
template <int D1 = 0, int D2 = 0, ..., int D_N = 0>
struct join_digits
{
   typedef join_digits<D2, ..., D_N> next_t;
   static const int pow10 = 10 * next_t::pow10;
   static const int value = next_t::value + D1*pow10;
};

template <int D1>
struct join_digits<D1>
{
   static const int value = D1;
   static const int pow10 = 1;
};

join_digits<3,2,1>::value;        // now really gives 321
```

Template rotation can be used in two ways:

- Direct rotation of the main template (as shown previously):

```
template <int D1 = 0, int D2 = 0, ..., int D_N = 0>
struct join_digits
{ ... };

template <int D1>
struct join_digits<D1>
{ ... };
```

- Rotation on a parameter. This adds an extra "indirection":

```
template <int D1 = 0, int D2 = 0, ..., int DN = 0>
struct digit_group
{
   // empty
};

template <typename T>
struct join_digits;      // primary template not defined

template <int D1, int D2, ..., int DN>
struct join_digits< digit_group<D1, ..., DN> >
{
   // as above
};

template <>
struct join_digits< digit_group<> >
{
   // as above
};
```

The first solution is usually simpler to code. However, the second has two serious advantages:

- Type T, which "carries" the tuple of template parameters, can be reused. T is usually a type container of some kind.
- Suppose for the moment that `join_digits<...>` is a true class (not a metafunction), and it is actually instantiated. It will be easy to write generic templates accepting any instance of `join_digits`. They just need to take `join_digits<X>`. But, if `join_digits` has a long and unspecified number of parameters, clients will have to manipulate it as X.[26]

5.8. Agglomerates

rotation technique encapsulated in `pop_front` can be used to create tuples as *agglomerate objects*.
In synthesis, an agglomerate A is a class that has a type container C in its template parameters. The class s `front<C>` and recursively inherits from `A< pop_front<C> >`. The simplest way to "use" the front type is eclare a member of that type. In pseudo-code:

```
plate <typename C>
ss A : public A<typename pop_front<C>::type>

typename front<C>::type member_;

ic:
/ ...
```

s need not be a problem' if `join_digits` were a functor, clients would likely take it as X anyway.

```
template < >
class A<empty>
{
};

template < >
class A< typearray<> >
{
};
```

- Inheritance can be public, private, or even protected.
- There are two possible recursion stoppers: A<empty_typelist> and A<empty_typearray>.

So, an agglomerate is a package of objects whose type is listed in the container. If C is typearray<int, double, std::string>, the layout of A would be as shown in Figure 3-4.

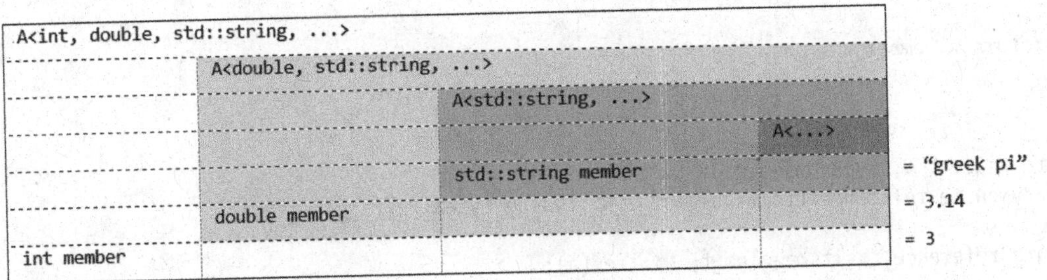

Figure 3-4. Layout of the agglomerate A

Note that in the implementation under review, the memory layout of the objects is reversed with respect to the type container.

To access the elements of the package, you use rotation again. Assume for the moment that all memb are public. You'll get a reference to the Nth member of the agglomerate via a global function and the collaboration of a suitable traits class.

There are two equally good development strategies: *intrusive traits* and *non-intrusive traits.*

Intrusive traits require the agglomerate to expose some auxiliary information:

```
template <typename C>
struct A : public A<typename pop_front<C>::type>
{
    typedef typename front<C>::type value_type;
    value_type member;

    typedef typename pop_front<C>::type tail_t;
};
```

```
emplate <typename agglom_t, size_t N>
truct reference_traits

  typedef reference_traits<typename agglom_t::tail_t, N-1> next_t;
  typedef typename next_t::value_type value_type;

  static value_type& ref(agglom_t& a)
  {
     return next_t::ref(a);
  }


mplate <typename agglom_t>
ruct reference_traits<agglom_t, 0>

 typedef typename agglom_t::value_type value_type;

 static value_type& ref(agglom_t& a)
 {
    return a.member;
 }


nplate <size_t N, typename agglom_t>
line typename reference_traits<agglom_t,N>::value_type& ref(agglom_t& a)

 return reference_traits<agglom_t, N>::ref(a);
```

A quick example:

```
edef typearray<int, double, std::string> C;
> a;

<0>(a) = 3;
<1>(a) = 3.14;
<2>(a) = "3.14";
```

Non-intrusive traits instead determine the information with partial specializations:

```
plate <typename agglom_t, size_t N>
uct reference_traits;

late <typename C, size_t N>
ct reference_traits< A<C>, N >

typedef reference_traits<typename pop_front<C>::type, N-1> next_t;
typedef typename front<C>::type value_type;
```

When feasible, non-intrusive traits are preferred. It's not obvious that the author of `reference_traits` can modify the definition of `A`. However it's common for traits to require reasonable "cooperation" from objects. Furthermore, auto-deduction code is a duplication of class `A` internals and auto-deduced values tend to be "rigid," so intrusiveness is not a clear loser.

A special case is an agglomerate modeled on a typelist *containing no duplicates*. The implementation is much simpler, because instead of rotation, a pseudo-cast suffices:

```
template <typename T, typename tail_t>        // cast-like syntax
T& ref(A< typepair<T, tail_t> >& a)           // T is non-deduced
{
   return a.member;
}

typedef  typepair<int, typepair<double, typepair<std::string, empty> > >  C;
A<C> a;

ref<double>(a) = 3.14;
ref<std::string>(a) = "greek pi";
ref<int>(a) = 3;
```

The cast works because the syntax `ref<T>(a)` fixes the first type of the pair and lets the compiler matc the tail that follows. This is indeed possible, due to the uniqueness hypothesis.

In fact, the C++ Standard allows one derived-to-base cast before argument deduction, if it's a necessar and sufficient condition for an exact match.

Here, the only way to bind an argument of type `A<C>` to a reference to `A< typepair<std::string, tail_t> >` is to cast it to `typepair<std::string, empty>` and then deduce `tail_t = empty`.

To store a value extracted from an agglomerate, declare an object of type `reference_traits<agglom_t,N>::value_type`.

Finally, with a little more intrusiveness, you just add a member function to `A`:

```
template <typename C>
struct A : public A< typename pop_front<C>::type >
{
   typedef typename front<C>::type value_type;
   value_type member;

   typedef typename pop_front<C>::type tail_t;

   tail_t& tail() { return *this; }
};

template <typename agglom_t, size_t N>
struct reference_traits
{
   // ...

   static value_type& get_ref(agglom_t& a)
   {
      return next_t::get_ref(a.tail());
   }
};
```

Invoking a member function instead of an implicit cast allows you to switch to private inheritance or ven to a has-a relationship:

```
emplate <typename C>
lass A

ublic:
  typedef typename pop_front<C>::type tail_t;
  typedef typename front<C>::type value_type;

ivate:
  A<tail_t> tail_;
  value_type member;

blic:
  tail_t& tail() { return tail_; }

  // ...
```

The memory layout of the object is now in the same order as the type container.

6.9. Conversions

ny algorithms in fact require a linear number of recursion steps, both for typelists and for type arrays. In ctice, the typepair representation suffices for most practical purposes except one—: the declaration of a elist is indeed unfeasible.

As anticipated, it's very easy to convert from a type array to typelist and vice versa.

It is an interesting exercise to provide a unified implementation[27]:

```
plate <typename T>
uct convert

typedef typename pop_front<T>::type tail_t;
typedef typename front<T>::type head_t;

typedef
  typename push_front<typename convert<tail_t>::type, head_t>::type
  type;


plate <>
ct convert< typearray<> >

typedef empty type;
```

another exercise of type dismantling; note also that using push_back instead of push_front would reverse ontainer.

```
template <>
struct convert< empty >
{
   typedef typearray<> type;
};
```

Note that T in this code is a generic type container, not a generic type.

Before, you used partial template specialization as a protection against *bad static argument types*. For example, if you try `front<int>::type`, the compiler will output that `front` cannot be instantiated on in (if you did not define the main template) or that it does not contain a member `type` (if it's empty).

However, such a protection is not necessary here. `convert` is built on top of `front` and `pop_front`, and they will perform the required argument validation. In this case, the compiler will diagnose that `front<int` instantiated inside `convert<int>`, is illegal.

The problem is just a less clear debug message. Among the options you have to correct the problem, yo can write type traits to identify type containers and then place assertions:

```
template <typename T>
struct type_container
{
   static const bool value = false;
};

template <typename T1, typename T2>
struct type_container< typepair<T1, T2> >
{
   static const bool value = true;
};

template <>
struct type_container<empty>
{
   static const bool value = true;
};

template <MXT_LIST_32(typename T)>
struct type_container< typearray<MXT_LIST_32(T)> >
{
   static const bool value = true;
};

template <typename T>
struct convert
   : static_assert< type_container<T>::value >
{
   //...
```

Very likely, the compiler will emit the first error pointing to the assertion line.

Note Section 5.2 is fully devoted to bad static argument types. You will meet function templates that atically restrict their template parameters to those having a particular interface.

It can be useful to extend type container traits by inserting a type representing the empty container of at kind (the primary template is unchanged).

```
emplate <typename T1, typename T2>
ruct type_container< typepair<T1, T2> >

 static const bool value = true;
 typedef empty type;


mplate <>
ruct type_container<empty>

 static const bool value = true;
 typedef empty type;


mplate <MXT_LIST_32(typename T)>
ruct type_container< typearray<MXT_LIST_32(T)> >

 static const bool value = true;
 typedef typearray<> type;
```

When enough "low-level" metafunctions—such as `front`, `back`, `push_front`, and so on—are available, st meta-algorithms will work on arrays and lists. You just need two different recursion terminations, as l as a specialization for `typearray<>` and one for `empty`.

Another option is *the empty-empty idiom*: Let a helper class take the original type container as T and a ond type, which is the empty container of the same kind (obtained from traits). When these are equal, stop.

```
plate <typename T>
uct some_metafunction
tatic_assert<type_container<T>::value>
elper<T, typename type_container<T>::type>



late <typename T, typename E>
ct helper

/ general case:
/ T is a non-empty type container of any kind
/ E is the empty container of the same kind
```

```
template <typename E>
struct helper<E, E>
{
   // recursion terminator
};
```

3.6.10. Metafunctors

User functors, predicates, and binary operations can be replaced by template-template parameters. Here is simple metafunctor:

```
template <typename T>
struct size_of
{
   static const size_t value = CHAR_BIT*sizeof(T);
};

template <>
struct size_of<void>
{
   static const size_t value = 0;
};
```

Here is a simple binary metarelation:

```
template <typename X1, typename X2>
struct less_by_size : selector<(sizeof(X1) < sizeof(X2))>
{
};

template <typename X>
struct less_by_size<void, X> : selector<true>
{
};

template <typename X>
struct less_by_size<X, void> : selector<false>
{
};

template <>
struct less_by_size<void, void> : selector<false>
{
};
```

And here's the skeleton of a metafunction that might use it:

```
emplate <typename T, template <typename X1, typename X2> class LESS>
truct static_stable_sort
static_assert< type_container<T>::value >

 // write LESS<T1, T2>::value instead of "T1<T2"

 typedef [[RESULT]] type;
```

Instead of describing an implementation, this section sketches a possible application of `static_stable` `rt`. Suppose our source code includes a collection of random generators that return unsigned integers:

```
ass linear_generator

 typedef unsigned short random_type;
 ...

ass mersenne_twister

 typedef unsigned int random_type;
 ...

ss mersenne_twister_64bit

 typedef /* ... */ random_type;
 ...
```

The user will list all the generators in a type container, in order from the best (the preferred algorithm) he worst. This container can be sorted by `sizeof(typename T::random_type)`. Finally, when the user s for a random number of type X, you scan the sorted container and stop on the first element whose `dom_type` has at least the same size as `X`. You then use that generator to return a value. Since sorting is ole, the first suitable type is also the best in the user preferences.

As promised earlier, I turn now to the problem of selecting unsigned integers by size (in bit).

First, you put all candidates in a type container:

```
edef typearray<unsigned char, unsigned short, unsigned int,
               unsigned long, unsigned long long> all_unsigned;
```

You have to scan the list from left to right and use the first type that has a specified size (it's also possible opend to the list a compiler-specific type).

■ **Note** A little algebra is necessary here. By definition of the sign function, for any integer, you have the identity δ·sign(δ)=|δ|. On the other hand, if S is a prescribed constant in `{-1, 0, 1}`, the equality δ·S=|δ| implies respectively δ≤0, δ=0, δ≥0. This elementary relationship allows you to represent three predicates (less-or-equal-to-zero, equal-to-zero, and greater-or-equal-to-zero) with an integer parameter.

In the following code, T is any type container:

```
#define MXT_M_ABS(a)        ((a)<0 ? -(a) : (a))

enum
{
   LESS_OR_EQUAL = -1,
   EQUAL = 0,
   GREATER_OR_EQUAL = +1
};

template
<
   typename T,
   template <typename X> class SIZE_OF,
   int SIGN,
   size_t SIZE_BIT_N
>
struct static_find_if
: static_assertion< type_container<T>::value >
{
   typedef typename front<T>::type head_t;

   static const int delta = (int)SIZE_OF<head_t>::value - (int)SIZE_BIT_N;

   typedef typename typeif
   <
      SIGN*delta == MXT_M_ABS(delta),
      front<T>,
      static_find_if<typename pop_front<T>::type,
                     SIZE_OF, SIGN, SIZE_BIT_N>
   >::type aux_t;

   typedef typename aux_t::type type;
};

// define an unsigned integer type which has exactly 'size' bits

template <size_t N>
struct uint_n
: static_find_if<all_unsigned, size_of, EQUAL, N>
{
};
```

```
/ defines an unsigned integer type which has at least 'size' bits

emplate <size_t N>
truct uint_nx
 static_find_if<all_unsigned, size_of, GREATER_OR_EQUAL, N>



pedef uint_n<8>::type uint8;
pedef uint_n<16>::type uint16;
pedef uint_n<32>::type uint32;
pedef uint_n<64>::type uint64;

pedef uint_nx<32>::type uint32x;
```

Note that the order of template parameters was chosen to make clear the line that *uses* static_find_if, t static_find_if itself.[28]

What happens if a suitable type is not found? Any invalid use will unwind a long error cascade (the code s been edited to suppress most of the noise):

```
nt_n<25>::type i0 = 8;
nt_nx<128>::type i1 = 8;

ror C2039: 'type' : is not a member of 'front<typearray<>>'
                              : see declaration of 'front<typearray<>>'
                              : see reference to class template instantiation
atic_find_if<T,SIZE_OF,SIZE_BIT_N,SIGN>' being compiled
      with
      [
op_front<pop_front<pop_front<pop_front<pop_front<all_unsigned>::type>::type>::type>::
e>::type,
      ]
                          : see reference to class template instantiation
atic_find_if<T,SIZE_OF,SIZE_BIT_N,SIGN>' being compiled
      with
      [
=pop_front<pop_front<pop_front<pop_front<all_unsigned>::type>::type>::type>::type,
      ]
                          : see reference to class template instantiation
atic_find_if<T,SIZE_OF,SIZE_BIT_N,SIGN>' being compiled
      with
      [
p_front<pop_front<pop_front<all_unsigned>::type>::type>::type,
      ]
]
                     : see reference to class template instantiation
```

dopted the name find_if with some abuse of notation; a genuine static_find_if would be static_find_ ypename T, template <typename X> class F>, which returns the first type in T where F<X>::value is true.

```
'static_find_if<T,SIZE_OF,SIZE_BIT_N,SIGN>' being compiled
        with
        [
            T=all`unsigned,
        ]
                        : see reference to class template instantiation
'uint_n<SIZE_BIT_N>' being compiled
        with
        [
            SIZE_BIT_N=25
        ]
```

Basically, the compiler is saying that, during deduction of `uint_n<25>::type`, after applying `pop_front` to the type array five times, it ended up with an empty container, which has no `front` type.

However it's easy to get a more manageable report. You just add an undefined type as a result of the recursion terminator:

```
template
<
   template <typename X> class SIZE_OF,
   int SIGN,
   size_t SIZE_BIT_N
>
struct static_find_if<typearray<>, SIZE_OF, SIGN, SIZE_BIT_N>
{
   typedef error_UNDEFINED_TYPE type;
};
```

Now the error message is more concise:

```
error C2079: 'i0' uses undefined class 'error_UNDEFINED_TYPE'
error C2079: 'i1' uses undefined class 'error_UNDEFINED_TYPE'
```

3.7. A Summary of Styles

When programming metafunctions, identify:

- A suggestive name and syntax.
- Which template parameters are needed to express the concept.
- Which atomic actions the algorithm depends on.
- A recursive efficient implementation.
- Special cases that must be isolated.

If the metafunction name is similar to a classic algorithm (say, `find_if`), then you can adopt a similar na (`static_find_if`) or even an identical one if it resides in a specific namespace (say, `typelist::find_if`).

Some authors append an underscore to pure static algorithms, because this allows mimicking real keywords (`typeif` would be called `if_`).

If several template parameters are necessary, write code so that the users will be able to remember their ıeaning and order. It's a good idea to give a syntax hint through the name:

```
static_find_if<all_unsigned, size_of, GREATER_OR_EQUAL, N>
```

Many unrelated parameters should be grouped in a traits class, which should have a default nplementation that is easy to copy.

Finally, the following table may help you translate a classic algorithm to a static one.

	Classic C++ Function	Static Metaprogramming
`at they manipulate`	Instances of objects	Types
`gument handling`	Via argument public interface	Via metafunctions
`aling with different guments`	Function overload	Partial template specializations
`turn result`	Zero or one `return` statement	Zero or more static data (type or constant), usually inherited
`ror trapping`	`try...catch` block	Extra template parameter `ERR`
`er-supplied callbacks`	Functors	Template-template parameters
`nporary objects`	Local variables	Private `typedef/static const`
`ıction calls`	Yes, as subroutines	Yes, also via derivation
`;orithm structure`	Iteration or recursion	Static recursion, stopped with suitable full/partial template specializations
`ıditional decisions`	Language constructs (`if`, `switch`)	Partial specializations
`or handling`	• Throw an exception • Return `false`	• Abort compilation • Return no result • Set result to an incomplete type

CHAPTER 4

Overload Resolution

This chapter presents TMP techniques based on overload resolution.

The common underlying schema is as follows:

- You want to test if type T satisfies a condition.
- You write several static functions with the same name, say `test`, and pass them a dummy argument that "carries" type T (in other words, an argument that allows deduction of T, such as T*).
- The compiler selects the best candidate, according to C++ language rules.
- You deduce which function was used, either using the return type or indirectly from a property of this type, and eventually make a decision.

The first section introduces some definitions.

4.1. Groups

A *group* is a class that provides optimized variants of a single routine. From the outside, a group acts as a monolithic function that automatically picks the best implementation for every call.

A group is composed of two entities:

- A template `struct` containing variants of a (single) static member function.
- A companion global function template that just forwards the execution to the correct member of the group, performing a static decision based on the auto-deduced template parameter and on some framework-supplied information.

The group itself is usually a template, even if formally unnecessary (it may be possible to write the gro as a normal class with template member functions).

Finally, observe that groups and traits are somehow orthogonal. Traits contain all the actions of a specific type, while groups contain a single action for many types.

```
Traits<T1>          Traits<T2>                      Group_F1        Group_F2
{                   {                               {               {
  Func1(T1);          Func1(T2);        <->           Func1(T1);      Func2(T1);
  Func2(T1);          Func2(T2);                      Func1(T2);      Func2(T2);
}                   }                               }               }
```

.1.1. From Overload to Groups

group is the evolution of a set of overloaded functions.

Step 1: You realize that a default template implementation can handle most cases, so you just add verloaded variants:

```
mplate <typename T>
ol is_product_negative(T x, T y)

 return x<0 ^ y<0;


ol is_product_negative(short x, short y)

 return int(x)*int(y) < 0;


ol is_product_negative(unsigned int x, unsigned int y)

 return false;


l is_product_negative(unsigned long x, unsigned long y)

 return false;
```

Step 2: Implementation is clustered in several templates that are picked using tags.

```
plate <typename T>
l is_product_negative(T x, T y, selector<false>)

return x<0 ^ y<0;


plate <typename T>
l is_product_negative(T x, T y, selector<true>)

return int(x)*int(y) < 0;


plate <typename T>
 is_product_negative(T x, T y)

ypedef selector<(sizeof(T)<sizeof(int))> small_int_t;
eturn is_product_negative(x, y, small_int_t());
```

Step 3: Group all the auxiliary functions in a class and leave a single function outside that dispatches the work:

```
// companion function

template <typename T>
bool is_product_negative(T x, T y)
{
   return is_product_negative_t<T>::doIt(x, y);
}

template <typename T>
struct is_product_negative_t
{
   static bool doIt(T x, T y)
   { ... }

   static bool doIt(unsigned, unsigned)
   { return false; }
};
```

Here is another very simple group:

```
struct maths
{
   template <typename T>
   inline static T abs(const T x)
   {
      return x<0 ? -x : x;
   }

   inline static unsigned int abs(unsigned int x)
   {
      return x;
   }
};

template <typename T>
inline T absolute_value(const T x)
{
   return maths::abs(x);
}
```

■ **Note** Remember that the group class, being a non-template, is always fully instantiated. Furthermore, a non-template function in a header file must be declared inline.

Suppose further that you have a metafunction named has_abs_method, such that as_abs_method<T>::value is true if the absolute value of an object x of type T is given by x.abs().[1]
This allows your group to grow a bit more complex. In the next example, you'll specialize the whole roup for double, and the specialization will ignore the actual result of has_abs_method<double>.[2]

```
emplate <typename scalar_t>
truct maths

 static scalar_t abs(const scalar_t& x, selector<false>)
 {
    return x<0 ? -x : x;
 }

 static scalar_t abs(const scalar_t& x, selector<true>)
 {
    return x.abs();
 }


mplate <>
ruct maths<double>

 template <bool UNUSED>
 static double abs(const double x, selector< UNUSED >)
 {
    return std::fabs(x);
 }


plate <typename scalar_t>
ine scalar_t absolute_value(const scalar_t& x)

typedef selector< has_abs_method<scalar_t>::value > select_t;
return maths<scalar_t>::abs(x, select_t());
```

Too many overloads will likely conflict. Remember that a non-template function is preferred to a matching plate, but this does not hold for a member function that uses the template parameter of the class:

```
plate <typename scalar_t>
uct maths

static scalar_t abs(const scalar_t& x, selector<false>)
{
   return x<0 ? -x : x;
}
```

ions 5.3 and 5.3.1 show how to detect if T has a member function T T::abs() const.

ourse, you could have written a method that takes selector<false>, but using a template as a replacement for ipsis can be of some interest.

```
    static int abs(const int x, selector<false>)
    {
        return std::abs(x);
    }
}
```

```
error: ambiguous call to overloaded function, during instantiation of absolute_value<int>
```

This is precisely the advantage of a "double-layer" template selection. "Layer one" is the automatic deduction of scalar_t in the companion function and "layer two" is the overload selection, performed inside a class template (the group) whose parameter has already been fixed:

```
template <typename scalar_t>
inline scalar_t absolute_value(const scalar_t& x)
{
    // collect auxiliary information, if needed
    return math<scalar_t>::abs(x, ...);
}
```

Combining them, you have fewer global function templates (too many overloads are likely to cause "ambiguous calls"). In addition, the group can have subroutines (private static member functions).

The user has several expansion choices:

- Specialize the whole group (if it's a template)
- Specialize the global companion function
- Model types to take advantage of the existing framework (for example, specialize has_abs_method)

The selection part can be even subtler, with additional layers in the middle. As the following example shows, the right member of the group is chosen via an implicit argument promotion:

```
#include <cmath>

struct tag_floating
{
    tag_floating() {}
    tag_floating(instance_of<float>) {}
    tag_floating(instance_of<double>) {}
    tag_floating(instance_of<long double>) {}
};

struct tag_signed_int
{
    tag_signed_int() {}
    tag_signed_int(instance_of<short>) {}
    tag_signed_int(instance_of<int>) {}
    tag_signed_int(instance_of<long>) {}
};
```

```
truct tag_unsigned_int

  tag_unsigned_int() {}
  tag_unsigned_int(instance_of<unsigned short>) {}
  tag_unsigned_int(instance_of<unsigned int>) {}
  tag_unsigned_int(instance_of<unsigned long>) {}
;

emplate <typename scalar_t>
ruct maths

 inline static scalar_t abs(const scalar_t x, tag_signed_int)
 {
    return x<0 ? -x : x;
 }

 inline static scalar_t abs(const scalar_t x, tag_unsigned_int)
 {
    return x;
 }

 inline static scalar_t abs(const scalar_t x, tag_floating)
 {
    return fabs(x);
 }


nplate <typename scalar_t>
ine scalar_t absv(const scalar_t& x)

return maths<scalar_t>::abs(x, instance_of<scalar_t>());
```

The same effect could be obtained with a reversed selector hierarchy (for example, letting tance_of<double> derive from scalar_floating), but instance_of is a general-purpose template and eat it as non-modifiable.

You could also introduce intermediate selectors (unfortunately, you have to write the constructors and):

```
uct tag_int

tag_int() {}
tag_int(instance_of<short>) {}
tag_int(instance_of<int>) {}
tag_int(instance_of<long>) {}
tag_int(instance_of<unsigned short>) {}
tag_int(instance_of<unsigned int>) {}
tag_int(instance_of<unsigned long>) {}
```

```
template <typename scalar_t>
struct maths
{
   static scalar_t mod(const scalar_t x, const scalar_t y, tag_int)
   {
      return x % y;
   }

   static scalar_t mod(const scalar_t& x, const scalar_t& y, tag_floating)
   {
      return fmod(x, y);
   }
};

template <typename scalar_t>
inline scalar_t mod(const scalar_t& x, const scalar_t& y)
{
   return maths<scalar_t>::mod(x, y, instance_of<scalar_t>());
}
```

Note in this code that `maths<double>` contains a method that must not be called (there's no `operator%` for double). Had `operation` been a non-template class, it would have been instantiated anyway, thus yielding a compiler error.

However, when parsing an expression depending on a template parameter, the compiler, not knowing the actual type involved, will accept any formally legal C++ statement.[3] So if at least one of the two arguments `x` and `y` has generic type `T`, `x % y` is considered valid until instantiation time.

The former example works unambiguously because the companion function restricts the call to members of `maths<double>` named `mod`, and for any type `T`, `instance_of<T>` can be promoted to at most one of either `tag_int` or `tag_floating`.

Sometimes groups are associated with a special header file that detects platform information using macro blocks and translates it in C++ using `typedefs`:

```
// file "root.hpp"
// note: this code is fictitious

struct msvc {};
struct gcc {};

#if defined(__MSVC)              // preprocessor compiler detection...
typedef msvc compiler_type;      // ...translated in c++
#elif defined(__GCC__)
typedef gcc compiler_type;
#endif

// from here on, there's a global type tag named "compiler_type"
```

[3]An illegal statement would be, for example, a call to an undeclared function. Recall that compilers are not required to diagnose errors in templates that are not instantiated. MSVC skips even some basic syntax checks, while GCC does forbid usage of undeclared functions and types. See also Section 5.2.3 about platform specific traits.

In different platforms, the same function could have a different "best" implementation, so you can elect the most suitable one using compiler_type as a tag (but *all* functions must be legal C++ code):

```
emplate <typename scalar_t, typename compiler_t>
truct maths

 static scalar_t multiply_by_two(const scalar_t x)
 { return 2*x; }


emplate < >
ruct maths<unsigned int, msvc>

 static unsigned int multiply_by_two(const unsigned int x)
 { return x << 1; }


mplate <typename scalar_t>
line scalar_t multiply_by_two(const scalar_t& x)

 return maths<scalar_t, compiler_type>::multiply_by_two(x);
```

Note that you can branch the selection of member functions as you wish—either simultaneously on ltiple tags or hierarchically.

As a rule, you might want to use the "compiler tag" whenever you need to manipulate the result of a ndard function that is defined as compiler-specific to some extent, for example, to pretty-print a string en by typeid(...).name().

Consider a real-world example. According to the standard, if A and B are both signed integers, *not both itive*, the sign of A % B is undefined (if instead A>0 and B>0, the standard guarantees that A % B > 0). For example, -10 % 3 can yield either -1 or +2, because -10 can be written as 3*(-3)+(-1) or 3*(-4)+(+2) l both |-1|<3 and |2|<3. In any case, both solutions will differ by 3.

However, operator% is often implemented so that A and (A % B) both have the same sign (which, in fact, e same rule used for fmod). It therefore makes sense to write a reminder function that grants this condition.

Since (-A) % B == -(A % B) and A % (-B) == A % B, you can deduce that you can return n(A)*(|A| % |B|) when the native implementation of A % B yields a different result.

A simple implementation can rely on (-3) % 2 being equal to +1 or -1. (Note that the following code is 100% bulletproof, but it's a good compromise.)

```
plate <typename T, int X = (-3)%2, int Y = (-3)%(-2), int Z = 3%(-2)>
uct modgroup;

if X=+1, Y=-1, Z=+1 then operator% already does what we want
(strictly speaking, we tested only int)

plate <typename T>
ct modgroup<T, 1, -1, 1>

tatic scalar_t mod(const T x, const T y)

  return x % y;
```

```
// in any other case, fall back to the safe formula

template <typename T, int X, int Y, int Z>
struct modgroup
{
   static scalar_t mod(const T x, const T y)
   {
      const T result = abs(x) % abs(y);
      return x<0 ? -result : result;
   }
};

template <typename scalar_t>
struct maths
{
   static scalar_t mod(const scalar_t x, const scalar_t y,
                       tag_int)
   {
      return modgroup<scalar_t>::mod(x, y);
   }

   static scalar_t mod(const scalar_t& x, const scalar_t& y,
                       tag_floating)
   {
      return fmod(x, y);
   }
};

template <typename scalar_t>
inline scalar_t mod(const scalar_t& x, const scalar_t& y)
{
   return maths<scalar_t>::mod(x, y, instance_of<scalar_t>());
}
```

4.1.2. Runtime Decay

A type tag may implement a special cast operator so that if no overload in the group matches the tag exactl the execution continues in a default function, which usually performs some work at runtime. The prototyp is a static integer that decays into a normal integer if there's no better match.

Suppose you want to fill a C array with zeroes:

```
template <typename T, T VALUE>
struct static_value
{
   // ...

   operator T() const
   {
      return VALUE;
   }
};
```

```
emplate <typename T>
truct zeroize_helper

  static void apply(T* const data, static_value<int, 1>)
  {
     *data = T();
  }

  static void apply(T (&data)[2], static_value<int, 2>)
  {
     data[0] = data[1] = T();
  }

  static void apply(T* const data, const int N)
  {
     std::fill_n(data, N, T());
  }

mplate <typename T, int N>
id zeroize(T (&data)[N])

 zeroize_helper<T>::apply(data, static_value<int, N>());
```

- Instead of 0, you write `T()`, which works for a broader range of types.
- If N is larger than 2, the best match is the third member.
- Each function in the group can decide freely to cast, or even to ignore, the `static_value`.
- The default case may accept every `static_value` not necessarily performing all the work at runtime, but with another template function:

```
plate <>
uct zeroize_helper<char>

template <int N>
struct chunk
{
   char data[N];
};

template <int N>
static void apply(char* const data, static_value<int, N>, selector<true>)

   *reinterpret_cast<chunk<N>*>(data) = chunk<N>();
```

```
    template <int N>
    static void apply(char* const data, static_value<int, N>, selector<false>)
    {
       memset(data, N, 0);
    }

    template <int N>
    static void apply(char* const data, static_value<int, N> S)
    {
       apply(data, S, selector<sizeof(chunk<N>) == N>());
    }
};
```

4.2. More Traits

This section completes the review of traits.

This time you are going to use traits restricted for static programming, but also as function groups. Let's start with a concrete case.

4.2.1. A Function Set for Strings

Suppose you are going to write some generic algorithms for strings. Surely you can use iterators, in particul random-access iterators, right? Most STL implementations have char-optimized algorithms, such as `std::find`, `std::copy`, and so on.

The only burden on the user is a large number of calls to `strlen` to find the end of range. `strlen` is a *very* fast function, but this is a violation of STL assumptions, as "end" is assumed to be obtained in constan time, not linear time.

```
const char* c_string = "this is an example";

// can we avoid this?
std::copy(c_string, c_string+strlen(c_string), destination);
```

You can squeeze in even more optimization using traits:

```
template <typename string_t>
struct string_traits
{
   typedef /* dependent on string_t */ const_iterator;
   typedef const string_t& argument_type;

   const_iterator begin(argument_type s);
   const_iterator end  (argument_type s);

   static bool is_end_of_string(const_iterator i, argument_type s);
};
```

Assuming that for every meaningful string, string_traits has the same interface, you can write an lgorithm as follows:

```
emplate <typename string_t>
oid loop_on_all_chars(const string_t& s)

  typedef string_traits<string_t> traits_t;

  typename traits_t::const_iterator i = traits_t::begin(s);
  while (!traits_t::is_end_of_string(i, s))
  {
     std::cout << *(i++);
  }
```

The code is verbose but clear. Yet at this point it may not be evident what you accomplished. e semi-opaque interface of string_traits gives more freedom in doing comparisons:

```
mplate <typename char_t>
ruct string_traits< std::basic_string<char_t> >

 typedef char_t char_type;
 typedef
   typename std::basic_string<char_type>::const_iterator
   const_iterator;

 typedef const std::basic_string<char_type>& argument_type;

 static const_iterator begin(argument_type text)
 {
    return text.begin();
 }

 static const_iterator end(argument_type text)
 {
    return text.end();
 }

static bool is_end_of_string(const_iterator i, argument_type s);
{
   return i == s.end();
}


late <>
ict string_traits<const char*>

ypedef char char_type;

ypedef const char* const_iterator;
ypedef const char* argument_type;
```

```
    static const_iterator begin(argument_type text)
    {
        return text;
    }

    static const_iterator end(argument_type text)
    {
        return 0;    // constant-time
    }

    static bool is_end_of_string(const_iterator i, argument_type s);
    {
        // a constant-time "C" test for end of string
        return (i==0) || (*i==0);
    }
};
```

Since end is now constant-time, you save a linear-time pass (you'll meet this very same problem again and solve it with a different technique in Section 6.2.2.

You can easily extend string_traits to a full interface (some words have been renamed for ease of reading):

```
template <typename string_t>
struct string_traits
{

typedef /* ... */ char_type;

typedef /* ... */ const_iterator;
typedef /* ... */ argument_type; // either string_t or const string_t&

static size_t npos();

static size_t find1st(arg_t txt, const char_t c, size_t offset=0);
static size_t find1st(arg_t txt, const arg_t s, size_t offset=0);

static size_t findlast(arg_t txt, const char_t s, size_t offset);
static size_t findlast(arg_t txt, const arg_t s, size_t offset);

static size_t find1st_in(arg_t txt, const char_t* charset, size_t offs=0);
static size_t find1st_out(arg_t txt, const char_t* charset, size_t offs=0);

static size_t size(arg_t txt);

static const_iterator begin(arg_t txt);
static const_iterator end(arg_t txt);

static const char_t* c_str(arg_t txt);
```

```
tatic bool empty(const_iterator begin, const_iterator end);
tatic bool less(const_iterator begin, const_iterator end);
tatic size_t distance(const_iterator begin, const_iterator end);
;
```

To leverage the interface and take advantage of `std::string` member functions, consider the following onvention:

- All iterators are random-access.
- The `find` functions return either the index of the character (which is portable in all kind of strings) or `npos()`, which means "not found".

```
atic size_t find1st(arg_t text, const char_type c, size_t offset=0)

 const char_t* pos = strchr(text+offset, c);
 return pos ? (pos-text) : npos();
```

In the specialization for `const char*`, you carry on the ambiguity on the end iterator, which can be a ll pointer to mean "until char 0 is found". Thus, you could implement distance as follows:

```
atic size_t distance(const_iterator begin, const_iterator end)

 return end ? end-begin : (begin ? strlen(begin) : 0);
```

Finally, you can inherit function sets via public derivation, as usual with traits, because they are teless (so the protected empty destructor can be omitted):

```
nplate <>
'uct string_traits<char*> : string_traits<const char*>
```

2.2. Concept Traits

You repeatedly saw in the first chapters, traits classes prescribe syntax, not precise entities. Code may row from traits in such a way that several different implementations are possible.

Suppose you have some kind of smart pointer class whose traits class is also responsible for ing memory:

```
plate <typename T, typename traits_t = smart_ptr_traits<T> >
ss smart_ptr

typedef typename traits_t::pointer pointer;
pointer p_;
```

```
public:

   ~smart_ptr()
   {
         traits_t::release(p_);
   }
   // ...
};
```

traits::release can be:

- A public static function (or functor); the relevant code is in the function body.

```
template <typename T>
struct smart_ptr_traits
{
   typedef T* pointer;

   static void release(pointer p)
   {
      delete p;
   }
```

- A public static function that triggers a conversion operator, which in fact runs the code.

```
template <typename T>
struct smart_ptr_traits
{
   static void release(bool)
   {
   };

   class pointer
   {
      // ...
      public:
         operator bool()
         { ... }
   };

   // ...
```

Using a slightly different syntax, you can rewrite this as follows:

```
template <typename T, typename traits_t = smart_ptr_traits<T> >
class smart_ptr
{
   typedef typename traits_t::pointer pointer;
   pointer p_;
```

```
  static void traits_release(typename traits_t::release)
  {
                      // note: empty body
  };

ublic:
  ~smart_ptr()
  {
          traits_release(p_);
  }
```

Release can now be a type, and the relevant code is in the (non-explicit) constructor body.

```
mplate <typename T>
ruct smart_ptr_traits

 typedef T* pointer;

 struct release
 {
    release(pointer p)
    {
       delete p;
    }
 };
```

The code can, again, trigger a conversion operator:

```
nplate <typename T>
:uct smart_ptr_traits

struct release
{
};

class pointer
{
   // ...
   public:

      operator release()
      {
         delete p_;
         return release();
      }
;
```

All these implementations are valid and you can choose the best positioning of the code that is ally executed.[4]

tly, the choice will depend on `release` and `pointer` being independent or provided by the same traits.

If traits::release is provided as a type, it may have static data that is easily shared with the rest of the program (you could, for example, log all the released pointers).

4.2.3. Platform-Specific Traits

Recall that traits classes can be "global" or "local". Global traits classes are visible everywhere and local traits should be passed as parameters.

Global traits are preferred to make some platform properties easily accessible to clients:

```
template <typename char_t>
struct textfile_traits
{
   static char_t get_eol() { return '\n'; }
   // ...
};
```

The following full example represents a timer object with a class template and borrows additional information from a "timer traits" class:

- How to get current time (in an unspecified unit)
- How to convert time into seconds (using a frequency)

```
template <typename traits_t>
class basic_timer
{
   typedef typename traits_t::time_type tm_t;
   typedef typename traits_t::difference_type diff_t;

   tm_t start_;
   tm_t stop_;

   inline static tm_t now()
   {
      return traits_t::get_time();
   }

   double elapsed(const tm_t end) const
   {
      static const tm_t frequency = traits_t::get_freq();
      return double(diff_t(end-start_))/frequency;
   }

public:
   typedef tm_t time_type;
   typedef diff_t difference_type;

   basic_timer()
   : start_()
   {}
```

```
difference_type lap() const
{ return now()-start_; }

time_type start()
{ return start_ = now(); }

difference_type stop()
{ return (stop_ = now())-start_; }

difference_type interval() const
{ return stop_-start_; }

double as_seconds() const
{ return elapsed(stop_); }

double elapsed() const
{ return elapsed(now()); }
```

Here is a sample traits class that measures clock time (in seconds):

```
nclude <ctime>
ruct clock_time_traits

typedef size_t time_type;
typedef ptrdiff_t difference_type;

static time_type get_time()
{
   time_t t;
   return std::time(&t);
}

static time_type get_freq()
{
   return 1;
}
```

Here's a different traits class that accounts for CPU time:

```
uct cpu_time_traits

typedef size_t time_type;
typedef ptrdiff_t difference_type;

static time_type get_time()

  return std::clock();
```

```
   static time_type get_freq()
   {
      return CLOCKS_PER_SEC;
   }
};
```

And a short use case:

```
basic_timer<clock_time_traits> t;
t.start();
// ...
t.stop();
std::cout << "I ran for " << t.as_seconds() << " seconds.";
```

The fundamental restriction of traits is that all member functions must contain valid C++ code, even if unused. You cannot use compiler-specific code in one of the functions.

Since different operating systems can expose more precise APIs for time measurement, you might be tempted to write specialized traits:

```
#include <windows.h>

struct windows_clock_time_traits
{
   typedef ULONGLONG time_type;
   typedef LONGLONG difference_type;

   static time_type get_time()
   {
      LARGE_INTEGER i;
      QueryPerformanceCounter(&i);
      return i.QuadPart;
   }

   static time_type get_freq()
   {
      LARGE_INTEGER value;
      QueryPerformanceFrequency(&value);
      return value.QuadPart;
   }
};

#include <sys/time.h>

struct macosx_clock_time_traits
{
   typedef uint64_t time_type;
   typedef int64_t difference_type;
```

```
static time_type get_time()
{
   timeval now;
   gettimeofday(&now, 0);
   return time_type(now.tv_sec) * get_freq() + now.tv_usec;
}

static time_type get_freq()
{
   return 1000000;
}
```

Apart from the typedefs for large integers, this traits interface is standard C++, so you might are mpted to isolate the preprocessor in a "factory header" and rely entirely on template properties later:

```
platform_detect.hpp

ruct windows {};
ruct macosx {};
ruct other_os {};

f defined(WIN32)
pedef windows platform_type;
lif defined(__APPLE__)
edef macosx platform_type;
lse
pedef other_os platform_type;
ndif

timer_traits.hpp

plate <typename platform_t>
uct clock_time_traits;

plate < >
uct clock_time_traits<windows>

// implementation with QPC/QPF


plate < >
uct clock_time_traits<macosx>

// implementation with gettimeofday
```

```
template < >
struct clock_time_traits<other_os>
{
   // implementation with std::time
};

typedef basic_timer< clock_time_traits<platform_type> > native_timer_type;
```

Unfortunately, the code is *non-portable* (if it compiles, however, it runs correctly).

According to the standard, a compiler is not required to diagnose errors in unused template member functions, but if it does, it requires that all mentioned entities be well-defined. In particular, GCC will report an error in `clock_time_traits<windows>::get_time`, because no function named `QueryPerformanceCounter` has been declared.

As the approach is attractive, some workarounds are possible:

- Define a macro with the same name and as many arguments as the function:

```
// define as nothing because the return type is void
// otherwise define as an appropriate constant, e.g. 0

#define QueryPerformanceCounter(X)

#if defined(WIN32)
#undef QueryPerformanceCounter        // remove the fake...
#include <windows.h>                  // ...and include the true function
#endif
```

- Declare—but do not define—the function. This is the preferred solution, because Windows traits should not link in other operating systems.

```
#if !defined(WIN32)
   void QueryPerformanceCounter(void*);
#endif
```

■ Note A common trick, if the function returns `void`, is to define the name of the function itself to <nothing>. The comma-separated argument list will be parsed as a comma operator.

This also allows ellipsis functions to be used:

```
#define printf

printf("Hello world, %f", cos(3.14));
```

However, there are a couple of potential issues. First, the macro changes the return type of the expression to `double` (the last argument). Furthermore, the program is still evaluating `cos(3.14)`. An alternative that also minimizes the runtime effort—although it's not totally bulletproof—is:

```
inline bool discard_everything(...) { return false };

#define printf                    false && discard_everything
```

.2.4. Merging Traits

specially when you're dealing with large traits, it's good practice to enable the users to customize naller parts of the traits class. Typically, the problem is solved by splitting the traits class into parts and ecombining them using public inheritance to form a traits default value.

Suppose you are grouping some comparison operators in traits:

```
mplate <typename T>
ruct binary_relation_traits

 static bool gt(const T& x, const T& y) { return x>y; }
 static bool lt(const T& x, const T& y) { return x<y; }

 static bool gteq(const T& x, const T& y) { return x>=y; }
 static bool lteq(const T& x, const T& y) { return x<=y; }

 static bool eq(const T& x, const T& y) { return x==y; }
 static bool ineq(const T& x, const T& y) { return x!=y; }
```

The general implementation of `binary_relation_traits` assumes that `T` defines all six comparison erators, but this example supports two important special cases, namely:

- `T` defines `operator<` only
- `T` defines `operator<` and `operator==` only

Without your support, the users will have to implement all the traits structure from scratch. So you must rrange the code as follows:

```
plate <typename T>
uct b_r_ordering_traits

static bool gt(const T& x, const T& y) { return x>y; }
static bool lt(const T& x, const T& y) { return x<y; }

static bool gteq(const T& x, const T& y) { return x>=y; }
static bool lteq(const T& x, const T& y) { return x<=y; }


plate <typename T>
uct b_r_equivalence_traits

static bool eq(const T& x, const T& y) { return x==y; }
static bool ineq(const T& x, const T& y) { return x!=y; }


late <typename T>
ct binary_relation_traits
blic b_r_ordering_traits<T>
blic b_r_equivalence_traits<T>
```

Then you have to write the alternative blocks, which can be combined:

```
template <typename T>
struct b_r_ordering_less_traits
{
   static bool gt(const T& x, const T& y) { return y<x; }
   static bool lt(const T& x, const T& y) { return x<y; }

   static bool gteq(const T& x, const T& y) { return !(x<y); }
   static bool lteq(const T& x, const T& y) { return !(y<x); }
};

template <typename T>
struct b_r_equivalence_equal_traits
{
   static bool eq(const T& x, const T& y) { return x==y; }
   static bool ineq(const T& x, const T& y) { return !(x==y); }
};

template <typename T>
struct b_r_equivalence_less_traits
{
   static bool eq(const T& x, const T& y) { return !(x<y) && !(y<x); }
   static bool ineq(const T& x, const T& y) { return x<y || y<x; }
};
```

Finally, you combine the pieces via derivation and a hidden template parameter.

```
enum
{
   HAS_JUST_OPERATOR_LESS,
   HAS_OPERATOR_LESS_AND_EQ,
   HAS_ALL_6_OPERATORS
};

template <typename T, int = HAS_ALL_6_OPERATORS>
struct binary_relation_traits
: b_r_ordering_traits<T>
, b_r_equivalence_traits<T>
{
};

template <typename T>
struct binary_relation_traits<T, HAS_JUST_OPERATOR_LESS>
: b_r_ordering_less_traits<T>
, b_r_equivalence_less_traits<T>
{
};
```

```
emplate <typename T>
truct binary_relation_traits<T, OPERATOR_LESS_AND_EQ>
 b_r_ordering_less_traits<T>
 b_r_equivalence_equal_traits<T>

;
```

Further, traits can be chained using appropriate enumerations and "bitwise-or" syntax.[5]

What if you wanted to provide an enumeration set, containing powers of two that will be combined ing the standard *flags idiom,* but at compile time:

```
tream fs("main.txt", ios::in | ios:out);

pedef binary_relation_traits<MyType, native::less | native::eq> MyTraits;
```

First, you let the flags start at 1, since you need powers of two.

```
mespace native

 enum
 {
     lt          = 1,
     lt_eq       = 2,
     gt          = 4,
     gt_eq       = 8,
     eq          = 16,
     ineq        = 32
 };
```

Second, you split the traits class into atoms, using partial specialization:

```
plate <typename T, int FLAG>
uct binary_relation_traits; // no body!

plate <typename T>
uct binary_relation_traits<T, native::lt>

static bool lt(const T& x, const T& y) { return x<y; }


plate <typename T>
uct binary_relation_traits<T, native::lt_eq>

static bool lteq(const T& x, const T& y) { return x<=y; }


nd so on...
```

Section 2.3.3.

If the user-supplied bitmask `FLAG` is set to (`native::ineq` | ...), `traits<T,FLAGS>` should derive from both `traits<T, native::ineq>` and `traits <T, FLAGS - native::ineq>`.

You need an auxiliary metafunction called `static_highest_bit<N>::value`, which returns the index of the highest bit set in a (positive) integer `N`, such as the exponent of the largest power of two less or equal to `N`.

Having this tool at your disposal, you come up with an implementation:

```
template <typename T, unsigned FLAG>
struct binary_relation_traits;

template <typename T>
struct binary_relation_traits<T, 0>
{
   // empty!
};

template <typename T>
struct binary_relation_traits<T, native::lt>
{
   static bool lt(const T& x, const T& y) { return x<y; }
};

template <typename T>
struct binary_relation_traits<T, native::gt>
{
   static bool gt(const T& x, const T& y) { return x>y; }
};

// write all remaining specializations
// then finally...

template <typename T, unsigned FLAG>
struct binary_relation_traits
: binary_relation_traits<T, FLAG & (1 << static_highest_bit<FLAG>::value)>
, binary_relation_traits<T,  FLAG - (1 << static_highest_bit<FLAG>::value)>
{
   // empty!
};
```

Now the user can select `binary_relation_traits` members at compile time:

```
typedef binary_relation_traits<MyType, native::less | native::eq>  MyTraits;

MyType a, b;
MyTraits::lt(a,b);      // ok.
MyTraits::lteq(a,b);    // error: undefined
```

[6] The details of `static_highest_bit` are in Section 3.4.1.

This technique is interesting in itself, but it does not meet the original requirements, since you can only ick "native" operators. But you can add more flags:

```
amespace native

  enum
  {
     lt       = 1,
     lt_eq    = 2,
     gt       = 4,
     gt_eq    = 8,
     eq       = 16,
     ineq     = 32
  };


mespace deduce

 enum
 {
    ordering    = 64,
    equivalence = 128,
    ineq        = 256
 };


nplate <typename T>
ruct binary_relation_traits<T, deduce::ordering>

 static bool gt(const T& x, const T& y) { return y<x; }

 static bool gteq(const T& x, const T& y) { return !(x<y); }
 static bool lteq(const T& x, const T& y) { return !(y<x); }


plate <typename T>
uct binary_relation_traits<T, deduce ::ineq>

static bool ineq(const T& x, const T& y) { return !(x==y); }


plate <typename T>
uct binary_relation_traits<T, deduce::equivalence>

static bool eq(const T& x, const T& y) { return !(x<y) && !(y<x); }
static bool ineq(const T& x, const T& y) { return x<y || y<x; }
```

```
typedef
  binary_relation_traits
  <
     MyType,
     native::less | deduce::ordering | deduce::equivalence
  >
  MyTraits;
```

Note that any unnecessary duplication (such that `native::ineq | deduce::ineq`) will trigger a compiler error *at the first use*. If `traits<T,N>` and `traits<T,M>` both have a member `x`, `traits<T,N+M>::x` is an ambiguous call.

4.3. SFINAE

The "substitution failure is not an error" (or SFINAE) principle is a guarantee that the C++ standard offers. You will see precisely what it means and how to remove function templates from an overload set when they do not satisfy a compile-time condition.

Remember that when a class template is instantiated, the compiler generates:

- Every member signature at class level
- Only strictly necessary function bodies

As a consequence, this code does not compile:

```
template <typename T>
struct A
{
   typename T::pointer f() const
   {
      return 0;
   }
};

A<int> x;
```

As soon as `A<int>` is met, the compiler will try to generate a signature for *every* member function, and will give an error because `int::pointer` is not a valid type. Instead, this would work:

```
template <typename T>
struct A
{
   int f() const
   {
      typename T::type a = 0;
      return a;
   }
};

A<int> x;
```

As long as A<int>::f() is unused, the compiler will ignore its body (and that is good news, because it ontains an error).

Furthermore, when the compiler meets f(x) and x has type X, it should decide which particular f is eing invoked, so it sorts all possible candidates from the best to the worst and tries to substitute X in any mplate parameter. If this replacement produces a function with an invalid signature (signature, not body!), e candidate is silently discarded. This is the SFINAE principle.

```
emplate <typename T>
ypename T::pointer f(T*);

t f(void*);

t* x = 0;
x);
```

The first f would be preferred because T* is a better match than void*; however, int has no member pe called pointer, so the second f is used. SFINAE applies only when the substitution produces an pression that is formally invalid (like int::pointer). Instead, it does not apply when the result is a type at does not compile:

```
mplate <typename T, int N>
ruct B

 static const int value = 100/N;


nplate <typename T>
, 0> f(T*);

 f(void*);
```

B<T, 0> is a valid type, but its compilation gives an error. The first f will be picked anyway, and the npiler will stop.

To take advantage of SFINAE, when you want to "enable" or "disable" a particular overload of a function nplate, you artificially insert in its signature a dependent name that may resolve to an invalid expression on-existent type like int::pointer).

If all candidates have been discarded, you get a compiler error (trivial uses of SFINAE look in fact like ic assertions).

There are two main applications of SFINAE: when f runs after being selected and when f is not cuted at all.

.1. SFINAE Metafunctions

g SFINAE and sizeof, you can write metafunctions that take a decision based on the interface of a T. This is very close to what is called *reflection* in different programming languages.

The basic ingredients are:

- Two (or more) types with different sizes; let's call them YES and NO.
- A set of overloaded functions f, where at least one must be a template, returning either YES or NO.
- A static constant defined in terms of sizeof(f(something)).

The following paradigm helps clarify this:

```
template <typename T>
class YES { char dummy[2]; };              // has size > 1

typedef char NO;                           // has size == 1

template <typename T>
class MF
{
   template <typename X>
   static YES<[[condition on X]]> test(X);

   static NO test(...);

   static T this_type();

public:
   static const bool value = sizeof(test(this_type())) != sizeof(NO);
};
```

The compiler has to decide which test is being called when the argument has type T. It will try to evaluate YES<[[condition on T]]> first (because void* and the ellipsis ... have very low priority). If this generates an invalid type, the first overload of test is discarded and it will select the other.

Note some important facts:

- The static functions *need not have a body*; only their signature is used in sizeof.
- YES<T> need not have size 2. It would be an error to write sizeof(test(this_type())) == 2. However, char *must* have size 1, so you could verify if sizeof(test(this_type()))>1.
- At least one of the test functions should be a template that depends on a *new* parameter X. It would be wrong to define test in terms of T (the parameter of MF), since SFINAE would not apply.
- You use a dummy function that returns T instead of, say, invoking test(T()) because T might not have a default constructor.

Some compilers will emit a warning because it's illegal to pass an object to an ellipsis function. Actually the code does not run, since sizeof wraps the whole expression, but warnings may be long and annoying. A good workaround is to pass pointers to functions:

```
template <typename X>
static YES<[[condition on X]]> test(X*);

static NO test(...);

static T* this_type();
```

If you switch to pointers:

- void becomes an admissible type (since T* exists).
- References become illegal (a pointer to a reference is an error).

So either way, you'll have to write some explicit specialization of MF to deal with corner cases.
SFINAE applies if *any* substitution of the template parameter produces an invalid type, not necessarily
the return type. Sometimes, in fact, it's more convenient to use arguments:

```
emplate <typename T>
lass MF

  template <typename X>
  static YES<void> test([[type that depends on X]]*);

  template <typename X>
  static NO test(...);

blic:
  static const bool value = sizeof(test<T>(0)) != sizeof(NO);
```

If the substitution of X in the first expression produces a valid type, thus a valid pointer, `test<T>(0)`
es it as the preferred call. (It casts 0 to a typed pointer and returns `YES<void>` or whatever yes-type.)
herwise, 0 is passed without any cast (as integer) to test(...), which returns NO.
The explicit call `test<T>` works because the ellipsis test function has a dummy template parameter;
ierwise, it would never match.[7]
As a simple example, you can test if type T has a member type named pointer:

```
nplate <typename T>
ass has_pointer_type

 template <typename X>
 static YES<typename X::pointer> test(X*);

 static NO test(...);

 static T* this_type();

lic:
static const bool value = sizeof(test(this_type())) != sizeof(NO);
```

almost) equivalently:[8]

```
plate <typename T>
ss has_pointer_type

template <typename X>
static YES<void> test(typename X::pointer*);
```

Section 1.2.1.

would fail if X::pointer were a reference; at the moment, you don't need to worry about this.

```
    template <typename X>
    static NO test(...);

public:
    static const bool value = sizeof(test<T>(0)) == sizeof(YES);
};
```

By modifying the template parameter of YES, you can check if T has a static constant named value. Once again, it's convenient to derive from a common yes-type:

```
// copied from Section 2.1.4
typedef char no_type;
typedef larger_than<no_type> yes_type;

template <int VALUE>
struct YES2 : yes_type
{
};

template <typename T>
class has_value
{
    template <typename X>
    static YES2<X::value> test(X*);

    // ...
};
```

Or you can check for the presence of a member function with a fixed name and signature[9]:

```
template <typename T, void (T::*F)(T&)>
struct YES3 : yes_type
{
};

template <typename T>
class has_swap_member
{
    template <typename X>
    static YES3<X, &X::swap> test(X*);

    // ...
};
```

[9]The swap-detection problem is actually much more difficult; it's discussed later in this section.

Finally, a popular idiom checks if T is a class or a fundamental type using a fake pointer-to-member. Literal zero can be cast to int T::* if T is a class, even if it has no member of type int.)

```
emplate <typename T>
lass is_class

  template <typename X>
  static yes_type test(int X::*);

  template <typename X>
  static no_type test(...);

blic:
  static const bool value = (sizeof(test<T>(0))!=sizeof(no_type));
```

.3.2. Multiple Decisions

e examples shown so far take a single yes/no decision path, but some criteria can be more complex. Let's ite a metafunction that identifies all signed integers[10]:

```
 (T is a class)
      return false

 (T is a pointer)
      return false

 (T is a reference)
      return false

 (we can have a non-type template parameter of type T)

      if (the expression "T(0) > T(-1)" is well-formed and true)
              return true
      else
              return false

e

      return false
```

: "main algorithm" alone would not suffice. It will work when T is a fundamental type. Some compilers evaluate the ession T(0) < T(-1) as true when T is a pointer; other compilers will give errors if T is a type with no constructor. 's why you add explicit specializations for pointers, references, and class types. Note, however, that this approach perior to an explicit list of specializations, because it's completely compiler/preprocessor independent.

```
template <typename X, bool IS_CLASS = is_class<X>::value>
class is_signed_integer;

template <typename X>
class is_signed_integer<X*, false> : public selector<false>
{
};

template <typename X>
class is_signed_integer<X&, false> : public selector<false>
{
};

template <typename X>
class is_signed_integer<X, true> : public selector<false>
{
};

template <typename X>
class is_signed_integer<X, false>
{
   template <typename T>
   static static_parameter<T, 0>* decide_int(T*);

   static void* decide_int(...);

   template <typename T>
   static selector<(T(0) > T(-1))> decide_signed(static_parameter<T, 0>*);

   static selector<false> decide_signed(...);

   static yes_type cast(selector<true>);
   static no_type cast(selector<false>);

   static X* getX();

public:
   static const bool value =
     sizeof(cast(decide_signed(decide_int(getX()))))==sizeof(yes_type);
};
```

cast maps all possible intermediate return types to yes_type or no_type, for the final sizeof test.

In general, it's possible to stretch this idea and return an enumeration (more precisely, a size_t), instead of bool. Suppose you had more intermediate decision cases:

```
static T1 decide(int*);
static T2 decide(double*);
...
static Tn decide(void*);
```

Then you can map T1, T2,... Tn to an enumeration using fixed_size:

```
  static fixed_size<1>::type& cast(T1);
  static fixed_size<2>::type& cast(T2);
  // ...

ublic:
  static const size_t value = sizeof(cast(decide(...)));
;
```

.3.3. Only_If

nother interesting use of SFINAE is in excluding elements from a set of overloaded (member) functions at are not compliant with some condition:

```
mplate <bool CONDITION>
ruct static_assert_SFINAE

 typedef void type;


mplate <>
ruct static_assert_SFINAE<false>
```

If a function has an argument of type pointer-to-X, where X is defined as static_assert_ INAE<...>::type, substitution of any CONDITION that evaluates to false generates an invalid expression. that particular function is removed from the set of overloads.

The fake pointer argument has a default value of 0, which means the user can safely ignore its existence.[11]

```
efine ONLY_IF(COND)   typename static_assert_SFINAE<COND>::type* = 0

plate <typename T>
d f(T x, ONLY_IF(is_integer<T>::value))



d f(float x)



later...

le x = 3.14;
; // calls f(float)
```

netimes it's desirable to document C++ code, not literally, but just as the user is supposed to use it. This kind of ional documentation is also a part of C++ style. The example illustrated here documents that f(T) is a single nent function, even if it's not. All the implementation details should be hidden.

This technique is often useful in universal-copy constructors of class templates:

```
template <typename T1>
class MyVector
{
public:
   // not used if T2 is T1

   template <typename T2>
   MyVector(const MyVector<T2>& that)
   {
   }
};
```

Restrictions on T2 may be easily introduced using ONLY_IF (has_conversion is fully documented in Section 4.4.

```
template <typename T2>
MyVector(const MyVector<T2>& that,
         ONLY_IF((has_conversion<T2,T1>::L2R)))
{
}
```

Another application is the "static cast" of static_value. You might need to convert, say, static_value<int, 3> to static_value<long, 3>:

```
template <typename T, T VALUE>
struct static_value
{
   static const T value = VALUE;

   static_value(const int = 0)
   {
   }

   template <typename S, S OTHER>
     static_value(const static_value<S, OTHER>,
                  typename only_if<VALUE==OTHER, int>::type = 0)
   {
   }
};
```

Sometimes it can be useful to apply the idiom, not to arguments, but to the return value:

```
template <bool CONDITION, typename T = void>
struct only_if
{
   typedef T type;
};
```

```
emplate <typename T>
truct only_if<false, T>

;

emplate <typename T>
ypename only_if<is_integer<T>::value,T>::type multiply_by_2(const T x)

  return x << 1;
```

This function is either ill-formed or takes a const T and returns T.

.3.4. SFINAE and Returned Functors

e various test functions you've seen so far have no use for their return type, whose size is all that matters. metimes they will instead return a functor that is immediately invoked. Consider a simple example, ere the function number_of_elem returns x.size() if x has a type member called size_type and erwise returns 1.

```
mplate <typename T, typename S>
ruct get_size

 S operator()(const T& x) const { return x.size(); }

 get_size(int) {}


uct get_one

 template <typename T>
 size_t operator()(const T&) const { return 1; }

 get_one(int) {}


plate <typename T>
_size<T, typename T::size_type> test(const T* x)    // SFINAE

return 0;


_one test(const void*)

return 0;
```

```
template <typename T>
size_t number_of_elem(const T& x)
{
   return test(&x)(x);
}

std::vector<int> v;
std::map<int, double> m;
double x;

number_of_elem(v);         // returns v.size()
number_of_elem(m);         // returns m.size()
number_of_elem(x);         // returns 1
```

You can use some techniques from the previous paragraph to describe an implementation of a logging callback, with a variable log level, based on metaprogramming.

In scientific computing, you can meet functions that run for a long time. So it's necessary to maintain some interaction with the function even while it's running, for example, to get feedback on the progress or to send an abort signal. Since there is no hypothesis on the environment (computational routines are usually portable), you cannot pass a pointer to a progress bar, and you have to design an equally portable interface.

A possible solution follows. The function internally updates a structure (whose type is known to its caller) with all the meaningful information about the state of the program, and it invokes a user functor regularly on the structure:

```
struct algorithm_info
{
   int iteration_current;
   int iteration_max;

   double best_tentative_solution;

   size_t time_elapsed;
   size_t memory_used;
};

template <..., typename logger_t>
void algorithm(..., logger_t LOG)
{
   algorithm_info I;
   for (...)
   {
      // do the work...

      I.iteration_current = ...;
      I.best_tentative_solution = ...;

      LOG(I);
   }
}
```

You can try to design some static interaction between the logger and the algorithm so that only some elevant portion of the information is updated. If LOG does nothing, no time is wasted updating I.

First, all recordable information is partitioned in levels. logger_t will declare a static constant named og_level and the algorithm loop will not update the objects corresponding to information in ignored levels.

By convention, having no member log_level or having log_level=0 corresponds to skipping the log.

```
emplate <int LEVEL = 3>
truct algorithm_info;

emplate <>
truct algorithm_info<0>



mplate <>
ruct algorithm_info<1> : algorithm_info<0>

 int iteration_current;
 int iteration_max;


mplate <>
ruct algorithm_info<2> : algorithm_info<1>

 double best_value;


nplate <>
ruct algorithm_info<3> : algorithm_info<2>

 size_t time_elapsed;
 size_t memory_used;
```

Second, you use SFINAE to query logger_t for a constant named log_level:

```
plate <int N>
uct log_level_t

operator int () const
{
   return N;
}


plate <typename T>
_level_t<T::log_level> log_level(const T*)

eturn log_level_t<T::log_level>();
```

```
inline int log_level(...)
{
   return 0;
}
```

Finally, a simple switch will do the work. If logger_t does contain log_level, SFINAE will pick the first overload of log_level, returning an object that's immediately cast to integer. Otherwise, the weaker overload will immediately return 0.

```
switch (log_level(&LOG))
{
   case 3:
      I.time_elapsed = ...;
      I.memory_used = ...;

   case 2: // fall through
      I.best_value = ...;

   case 1: // fall through
      I.iteration_current = ...;
      I.iteration_max = ...;

   case 0: // fall through
   default:
      break;
}

LOG(I);
```

This implementation is the simplest to code, but LOG still has access to the whole object I, even the pa that is not initialized.

The static information about the level is already contained in log_level_t, so it's appropriate to transform this object into a functor that performs a cast.

```
template <int N>
struct log_level_t
{
   operator int () const
   {
      return N;
   }

   typedef const algorithm_info<N>& ref_n;
   typedef const algorithm_info< >& ref;

   ref_n operator()(ref i) const
   {
      return i;
   }
};
```

```
emplate <typename T>
og_level_t<T::log_level> log_level(const T*)

  return log_level_t<T::log_level>();


line log_level_t<0> log_level(...)

  return log_level_t<0>();


  switch (log_level(&LOG))
  {
     // as above...
  }

  LOG(log_level(&LOG)(I));
```

This enforces LOG to implement an operator() that accepts exactly the right "slice" of information.

3.5. SFINAE and Software Updates

e of the many uses of SFINAE-based metafunctions is conditional requirement detection.

TMP libraries often interact with user types and user functors, which must usually satisfy some inimal) interface constraint. New releases of these libraries could in principle impose additional uirements for extra optimizations, but this often conflicts with backward compatibility.

Suppose you sort a range by passing a custom binary relation to an external library function, called std::sort:

```
uct MyLess

bool operator()(const Person& x, const Person & y) const
{
   // ...
 }


::vector<Person> v;
std::sort(v.begin(), v.end(), MyLess());
```

Version 2.0 of the sorting library requires MyLess to contain an additional function called static void pareAndSwap(Person& a, Person& b), so this code will not compile.

Instead, the library could easily detect if such a function is provided, and, if so, automatically invoke a er parallel CAS-based algorithm.

This "self-detection" of features allows *independent upgrades* of the underlying libraries.

This applies also to traits:

```
struct MyTraits
{
   static const bool ENABLE_FAST_ALLOCATOR = true;
   static const bool ENABLE_UTF8 = true;
   static const bool ENABLE_SERIALIZATION = false;
};

typedef nonstd::basic_string<char, MyTraits> MyString;
```

Version 2.0 of the string library has a use for an extra member:

```
struct MyTraits
{
   static const bool ENABLE_FAST_ALLOCATOR = true;
   static const bool ENABLE_UTF8 = true;
   static const bool ENABLE_SERIALIZATION = false;

   static const size_t NUMBER_OF_THREADS = 4;
};
```

But the author of the library should not assume that this new constant is present in the traits class he receives. However, he can use SFINAE to indirectly extract this value, if it exists, or use a default:

```
template <typename T, size_t DEFAULT>
class read_NUMBER_OF_THREADS
{
   template <typename X>
   static static_value<size_t, X::NUMBER_OF_THREADS> test(X*);

   static static_value<size_t, DEFAULT> test(void*);

   template <size_t N>
   static typename fixed_size<N+1>::type& cast(static_value<size_t,N>);

   static T* getT();

public:
   static const size_t value = sizeof(cast(test(getT()))) - 1;
};
```

The +1/-1 trick is necessary to avoid arrays of length zero.

The author of nonstd::basic_string will write:

```
emplate <typename char_t, typename traits_t>
lass basic_string

  // ...

  int n = read_NUMBER_OF_THREADS<traits_t, 4>::value;
```

So this class compiles even with older traits.

As a rule, you don't need to check that NUMBER_OF_THREADS has indeed type (static const) size_t. ny integer will do. It's possible to be more rigorous, but it is generally not worth the machinery. I am going show all the details, but you should consider the rest of this section an exercise. You need *three* additional etafunctions:

- Detect if T has any constant named NUMBER_OF_THREADS, with the usual techniques.
- If this is false, the result is immediately false (line #2).
- Otherwise, use a different specialization, where it's legal to write T::NUMBER_OF_THREADS. You pass this "item" to a test function (line #1). The best choice is a non-template function with an argument of type REQUIRED_T; the other option is a template that will match everything else, so no cast can occur.

```
nplate <typename T>
ruct has_any_NUMBER_OF_THREADS

 template <typename X>
 static static_value<size_t, X::NUMBER_OF_THREADS> test(X*);

 static no_type test(void*);

 template <size_t N>
 static yes_type cast(static_value<size_t, N>);

 static no_type cast(no_type);

 static T* getT();

 static const bool value = (sizeof(cast(test(getT()))) > 1);


plate <typename REQUIRED_T, typename T, bool>
uct check_NUMBER_OF_THREADS_type;

plate <typename REQUIRED_T, typename T>
uct check_NUMBER_OF_THREADS_type<REQUIRED_T, T, true>

static yes_type test(REQUIRED_T);

emplate <typename X>
static no_type test(X);
```

```
    static const bool value
        = sizeof(test(T::NUMBER_OF_THREADS))>1; // line #1
};

template <typename REQUIRED_T, typename T>
struct check_NUMBER_OF_THREADS_type<REQUIRED_T, T, false>
{
    static const bool value = false; // line #2
};

template <typename T>
struct has_valid_NUMBER_OF_THREADS
: check_NUMBER_OF_THREADS_type<size_t, T,
                                has_any_NUMBER_OF_THREADS<T>::value>
{
};
```

4.3.6. Limitations and Workarounds

SFINAE techniques ultimately rely on the compiler handling an error gracefully, so they are especially vulnerable to compiler bugs.

If the correct code does not compile, here's a checklist of workarounds:

- Give all functions a body.
- Move static functions outside of the class, in a private namespace.
- Remove `private` and use `struct`.
- Think of a simpler algorithm.

able 4-1. *side-by-side comparison of the code, before and after the workarounds*

```
mplate <typename X>
ass is_signed_integer

emplate <typename T>
tatic static_value<T, 0>* decide_int(T*);

tatic void* decide_int(...);

emplate <typename T>
tatic selector<(T(0)>T(-1))>
decide_signed(static_value<T,0>*);

tatic selector<false> decide_signed(...);

atic yes_type cast(selector<true>);
atic no_type cast(selector<false>);

atic X* getX();

ublic:
tatic const bool value =
  sizeof(cast(decide_signed(decide_int(getX()))))
  == sizeof(yes_type);
```

```
namespace priv {

template <typename T>
static_value<T, 0>* decide_int(T*);

void* decide_int(...);

template <typename T>
selector<(T(0)>T(-1))>
  decide_signed(static_value<T, 0>*);

selector<false> decide_signed(...);

yes_type cast(selector<true>);
no_type cast(selector<false>);

template <typename X>
struct is_signed_integer_helper
{
  X* getX();

  static const bool value =
    sizeof(cast(decide_signed(decide_int(getX()))))
    ==sizeof(yes_type);
};

} // end of namespace

template <typename T>
struct is_signed_integer
: public selector<priv::is_signed_integer_
helper<T>::value>
{
};
```

A corner case in the standard is a substitution failure inside a `sizeof` that should bind to a template ameter. The following example usually does not compile:

```
plate <typename T>
ss is_dereferenceable

template <size_t N>
class YES { char dummy[2]; };

template <typename X>
  static YES<sizeof(*X())> test(X*);
```

```
    static NO test(...);

    static T* this_type();

public:
    static const bool value = sizeof(test(this_type()))>1;
};
```

Detection of member functions is extremely problematic. Let's rewrite the metafunction here.

```
template <typename S>
class has_swap_member
{
    template <typename T, void (T::*)(T&) >
    class YES { char dummy[2]; };

    typedef char NO;

    template <typename T>
    static YES<T, &T::swap> test( T* );

    static NO test(...);

    static S* ptr();

public:
    static const bool value = sizeof(test(ptr()))>1;
};
```

Suppose that classes `D1` and `D2` have a public template base called `B<T1>` and `B<T2>`, and they have no data members of their own. `swap` will likely be implemented only once in `B`, with signature `void B<T>::swap(B<T>&)`, but the users will see it as `D1::swap` and `D2::swap` (an argument of type `D1` will be cas to `B<T1>&`).[12]

However, `has_swap_member<D1>::value` is `false` because `YES<D1, &D1::swap>` does not match `YES<T, void (T::*F)(T&)>`.

Hypothetically, it would match either `YES<T1,void(T2::*F)(T2&)>` or even `YES<T1,void(T1::*F)(T2&)>`, but this pointer cast is out of scope, because `T2` is unknown.

Furthermore, the standard explicitly says that you cannot take a pointer to a member function of a library object, because the implementation is allowed to modify the prototype, as long as the syntax works expected. For example, you could have a perfectly valid `void T::swap(T&, int = 0)`.

So the fact that `has_swap_member<T>::value` is `false` does not mean that the syntax `a.swap(b)` is illega

The best you can do is integrate the detection phase with the swap itself and create a function that swaps two references with the best-known method. When swap detection fails, ADL will usually find an equivalent routine in the right namespace (at least for all STL containers; see Section 1.4.2.

[12]This may look like a corner case, but it's quite common. In popular STL implementation, let `D1=std::map`, `D2=std::` and `B<T>` be an undocumented class that represents a balanced tree.

```
sing std::swap;

truct swap_traits

   template <typename T>
   inline static void apply(T& a, T& b)
   {
      apply1(a, b, test(&a));
   }

ivate:

   template <typename T, void (T::*F)(T&)>
   struct yes : public yes_type
   {
      yes(int = 0)
      {}
   };

   template <typename T>
   static yes<T, &T::swap> test(T*)
   { return 0; }

   static no_type test(void*)
   { return 0; }


   template <typename T>
   inline static void apply1(T& a, T& b, no_type)
   {
      swap(a, b);
   }

   template <typename T>
   inline static void apply1(T& a, T& b, yes_type)
   {
      a.swap(b);
   }


plate <typename T>
ine void smart_swap(T& x, T& y)

swap_traits::apply(x, y);
```

Note that all functions have a body, as they are truly invoked.

The workflow is as follows. `smart_swap(x,y)` invokes `apply`, which in turn is `apply1(x,y,[[condition on T]])`. `apply1` is an ADL swap when the condition is no and a member swap invocation otherwise.

```
#include <map>

struct swappable
{
   void swap(swappable&)
   {
   }
};

int main()
{
   std::map<int, int> a, b;
   smart_swap(a, b);          // if it fails detection of map::swap
                              // then it uses ADL swap, which is the same

   swappable c, d;
   smart_swap(c, d);          // correctly detects and uses swappable::swap

   int i = 3, j = 4;
   smart_swap(i, j);          // correctly uses std::swap
}
```

■ **Note** The true solution requires the C++0x keyword `decltype`. See Section 12.2.

One final caveat is to avoid mixing SFINAE with private members.

The C++ 2003 Standard says that access control occurs *after* template deduction. So, if `T::type` exists but it's private, SFINAE will select an action based on the information that `T::type` actually exists, but a compiler error will generally occur immediately after (since `T::type` is inaccessible).[13]

```
template <typename T>
typename T::type F(int);

template <typename T>
char F(...);

class X
{
        typedef double type;  // note: private, by default
};
```

[13]This was changed in the C++11 Standard. See http://www.open-std.org/jtc1/sc22/wg21/docs/cwg_defects.html#1170.

```
/ A condensed version of the usual SFINAE machinery...
/ We would expect the code to compile and N==1.
/ This occurs only in C++0x
nt N = sizeof(F<X>(0));

rror: type "X::type" is inaccessible
 typename T::type F(int);
                  ^
         detected during instantiation of "F" based on template argument <X>
```

.3.7. SFINAE with Partial Specializations

INAE applies also to partial specialization of class templates. When a condition that should be used select the partial specialization is ill-formed, that specialization is silently removed from the set of ndidates. This section shows a practical application with an example.[14]

Suppose you have a template class called A<T>, which you want to specialize when type T contains a pedef called iterator.

You start by adding a second template parameter to A and a partial specialization on the second ou will define DEFAULT_TYPE and METAFUNC later):

```
mplate <typename T, typename X = DEFAULT_TYPE>
ruct A
.. };

mplate <typename T>
ruct A<T, typename METAFUNC<typename T::iterator>::type >
.. };
```

According to SFINAE, when T::iterator does not exist, the specialization is ignored and the general nplate is used. However, when T::iterator indeed exists (and METAFUNC is well defined), both definitions valid. But according to the C++ language rules, if DEFAULT_TYPE happens to be the same as METAFUNCTION :iterator>::type, the specialization of A is used. Let's rewrite the example more expliticly:

```
plate <typename T>
uct METAFUNC

typedef int type;


plate <typename T, typename X = int>
uct A
.. };

plate <typename T>
uct A<T, typename METAFUNC<typename T::iterator>::type >
.. };

t> a1; // uses the general template
d::vector<int>> a2; // uses the specialization
```

---

ter Brown recently made this technique popular. See http://www.open-std.org/jtc1/sc22/wg21/docs/ rs/2014/n3911.

4.4. Other Classic Metafunctions with Sizeof

An overload may be selected because the argument can be cast successfully.

This section shows a metafunction that returns three Boolean constants—`has_conversion<L,R>::L2R` is true when `L` (left) is convertible to `R` (right) and `has_conversion<L,R>::identity` is true when `L` and `R` ar the same type.[15]

```
template <typename L, typename R>
class has_conversion
{
   static yes_type test(R);
   static no_type test(...);
   static L left();

public:
   static const bool L2R = (sizeof(test(left())) == sizeof(yes_type));
   static const bool identity = false;
};

template <typename T>
class has_conversion<T, T>
{
public:
   static const bool L2R = true;
   static const bool identity = true;
};
```

This code passes a fake instance of `L` to `test`. If `L` is convertible to `R`, the first overload is preferred, and the result is `yes_type`.

Following Alexandrescu,[16] you can deduce whether a type publicly derives from another:

```
template <typename B, typename D>
struct is_base_of
{
   static const bool value =
   (
      has_conversion<const D*, const B*>::L2R &&
      !has_conversion<const B*, const void*>::identity
   );
};
```

Implicit promotion techniques have been extensively used by David Abrahams.[17] The key point is to overload an operator at namespace level, not as a member.

---

[15]The left-right notation may not be the most elegant, but it's indeed excellent for remembering how the class works.

[16]See the bibliography.

[17]`boost::is_incrementable` correctly strips qualifiers from `T`, but it allows `operator++` to return `void`, which in ge is not desirable. In this case, the simpler version presented here gives a compile-time error.

```
truct fake_incrementable

  template <typename T>
  fake_incrementable(T);    // non-explicit universal constructor
;

ake_incrementable operator++(fake_incrementable);      // line #1

es_type test(fake_incrementable);

emplate <typename T>
_type test(T);

emplate <class T>
ruct has_preincrement

  static T& getT();

  static const bool value = sizeof(test(++getT())) == sizeof(no_type);
```

The ++getT() statement can either resolve to x's own operator++ or (with lower priority) resolve to
onversion to fake_incrementable, followed by fake_incrementable increment. This latter function is
ible, because, as anticipated, it is declared as a global entity in the namespace, not as a member function.

To test post-increment, replace line #1 with:

```
ke_incrementable operator++(fake_incrementable, int);
```

Note that the computation of sizeof(test(++x)) must be done in the namespace where
e_incrementable lives. Otherwise, it will fail:

```
espace aux {

uct fake_incrementable

 template <typename T>
 fake_incrementable(T);


e_incrementable operator++(fake_incrementable);

_type test(fake_incrementable);

plate <typename T>
type test(T);
```

```
template <typename T>
struct has_preincrement
{
   static T& getT();
   static const bool value
      = sizeof(aux::test(++getT())) == sizeof(no_type);
};
```

You can also move the computation inside the namespace and recall the result outside:

```
namespace aux {

// ... (all as above)

template <typename T>
struct has_preincrement_helper
{
   static T& getT();
   static const bool value = sizeof(test(++getT())) == sizeof(no_type);
};

}

template <typename T>
struct has_preincrement : selector<aux::has_preincrement_helper<T>::value>
{
};
```

4.5. Overload on Function Pointers

One of the most convenient tag objects used to select an overloaded function is a function pointer, which is then discarded.

A pointer is cheap to build yet can convey a lot of static information, which makes it suitable for template argument deduction.

4.5.1. Erase

The following is the primary example. It iterates over an STL container, so you need to erase the element pointed to by iterator `i`. Erasure should advance (not invalidate) the iterator itself. Unfortunately, the syntax differs. For some containers, the right syntax is `i = c.erase(i)`, but for associative containers it is `c.erase(i++)`.

Taking advantage of the fact that `C::erase` must exist (otherwise you wouldn't know what to do and the call to `erase_gap` would be ill formed), you just pick the right one with a dummy pointer:

```
template <typename C, typename iterator_t, typename base_t>
void erase_gap2(C& c, iterator_t& i, iterator_t (base_t::*)(iterator_t))
{
   i = c.erase(i);
}
```

```
emplate <typename C, typename iterator_t, typename base_t>
oid erase_gap2(C& c, iterator_t& i, void (base_t::*)(iterator_t))

  c.erase(i++);


emplate <typename C>
oid erase_gap(C& c, typename C::iterator& i)

  erase_gap2(c, i, &C::erase);


t main()

  for (i = c.begin(); i != c.end(); )
  {
     if (need_to_erase(i))
        erase_gap(c, i);
     else
        ++i;
  }
```

Observe that erasure is *not* invoked via the pointer. It's just the type of the pointer that matters. Also, the type of erase may not be ... (C::*)(...), because a container could have a "hidden base". e exact type is therefore left open to compiler deduction.

5.2. Swap

e previous technique can be extended via SFINAE to cases where it's unknown if the member function sts. To demonstrate, you need to extend swap_traits (introduced in Section 4.3.6) to perform the owing[18]:

- If T has void T::swap(T&), use a.swap(b).
- If T has static void swap(T&,T&), use T::swap(a,b).
- If T has both swaps, the call is ambiguous.
- In any other case, use ADL swap.

The first part simply reuses the techniques from the previous sections. In particular, observe that all -types derive from a common "yes-base," because the first test is meant only to ensure that the possible p member functions exist.

s extension is to be considered an exercise, but not necessarily a good idea.

```
struct swap_traits
{
   template <typename T, void (T::*F)(T&)>
   class yes1 : public yes_type {};

   template <typename T, void (*F)(T&, T&)>
   class yes2 : public yes_type {};


   template <typename T>
   inline static void apply(T& a, T& b)
   {
      apply1(a, b, test(&a));
   }

private:
   // first test: return a yes_type* if any allowed T::swap exists

   template <typename T>
   static yes1<T, &T::swap>* test(T*)
   { return 0; }

   template <typename T>
   static yes2<T, &T::swap>* test(T*)
   { return 0; }

   static no_type* test(void*)
   { return 0; }
```

When the test is false, call ADL swap. Otherwise, perform a *function-pointer based* test. Call apply2 by taking the address of swap, which is known to be possible because at least one swap exists.

```
private:

   template <typename T>
   inline static void apply1(T& a, T& b, no_type*)
   {
      swap(a, b);
   }

   template <typename T>
   inline static void apply1(T& a, T& b, yes_type*)
   {
      apply2(a, b, &T::swap);
   }

   template <typename T>
   inline static void apply2(T& a, T& b, void (*)(T&, T&))
   {
      T::swap(a, b);
   }
```

```
template <typename T, typename BASE>
inline static void apply2(T& a, T& b, void (BASE::*)(BASE&))
{
   a.swap(b);
}

template <typename T>
inline static void apply2(T& a, T& b, ...)
{
   swap(a, b);
}
```

.5.2. Argument Dominance

hen a function template has several arguments whose type must be deduced, you may incur ambiguities:

```
mplate <typename T>
max(T a1, T a2) { ... }

x(3, 4.0); // error: ambiguous, T may be int or double
```

It's often the case that one argument is more important, so you can explicitly instruct the compiler to ore everything else during type deduction:

```
here T must be the type of arg1

nplate <typename T>
id add_to(T& a1, T a2) { ... }

ble x = 0;
_to(x, 3); // we would like this code to compile
```

The solution to this is to replace T with an indirect metafunction that yields the same result. Type luction is performed only on non-dependent names, and the compiler then ensures that the result is npatible with any other dependent name:

```
plate <typename T>
d add_to(T& a1, typename instance_of<T>::type a2)
.. }
```

In this example, T& is viable for type-detection. T=double is the only match. instance_of<double> does eed contain a type called type (which is double), so the match is feasible. So the function automatically s a2 to double.

This idiom is very popular when a1 is a function pointer and a2 is the argument of a1:

```
template <typename A, typename R>
R function_call(R (*f)(A), R x)
{ return f(x); }
```

The function pointer is a dominating argument, because you can call f on everything that is convertibl
You should therefore consider disabling the detection on x:

```
template <typename A, typename R>
R function_call(R (*f)(A), typename instance_of<R>::type x)
{ return f(x); }
```

CHAPTER 5

Interfaces

Templates are used as interfaces in two different ways: to provide sets of atomic functions and to obtain *compile-time polymorphism*.

If several functions use the same portion of the interface of an object, you can factor them out in a sing template:

```
void do_something(std::vector<double>& v)
{
   if (v.empty())
      // ...

   ... v.size();

   for_each(v.begin(), v.end(), my_functor());
   ...
}

void do_something(std::list<double>& L)
{
   if (L.empty())
      // ...

   ... L.size();

   for_each(L.begin(), L.end(), my_functor());
   ...
}
```

becomes:

```
template <typename T>
void do_something(T& L)
{
   if (L.empty())
      // ...

   ... L.size();

   for_each(L.begin(), L.end(), my_functor());
   ...
}
```

This code unification is simpler when you follow common guidelines for containers (as listed in Section 1.4). If necessary, as described in Section 3.4.3, you can replace calls to *member* functions with calls to small *lobal* functions. Assume you have a third `do_something` that executes a slightly different test:

```
oid do_something(MyContainer<double>& M)

  if (M.size() == 0)
  ...
```

It's better to isolate the test for "emptiness" in a different function:

```
mplate <typename T>
ol is_empty(const T& c)

 return c.empty();


mplate <typename T>
ol is_empty(const MyContainer<T>& c)

 return c.size() == 0;


mplate <typename T>
id do_something(T& L)

 if (is_empty(L))
  ...
```

1. Wrapping References

lass template and its specializations can be used to make interfaces uniform:

```
ss Dog

public:
   void bark();
   void go_to_sleep();


ss Professor

public:
   void begin_lesson();
   void end_lesson();
```

```
template <typename T>
class Reference
{
   T& obj_;

public:
   Reference(T& obj) : obj_(obj) {}
   void start_talking() { obj_.talk(); }
   void end_talking() { obj_.shut(); }
};

template <>
class Reference<Dog>
{
   Dog& obj_;

public:
   Reference(Dog& obj) : obj_(obj) {}

   void start_talking() { for (int i=0; i<3; ++i) obj_.bark(); }
   void end_talking() { obj_.go_to_sleep(); }
};

template <>
class Reference<Professor>
{
   Professor& obj_;

public:
   Reference(Professor& obj) : obj_(obj) {}

   void start_talking() { obj_.begin_lesson(); }
   void end_talking() { obj_.end_lesson(); }
};
```

Note that the wrapper may indeed contain some logic. Finally:

```
template <typename T>
void DoIt(T& any)
{
   Reference<T> r(any);
   r.start_talking();
   // ...
   r.end_talking();
}
```

5.2. Static Interfaces

Vhen a function template manipulates an object of unspecified type T, it actually forces the object to nplement an interface. For example, this very simple function contains a lot of hidden assumptions about ne (unknown) types involved:

```
emplate <typename iter1_t, typename iter2_t>
ter2_t copy(iter1_t begin, const iter1_t end, iter2_t output)

  while (begin != end)
     *(output++) = *(begin++),

  return output;
```

Here, iter1_t and iter2_t must have a copy constructor, called operator++(int). iter1_t also needs erator!=. Furthermore, every operator++ returns a dereferenceable entity, and in the case of iter2_t, the al result is an l-value whose assignment blindly accepts whatever *(begin++) returns.

In short, template code pretends that all instructions compile, until the compiler can prove they don't.

In general, it's too verbose and/or generally not useful to list the assumptions on a type interface. In the evious example, iter1_t::operator++ will likely return iter1_t, which also implements operator*, but it ed not be *exactly* the case (for instance, copy would work if, say, iter1_t::operator++ returned int*).

So you must try to list explicitly a minimal set of *concepts* that the template parameter must satisfy. ormally, a concept is a requirement on the type that implies that a C++ statement is legal, whatever its plementation.[1]

For example, this object will happily play the role of iter2_t:

```
ruct black_hole_iterator

 const black_hole_iterator& operator++ () const
 {
    return *this;
 }

 const black_hole_iterator& operator++ (int) const
 {
    return *this;
 }

 const black_hole_iterator& operator* () const
 {
    return *this;
 }
```

notion of *concept* was introduced in Section 2.2.4.

```
    template <typename T>
    const black_hole_iterator& operator= (const T&) const
    {
       return *this;
    }
};
```

Here, the concept of "the object returned by operator* must be an l-value" is satisfied, even if in an unusual way (the assignment does not modify the black hole).

Generally, you won't list the exact concepts for any generic function. However, some sets of concepts have a standard name, so whenever possible, you'll adopt it, even if it's a superset of what is actually needed.

In the previous copy template, it's best to use an *input iterator* and an *output iterator*, because these are the smallest universally known labels that identify a (super-)set of the concepts. As you will read in Chapter 6, a true output iterator satisfies a few more properties (for example, it must provide some typedefs, which are irrelevant here); however, this is a fair price for reusability.[2]

Authors of template code often need to make concepts explicit. If they have a simple name, they can be used as template parameters:

```
template <typename FwdIter, typename RandIter>
FwdIter special_copy(RandIter beg, RandIter end, FwdIter output);
```

Note that in this function, nothing constrains beg to be an iterator except names (which are hints for humans, not for the compiler). The template argument FwdIter will match *anything*, say double or void*, and if you are lucky, the body of the function will report errors. It may happen that you pass a type that works, but it does not behave as expected.[3]

On the other hand, classic C++ does offer a tool to constrain types: inheritance. You write pieces of code that accept a BASE* and at runtime they invoke the right virtual functions.

Static interfaces are their equivalent in TMP. They offer less generality than a "flat" type T, but have the same level of static optimizations.

A *static interface* is a skeleton class that limits the scope of validity of a template to types derived from the interface, and at the same time it provides a default (static) implementation of the "virtual" callback mechanism.

The details follow.

5.2.1. Static Interfaces

The original language idiom was called the "curiously recurring template" pattern (*CRTP*) and it is based on the following observation: a static_cast can traverse a class hierarchy using only compile-time information. Put simply, static_cast can convert BASE* to DERIVED*. If the inheritance relationship between DERIVED and BASE is incorrect or ambiguous, the cast will not compile. However, the result will be valid only if at runtime BASE* is pointing to a true DERIVED object.

---

[2]The black hole iterator is a hack, not a perfect output iterator.

[3]This is why, for example, the standard describes carefully what happens to functors passed to STL algorithms, such as how many times they are copied, and so on.

As a special case, there's an easy way to be sure that the cast will succeed; that is, when each derived lass inherits from a "personal base":

```
emplate <typename DERIVED_T>
lass BASE

  protected:
     ~BASE() {}
;

.ass DERIVED1 : public BASE<DERIVED1>


ass DERIVED2 : public BASE<DERIVED2>
```

An object of type BASE<T> is guaranteed to be the base of a T, because thanks to the protected structor, nobody except a derived class can build a BASE<T>, and only T itself derives from BASE<T>. So BASE<T> can cast itself to T and invoke functions:

```
nplate <typename DERIVED_T>
ruct BASE

 DERIVED_T& true_this()
 {
    return static_cast<DERIVED_T&>(*this);
 }

 const DERIVED_T& true_this () const
 {
    return static_cast<const DERIVED_T&>(*this);
 }

 double getSomeNumber() const
 {
    return true_this().getSomeNumber();
 }


uct DERIVED_rand : public BASE<DERIVED_rand>

double getSomeNumber() const
{
   return std::rand();
}
```

```
struct DERIVED_circle : public BASE<DERIVED_circle>
{
   double radius_;

   double getSomeNumber() const
   {
      return 3.14159265359 * sq(radius_);
   }
};
```

Exactly as for virtual functions, normal calls via the derived class interface are inexpensive:

```
DERIVED_rand d;
d.getSomeNumber();           // normal call; BASE is completely ignored
```

However, you can write a function template that takes a reference-to-base and makes an inexpensive call to the derived member function. `true_this` will produce no overhead.

```
template <typename T>
void PrintSomeNumber(BASE<T>& b)       // crucial: pass argument by reference
{
   // here BASE methods will dispatch to the correct T equivalent
   std::cout << b.getSomeNumber();
}

DERIVED_circle C;
DERIVED_rand R;
...
PrintSomeNumber(C); // prints the area of the circle
PrintSomeNumber(R); // prints a random number
```

Conceptually, the previous function is identical to the simpler (but vaguer) function here:

```
template <typename T>
void PrintSomeNumber(T& b)
{
   std::cout << b.getSomeNumber();
}
```

However, the replacement looks acceptable because `PrintSomeNumber` is a named function, not an operator (think about writing a global `operator+` with two arguments of type T). The following example demonstrates the use of static interfaces with operators.[4] It will implement only `operator+=` and have `operator+` for free, simply deriving from the `summable<...>` interface.

---

[4]The `boost` library contains some more general code. See `http://www.boost.org/doc/libs/1_57_0/libs/utility/operators.htm`.

```
emplate <typename T>
truct summable

  T& true_this()
  {
     return static_cast<T&>(*this);
  }

  const T& true_this () const
  {
     return static_cast<const T&>(*this);
  }

  T operator+ (const T& that) const
  {
      T result(true_this());
      result += that;        // call dispatch to native T::operator+=
      return result;
  }

ruct complex_number : public summable<complex_number>

 complex_number& operator+= (const complex_number& that)
 {
    ...
 }

nplex_number a;
nplex_number b;

nplex_number s = a+b;
```

The (apparently simple) last line performs the following compile-time steps:

- a does not have an `operator+` of its own, so cast a to its base that has it, namely `const summable<complex_number>&`.
- `const summable<complex_number>&` can be summed to a `complex_number`, so b is fine as is.
- `summable<complex_number>::operator+` builds a `complex_number` named `result`, which is a copy of `true_this`, because `true_this` is a `complex_number`.
- Dispatching execution to `complex_number::operator+=`, the result is computed and returned.

Note that you could rewrite the base class as:

```
template <typename T>
struct summable
{
   // ...

   T operator+ (const summable<T>& that) const
   {
      T result(true_this());
      result += that.true_this();
      return result;
   }
};
```

Let's call *interface* the base class and *specializations* the derived classes.

5.2.2. Common Errors

You just met a situation where the interface class makes a specialized copy of itself:

```
T result(true_this());
```

This is not a problem, since the interface, which is static, knows its "true type" by definition. However, the correct behavior of true_this can be destroyed by *slicing*:

```
template <typename DERIVED_T>
void PrintSomeNumber(BASE<DERIVED_T> b)// argument by value
{
   std::cout << b.getSomeNumber();        // error: slicing
                                          // b is not a DERIVED_T any more
}
```

Usually, it's necessary to declare BASE destructor non-virtual and protected, and sometimes it's a good idea to extend protection to the copy constructor. Algorithms should not need to make a copy of the static interface. If they need to clone the object, the correct idiom is to call the DERIVED_T constructor and pass true_this(), as shown previously.

```
template <typename DERIVED_T>
struct BASE
{
   DERIVED_T& true_this()
   {
      return static_cast<DERIVED_T&>(*this);
   }

   const DERIVED_T& true_this() const
   {
      return static_cast<const DERIVED_T&>(*this);
   }
```

```
rotected:
  ~BASE()
  {
  }

  BASE(const BASE&)
  {
  }
;
```

The interface of DERIVED is visible only inside the body of BASE member functions:

```
emplate <typename DERIVED_T>
ruct BASE

 // ...

 typedef DERIVED_T::someType someType;        // compiler error

 void f()
 {
    typedef DERIVED_T::someType someType;     // ok here
 }


ass DERIVED : public BASE<DERIVED>

 ....
```

Typedefs and enums from DERIVED are not available at class level in BASE. This is obvious, because
IVED is compiled after its base, which is BASE<DERIVED>. When BASE<DERIVED> is processed, DERIVED is
own, but still incomplete.

It's a good idea (not an error) to make BASE expose a typedef for DERIVED_T. This allows external
ctions to make a specialized copy of BASE.

```
plate <typename DERIVED_T>
uct BASE

typedef DERIVED_T static_type;
```

However, DERIVED cannot access BASE members without full qualification, because a template base
s is out of scope for the derived objects.[5]

```
plate <typename DERIVED_T>
uct BASE

typedef double value_type;
```

---

[2] page 135.

```
  value_type f() const
  {
     return true_this().f();
  }

  // ...
};

struct DERIVED1 : public BASE<DERIVED1>
{
   value_type f() const         // error: value_type is undefined
   {
      true_this();              // error: true_this is undefined
      return 0;
   }
};

struct DERIVED2 : public BASE<DERIVED2>
{
   BASE<DERIVED2>::value_type f() const     // ok
   {
      this->true_this();                    // ok
      return 0;
   }
};
```

Note once again that scope restriction holds only "inside" the class. External users will correctly see `DERIVED1::value_type`:

```
template <typename T>
struct value_type_of
{
   typedef typename T::value_type type;
};

value_type_of<DERIVED1>::type Pi = 3.14;       // ok, Pi has type double
```

Finally, the developer must ensure that all derived classes correctly announce their names to the base in order to avoid a classic copy and paste error:

```
class DERIVED1 : public BASE<DERIVED1>
{
};

class DERIVED2 : public BASE<DERIVED1>
{
};
```

enefits	Problems
rite algorithms that take "not too generic objects" nd use them with a statically known interface.	The developer must ensure that all algorithms take arguments by reference and avoid other common errors.
nplement only some part of the code in the derived pecialized) class and move all common code in e base.	Experimental measurements suggest that the presence of non-virtual protected destructors and multiple inheritance may inhibit or degrade code optimizations.

.2.3. A Static_Interface Implementation

any of the previous ideas can be grouped in a class:

```
mplate <typename T>
ruct clone_of

 typedef const T& type;


mplate <typename static_type, typename aux_t = void>
ass static_interface

lic:
 typedef static_type type;

 typename clone_of<static_type>::type clone() const
 {
    return true_this();
 }

tected:
 static_interface() {}
 ~static_interface() {}

 static_type& true_this()
 {
    return static_cast<static_type&>(*this);
 }

 const static_type& true_this() const
 {
    return static_cast<const static_type&>(*this);
 }
```

You'll come back to the extra template parameter later in this chapter.

The helper metafunction clone_of can be customized and returning const reference is a reasonable default choice. For small objects, it may be faster to return a copy:

```
template <typename T, bool SMALL_OBJECT = (sizeof(T)<sizeof(void*))>
struct clone_of;

template <typename T>
struct clone_of<T, true>
{
   typedef T type;
};

template <typename T>
struct clone_of<T, false>
{
   typedef const T& type;
};
```

First, you make some macros available to ease interface declaration.

An interface is defined by

```
#define MXT_INTERFACE(NAME)                                  \
                                                             \
template <typename static_type>                              \
class NAME : public static_interface<static_type>

#define MXT_SPECIALIZED       this->true_this()
```

Here's a practical example. The interface macro is similar to a normal class declaration.[6]

```
MXT_INTERFACE(random)
{
protected:

   ~random()
   {
   }

public:
   typedef double random_type;

   random_type max() const
   {
      return MXT_SPECIALIZED.max();
   }
```

[6]The downside of this technique is that the macro may confuse some IDEs that parse headers to build a graphical representation of the project.

```
  random_type operator()() const
  {
     return MXT_SPECIALIZED();    // note operator call
  }
;
```

- random can access true_this() only with explicit qualification (as MXT_SPECIALIZED does).
- random needs to declare a protected destructor.
- static_type is a valid type name inside random, even if static_interface is out of scope, because it's the template parameter name.

Now let's implement some random algorithms:

```
efine MXT_SPECIALIZATION(S, I)                    class S : public I< S >

T_SPECIALIZATION(gaussian, random)

 public:

    double max() const
    {
       return std::numeric_limits<double>::max();
    }

    double operator()() const
    {
       // ...
    }

_SPECIALIZATION(uniform, random)

public:

    double max() const
    {
       return 1.0;
    }

    // ...
```

What if you need a template static interface, such as:

```
plate <typename RANDOM_T, typename SCALAR_T>
ss random

ublic:
   typedef SCALAR_T random_type;

   // ...
```

```
template <typename T>
class gaussian : public random<gaussian<T>, T>
{
   // ...
};
```

It's easy to provide more macros for template static interfaces (with a small number of parameters). A naïve idea is:

```
#define MXT_TEMPLATE_INTERFACE(NAME,T)                           \
                                                                 \
template <typename static_type, typename T>                      \
class NAME : public static_interface<static_type>

#define MXT_TEMPLATE_SPECIALIZATION(S,I,T)                       \
                                                                 \
template <typename T>                                            \
class S : public I< S<T> >
```

Which is used like this:

```
MXT_TEMPLATE_INTERFACE(pseudo_array, value_t)
{
protected:

   ~pseudo_array()
   {
   }

public:
   typedef value_t value_type;

   value_type operator[](const size_t i) const
   {
      return MXT_SPECIALIZED.read(i, instance_of<value_type>());
   }

   size_t size() const
   {
      return MXT_SPECIALIZED.size(instance_of<value_type>());
   }
};
```

A non-template class can use a template static interface. For example, you could have a bitstring class that behaves like an array of bits, an array of nibbles, or an array of bytes:

```
typedef bool bit;
typedef char nibble;
typedef unsigned char byte;
```

```
lass bitstring
 public pseudo_array<bitstring, bit>
 public pseudo_array<bitstring, nibble>
 public pseudo_array<bitstring, byte>

  ...
```

An interface need not respect the same member names as the true specialization. In this case, erator[] dispatches execution to a function template read. This makes sense, because the underlying tstring can read the element at position i in many ways (there are three distinct i-th elements). But side pseudo_array, the type to retrieve is statically known, so using a bitstring as a pseudo_array is uivalent to “slicing” the bitstring interface. This makes code much simpler.

The first problem you need to solve is that when the macro expands, the compiler reads:

```
mplate <typename static_type, typename value_t>
ass pseudo_array : public static_interface<static_type>
```

Thus bitstring inherits multiple times from static_interface<bitstring>, which will make the atic_cast in true_this ambiguous.

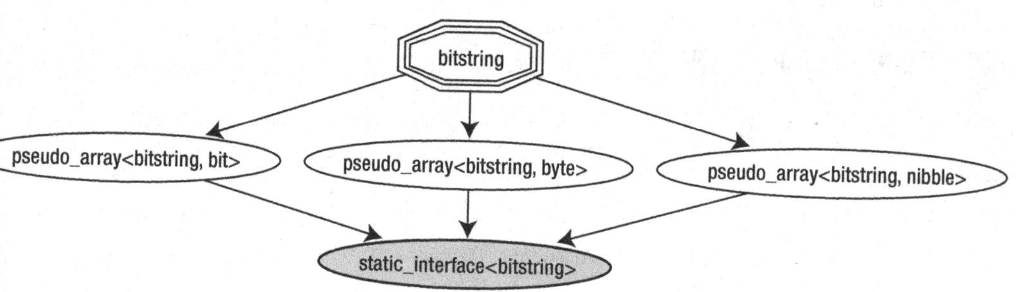

ure 5-1. *Ambiguous inheritance diagram*

To avoid this issue, use an extra parameter in the static interface for disambiguation. The most mbiguous type names are either T or the whole interface (pseudo_array<bitstring, T>). The macro omes:

```
fine MXT_TEMPLATE_INTERFACE(NAME,T)                        \
                                                           \
plate <typename static_type, typename T>                   \
ss NAME                                                    \
ublic static_interface<static_type, NAME<static_type, T> >

fine MXT_TEMPLATE_SPECIALIZATION(S,I,T)                     \
                                                            \
late <typename T>                                           \
ss S : public I< S<T>, T >
```

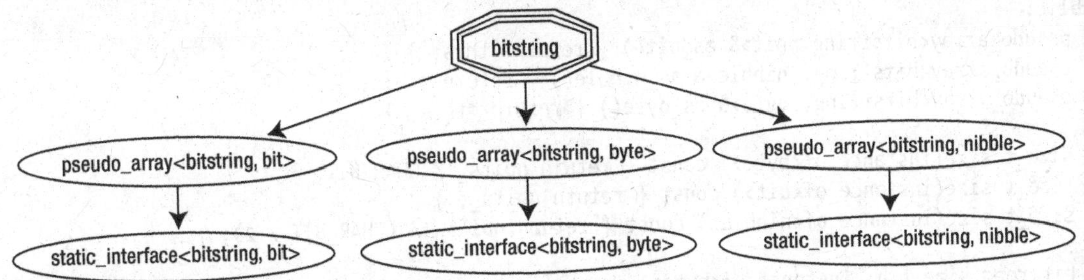

***Figure 5-2.** Improved inheritance diagram*

5.2.4. The Memberspace Problem

Up to now, static interfaces have been described as techniques that limit the scope of some template parameters. So instead of `F(T)`, you write `F(random<T>)` where `T` is a special implementation of a random generator. This is especially useful if `F` is indeed a (global) operator.

A second application of static interfaces is the *memberspace* problem.[7] The name memberspace is the equivalent of a namespace, relative to the member functions of a class. In other words, it's sort of a subspace where a class can put member functions with duplicate names.

Assume that `C` is a container that follows the STL conventions, so the first element of `C` is `*begin()` and the last is `*rbegin()`.

This is the classic solution to partition an interface where function names have a unique prefix/suffix, such as `push+front`, `push+back`, `r+begin`, and so on.

It's better to have a real partition, where `front` and `back` are both containers with their own interfaces:

```
C MyList;
// ...

first = MyList.front.begin();
last  = MyList.back.begin();

MyList.front.push(3.14);
MyList.back.push(6.28);
MyList.back.pop();
```

Indeed, you can use static interfaces to write code such as:[9]

```
class bitstring
: public pseudo_array<bitstring, bit>
, public pseudo_array<bitstring, nibble>
, public pseudo_array<bitstring, byte>
{
   char* data_;
   size_t nbits_;
```

---

[7]Apparently, the term "memberspace" was introduced by Joaquín M López Muñoz in "An STL-Like Bidirectional Ma (see `www.codeproject.com/vcpp/stl/bimap.asp`). Also, the double-end queue example is from the same author.
[8]In the pseudo-code that follows, you should pretend that C is a class; of course a non-template container would be an unusual beast.
[9]This code does not compile, because for conciseness, we removed all `const` versions of the member functions. However, the fix should be obvious.

```
ublic:
  pseudo_array<bitstring, bit>& as_bit() { return *this; }
  pseudo_array<bitstring, nibble>& as_nibble() { return *this; }
  pseudo_array<bitstring, byte>& as_byte() { return *this; }

  size_t size(instance_of<byte>) const { return nbits_ / CHAR_BIT; }
  size_t size(instance_of<bit>) const { return nbits_; }
  size_t size(instance_of<nibble>) const { return nbits_ / (CHAR_BIT / 2); }

  bit read(size_t n, instance_of<byte>) const { return ...; }
  nibble read(size_t n, instance_of<bit>) const { return ...; }
  byte read(size_t n, instance_of<nibble>) const { return ...; }


tstring b;

t n1 = b.as_bit().size();
t n2 = b.as_byte().size();
```

Compare that with:

```
tstring b;

t n1 = b.size(instance_of<bit_tag>());
```

b.as_bit() is also sort of a container of its own, and it can be passed by reference to algorithms:

```
nplate <typename T, typename X>
arity(pseudo_array<T, X>& data)

 X result = 0;
 for (size_t i=0; i<data.size(); ++i)
    result ^= data[i];

 return result;
```

This technique is excellent, but it suffers from a limitation. As mentioned, typedefs *provided in specialization are not available in the static interface,* thus you have no way of declaring a member ction returning an iterator. This is because the static interface has to borrow the iterator type from the cialization.

```
_INTERFACE(front)

typename static_type::iterator begin()          // <-- error here
{
   return MXT_SPECIALIZED.begin();
```

```
    typename static_type::iterator end()          // <-- error again
    {
        return MXT_SPECIALIZED.end();
    }
};

MXT_INTERFACE(back)
{
    typename static_type::reverse_iterator begin() // <-- another error
    {
        return MXT_SPECIALIZED.rbegin();
    }

    typename static_type::reverse_iterator end()   // <-- lots of errors
    {
        return MXT_SPECIALIZED.rend();
    }
};

class C : public front<C>, public back<C>
{
    // ...

public:

    front<C>& front()
    { return *this; }

    back<C>& back()
    { return *this; }

};

C MyList;
MyList.front().begin();       // error
MyList.back().begin();        // error
// ...
```

Note that it's not a matter of syntax. Since C is still incomplete, `C::iterator` does not yet exist. However, there are some *design* fixes:

- Define iterator before C:

```
class C_iterator
{
    // ...
};

class C
{
    // container implementation

    typedef C_iterator iterator;
};
```

- Insert an additional layer between C and the interfaces, so that the static interface compiles after C (and before the wrapper class):

```
lass C

  // container implementation

  class iterator { ... };
;

(T_TEMPLATE_INTERFACE(front, impl_t)

  typename impl_t::iterator begin()
  {
     return MXT_SPECIALIZED.begin();
  }

  typename impl_t::iterator end()
  {
     return MXT_SPECIALIZED.end();
  }


 ...

ass C_WRAPPER : public front<C_WRAPPER, C>, public back<C_WRAPPER, C>

 C c_;

lic:
 // reproduce C's interface
 // dispatch all execution to c_

 typename C::iterator begin()
 {
    return c_.begin();
 }

 // ....
```

.5. Member Selection

same technique used in merging traits (see Section 4.2.4 can be successfully applied to value objects. next listing, which is intentionally incomplete, suggests a possible motivation:

```
n

mpty     = 0,
ear      = 1,
```

```
    month     = 2,
    day       = 4,
    // ...
};

template <unsigned CODE> struct time_val;

template <> struct time_val<empty> { }; // empty, I really mean it ☺
template <> struct time_val<year>  { int year; };
template <> struct time_val<month> { short month; };

// ...

template <unsigned CODE>
struct time_val
: public time_val<CODE & static_highest_bit<CODE>::value>
, public time_val<CODE - static_highest_bit<CODE>::value>
{
};

// an algorithm

template <unsigned CODE>
time_val<(year | month | day)> easter(const time_val<CODE>& t)
{
   time_val<(year | month | day)> result;

   result.year = t.year;
   result.month = compute_easter_month(t.year);
   result.day = compute_easter_day(t.year);

   return result;
}

   time_val<year | month> tv1;
   time_val<month | day> tv2;

   easter(tv1);    // ok.
   easter(tv2);    // error: tv2.year is undefined.
```

Note that the algorithm acts unconditionally as if any `time_val<CODE>` had a member year. When necessary, you can isolate this assumption using a wrapper:

```
template <unsigned CODE>
time_val<year | month | day> easter(const time_val<CODE>& t, selector<true>)
{
   // implementation
}
```

```
emplate <int CODE>
ime_val<year | month | day> easter(const time_val<CODE>& t, selector<false>)

  // put whatever here: throw exception, static assert...


emplate <int CODE>
ime_val<year | month | day> easter(const time_val<CODE>& t)

  return easter(t, selector<CODE & year>());
```

.3. Type Hiding

assic C++ programs transform instances of objects into other instances that have possibly different types ia function calls).

```
t i = 314;
uble x = f(i);   // transform an instance of int into an instance of double
```

Using templates, C++ can manipulate instances, compile-time constants, and types (constants are in e middle because they share some properties with both). You can transform types and constants into tances (trivially), types into types (via traits and metafunctions), types into constants (via metafunctions d other operators, such as `sizeof`), instances into constants (via `sizeof`), and types into some special tem objects (using `typeid`). However, classic C++ has very limited language tools to transform an instance o a type.[10]

The most common example comes from iterator handling:

```
: = *begin;       // store a copy of the first element
                  // who is T?
```

At the moment, a suitable type is provided by metafunctions:

```
ename std::iterator_traits<iterator_t>::value_type t = *begin;
```

There are tricks, which essentially avoid direct knowledge of `T`. The simplest option is to pass `*begin` as ımmy unused parameter to a template function that will deduce its type:

```
plate <typename iterator_t>
d f(iterator_t beg, iterator_t end)

if (beg == end)
   return;

f_helper(beg, end, *beg);
```

---

dern C++ offers two new keywords: `decltype` and `auto`. The former returns the exact type of any expression, arly to `sizeof`. The latter allows an instance to "copy" the type of its initializer, so `auto i = f()` would declare a ble `i` having the best possible type to store the result of `f() locally`. See Chapter 12 for more details.

```
template <typename iterator_t, typename value_t>
void f_helper(iterator_t beg, iterator_t end, const value_t& )
{
 // for most iterators,
 // value_t ~ iterator_traits<iterator_t>::value_type

 // however if *beg returns a proxy, value_t is the type of the proxy
 // so this may not work with std::vector<bool> and in general,
 // where value_t just stores a reference to the value.
}
```

In classic C++, there are two ways to store an object without knowing its type:

- Pass it to a template function, as shown previously. However, the lifetime of the object is limited.
- Cancel its interface, possibly via a combination of templates and virtual functions. In the simplest case, the object can be *merely stored* and nothing else:[11]

```
class wrapper_base
{
   public:
     virtual ~wrapper_base() {}

     virtual wrapper_base* clone() const = 0;
};

template <typename T>
class wrapper : public wrapper_base
{
      T obj_;

   public:
      wrapper(const T& x)
      : obj_(x) {}

      wrapper<T>* clone() const
      {
         return new wrapper<T>(obj_);
      }
};

template <typename T>
wrapper_base* make_clone(const T& x)
{
   return new wrapper<T>(x);
}
```

[11]This example is important and it will be analyzed again in Section 5.4.1.

Sometimes it's desirable to provide a common interface for several types. The most famous example is iven by *variant objects (also known as discriminated unions)*, which are classes whose static types are fixed, ut whose internal storage can transport different types.

The rest of this section discusses in detail the problem of command-line parsing. Assume you are oding a tool that gets options from the command line. Each option has a name and an associated value of ome fixed type. Options come first, and everything else is an argument:

```
ol.exe -i=7 -f=3.14 -d=6.28 -b=true ARGUMENT1 ARGUMENT2 ... ARGUMENTn
```

here `i` is an `int`, `f` is a `float`, and so on.

Ideally, you need a sort of `map<string, T>`, where `T` can vary for each pair. Also, you should be able to ery such a map for values having the right type, so that you can accept `-f=3.14` but reject `-f="hello world"`.

Assume, for extra simplicity, that you start with an array of strings, where each string is either `[prefix]` ame] or `[prefix][name]=[value]`,[12] and that each parameter value will be obtained via stream extraction perator>>).

You can produce two containers. The first, named `option_map`, stores name-value pairs, like `std::map`, t each value has an arbitrary type. The second container, named `option_parser`, is another map that ows the desired pairing name-type (for example, "f" is a float) before parsing the command line. The get is writing code like:

```
t main(int argc, char* argv[])

 option_parser PARSER;

 PARSER.declare_as<float>("f"); // we tell the parser what it should
 PARSER.declare_as<int>("i");   // expect, i.e. that "d" is a double,
 PARSER.declare_as<double>("d");// etc. etc.

 option_map<std::string> CL;    // only key_type is a template parameter

 try
 {
    const char* prefix = "-";

    char** opt_begin = argv+1;
    char** opt_end   = argv+argc;

    // finally we ask the parser to fill a map with the actual values
    // this may throw an exception...

    char** arg_begin = PARSER.parse(CL, opt_begin, opt_end, prefix);

    double d;
    if (!CL.get(d, "d"))
    {
       // the user did not specify a value for "d"
       d = SOME_DEFAULT_VALUE;
    }
```

---

prefix is a fixed character sequence, usually "-", "--", or "/".

```
   }
   catch (std::invalid_argument& ex)
   {
      // ...
   }
}
```

5.3.1. Trampolines

The core technique for this kind of "polymorphism" is the use of *trampolines*.

Formally, a trampoline is a local class inside a function template, but the meaning of "local" should not be taken literally.

The class has only static member functions. Its public interface accepts parameters of a fixed type (say, `void*`), but being nested in a template, the body of the trampoline is aware of the "outer" template parameter and uses it to perform safe static casts.

Here is a bare bones example—a naked `struct` that holds untyped pointers and a function template that knows the static type of the object and apparently loses information.

```
struct generic_t
{
   void* obj;
   void (*del)(void*);
};

template <typename T>                    // outer template parameter
generic_t copy_to_generic(const T& value)
{
   struct local_cast                     // local class
   {
      static void destroy(void* p)       // void*-based interface
      {
         delete static_cast<T*>(p);      // static type knowledge
      }
   };

   generic_t p;
   p.obj = new T(value);              // information loss: copy T* to void*
   p.del = &local_cast::destroy;

   return p;
}
```

Actually, `p.obj` alone does not know how to destroy its attached object, but `p.del` points to (in pseudo code) `copy_to_generic<T>::local_cast::destroy` and this function will do the right thing, namely cast `void*` back to `T*` just before deleting it.

```
p.del(p.obj);                            // it works!
```

del is the functional equivalent of a virtual destructor. The analogy between trampolines and virtual ınction tables is correct, but:

- Trampoline techniques allow you to work with *objects*, not with *pointers* (a classic factory would have returned pointer-to-base, while copy_to_generic produces an object).
- Trampoline pointers can be tested and modified at runtime. For example, del can be replaced anytime with a do-nothing function if ownership of the pointer is transferred.
- Trampolines are much less clear (that is, more difficult to maintain) than abstract class hierarchies.

The advantage of structures like generic_t is that their type is statically known, so they can be used in andard containers, and they are classes, so they can manage their own resources and invariants.

Unfortunately, while type T is known *internally*, it cannot be exposed. Function pointers like del cannot ve T anywhere in their signature. The interface of the trampoline class must be independent of T and it nnot have template member functions (thus, for example, you cannot have a trampoline member that kes a functor and applies it to the pointee).

Next, you'll need another tool—a wrapper for std::type_info.

3.2. Typeinfo Wrapper

e typeid operator is a less-known C++ operator that determines the type of an expression at runtime and urns a constant reference to a system object of type std::type_info.

type_info::before is a member function that can be used to simulate a total (but unspecified) lering on types.

Several wrappers have been proposed to give std::type_info value semantics. This code is similar to elegant implementation found in [1] but the comparison operator ensures that a default-constructed ıll) typeinfo is less than any other instance.[13]

```
ss typeinfo

const std::type_info* p_;

lic:
typeinfo()
   : p_(0)
{}

typeinfo(const std::type_info& t)
   : p_(&t)
{}

inline const char* name() const
{
   return p_ ? p_->name() : "";
}
```

e implementation uses short-circuit to prevent null pointer dereferencing, and it's extremely concise. See also an cise in Appendix B.

```
    inline bool operator<(const typeinfo& that) const
    {
        return (p_ != that.p_) &&
            (!p_ || (that.p_ && static_cast<bool>(p_->before(*that.p_))));
    }

    inline bool operator==(const typeinfo& that) const
    {
        return (p_ == that.p_) ||
            (p_ && that.p_ && static_cast<bool>(*p_ == *that.p_));
    }
};
```

5.3.3. Option_Map

Recall that option_map was introduced in Section 5.3 as a container to store values parsed from the command line, together with their type. The interface for option_map is indeed very simple.

```
template <typename userkey_t>
class option_map
{
public:
// typed find:
// MAP.find<T>("name") returns true
// if "name" corresponds to an object of type T

   template <typename T>
   bool find(const userkey_t& name) const;

// typeless find:
// MAP.scan("name") returns true if "name" corresponds to any object

   bool scan(const userkey_t& name) const;

// checked extraction:
// MAP.get(x, "name") returns true
// if "name" corresponds to an object of type T;
// in this case, x is assigned a copy of such object;
// otherwise, x is not changed

   template <typename T>
   bool get(T& dest, const userkey_t& name) const;

// unchecked extraction:
// MAP.get<T>("name") returns either the object of type T
// corresponding to "name", or T().

   template <typename T>
   T get(const userkey_t& name) const;
```

```
/ insertion
/ MAP.put("name", x) inserts a copy of x into the map

  template <typename T>
  bool put(const userkey_t& name, const T& value);

  size_t size() const;

  ~option_map();
```

Now for the implementation details—the idea of `generic_t` is developed a bit further, giving it the
ility to copy and destroy:

```
mplate <typename userkey_t>
ass option_map

 struct generic_t
 {
    void* obj;
    void (*copy)(void* , const void*);
    void (*del)(void*);
 };
```

Since you'll want to search the container both by name and by pair (name, type), you should pick the
ter structure as key, using the `typeinfo` wrapper class.

```
edef std::pair<userkey_t, typeinfo> key_t;
edef std::map<key_t, generic_t> map_t;
edef typename map_t::iterator iterator_t;

_t map_;
```

The insertion routine is almost identical to the prototype example:

```
plate <typename T>
l put(const userkey_t& name, const T& value)

struct local_cast
{
   static void copy(void* dest, const void* src)
   {
      *static_cast<T*>(dest) = *static_cast<const T*>(src);
   }

   static void destroy(void* p)
   {
      delete static_cast<T*>(p);
   }
;

generic_t& p = map_[key_t(name, typeid(T))];
```

```
    p.obj = new T(value);
    p.copy = &local_cast::copy;
    p.del = &local_cast::destroy;

    return true;
}
```

Some functions come for free on the top of `std::map`:

```
size_t size() const
{
   return map_.size();
}
```

Here is the typed `find`:

```
template <typename T>
bool find(const userkey_t& name) const
{
   return map_.find(key_t(name, typeid(T))) != map_.end();
}
```

To retrieve data from the `option_map`, you use the copy function. First, you do a typed `find`. If it succeeds and the object is non-null, you perform the copy over the user-supplied reference:

```
template <typename T>
bool get(T& dest, const userkey_t& name) const
{
   const typename map_t::const_iterator i = map_.find(key_t(name, typeid(T)));

   const bool test = (i != map_.end());
   if (test && i->second.obj)
      i->second.copy(&dest, i->second.obj);

   return test;
}
```

The unchecked retrieval is a shortcut implemented for convenience:

```
template <typename T>
T get(const userkey_t& name) const
{
   initialized_value<T> v;
   get(v.result, name);
   return v.result;
}
```

At this moment, you simply let the destructor wipe out all the objects.[14]

```
option_map()

  iterator_t i = map_.begin();
  while (i != map_.end())
  {
     generic_t& p = (i++)->second;
     if (p.del)
        p.del(p.obj);
  }
```

Finally, you can take advantage of the ordering properties of `typeinfo` for the typeless find. Due to the
ay pairs are ordered, the map is sorted by name and entries with the same names are sorted by `typeinfo`.
st, you search for the upper bound of `(name, typeinfo())`. Any other pair with the same name will be
ger, because `typeinfo()` is the least possible value. So, if the upper bound exists and has the same name
u are looking for, it returns `true`.

```
ol scan(const userkey_t& name) const

 const typename map_t::const_iterator i
    = map_.upper_bound(key_t(name, typeinfo()));

 return i != map_.end() && i->first.first == name;
```

Note that the container may hold more objects of different types having the same name.

3.4. Option_Parser

`ion_parser` is not described in full, since it does not add anything to the concepts used in building
`ion_map`. However, note that a trampoline may have parameters whose type is not `void*`. We leave some
ails for exercise.

```
ss option_parser

ypedef option_map<std::string> option_map_t;
ypedef bool (*store_t)(option_map_t&, const char*, const char*);

ypedef std::map<std::string, store_t> map_t;
ap_t map_;
```

[14] implementation is obviously faulty; `option map` cannot be safely copied/assigned. To keep the code as simple
ssible, and even simpler, the discussion of this topic is deferred to Section 5.35.

```
public:

  template <typename T>
    void declare_as(const char* const name)
  {
    struct local_store
    {
      static bool store(option_map_t& m,
                        const char* name, const char* value)
      {
        std::istringstream is(value);
        T temp;
        return (is >> temp) && m.put(name, temp);
      }
    };

    map_[name] = &local_store::store;
  }
```

Note that `local_store::store` does not take `void*` arguments. The only requirement for a trampoline is to publish an interface independent of `T`.

```
template <typename iterator_t>
iterator_t parse(option_map_t& m, iterator_t begin, iterator_t end)
{
  for every iterator i=begin...end
  {
     get the string S = *i;
     if S has no prefix
        stop and return i;
     else
        remove the prefix

     if S has the form "N=V"
        split S in N and V
     else
        set N = S
        set V = <empty string>

     if N is not contained in map_
        throw exception "unknown option"
     else
        set F := local_store::store
        execute F(m, N, V)
        if it fails, throw exception "illegal value"
  }
}
```

.3.5. Final Additions

ue to the way declare_as works, every type that can be extracted from a string stream is acceptable in the ommand-line parser.

To include parameterless options, simply add an empty class:

```
truct option

;

line std::istream& operator>>(std::istream& is, option&)

 return is;
```

This will enable a command-line switch, such as:

```
ol.exe -verbose
```

If the name is unique, the simplest way to retrieve the value of the switch is using a typeless find. This l yield false if the switch is omitted.

```
RSER.declare_as<option>("verbose");

ar** arg_begin = PARSER.parse(CL, opt_begin, opt_end, prefix);
 (CL.scan("verbose"))

 // ...
```

Trampoline techniques can be easily optimized for space. Instead of creating one pointer for each rtual function," you can group functions for type T in a static instance of a structure and therefore have a gle pointer, exactly as in the traditional implementation of virtual function tables.

This approach is also scalable. Should you need to add an extra "capability" to the interface, it requires er modifications and almost no extra memory (since you have a single pointer table, as opposed to many nters per instance).

```
uct virtual_function_table

 void (*copy)(void* , void*);
 void (*del)(void*);
 void* (*clone)(const void*);

struct generic_t
{
   void* obj;
   const virtual_function_table* table; // single pointer-to-const
};
```

```
// identical implementation, but not a local class any more...

   template <typename T>
   struct local_cast
   {
      static void copy(void* dest, void* src)
      {
         *static_cast<T*>(dest) = *static_cast<T*>(src);
      }

      static void destroy(void* p)
      {
         delete static_cast<T*>(p);
      }

      static void* clone(const void* p)
      {
         return new T(*static_cast<const T*>(p));
      }
   };

   template <typename T>
      bool put(const userkey_t& name, const T& value)
   {
      static const virtual_function_table pt =
      {
         &local_cast<T>::copy,
         &local_cast<T>::destroy,
         &local_cast<T>::clone
      };

      generic_t& p = map_[key_t(name, typeid(T))];

      p.obj = new T(value);
      p.table = &pt;

      return true;
   }
```

Of course, instead of `p.del`, you should write `p.table->del` and pay an extra indirection.

Finally, you make `generic_t` a true value by the rule of three: implementing copy constructor, assignment, and destructor.

```
struct generic_t
{
   void* obj;
   const virtual_function_table* table;

   generic_t()
      : obj(0), table(0)
   {
   }
```

```
generic_t(const generic_t& that)
   : table(that.table)
{
   if (table)
      obj = table.clone(that.obj);
}

generic_t& operator=(const generic_t& that)
{
   generic_t temp(that);
   swap(obj, temp.obj);
   swap(table, temp.table);
   return *this;
}

~generic_t()
{
   if (table && obj)
      (table->del)(obj);
}
```

3.6. Boundary Crossing with Trampolines

is section briefly summarizes the last paragraphs. A trampoline function is used as a companion to a void inter when it contains enough information to recover the original type:

```
id* myptr_;
id (*del_)(void*);

nplate <typename T>
uct secret_class

static void destroy(void* p)
{
   delete static_cast<T*>(p);
}


tr_ = [[a pointer to T]];
_ = &secret_class<T>::destroy;
```

The information about T cannot be returned to the caller, because T cannot be present in the trampoline rface.

So you will generally tackle the issue requiring the caller to specify a type T, and the trampoline ensures it's the same as the original type (calling `typeid`, for example, see the "typed find"). This is rmally called an *exact cast*.

In short, an exact cast will fail if the type is not precisely what the program expects:

```
template <typename T>
T* exact_cast() const
{
   return &secret_class<T>::destroy == del_ ?
      static_cast<T*>(myptr_) : 0;
}
```

A second possibility is to throw an exception:

```
template <typename T>
struct secret_class
{
   static void throw_T_star(void* p)
   {
      throw static_cast<T*>(p);
   }
};

struct myobj
{
   void* myptr_;
   void (*throw_)(void*);

   template <typename T>
   myoby(T* p)
   {
      myptr_ = p;
      throw_ = &secret_class<T>::throw_T_star;
   }

   template <typename T>
   T* cast_via_exception() const
   {
      try
      {
         (*throw_)(myptr_);
      }
      catch (T* p)    // yes, it was indeed a T*
      {
         return p;
      }
      catch (...)     // no, it was something else
      {
         return 0;
      }
   }
};
```

This approach is several orders of magnitude slower (a `try...catch` block may not be cheap), but it dds an interesting new feature. You can cast not only to the original type `T`, but also to any *base class* of `T`. /hen the trampoline function throws `DERIVED*`, the exception handler will succeed in catching `BASE*`.

Remember that it's not possible to `dynamic_cast` a `void*` directly, so this is actually the best you can o. If efficiency is an issue, in practice you might want to adopt a scheme where you perform an exact cast to ASE* using trampolines and execute a dynamic cast on the result later (after the trampoline code).

Observe also that, depending on the precise application semantics, you can sometimes limit the ımber of "destination" types to a small set and hardcode them in the trampoline:

```
:ruct virtual_function_table

 bool (*safe_to_double)(void*, double&);
 std::string (*to_string)(void*);


mplate <typename T1, typename T2>
ruct multi_cast

 static T2 cast(void* src)
 {
    return has_conversion<T1,T2>::L2R ?
       T2(*static_cast<T1*>(src)) : T2();
 }

 static bool safe_cast(void* src, T2& dest)
 {
    if (has_conversion<T1,T2>::L2R)
       dest = *static_cast<T1*>(src);

    return has_conversion<T1,T2>::L2R;
 }


to_double = &multi_cast<T, double>::safe_cast;
to_string = &multi_cast<T, std::string>::cast;
```

4. Variant

key point in type-hiding techniques is deciding who remembers the correct type of the objects. In example, the client of `option_map` is responsible for declaring and querying the right types, by calling `ion_map::get<T>("name")`.

In some cases, the client needs or prefers to ignore the type and blindly delegate the "opaque" object. s way, it performs the right action, whatever the stored object is.

5.4.1. Parameter Deletion with Virtual Calls

If you simply need to transport a copy of an object of arbitrary type, you can wrap it in a custom class template, thereby "hiding" the template parameter behind a non-template abstract base class.

The following rough code snippet will help clarify this idea:

```
struct wrapper_base
{
   virtual ~wrapper_base()
   {
   }

   virtual wrapper_base* clone() const = 0;

   // add more virtual functions if needed

   virtual size_t size() const = 0;
};

template <typename T>
struct wrapper : wrapper_base
{
   T obj_;

   wrapper(const T& that)
      : obj_(that)
   {
   }

   virtual wrapper_base* clone() const
   {
      return new wrapper<T>(obj_);
   }

   // implement virtual functions delegating to obj_

   virtual size_t size() const
   {
      return obj_.size();
   }
};

class transporter
{
   wrapper_base* myptr_;

public:
   ~transporter()
   {
      delete myptr_;
   }
```

```
transporter(const transporter& that)
: myptr_(that.myptr_ ? that.myptr_->clone() : 0)
{
}

transporter()
: myptr_(0)
{
}

template <typename T>
transporter(const T& that)
   : myptr_(new wrapper<T>(that))
{
}

// implement member functions delegating to wrapper_base

size_t size() const
{
   return myptr_ ? myptr_->size() : 0;
}
```

You can also add a custom (friend) dynamic cast:

```
nplate <typename T>
atic T* transporter_cast(transporter& t)

if (wrapper<T>* p = dynamic_cast<wrapper<T>*>(t.myptr_))
   return &(p->obj_);
else
   return 0;
```

4.2. Variant with Visitors

aque interfaces often make use of the visitor pattern. The *visitor* is a functor of unspecified type that is epted by the interface and is allowed to communicate with the real objects, whose type is otherwise hidden.

In other words, you need a way to pass a generic functor through the non-template trampoline interface.

As a prototype problem, you will code a concept class that can store any object of size not greater than a d limit.[15]

```
plate <size_t N>
ss variant;
```

s is also known as an *unbounded discriminated union*. The code should be taken as a proof-of-concept, not as uction ready. Two big issues are not considered: `const`-ness and aligned storage. I suggest as a quick-and-dirty fix you put `variant::storage_` in a union with a dummy structure having a single member `double`. See. A. andrescu's "An Implementation of Discriminated Unions in C++".

First, you define the required trampolines. variant will have some fixed-size storage where you place the objects:

```
template <size_t N>
class variant
{
   char storage_[N];
   const vtable* vt;
};
```

Again from the rule of three, the tentative interface has three functions:

```
struct vtable
{
   void (*construct)(void*, const void*);
   void (*destroy)(void*);
   void (*assign)(void*, const void*);
};

template <typename T>
struct vtable_impl
{
   static void construct(void* dest, const void* src)
   {
      new(dest) T(*static_cast<const T*>(src));
   }

   static void destroy(void* dest)
   {
      static_cast<T*>(dest)->~T();
   }

   static void assign(void* dest, const void* src)
   {
      *static_cast<T*>(dest) = *static_cast<const T*>(src);
   }
};

template <>
struct vtable_impl<void>
{
   static void construct(void* dest, const void* src)
   {
   }

   static void destroy(void* dest)
   {
   }
```

```
  static void assign(void* dest, const void* src)
  {
  }
;

emplate <typename T>
truct vtable_singleton

  static const vtable* get()
  {
     static const vtable v =
     {
        &vtable_impl<T>::construct,
        &vtable_impl<T>::destroy,
        &vtable_impl<T>::assign
     };

     return &v;
  }


mplate <size_t N>
ass variant

 char storage_[N];
 const vtable* vt;

blic:
 ~variant()
 {
    (vt->destroy)(storage_);
 }

 variant()
    : vt(vtable_singleton<void>::get())
 {
 }

 variant(const variant& that)
    : vt(that.vt)
 {
    (vt->construct)(storage_, that.storage_);
 }

 template <typename T>
 variant(const T& that)
    : vt(vtable_singleton<T>::get())
 {
    MXT_ASSERT(sizeof(T)<=N);
    (vt->construct)(storage_, &that);
 }
```

The constructors initialize the "virtual function table pointer" and invoke the construction over raw memory.[16]

The assignment operator depends on a subtle issue: exceptions. If a constructor throws an exception, since the object was never fully constructed it won't be destroyed either, and that's exactly what you need. However, if you need to overwrite an instance of T1 with an instance of T2, you destroy T1 first, but construction of T2 may fail.

Thus, you need to reset the virtual table pointer to a no-op version, destroy T1, construct T2, and then eventually store the right pointer.

```
void rebuild(const void* src, const vtable* newvt)
{
   const vtable* oldvt = vt;
   vt = vtable_singleton<void>::get();
   (oldvt->destroy)(storage_);

   // if construct throws,
   // then variant will be in a consistent (null) state

   (newvt->construct)(storage_, src);
   vt = newvt;
}
```

Thanks to rebuild, you can copy another variant and any other object of type T:

```
variant& operator=(const variant& that)
{
   if (vt == that.vt)
      (vt->assign)(storage_, that.storage_);
   else
      rebuild(that.storage_, that.vt);

   return *this;
}

template <typename T>
variant& operator=(const T& that)
{
   MXT_ASSERT(sizeof(T)<=N);

   if (vt == vtable_singleton<T>::get())
      (vt->assign)(storage_, &that);
   else
      rebuild(&that, vtable_singleton<T>::get());

   return *this;
}
};
```

[16]We got rid of the " `if pointer is null` " tests initializing members with a dummy trampoline.

This variant is only pure storage, but consider this addition:

```
lass variant

 // ...

 template <typename visitor_t>
 void accept_visitor(visitor_t& v)
 {
    // ???
 }
```

Since trampolines need to have a fixed non-template signature, here the solution is *virtual inheritance*. ou define an interface for any unspecified visitor and another interface for a visitor who visits type T. Since e trampoline knows T, it will try one dynamic cast.

Virtual inheritance is necessary because visitors may want to visit more than one type.

```
ass variant_visitor_base

blic:
virtual ~variant_visitor_base()
{
}


nplate <typename T>
ass variant_visitor : public virtual variant_visitor_base

lic:
virtual void visit(T&) = 0;

virtual ~variant_visitor()




uct bad_visitor



uct vtable

/ ...

oid (*visit)(void*, variant_visitor_base*);
```

```
template <typename T>
struct vtable_impl
{
   // ...

   static void visit(void* dest, variant_visitor_base* vb)
   {
     if (variant_visitor<T>* v = dynamic_cast<variant_visitor<T>*>(vb))
       v->visit(*static_cast<T*>(dest));
     else
       throw bad_visitor();
   }
};

template <>
struct vtable_impl<void>
{
   // ...

   static void visit(void* dest, variant_visitor_base* vb)
   {
   }
};

template <size_t N>
class variant
{
public:
   variant& accept_visitor(variant_visitor_base& v)
   {
      (vt->visit)(storage_, &v);
      return *this;
   }
```

Finally, here's a concrete visitor (which will visit three types, hence the importance of the virtual base class):

```
struct MyVisitor
: public variant_visitor<int>
, public variant_visitor<double>
, public variant_visitor<std::string>
{
   virtual void visit(std::string& s)
   {
      std::cout << "visit: {s}" << s << std::endl;
   }

   virtual void visit(int& i)
   {
      std::cout << "visit: {i}" << i << std::endl;
   }
```

```
  virtual void visit(double& x)
  {
     std::cout << "visit: {d}" << x << std::endl;
  }
;

     variant<64> v1, v2, v3;
     std::string s = "hello world!";
     double x = 3.14;
     int j = 628;

     v1 = s;
     v2 = x;
     v3 = j;

     MyVisitor mv;

     v1.accept_visitor(mv);
     v2.accept_visitor(mv);
     v3.accept_visitor(mv);
```

```
sit: {s}hello world!
sit: {d}3.14
sit: {i}628
```

Note for the sake of completeness that *bounded* discriminated unions, such as `boost::variant`, adopt ifferent approach. `variant` is a class template with N type parameters `T1...Tn`. At any time, `variant` holds ctly one instance of `Tj`. The constructor can take any object of type T having an unambiguous conversion exactly one `Tj`, or it fails.

5. Wrapping Containers

w containers are often built on top of classical STL objects:

```
plate <typename T, typename less_t = std::less<T> >
ss sorted_vector

typedef std::vector<T> vector_t;
vector_t data_;
```

The sorted vector basically is equivalent to a set of functions that manipulates a vector, enforcing some riant (namely, preserving the ordering). So, a `sorted_vector` is a kind of a *container adapter*, because it gates the actual storage and it only alters the way data is stored.

Suppose you already have a vector and want to treat it as a sorted vector. Remember that it's a bad idea xpose the internals of the class (recall Section 1.4.4).

```
template <typename T, typename less_t = std::less<T> >
class sorted_vector
{
public:
   vector_t& base()                    // very bad
   { return data_; }

   const vector_t& base() const        // moderately bad
   { return data_; }
};

void causeDamage(sorted_vector<double>& s)
{
   std:random_shuffle(s.base().begin(), s.base().end());
   laugh();   // evil laugh here
}
```

You can instead have an additional parameter that defines the storage, analogous to the container type of std::stack and similar to the allocator parameter for std::vector.

```
template <typename T, typename less_t = ..., typename vector_t = std::vector<T> >
class sorted_vector
{
   vector_t data_;

public:
   sorted_vector(vector_t data)
      : data_(data)
   {
   }
};

void treatVectorAsSorted(vector<double>& v)
{
   sorted_vector<double, less<double>, vector<double>&> sorted_v(v);
   // ...
}
```

When you write the code of sorted_vector, you should behave as if vector_t is std::vector, whose interface is defined unambiguously. Any replacement type will have to satisfy the same contract.

Anyway, this solution is the most complex to code, since you need reference-aware functions. You should explicitly support the case of vector_t being a reference to some vector, and this is likely to cause problems when deciding to take arguments by value/by reference. This would be a good case for traits.

```
template <typename T>
struct s_v_storage_traits
{
   typedef const T& argument_type;
   typedef T value_type;
};
```

```
emplate <typename T>
truct s_v_storage_traits<T&>

  typedef T& argument_type;
  typedef T& value_type;
;

emplate <typename T, typename less_t = ..., typename vector_t = vector<T> >
lass sorted_vector

  typename s_v_storage_traits<vector_t>::value_type data_;

blic:
  sorted_vector(typename
                s_v_storage_traits<vector_t>::argument_type data)
  : data_(data)
  {
  }
```

A strong need to isolate the storage parameter comes from serialization. Modern operating systems can sily map memory from arbitrary storage devices into the program address space at no cost.

In other words, you can get a pointer (or a pointer-to-const) from the OS that *looks* like ordinary emory, but that's actually pointing somewhere else, for example, to the hard drive.

Now you can create a `sorted_vector` that points directly to the mapped memory, plugging a suitable ss as `vector_t`:[17]

```
nplate <typename T>
ass read_only_memory_block

 const T* data_;
 size_t size_;

lic:
 // constructor, etc....

 // now implement the same interface as a const vector
 typedef const T* const_iterator;

 const_iterator begin() const { return data_; }
 const_iterator end() const { return data_ + size_; }

 const T& operator[](size_t i) const { return data_[i]; }
 // ...
```

Observe that you don't need a true drop-in replacement for vector. If you just call `const` member ctions, a subset of the interface will suffice.

---

e mapped memory area is usually not resizable. Merely for simplicity, we assume it's `const`, but that need not be the . A vector needs to store three independent pieces of data (for example, "begin," "size," and "capacity"; everything can be deduced). A `read_write_memory_block` would also need these members, but the capacity would be a tant and equal to "max size" from the beginning.

CHAPTER 6

Algorithms

The implementation of an algorithm needs a generic I/O interface. You need to decide how and where functions get data and write results, and how and what intermediate results are retained. Iterators are an existing abstraction that helps solve this problem.

An *iterator* is a small data type that offers a sequential view over a dataset. Put simply, it's a class that implements a subset of the operations that pointers can perform.

The importance of iterators is that they decouple functions from the actual data storage. An algorithm reads its input via a couple of iterators `[begin...end)` of unspecified type and often writes its output to another range:

```
template <typename iterator_t>
... sort(iterator_t begin, iterator_t end);

template <typename iter1_t, typename iter2_t >
... copy(iter1_t input_begin, iter1_t input_end, iter2_t output_begin);
```

It's possible to write a rough classification of algorithms based on their I/O interface. *Non-mutating algorithms* iterate on one or more read-only ranges. There are two sub-families:

- "find" algorithms return an iterator that points to the result (such as `std::min_element`) or to end if no result exists.
- "accumulate" algorithms return an arbitrary value, which need not correspond to any element in the range.

Selective copying algorithms take an input read-only range and an output range, where the results are written. The output range is assumed to be writable. If the output range can store an arbitrary number of elements or simply as many elements as the input range, only the left-most position is given (such as `std::copy`).

- Usually each algorithm describes what happens if input and output ranges overlap. "transform" algorithms accept an output range that's either disjoint or entirely coincident with `begin...end`.

Reordering algorithms shuffle the elements of the input range and ensure that the result will be in so[me] special position, or equivalently, that the result will be a particular sub-range (for example, `std::nth_element` and `std::partition`).

- "shrinking" algorithms (`std::remove_if`) rearrange the data in `begin...end` and, if the result is shorter than the input sequence, they return a new `end1`, leaving unspecified elements in range `end1..end`.

Writing algorithms in terms of iterators can offer significant advantages:

- All containers, standard and nonstandard, can easily provide iterators, so it's a way to decouple algorithms and data storage.
- Iterators have a default and a convenient way to signal "failure," namely by returning end.
- It may be feasible, depending on the algorithm's details, to ignore the actual "pointed type" under the iterators.

On the other hand, there are two difficulties:

- Iterators are a view over a dataset. You'll often need to adapt a given view to match what another algorithm expects. For example, you write a function that gets as input a sequence of `pair<X, Y>` but internally you may need to invoke a routine that needs a sequence of X. In some cases, changing the view requires a lot of effort.
- The exact type of the iterator should be avoided whenever possible. Assume that v is a const-reference to a container and compare the following two ways to iterate over all elements (let's informally say two "loops").

```
for (vector<string>::const_iterator i = v.begin(); i != v.end(); ++i)
{ ... }

std::for_each(v.begin(), v.end(), ...);
```

The first "loop" is less generic and more verbose. It is strongly tied to the exact container that you e using (namely, `vector<string>`). If you replace the data structure, this code won't compile any more. ditionally, it recomputes `v.end()` once per iteration.[1]

The second loop has its disadvantages as well. You have to pass a function object as the "loop body," ich may be inconvenient.

1. Algorithm I/O

orithms are usually functions that perform their input/output operations via generic ranges. In this case, a ge is represented by a pair of iterators of generic type `iterator_t`, and the function assumes that `iterator_t` ports all the required operations. You'll see, however, that this assumption is not only a convenient plification, it's often the best you have, as it's extremely hard to *detect* if a generic type T is an iterator.

The hypotheses are:

- `*i` returns `std::iterator_traits<T>::reference`, which behaves like a reference to the underlying object.[2]
- Whatever `*i` returns, a copy of the pointed value can be stored as an `std::iterator_traits<T>::value_type`; often, you'll impose further that this type is assignable or swappable.[3]

---

nodern C++, there are member functions called `cbegin()` and `cend` that always return const-iterators, and so the would be `for (auto i = v.cbegin(); i != v.cend(); ++i)`.

C++ Standard guarantees that `*i` is a real reference, but it may be useful not to assume this unless necessary. all containers are standard-compliant, and in fact not even `std::vector<bool>` is.

ue_type is granted by the standard to be non-const qualified, but this is not enough. For example, `std::map`'s e_type is `pair<const key_type, mapped_type>` which is not assignable; more about this problem is in Section 6.3.

- Any elementary manipulation of i (copy, dereference, increment, and so on) is inexpensive.
- You can dispatch specialized algorithms for iterators of different types using std::iterator_traits<T>::iterator_category as a type tag.
- All increment/decrement operators that are valid on i return a dereferenceable object (usually, another instance of T). This allows you to write safely *(i++).

Sometimes you'll implicitly assume that two copies of the same iterator are independent. This is usually violated by I/O-related iterators, such as objects that read/write files or memory, like std::back_insert_iterator, because *i conceptually allocates space for a new object; it does not retrieve an existing element of the range.

6.1.1. Swap-Based or Copy-Based

As a consequence of the basic assumptions, most (if not all) I/O in the algorithm should be written without explicitly declaring types. Using reference and value_type should be minimized, if possible, usually via swaps and direct dereference-and-assign.

For example, copy tackles the problem of output. It simply asks a valid iterator where the result is written:

```
template <typename iter1_t, typename iter2_t>
iter2_t copy(iter1_t begin, iter1_t end, iter2_t output)
{
   while (begin != end)
      *(output++) = *(begin++);        // dereference-and-assign

   return output;
}
```

Not knowing what the elements are, you can assume that a swap operation is less heavy than an ordinary assignment. A POD swap performs three assignments, so it is slightly worse, but if objects contain resource handles (such as pointers to heap allocated memory), swaps are usually optimized to avoid construction of temporary objects (which may fail or throw). If s1 is a short string and s2 is a very long string, the assignment s1=s2 will require a large amount of memory, while swap(s1,s2) will cost nothing.

For example, an implementation of std::remove_if could overwrite out-of-place elements with a smart_swap.

move is a destructive copy process, where the original value is left in a state that's consistent but unknown to the caller.

```
template <typename iterator_t>
void move_iter(iterator_t dest, iterator_t source)
{
   if (dest == source)
      return;

   if (is_class<std::iterator_traits<iterator_t>::value_type>::value)
      smart_swap(*dest, *source);
   else
      *dest = *source;
}
```

```
emplate <typename iterator_t, typename func_t>
terator_t remove_if(iterator_t begin, iterator_t end, func_t F)

  iterator_t i = begin;

  while (true)
  {
     while (i != end && F(*i))
        ++i;

     if (i == end)
        break;

     move_iter(begin++, i++);
  }

  return begin;
```

This algorithm returns the new end of range. It will use an assignment to "move" a primitive type d a swap to "move" a class. Since the decision rule is hidden,[4] it follows that the algorithm will leave predictable objects between the new and old ends of range:

```
ruct less_than_3_digits

 bool operator()(const std::string& x) const
 {
    return x.size()<3;
 }

 bool operator()(const int x) const
 {
    return x <= 99;
 }

::string A1[] = { "111", "2", "3", "4444", "555555", "66" };
         A2[] = {  111 ,  2 ,  3 ,  4444 ,  555555 ,  66  };

ove_if(A1, A1+6, less_than_3_digits());
ove_if(A2, A2+6, less_than_3_digits());
```

possibly suboptimal, but this is not really relevant here.

After executing this code, the arrays A1 and A2 will be different. The trailing range is filled with unspecified objects, and they do vary.

[0]	111	"111"
[1]	4444	"4444"
[2]	555555	"555555"
[3]	4444	"2"
[4]	555555	"3"
[5]	66	"66"

■ **Note** C++0x has a language construct for move semantics: R-value references.

A function argument declared as an R-value reference-to-T (written T&&) will bind to a non-constant temporary object. Being temporary, the function can freely steal resources from it. In particular, you can write a special "move constructor" that initializes a new instance from a temporary object.

Furthermore, casting a reference to an R-value reference has the effect of marking an existing object as "moveable" (this cast is encapsulated in the STL function std::move).

Combining these features, the three-copy swap can be rewritten as:

```
void swap(T& a, T& b)
{
   T x(std::move(a));
   a = std::move(b);
   b = std::move(x);
}
```

So if T implements a move constructor, this function has the same complexity as a native swap.

Other implementations of move_iter could:

- Test if (!has_trivial_destructor<...>::value). It's worth swapping a class that owns resources, and such a class should have a non-trivial destructor. Observe, however, that if the type is not swappable, this approach may be slower, because it will end up calling the three-copy swap, instead of one assignment.
- Test the presence of a swap member function and use assignment in any other case.

```
template <typename iterator_t>
void move_iter(iterator_t dest, iterator_t source, selector<true>)
{
   dest->swap(*source);
}

template <typename iterator_t>
void move_iter(iterator_t dest, iterator_t source, selector<false>)
{
   *dest = *source;
}
```

```
emplate <typename iterator_t>
oid move_iter(iterator_t dest, iterator_t source)

 typedef typename std::iterator_traits<iterator_t>::value_type val_t;
 if (dest != source)
   move_iter(dest, source, has_swap<val_t>());
```

.1.2. Classification of Algorithms

ecall the distinction between non-mutating, selective copy and reordering algorithms. This section shows ow sometimes, even when the mathematical details of the algorithm are clear, several implementations are ossible, and it discusses the side effects of each.

Let's say you want to find the minimum and the maximum value of a range simultaneously. If the range s N elements, a naïve algorithm uses ~2N comparisons, but it's possible to do better. While iterating, you n examine two consecutive elements at a time and then compare the larger with the max and the smaller th the min, thus using three comparisons per two elements, or about 1.5*N comparisons total.

First, consider a non-mutating function (the macro is only for conciseness)[5]:

```
efine VALUE_T   typename std::iterator_traits<iterator_t>::value_type

mplate <typename iterator_t, typename less_t>
d::pair<VALUE_T, VALUE_T> minmax(iterator_t b, iterator_t e, less_t less)
```

minmax(begin, end) scans the range once from begin to end, without changing any element, and it urns a pair (min, max). If the range is empty, you can either return a default-constructed pair or break the sumption that result.first < result.second, using std::numeric_limits.

Here's a reasonable implementation, which needs only forward iterators:

```
nplate <typename scalar_t, typename less_t>
.ine scalar_t& mmax(scalar_t& a, const scalar_t& b, less_t less)

return (less(a, b) ? a=b : a);


plate <typename scalar_t, typename less_t>
ine scalar_t& mmin(scalar_t& a, const scalar_t& b, less_t less)

return (less(b, a) ? a=b : a);


plate <typename iterator_t, typename less_t>
::pair<...> minmax(iterator_t begin, const iterator_t end,
                   less_t less)

typedef
  typename std::iterator_traits<iterator_t>::value_type value_type;
```

milar function is part of the modern C++ standard. See http://en.cppreference.com/w/cpp/algorithm/minmax.

```
    std::pair<value_type, value_type> p;

    if (begin != end)
    {
      p.first = p.second = *(begin++);
    }

    while (begin != end)
    {
      const value_type& x0 = *(begin++);
      const value_type& x1 = (begin != end) ? *(begin++) : x0;

      if (less(x0, x1))
      {
         mmax(p.second, x1, less);
         mmin(p.first , x0, less);
      }
      else
      {
         mmax(p.second, x0, less);
         mmin(p.first , x1, less);
      }
    }
    return p;
}
```

As a rule, it's more valuable to return iterators, for two reasons. First, the objects may be expensive to copy, and second, if no answer exists, you return end.

So, given that dereferencing an iterator is inexpensive, a possible refinement can be:

```
template <typename iterator_t, typename less_t>
std::pair<iterator_t, iterator_t> minmax(...)
{
      std::pair<iterator_t, iterator_t> p(end, end);

      if (begin != end)
      {
         p.first = p.second = begin++;
      }

      while (begin != end)
      {
         iterator_t i0 = (begin++);
         iterator_t i1 = (begin != end) ? (begin++) : i0;

         if (less(*i1, *i0))
            swap(i0, i1);

         // here *i0 is less than *i1
```

```
        if (less(*i0, *p.first))
            p.first = i0;

        if (less(*p.second, *i1))
            p.second = i1;

    }
    return p;
```

Note that you never mention value_type any more.
Finally, you can outline the reordering variant:

```
emplate <typename iterator_t>
oid minmax(iterator_t begin, iterator_t end);
```

The function reorders the range so that, after execution, *begin is the minimum and *(end-1) is the aximum. All the other elements will be moved to an unspecified position. Iterators are bidirectional, so d-1 is just a formal notation.

Suppose F takes a range [begin...end). It compares the first and the last element, swaps them if they e not in order, and then it proceeds to the second and the second to last. When the iterators cross, it stops d it returns an iterator H, which points to the middle of the range. F executes about N/2 "compare and ap" operations, where N is the length of the range.

Obviously, the maximum cannot belong to the left half and the minimum cannot belong to the right lf. You must invoke again F on both half-intervals and let HL=F(begin, HL) and HR=F(HR, end).

When there's a single element in one of the intervals, it has to be the extreme.

If a unit of complexity is a single "compare and swap," the algorithm performs N/2 at iteration 0 to find ·(N/4) for the second partition, 2· (N/8) for the third, and so on, so the total number of operations is again out 3/2·N.

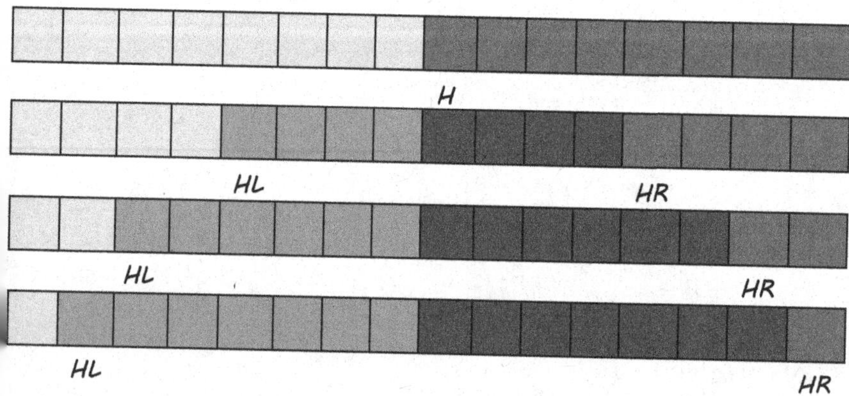

ure 6-1. *A graphical representation of the reordering minmax algorithm*

6.1.3. Iterator Requirements

Algorithms have requirements about the kind of operation the iterator must provide. As a rule of thumb, the "average" iterator is bidirectional.[6] It supports single increment and decrement (++ and --), equality/inequality (== and !=). However, it does not offer additions of arbitrary integers, difference, and operator<. Random-access iterators are used wherever maximum speed is needed, and for sorting, so they usually deserve a special treatment with specialized algorithms.

As previously mentioned, you can ensure that a requirement on the iterator is met by dispatching to another function that accepts an additional formal argument of type "iterator category":

```
template <typename iter_t>
void do_something(iter_t begin, iter_t end)
{
    return do_something(begin, end,
        typename std::iterator_traits<iter_t>::iterator_category());
}

template <typename iter_t>
void do_something(iter_t begin, iter_t end, std::bidirectional_iterator_tag)
{
    // do the work here
}
```

This technique was invented for invoking optimized versions of the algorithm for any iterator type, but it can be used to restrict the invocation as well. Standard iterator tags form a class hierarchy, so a "strong" tag can be cast nicely to a "weaker" requirement.

Here are some guidelines:

- Sometimes you'll write an algorithm first and *then* deduce which iterator is required for the algorithm to work. While deduction a posteriori is perfectly acceptable, it is easy to underestimate the requirements imposed by subroutines.
- It's usually good design to separate algorithms that have different requirements. For example, instead of sorting *and then* iterating, just prescribe that the range should be already sorted. This may bring down the requirements to bidirectional iterators.

```
template <typename iterator_t>
void do_something(iterator_t begin, iterator_t end)
{
    // the following line has stronger requirements than all the rest

    std::sort(begin, end, std::greater<...>());
    std::for_each(begin, end, ...);
}

template <typename iterator_t>
void do_something_on_sorted_range(iterator_t begin, iterator_t end)
{
    // much better: all lines have the same complexity
```

[6]This is of course fair, but arbitrary. About half the STL containers have bidirectional iterators and half random-access. However, if you weight them by usage and include plain pointers, the average iterator would be more random-access.

```
std::reverse(begin, end);
std::for_each(begin, end, ...);
```

.1.4. An Example: Set Partitioning

ıppose you are given a set of integers X and you need to partition it into two subsets so that the sum in each as roughly the same value.[7]

For this problem, heuristic algorithms are known that quickly find an acceptable partition (possibly ıboptimal). The simplest is the greedy algorithm, which states that:

```
et P1={} and P2={} be empty sets;
ile X is not empty, repeat:

  Assign the largest remaining integer in X to the set Pi which currently has the lower sum
  (break ties arbitrarily);
```

This prescription sounds like reordering, so you can consider a mutating algorithm. You reorder the input nge and return an iterator h, so that [begin, h) and [h, end) are the required partitions. Also, as an additional nus, you can compute the difference of the sums of both partitions $\left|\sum_{i\in[begin,h)} *i - \sum_{i\in[h,end)} *i\right|$, ıich is the objective to be minimized. Thus, the result will be std::pair<iterator, value_type>.

The implementation behaves like this:

- The range is divided in three logical blocks: partition A [begin, end_of_A) on the left, partition B on the right [begin_of_B, end), and a residual middle block M.
- A and B are initially empty and M = [begin, end).
- While M is non-empty, repeat:
  - Elements of M are sorted in decreasing order.
  - Iterate over the elements of M. Objects assigned to A are swapped to the right of A (in position "end of A") and objects assigned to B are swapped to the left of B (in position "begin of B minus 1").[8]

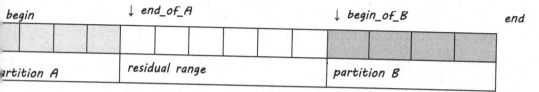

begin ↓ end_of_A ↓ begin_of_B end

ırtition A | residual range | partition B

ılly, you would like these sums to differ by 0 or 1. This is a NP-hard problem, anyway.

swapping process will leave some elements behind. That's the reason for the loop on the size of M. In the worst , about half of the members of M will be skipped, so the algorithm complexity is still superlinear; that is, it takes time ortional to ~ n·log(n) when processing n elements.

This code is a concise example of a mutating algorithm:

- It does not allocate temporary memory
- Its runtime complexity is documented

```
#define mxt_value_type(T)  typename std::iterator_traits<T>::value_type

template <typename iterator_t>
std::pair<iterator_t, mxt_value_type(iterator_t)>
         equal_partition (iterator_t begin, iterator_t end)
{
   typedef mxt_value_type(iterator_t)> scalar_t;

   scalar_t sum_a = 0;
   scalar_t sum_b = 0;
   iterator_t end_of_A = begin;
   iterator_t beg_of_B = end;

   while (end_of_A != beg_of_B)
   {
      std::sort(end_of_A, beg_of_B, std::greater<scalar_t>());

      iterator_t i = end_of_A;
      do
      {
         if (sum_b < sum_a)
         {
            sum_a = sum_a - sum_b;
            sum_b = *i;
            smart_swap(*i, *(--beg_of_B));
         }
         else
         {
            sum_b = sum_b - sum_a;
            sum_a = *i;
            smart_swap(*i, *(end_of_A++));
         }
      }
      while ((i != beg_of_B) && (++i != beg_of_B));
   }
   return std::make_pair(end_of_A,
                         sum_a<sum_b ? sum_b-sum_a : sum_a-sum_b);
}
```

Let's examine the implementation to determine the requirements on iterators and types.

- At a first glance, it may look like a bidirectional `iterator_t` suffices, because the code only uses copy construction, inequality, ++, and `--`. However, `std::sort` requires random access iterators.[9]
- The underlying `scalar_t` needs to implement `operator<` and binary `operator-`. Note that there's a small difference between these lines:

```
sum_b = sum_b - sum_a;
sum_b -= sum_a;
```

The second option would introduce a new requirement (namely `operator-=`).

.1.5. Identifying Iterators

ıe metafunction `std::iterator_traits<T>` returns several types if `T` is an iterator or a pointer (in this case, pes are trivially deduced). It also is the most reliable way to ensure that `T` is an iterator, because for most her types it will not compile:

```
mplate

 typename T,
 typename IS_ITERATOR = std::iterator_traits<T>::value_type

ass require_iterator

 // similar to a static assertion,
 // this will compile only if T is a compliant iterator
```

You can take an educated guess as to whether a type is a conforming iterator by using the *five basic* *edefs* that iterators are required to supply.[10]

Using the SFINAE techniques[11] again, you would write:

```
ıplate <typename T>
uct is_iterator

static const bool value =
   static_AND
   <
      has_type_value_type<T>,
      static_AND
      <
```

---

fastest classical algorithms, *quicksort* and *heapsort*, can sort a random-access container in place in superlinear time ally `std::sort` is a combination of both). *mergesort* is a third superlinear method that works with forward iterators, t requires extra memory to hold a copy of the whole input. In practice, however, if such extra memory is available, ıy be convenient to copy/swap the input in a vector, sort the vector, and put the result back.

fer to the excellent description in Chapter 3 of [6].

Section 4.3.1 on SFINAE.

```
        has_type_reference<T>,
        static_AND
        <
           has_type_pointer<T>,
           static_AND
           <
              has_type_iterator_category<T>,
              has_type_difference_type<T>
           >
        >
     >
   >::value;
};

template <typename T>
struct is_iterator<T*>
{
   static const bool value = true;
};
```

The rational for the heuristic is as follows:

- std::map is not an iterator, but it defines all types except iterator_category. Therefore, you really need to test that all five types are present.
- You cannot test if std::iterator_traits is well defined, because it will not compile if T is invalid.
- There exist types where is_iterator is true, but they are not even dereferenceable (trivially, let T be std::iterator_traits<int*>).

Here's a test that, with good precision, will identify non const-iterators.[12]

The key motivation is the following:

- An iterator will define a value type T and a reference type, usually T& or const T&.
- T& is convertible to T, but not vice versa
- const T& and T are mutually convertible.[13]

There are several possible cases:

- If T is not an iterator, it's not even a mutable iterator (that's handled by the last partial specialization).
- If reference is value_type& then the answer is true (this case is handled by the helper class).
- If reference is convertible to value_type, but not vice versa, the answer is again true.

[12]Of course, if a metafunction is known to fail for some specific type, it's always possible for the user to specialize it explicitly. Note also that the boost library takes another approach: if x is an instance of T, it checks if *x can be conve to T's value_type. See boost::is_readable_iterator.

[13]Remember that X is convertible to Y if given two functions void F(X) and Y G(), the call F(G()) is legal. If X=T an Y=T& or Y=const T&, the call is fine. Alternatively, if X=T& and Y=T, the call is invalid. That's precisely the way has_ conversion works.

```
emplate <typename T1, typename T2>
truct is_mutable_iterator_helper

  static const bool value = false;
;

emplate <typename T>
truct is_mutable_iterator_helper<T&, T>

  static const bool value = true;


emplate <typename T, bool IS_ITERATOR = is_iterator<T>::value>
.ass is_mutable_iterator

  typedef typename std::iterator_traits<T>::value_type val_t;
  typedef typename std::iterator_traits<T>::reference ref_t;

blic:
  static const bool value =
     static_OR
     <
        is_mutable_iterator_helper<ref_t, val_t>,
        selector
        <
           has_conversion<ref_t, val_t>::L2R &&
           !has_conversion<val_t, ref_t>::L2R
        >
     >::value;



nplate <typename T>
ss is_mutable_iterator<T, false>

lic:
static const bool value = false;
```

- `Has_conversion<ref_t, val_t>::L2R` should be true by definition of `value_type`.
- You wrap a static bool in a `selector`, since `static_OR` needs two types, not constants.

Some iterators are known to be views on sorted sets, for example, `set<T>::iterator`. Can you detect them? As is, the question is ill-formed: `set<T>::iterator` is a dependent type, and in C++ there's no "reverse ching" to deduce `T`, given `iterator`.[14]

---

remarked in Chapter 1, there is actually a way to do this, but it does not scale well and it's intrusive. It requires eration from the author of `std::set`; such a technique is the topic of Section 6.6.

```
template <typename T>
void wrong(std::set<T>::iterator i)       // error: T is non-deducible
{
}
```

However, you can make the problem easier if you limit the options to some special candidates. In fact, a set is declared as `set<T, L, A>`, but in some contexts you might take a guess on `L` and `A`.

A practical example is given in the following code:

```
template <typename T, typename less_t, typename alloc_t = std::allocator<T> >
class sorted_vector
{
   std::vector<T, alloc_t> data_;
   less_t less_;

public:
   template <typename iterator_t>
   sorted_vector(iterator_t begin, iterator_t end, less_t less = less_t())
   : data_(begin, end), less_(less)
   {
      // this is unnecessary if begin...end is already sorted

      std::sort(data_.begin(), data_.end(), less_);
   }
};
```

Since the underlying sort algorithm will consume CPU even when the range is already sorted, try to guess if this step can be avoided.[15]

There are two distinct tests. First, some iterators guarantee that the range they point to is sorted (this is a "static test," as it depends only on the iterator type); second, any iterator pair can happen to point at a sorted range (this is a "runtime test"). You can combine the static and runtime tests in this order:

```
if (!is_sorted_iterator<iterator_t, less_t>::value)
{
   if (!is_sorted(begin, end, less_)
      std::sort(begin, end, less_);
}
```

A very important observation is that `is_sorted_iterator<iterator_t, less_t>` is allowed to return false negatives but not false positives. You can tolerate unnecessary sorts, but you must not let an unsorted range pass.

■ **Note** Testing if a range is already sorted takes linear time.

---

[15]Among all superlinear algorithms, only some mergesort variant may take advantage of a sorted input; quicksort and heapsort, on the other hand, do not depend significantly on the "entropy" of the initial data.

In C++0x, there's a dedicated algorithm:

```
emplate <typename FwdIter>
ool is_sorted(FwdIter begin, FwdIter end);

emplate <typename FwdIter, typename less_t>
ool is_sorted(FwdIter begin, FwdIter end, less_t LESS);
```

In classic C++, the implementation of the latter function is extremely concise:

```
ing std::adjacent_find;
ing std::reverse_iterator;
turn
 adjacent_find(reverse_iterator<FwdIter>(end), reverse_iterator<FwdIter>(begin), LESS)
 == reverse_iterator<FwdIter>(begin);
```

is_sorted_iterator<iterator_t, less_t> could simply try to match iterator_t against some ecial standard iterators:

```
efine ITER(C,T1)          typename std::C<T1,less_t>::iterator
efine CONST_ITER(C,T1)    typename std::C<T1,less_t>::const_iterator

mplate

 typename iter_t,
 typename less_t,
 typename value_t = typename std::iterator_traits<iter_t>::value_type

ruct is_sorted_iterator

tic const bool value =
 static_OR
 <
    static_OR
    <
     typeequal<iter_t, ITER(set, value_t)>,
     typeequal<iter_t, CONST_ITER(set, value_t)>
    >,
    static_OR
    <
     typeequal<iter_t, ITER(multiset, value_t)>,
     typeequal<iter_t, CONST_ITER(multiset, value_t)>
    >
>::value;
```

There's a partial specialization for maps:

```
#define ITER(C,T1,T2)           typename std::C<T1,T2,less_t>::iterator
#define CONST_ITER(C,T1,T2)     typename std::C<T1,T2,less_t>::const_iterator

template
<
   typename iter_t,
   typename less_t,
   typename T1,
   typename T2
>
struct is_sorted_iterator< iter_t, less_t, std::pair<const T1, T2> >
{
   static const bool value =
   static_OR
   <
      static_OR
      <
         static_OR
         <
          typeequal<iter_t, ITER(map,T1,T2)>,
          typeequal<iter_t, CONST_ITER(map,T1,T2)>
         >,
         static_OR
         <
          typeequal<iter_t, ITER(multimap,T1,T2)>,
          typeequal<iter_t, CONST_ITER(multimap,T1,T2)>
         >
      >,
      static_OR
      <
         static_OR
         <
          typeequal<iter_t, ITER(map,const T1,T2)>,
          typeequal<iter_t, CONST_ITER(map,const T1,T2)>
         >,
         static_OR
         <
          typeequal<iter_t, ITER(multimap,const T1,T2)>,
          typeequal<iter_t, CONST_ITER(multimap,const T1,T2)>
         >
      >
   >::value;

};
```

5.1.6. Selection by Iterator Value Type

function that takes iterators may want to invoke another template, tagging the call with the iterator value ype. In particular, this allows some mutating algorithms to deal with anomalies, such as mutable iterators hat have constant references (for example, `std::map`).

```
emplate <typename iterator_t>
terator_t F(iterator_t b, iterator_t e)

  typedef typename std::iterator_traits<iterator_t>::value_type value_type;
  return F(b, e, instance_of<value_type>());

emplate <typename iterator_t, typename T1, typename T2>
erator_t F(iterator_t b, iterator_t e, instance_of< std::pair<const T1, T2> >)

 // modify only i->second

mplate <typename iterator_t, typename T>
erator_t F(iterator_t b, iterator_t e, instance_of<T>)

 // modify *i
```

Selective-copy algorithms may use the *output* iterator value type to decide what to return. Suppose omputation produces a series of values and the corresponding weights; if the output type is a pair, the mp writes both; otherwise, it writes only the value:

```
mplate <[...], typename iterator_t>
id do_it([...], iterator_t out_begin, iterator_t out_end)

 typedef typename
   std::iterator_traits<iterator_t>::value_type value_type;

 // ...
 dump([...], out_begin, out_end, instance_of<value_type>());

vate:
plate <[...], typename iterator_t, typename T1, typename T2>
d dump([...], iterator_t b, iterator_t e, instance_of< std::pair<T1, T2> >)

for (i=b; i!=e; ++i)
   // write value in b->first and weight in b->second

plate <typename iterator_t, typename T>
d dump([...], iterator_t b, iterator_t e, instance_of<T>)

for (i=b; i!=e; ++i)
   // write value in *b
```

Note that the implementations may be unified using accessors. See the next section for details.

6.2. Generalizations

This section discusses alternative ways of coding functions, with different I/O interfaces. Since iterators offer a view over data, they may not be flexible enough, especially for algorithms that have special semantics.

Some computations may be described in terms of properties, such as "find the object whose *price* is the minimum". Surely, you will need iterators to scan the objects, but how is a price read?

6.2.1. Properties and Accessors

An algorithm that accepts iterators may not use the actual interface of the pointed type. Usually, they have two versions, one where the required operations are handled directly by the pointed type, and one that take an extra functor that completely supersedes the object interface.

For example, `std::sort(b, e)` assumes that the pointed type is less-than comparable and it uses the pointer's `operator<`, while `std::sort(b, e, LESS)` uses an external binary predicate for all the comparisons, and `operator<` may not exist at all.

As a generalization of this concept, algorithms may be defined in terms of *properties*.

Properties generalize data members: a (read-only) *property* is simply a non-void function of a single (`const`) argument, which by default invokes a `const` member function of the argument or returns a copy of data member of the argument. Here's a trivial example.

```
template <typename T>
struct property_size
{
   typedef size_t value_type;

   value_type operator()(const T& x) const
   {
      return x.size();
   }
};
```

An instance of `property_size` passed to an algorithm is called the *accessor* of the property.

Many computational algorithms can be defined in terms of properties. They ignore the pointed type, but they need to read "its size"; thus, they require a suitable accessor.

By hypothesis, applying an accessor is inexpensive.

■ **Note** A property is a functor, thus the right `typedef` should be `result_type`, but the user needs to store copy of the property value, which conceptually lies in the object and is only "accessed" by the functor. Therefore, `value_type` is preferred.

A *read-write property* has an additional member that writes back a value:

```
template <typename T>
struct property_size
{
   typedef size_t value_type;
```

```
value_type operator()(const T& x) const
{
   return x.size();
}

value_type operator()(T& x, const value_type v) const
{
   x.resize(v);
   return x.size();
}
```

Accessors are useful in different contexts. In the simplest case, they save calls to `std::transform` or to ıstom binary operators.

Suppose you have a range of `std::string`, and need to find the total size and the maximum size. Using e classical STL, you can write a custom "sum" and a custom "less". The transformation from string to teger (the size) is performed inside these functors.

```
ruct sum_size

size_t operator()(size_t n, const std::string& s) const
{
   return n + s.size();
}


ruct less_by_size

bool operator()(const std::string& s1, const std::string& s2) const
{
   return s1.size() < s2.size();
}


assume beg!=end

e_t tot = std::accumulate(beg, end, 0U, sum_size());
e_t max = std::max_element(beg, end, less_by_size())->size();
```

Using accessors, you would have more code reuse:

```
fine VALUE   typename accessor_t::value_type

plate <typename iterator_t, typename accessor_t>
UE accumulate(iterator_t b, iterator_t e, accessor_t A, VALUE init = 0)

while (b != e)
   init = init + A(*b++);

return init;
```

```
template <typename iterator_t, typename accessor_t>
iterator_t max_element(iterator_t b, iterator_t e, accessor_t A)
{
   if (b == e)
      return e;

   iterator_t result = b;
   while ((++b) != e)
   {
      if (A(*result) < A(*b))
         result = b;
   }

   return result;
}

size_t tot = accumulate(beg, end, property_size<std::string>());
size_t max = max_element(beg, end, property_size<std::string>());
```

The default accessor returns the object itself:

```
template <typename T>
struct default_accessor
{
   typedef T value_type;

   T& operator()(T& x) const
   {
      return x;
   }
};
```

Accessors offer a good degree of abstraction in complex computational algorithms that need several "named properties" at a time. We cite the knapsack problem as an example.

Each object has two properties: a (nonnegative) price and a (nonnegative) quality. You are given an initial amount of money and your objective is to buy the subset of objects having maximal total quality. At the end of the computation, (part of) the result is a subset of the original range, so you choose a reordering algorithm. You return an iterator that partitions the range, paired with an additional by-product of the algorithm—in this case, the total quality.

The function prototype in terms of accessors is long, but extremely clear:

```
#define QUALITY    typename quality_t::value_type
#define PRICE      typename price_t::value_type

template <typename price_t, typename quality_t, typename iterator_t>
std::pair<iterator_t, QUALITY> knapsack(iterator_t begin, iterator_t end,
                                        PRICE budget,
                                        price_t price,
                                        quality_t quality)
```

`price_t` and `quality_t` are accessors for the required properties.

So the price of the element `*i` is simply `price(*i)`, and it can be stored in a variable having type `ypename price_t::value_type`.

To illustrate the usage, here's a non-mutating function that simply evaluates the total quality of the olution, assuming that you buy all elements possible starting from `begin`:

```
emplate <typename price_t, typename quality_t, typename iterator_t>
JALITY knapeval(iterator_t begin, iterator_t end, PRICE money,
                price_t price, quality_t quality)

  typename quality_t::value_type total_q = 0;
  while (begin != end)
  {
     const typename price_t::value_type p = price(*begin);
     if (p > money)
        break;

     money -= p;
     total_q += quality(*begin++);
  }
  return total_q;
```

For algorithm testing, you will usually have the accessors fixed. It can be convenient to generate a aceholder structure that fits:

```
ruct property_price

 typedef unsigned value_type;

 template <typename T>
 value_type operator()(const T& x) const
 {
    return x.price();
 }

uct price_tag_t {};
uct quality_tag_t {};

uct knapsack_object

property<unsigned, price_tag_t> price;
property<unsigned, quality_tag_t> quality;
```

The `property` class is described next.

The extra tag forbids assignment between different properties having the same underlying type example, `unsigned int`).

```
template <typename object_t, typename tag_t = void>
class property
{
   object_t data_;

public:
   property()
   : data_()   // default-constructs fundamental types to zero
   {}

   property(const object_t& x)
   : data_(x)
   {}

   const object_t& operator()() const
   {
      return data_;
   }

   const object_t& operator()(const object_t& x)
   {
      return data_ = x;
   }

   const char* name() const
   {
      return typeid(tag_t).name();
   }
};
```

6.2.2. Mimesis

Some general-purpose algorithms accept a range—that is, two iterators `[begin, end)` and an additional value—or a unary predicate. These algorithms are implemented twice. The latter version uses the predicate to test the elements and the former tests for "equality with the given value".

A classic example is `std::find` versus `std::find_if`.

```
template <typename iter_t, typename object_t>
iter_t find(iter_t begin, iter_t end, object_t x)
{
   for (; begin != end; ++begin)
   {
      if (*begin == x)
         break;
   }
   return begin;
}
```

```
template <typename iter_t, typename functor_t>
iter_t find_if(iter_t begin, iter_t end,
functor_t f)
{
   for (; begin != end; ++begin)
   {
      if (f(*begin))
         break;
   }
   return begin;
}
```

In principle, `find` could be rewritten in terms of `find_if`:

```
emplate <typename iter_t, typename object_t>
ter_t find(iter_t begin, const iter_t end, object_t x)

  std::equal_to<object_t> EQ;
  return std::find_if(begin, end, std::bind2nd(EQ, x));
```

But the converse is also possible:

```
mplate <typename functor_t>
ass wrapper

  functor_t f_;

blic:
  wrapper(functor_t f = functor_t())
  : f_(f)
  {
     // verify with a static assertion that
     // functor_t::result_type is bool
  }

  bool operator==(const typename functor_t::argument_type& that) const
  {
     return f_(that);
  }


plate <typename iter_t, typename functor_t>
r_t find_if(iter_t begin, const iter_t end, functor_t F)

return std::find(begin, end, wrapper<functor_t>(F));
```

A *mimesis object* for type `T` informally behaves like an instance of `T`, but internally it's a unary predicate. imesis implements `operator==(const T&)`, `operator!=(const T&)`, and operator "cast to T" operators being `const`).

To invoke a predicate, you write:

```
(f(x))
```

To invoke a mimesis, the equivalent syntax would be:

```
(f == x)
```

These requirements are slightly incomplete:

- The equality and inequality should take the mimesis itself and a T in any order, to prevent the undesired usage of “cast to T” for comparisons (you'll read more about this later).
- The cast operator should return a prototype value that satisfies the same criteria.

In other words, if M is a mimesis for type T, then the fundamental property for M is:

```
M<T> m;
assert(m == static_cast<T>(m));
```

The simplest mimesis for type T is T itself.

As a very simple case, let's implement a mimesis that identifies positive numbers:

```
template <typename scalar_t >
struct positive
{
   bool operator==(const scalar_t& x) const
   {
      return 0<x;
   }

   bool operator!=(const scalar_t& x) const
   {
      return !(*this == x);
   }

   operator scalar_t() const
   {
      return 1; // an arbitrary positive number
   }
};
```

Here's the first application where you don't need find_if any more.

```
double a[] = { -3.1, 2.5, -1.0 };
std::find(a, a+3, positive<double>()); // fine, returns pointer to 2.5
```

The key is that the value parameter in find has an independent template type, so positive<double> passed over as is, without casting.

A deduced template type, such as:

```
template <typename I>
iter_t find(I, I, typename std::iterator_traits<I>::value_type x)
```

would have caused the mimesis to decay into its default value (and consequently, would return a wrong fi result).

The mimesis interface can in fact be richer:

```
emplate <typename scalar_t, bool SIGN = true>
truct positive

  bool operator==(const scalar_t& x) const
  {
     return (0<x) ^ (!SIGN);
  }

  bool operator!=(const scalar_t& x) const
  {
     return !(*this == x);
  }

  operator scalar_t() const
  {
     // arbitrary positive and non-positive numbers
     return SIGN ? +1 : -1;
  }

  positive<scalar_t, !SIGN> operator!() const
  {
     return positive<scalar_t, !SIGN>();
  }

mplate <typename scalar_t, bool SIGN>
line bool operator==(const scalar_t& x, const positive<scalar_t, SIGN> p)

 return p == x;

mplate <typename scalar_t, bool SIGN>
.ine bool operator!=(const scalar_t& x,
                     const positive<scalar_t, SIGN> p)

 return p != x;
```

Thus `positive<double, true>` will compare equal to any strictly positive double and it will convert .0 when needed. On the other hand, `positive<double, false>` will compare equal to non-positive nbers, and it will return -1.0.

Note that the user will simply write `positive<T>()` or `!positive<T>()`.

```
::find(a, a+3, !positive<double>());
```

You have seen that writing a mimesis takes more effort than a functor, but it's worth it, especially for eralizing functions that take a special value as an argument. The next section offers another application.

6.2.3. End of Range

Iterator-based algorithms cannot compute the end of a range dynamically. For example, you cannot express the concept "find 5.0 but stop on the first negative number," because the range is pre-computed. You need two function calls.

```
using namespace std;
find(begin, find_if(begin, end, bind2nd(less<double>(), 0.0)), 5.0)
```

The canonical example of range inefficiency is given by C strings. Suppose you are copying a C string and you get an output iterator to the destination:

```
const char* c_string = "this is an example";

// can we avoid strlen?
std::copy(c_string, c_string+strlen(c_string), destination);
```

`strlen` has to traverse the string looking for the terminator, then `copy` traverses it again. The process in practice is extremely fast, but it does an unnecessary pass.

Suppose for a moment that you rewrite `copy`. You don't change the function body, but just allow the endpoints of the range to have different types.

```
template <typename iter1_t, typename iter2_t, typename end_t>
iter2_t copy_2(iter1_t begin, end_t end, iter2_t output)
{
   while (begin != end)
      *(output++) = *(begin++),

   return output;
}
```

This is equivalent to asking that `end` be a mimesis for the type `iter1_t`.

Compare with the following code:

```
template <typename char_t, char_t STOP = 0>
struct c_string_end
{
   typedef char_t* iterator_t;

   operator iterator_t() const { return 0; }

   bool operator!=(const iterator_t i) const
   {
      return !(*this == i);
   }

   bool operator==(const iterator_t i) const
   {
      return i==0 || *i==STOP;
   }
};

// implement operator== and != with arguments in different order
// ...
```

```
onst char* begin = "hello world!";
opy_2(begin, c_string_end<const char>(), output); // ok and efficient!
opy_2(begin, begin+5, output);                     // also ok!
```

The latter invocation of copy_2 is equivalent to `std::copy`.

To sum up, a mimesis has two uses:

- Algorithms that accept a "test," which can be either a value or a predicate.
- Algorithms that process a range `begin...end`, where end is just a termination criteria (that is, it's not decremented).

Note the difference between the two. The "test" mentioned in the first point is a skip-and-continue ndition *on elements*; end is a terminate-and-exit criterion *on iterators*.

The cast operator in the interface of a mimesis turns out to be useful when the object acts as a skip-and-ntinue filter. Assume you are computing the average of all the elements that satisfy some criteria. First, you ite a tentative "classical" version.

```
mplate <class iter_t, class predicate_t>
pename std::iterator_traits<iter_t>::value_type
 average_if(iter_t begin, iter_t end, predicate_t f)

 size_t count = 0;
 typename std::iterator_traits<iter_t>::value_type result = 0;

 for (; begin != end; ++begin)
 {
    if (f(*begin))
    {
       result += *begin;
       ++count;
    }
 }
return count>0 ? result/count : [[???]];
```

If the predicate rejects all elements, you don't know what to return, except possibly `std::numeric_its<...>::quiet_NaN()` (hoping that `has_quiet_NaN` is true).

However, the best choice is to ask the functional object what to return. If F is seen as the rejection logic t the acceptance), it should be also responsible for providing a prototype of the rejected element, and t's exactly the fundamental property for a mimesis.

That's why you rewrite the algorithm using a mimesis standing for a `quiet_NaN`:[16]

```
plate <typename iter_t, typename end_t, typename nan_t>
ename std::iterator_traits<iter_t>::value_type
average(iter_t begin, const end_t end, nan_t NaN)

size_t count = 0;
typename std::iterator_traits<iter_t>::value_type result = 0;
```

e algorithm should now be named `average_if_not`.

```
   for (; begin != end; ++begin)
   {
      if (NaN != *begin)
      {
         result += *begin;
         ++count;
      }
   }
   return count>0 ? result/count : NaN;
}
```

A typical role of a mimesis is to represent an "exclusion filter":

```
template <typename scalar_t>
struct ieee_nan
{
   operator scalar_t() const
   {
      return std::numeric_limits<scalar_t>::quiet_NaN();
   }

   bool operator!=(const scalar_t& x) const
   {
      return x == x;
   }

   bool operator==(const scalar_t& x) const
   {
      return x != x;
   }
};
```

The dangerous downside of a cast operator is that it can be called unexpectedly. Consider again the example four pages ago:

```
template <typename iterator_t, char STOP = 0>
struct c_string_end
{
   // ...
};

// ooops. forgot to implement operator== and !=
// with arguments in different order

// later...
while (begin != end)
{
   // ...
}
```

begin!=end will actually call bool operator!=(const char*, const char*) passing begin, which is alread pointer, and applying a cast to end (which produces a null pointer). Therefore, the loop will never exit.

Note also that it's possible to wrap a mimesis and turn it into a predicate and vice versa.

5.3. Iterator Wrapping

Vriting STL-compliant iterators is a complex activity and it involves a lot of code duplication. Luckily, riting const_iterators is far easier.

A wrapped iterator, const or non-const, is a class that contains another iterator as a member. The wrapper rwards every "positioning operation" (for example, increments and decrements) to the member, but it intercepts ereferencing, changing the result so as to express a logical view on the underlying dataset.

Since the end user may not see actual data, but a custom-forged value, it's often impossible to modify e original objects through the view, so that wrapped iterators are mostly const_iterators.

Suppose you have a vector of integers and an iterator wrapper that returns the actual value ultiplied by 5.

```
emplate <typename iterator_t>
lass multiplier_iterator

 // ...


 Later...
t main()

 std::vector<int> data;
 data.push_back(8);

 multiplier_iterator<std::vector<int>::iterator> i(data.begin(), 5);

 int a = *i;              // now a = 5*8
 *i = 25;                 // what about data[0] now???
 assert(*i == 25);

 *i = 24;                 // what about data[0] now???
 assert(*i == 25);        // are you sure?
```

Even if multiplier_iterator could physically write an integer at position data[0], what should it do? re it smart enough, it would write 25/5=5, so that *i returns 25 from that point on.

However, the instruction *i = 24 is even more problematic. Should it throw an exception? Or do hing? Or set data[0]=(24+(5-1))/5 anyway?

A correct implementation of operator-> is indeed the hardest issue. A lucky wrapper will simply patch the execution to the wrapped iterator recursively, but since this usually reveals the "real" data lerneath, it may not be compatible with the wrapping logic.

Consider instead *omitting* operators that are less likely to be used. operator-> is the first candidate, ess their implementation is both trivial and correct.[17]

The arrow operator is used to access members of the pointed type, but in portions of code where this e is generic (for example, a template parameter may be deduced), these members are usually *not known*, he arrow should not be used.[18]

For example, std::vector::assign will generally work even on iterators having no operator->.

---

a rule, iterator wrappers need not be 100% standard-conforming, as there are some common issues that won't compromise functionality. The most common are lack of operator-> and operator* returning a value and not a reference (in other ls: iterator::reference and iterator::value_type are the same). On the other hand, the implementation with these lified features may be much easier. See the random_iterator example later in this chapter.

exception is std::map, which could legitimately call i->first and i->second.

6.3.1. Iterator Expander

Iterator wrappers will delegate most operations to the wrapped object, such as operator++.

The dispatching part is extremely easy to automate using a static interface,[19] which is named iterator_expander:

```
class wrapper
: public iterator_expander<wrapper>
, public std::iterator_traits<wrapped>
{
   wrapped w_;

public:
   wrapped& base()
   {
      return w_;
   }

   const wrapped& base() const
   {
      return w_;
   }

   wrapper(wrapped w)
      : w_(w)
   {
   }

   [...] operator* () const
   {
      // write code here
   }

   [...] operator-> () const
   {
      // write code here
   }
};
```

The iterator_expander interface (listed next) is responsible for all possible positioning (++, ++, += -=, +, and -) and comparison operators. They are all implemented, and as usual, they will be compiled only if used. If wrapped does not support any of them, an error will be emitted (no static assertion is necessary, as the cause of the error will be evident).

Note also that every operator in the interface returns true_this(), not *this, because otherwise a combined expression such as *(i++) would not work. iterator_expander does not implement operator but true_this() returns the actual wrapper.

[19]As usual, the Boost library offers a more complete solution, but this is simpler and fully functional.

```
emplate <typename iterator_t, typename diff_t = ptrdiff_t>
lass iterator_expander

rotected:
/ the static interface part, see Section 6.2

~iterator_expander() {}
 iterator_expander() {}

iterator_t& true_this()
{ return static_cast<iterator_t&>(*this); }

:onst iterator_t& true_this() const
 return static_cast<const iterator_t&>(*this); }

ıblic:
.terator_t& operator++() { ++true_this().base(); return true_this(); }
terator_t& operator--() { --true_this().base(); return true_this(); }

terator_t& operator+=(diff_t i)
 true_this().base() += i; return true_this(); }
terator_t& operator-=(diff_t i)
 true_this().base() -= i; return true_this(); }

terator_t operator++(int)
 iterator_t t(true_this()); ++(*this); return t; }
terator_t operator--(int)
 iterator_t t(true_this()); --(*this); return t; }

terator_t operator+(diff_t i) const
 iterator_t t(true_this()); t+=i; return t; }
:erator_t operator-(diff_t i) const
 iterator_t t(true_this()); t-=i; return t; }

.ff_t operator-(const iterator_expander& x) const
 return true_this().base() - x.true_this().base(); }

ol operator<(const iterator_expander& x) const
 return true_this().base() < x.true_this().base(); }

ol operator==(const iterator_expander& x) const
return true_this().base() == x.true_this().base(); }

ol operator!=(const iterator_expander& x) const
return !(*this == x); }
ol operator> (const iterator_expander& x) const
return x < *this; }
ol operator<=(const iterator_expander& x) const
return !(x < *this); }
ol operator>=(const iterator_expander& x) const
return !(*this < x); }
```

You also need an external operator:

```
template <typename iterator_t, typename diff_t>
iterator_t operator+(diff_t n, iterator_expander<iterator_t, diff_t> i)
{
   return i+n;
}
```

Note that difference_type is taken, not deduced. iterator_expander<T> cannot read types defined in T, because it's compiled before T since it's a base of T.

So the wrapper will be declared as follows:

```
template <typename iterator_t>
class wrapper
: public iterator_expander
         <
            wrapper<iterator_t>,
            typename std::iterator_traits<iterator_t>::difference_type
         >
{
   // ...
};
```

Here's a trivial practical example that also shows that the iterator base can be a simple integer.

```
class random_iterator
: public iterator_expander<random_iterator>
, public std::iterator_traits<const int*>
{
   int i_;

public:
   int& base() { return i_; }
   const int& base() const { return i_; }

   explicit random_iterator(const int i=0)
      : i_(i)
   {
   }

   int operator*() const
   {
      return std::rand();
   }
};

int main()
{
   std::vector<int> v;
   v.assign(random_iterator(0), random_iterator(25));

   // now v contains 25 random numbers
   //...
}
```

Note that this example skips the arrow operator and dereferencing returns a value, not a reference (but ince the class inherits `const int*` traits, it's still possible to bind a `reference` to `*iterator`, as `reference` is `onst int&`).

Note Don't store copies of values in iterators. While this actually allows returning genuine references and ointers, the referenced entity has a lifetime that is bound to the iterator, not to the "container" (in other words, estroying the iterator, the reference becomes invalid), and this will lead to subtle bugs. Here's some *bad* code:

```
lass random_iterator
 public iterator_expander<random_iterator>
 public std::iterator_traits<const int*>

  int i_;
  int val_; // bad

blic:
  const int& operator*() const
  {
     return val_ = std::rand(); // bad
  }

  const int* operator->() const
  {
     return &*(*this); // even worse
  }
```

Iterator wrappers solve the problem of iterating over values in a map (or equivalently, the problem of nst-iterating over keys).

This time, the example is going to be a true non-`const` iterator implementation, because you iterate r existing elements, so you can return pointers and references.

```
plate <typename T, int N>
uct component;

plate <typename T1, typename T2>
uct component<std::pair<T1, T2>, 1>

typedef T1 value_type;
typedef T1& reference;
typedef const T1& const_reference;
typedef T1* pointer;
typedef const T1* const_pointer;
```

```
template <typename T1, typename T2>
struct component<std::pair<const T1, T2>, 1>
{
   typedef T1 value_type;
   typedef const T1& reference;
   typedef const T1& const_reference;
   typedef const T1* pointer;
   typedef const T1* const_pointer;
};

template <typename T1, typename T2>
struct component<std::pair<T1, T2>, 2> : component<std::pair<T2, T1>, 1>
{
};
```

Assume that iterator_t (the wrapped type) points to a std::pair-like class. If that's not the case, the compiler will give an error when compiling one of the ref overloads.

```
template <typename iterator_t, int N>
class pair_iterator
: public iterator_expander< pair_iterator<iterator_t, N> >
{
   static const bool IS_MUTABLE =
      is_mutable_iterator<iterator_t>::value;

   iterator_t i_;

   typedef std::iterator_traits<iterator_t> traits_t;
   typedef component<typename traits_t::value_type, N> component_t;

   typedef typename component_t::reference ref_t;
   typedef typename component_t::const_reference cref_t;

   typedef typename component_t::pointer ptr_t;
   typedef typename component_t::const_pointer cptr_t;

   template <typename pair_t>
   static ref_t ref(pair_t& p, static_value<int, 1>)
   { return p.first;   }

   template <typename pair_t>
   static ref_t ref(pair_t& p, static_value<int, 2>)
   { return p.second; }

   template <typename pair_t>
   static cref_t ref(const pair_t& p, static_value<int, 1>)
   { return p.first; }

   template <typename pair_t>
   static cref_t ref(const pair_t& p, static_value<int, 2>)
   { return p.second; }
```

```
ublic:

  explicit pair_iterator(iterator_t i)
  : i_(i)
  {}

  iterator_t& base() { return i_; }
  const iterator_t& base() const { return i_; }

  typedef typename typeif<IS_MUTABLE, ref_t, cref_t>::type reference;
  typedef typename typeif<IS_MUTABLE, ptr_t, cptr_t>::type pointer;
  typedef typename component_t::value_type value_type;
  typedef typename traits_t::iterator_category iterator_category;
  typedef typename traits_t::difference_type difference_type;

  reference operator* () const
  {
     return ref(*i_, static_value<int, N>());
  }

  pointer operator->() const
  {
     return &*(*this);
  }
```

Here's a driver function:

```
nplate <int N, typename iterator_t>
line pair_iterator<iterator_t, N> select(iterator_t i)

 return pair_iterator<iterator_t, N>(i);
```

And finally some example code. The syntax for the driver is `select<N>(i)` where `N` is 1 or 2 and `i` is an ator whose `value_type` is a pair:

```
plate <typename T>
uct Doubler

void operator()(T& x) const
{
   x *= 2;
}
```

```
template <typename T>
struct User
{
   void operator()(const T& x) const
   {
      std::cout << x << ';';
   }
};

typedef std::map<int, double> map_t;

MXT_ASSERT(!is_mutable_iterator<map_t::const_iterator>::value);
MXT_ASSERT(is_mutable_iterator<map_t::iterator>::value);

map_t m;
const map_t& c = m;

m[3] = 1.4;
m[6] = 2.8;
m[9] = 0.1;

// print 3;6;9; via iterator
std::for_each(select<1>(m.begin()), select<1>(m.end()), User<int>());

// print 3;6;9; via const_iterator
std::for_each(select<1>(c.begin()), select<1>(c.end()), User<int>());

// multiplies by 2 each value in the map
std::for_each(select<2>(m.begin()), select<2>(m.end()), Doubler<double>());

std::vector<double> v1;
v1.assign(select<1>(c.begin()), select<1>(c.end()));

std::vector< std::pair<int, double> > v2(m.begin(), m.end());

// multiplies by 2 each key in the vector (the key is not constant)
std::for_each(select<1>(v2.begin()), select<1>(v2.end()), Doubler<int>());

// these two lines should give an error:
// std::for_each(select<1>(m.begin()), select<1>(m.end()), Doubler<int>());
// std::for_each(select<1>(c.begin()), select<1>(c.end()), Doubler<int>());
```

6.3.2. Fake Pairs

The inverse problem is "merging" two logical views and obtaining a single iterator that makes them look li pairs. With pair_iterator, you can build a vector of keys and a vector of values reading a map, but not th other way around.

```
std::vector<int> key;
std::vector<double> value;

std::map<int, double> m = /* ??? */;
```

Actually, you can extend the interface of iterator expander to allow the possibility that the derived class as more than one base. Simply let base have N overloads, taking a `static_value<size_t, N>`, and each can ossibly return a reference to an iterator of a different kind.

You can isolate the elementary modifiers to be applied to the bases and code a very simple statically-ecursive method.[20]

Since you do not know in advance what `base(static_value<size_t, K>)` is, you must introduce some uxiliary "modifier" objects with template member functions, as follows:

```
truct plusplus

  template <typename any_t>
     void operator()(any_t& x) const { ++x; }
;

ass pluseq

  const diff_t i_;

blic:
  pluseq(const diff_t i) : i_(i) {}

  template <typename any_t>
     void operator()(any_t& x) const { x += i_; }



mplate <typename iterator_t, size_t N, typename diff_t>
ass iterator_pack

otected:
  typedef static_value<size_t, N> n_times;

  ~iterator_pack() {}
  iterator_pack() {}

  iterator_t& true_this()
  {
     return static_cast<iterator_t&>(*this);
  }

  const iterator_t& true_this() const
  {
     return static_cast<const iterator_t&>(*this);
  }
```

brevity, all "subtractive" functions have been omitted.

```
    /* static recursion */

    template <typename modifier_t, size_t K>
    void apply(const modifier_t modifier, const static_value<size_t, K>)
    {
       modifier(true_this().base(static_value<size_t, K-1>()));
       apply(modifier, static_value<size_t, K-1>());
    }

    template <typename modifier_t>
    void apply(const modifier_t modifier, const static_value<size_t, 0>)
    {
    }

public:

    typedef diff_t difference_type;

    iterator_t& operator++()
    {
       apply(plusplus(), n_times());
       return true_this();
    }

    iterator_t& operator+=(const diff_t i)
    {
       apply(pluseq(i), n_times());
       return true_this();
    }
```

You need to add a few more member functions. For simplicity, some operators, such as comparisons, make use of the first element only: [21]

```
typedef static_value<size_t,0> default_t;

diff_t operator-(const iterator_pack& x) const
{
   const default_t d;
   return true_this().base(d) - x.true_this().base(d);
}

bool operator<(const iterator_pack& x) const
{
   const default_t d;
   return true_this().base(d) < x.true_this().base(d);
}

bool operator==(const iterator_pack& x) const
{
   const default_t d;
   return true_this().base(d)==x.true_this().base(d);
}
```

[21]In synthesis, an iterator pack is an iterator-like class that maintains synchronization between N different iterators. If such a pack, you can call P += 2 only if all iterators are random-access. Otherwise, the code will not compile. Howev if the first component is a random-access iterator, the pack will have a constant-time difference.

All other operators derive from the basic ones in the usual way—postfix ++ and operator+ from prefix + and += and other comparisons from < and ==.

With the new tool at your disposal, here's a not-fully-standard iterator that pretends to iterate over std::pair. First, some highlights:

- Here, pointer is void, because you don't want to support operator->, but to compile std::iterator_traits< iterator_couple<...> > pointer needs to be defined; however this definition will prevent any other use.
- iterator_category is the weaker of the two categories; however, you can statically-assert that both categories should be comparable so as to avoid unusual pairs (such as input/output iterators). Of course, the restriction could be removed.
- The main problem is how to define reference. Obviously, you have to rely on r1_t and r2_t but cannot use std::pair<r1_t, r2_t>. (Mainly because, in classic C++, std::pair does not support it and it will not compile.)[22]

```
efine TRAITS(N)    std::iterator_traits<iterator##N##_t>

mplate <typename iterator1_t, typename iterator2_t>
ass iterator_couple
public iterator_pack
        <
            iterator_couple<iterator1_t, iterator2_t>,
            2,
            typename TRAITS(1)::difference_type
        >

 typedef typename TRAITS(1)::value_type v1_t;
 typedef typename TRAITS(2)::value_type v2_t;
 typedef typename TRAITS(1)::reference r1_t;
 typedef typename TRAITS(2)::reference r2_t;
 typedef typename TRAITS(1)::iterator_category cat1_t;
 typedef typename TRAITS(2)::iterator_category cat2_t;

lic:
 iterator_couple(iterator1_t i1, iterator2_t i2)
 : i1_(i1), i2_(i2)
 {
 }

 typedef typename
    typeif
    <
       is_base_of<cat1_t, cat2_t>::value,
       cat1_t,
       cat2_t
    >::type iterator_category;

typedef std::pair<v1_t, v2_t> value_type;

typedef void pointer;
```

---

d::pair takes arguments in the constructor by const reference, but if either type is a reference, it creates a reference reference, and that's forbidden.

```
  struct reference
  {
     /* see below... */
  };

  iterator1_t& base(static_value<size_t, 0>) { return i1_; }
  iterator2_t& base(static_value<size_t, 1>) { return i2_; }

  const iterator1_t& base(static_value<size_t, 0>) const
  { return i1_; }
  const iterator2_t& base(static_value<size_t, 1>) const
  { return i2_; }

  reference operator* () const
  {
     MXT_ASSERT
     (
        (is_base_of<cat1_t, cat2_t>::value
            || is_base_of<cat2_t, cat1_t>::value)
     );
     return reference(*i1_, *i2_);
  }

private:
  iterator1_t i1_;
  iterator2_t i2_;
};
```

You have to emulate a pair of references, which std::pair does not allow:

```
struct reference
{
   r1_t first;
   r2_t second;

   reference(r1_t r1, r2_t r2)
      : first(r1), second(r2)
   {
   }

   operator std::pair<v1_t, v2_t>() const
   {
      return std::pair<v1_t, v2_t>(first, second);
   }

   template <typename any1_t, typename any2_t>
      operator std::pair<any1_t, any2_t>() const
   {
      return std::pair<any1_t, any2_t>(first, second);
   }
```

```
  reference& operator= (const std::pair<v1_t, v2_t>& p)
  {
     first = p.first;
     second = p.second;
     return *this;
  }

  void swap(reference& r)
  {
     swap(first, r.first);
     swap(second, r.second);
  }

  void swap(std::pair<v1_t, v2_t>& p)
  {
     swap(first, p.first);
     swap(second, p.second);
  }
```

The template cast-to-pair operator is needed since `std::map` will likely cast the reference not to `ir<V1,V2>`, but to `pair<const V1,V2>`.

This implementation may suffice to write code like this:

```
mplate <typename iter1_t, typename iter2_t>
erator_couple<iter1_t, iter2_t> make_couple(iter1_t i1, iter2_t i2)

 return iterator_couple<iter1_t, iter2_t>(i1, i2);


::vector<int> k;
::list<double> v1;
::vector<double> v2;

::map<int, double> m;

::pair<int, double> p = *make_couple(k.begin(), v1.begin());

nsert(make_couple(k.begin(), v1.begin()),
      make_couple(k.end(), v1.end()));

::vector< std::pair<int, double> > v;
ssign(make_couple(k.begin(), v2.begin()),
      make_couple(k.end(), v2.end()));
```

Note that the first `insert` gets a bidirectional iterator, whereas the last `assign` gets a random-access ator.[23]

---

erestingly, the use of a global helper function avoids all the nasty ambiguities between a constructor and a function aration. The problem is described and solved in "Item 6" of [7].

6.4. Receipts

Receipts are empty classes that can be created only by "legally authorized entities" and unlock the execution of functions, as required parameters. Some receipts can be stored for later use, but some instead must be passed on immediately.

In a very simple case, when you need to enforce that function F is called before G, you modify F and let it return a receipt R, which cannot be constructed otherwise. Finally, G takes R as an additional—formal—parameter.

Receipts are mostly useful in connection with hierarchy of classes, when a virtual member function foo in every DERIVED should invoke BASE::foo at some point.

Assume for the moment that foo returns void.

There are two similar solutions:

- In the public non-virtual/protected virtual technique, the base class implements a public non-virtual foo, which calls a protected virtual function when appropriate.

```
class BASE
{
protected:
   virtual void custom_foo()
   {
   }

public:
   void foo()
   {
      /* ... */
      custom_foo();
   }
};
```

- Use receipts. BASE::foo returns a secret receipt, private to BASE.

```
class BASE
{
protected:
   class RECEIPT_TYPE
   {
      friend class BASE;

      RECEIPT_TYPE() {}       // constructor is private
   };

public:
   virtual RECEIPT_TYPE foo()
   {
      /* ... */
      return RECEIPT_TYPE();
   }
};
```

```
lass DERIVED : public BASE

ublic:
  virtual RECEIPT_TYPE foo()
  {
     /* ... */

     // the only way to return is...
     return BASE::foo();
  }
;
```

If RECEIPT_TYPE has a public copy constructor, DERIVED can store the result of BASE::foo at any time. therwise, it's forced to invoke it on the return line.

Note that a non-void return type T can be changed into std::pair<T,RECEIPT_TYPE>, or a custom class, nich needs a receipt, but ignores it.

Receipts are particularly useful in objects, where you want to control the execution order of member nctions (*algors* are described in Section 8.6):

```
ass an_algor

blic:
 bool initialize();

 void iterate();

 bool stop() const;

 double get_result() const;


ble execute_correctly_algor(an_algor& a)

 if (!a.initialize())
    throw std::logic_error("something bad happened");

 do
 {
    a.iterate();
 } while (!a.stop());

return a.get_result();


ble totally_crazy_execution(an_algor& a)

if (a.stop())
   a.iterate();

if (a.initialize())
   return a.get_result();
else
   return 0;
```

In general, you want initialize to be called before iterate, and get_result after at least one iteration. So you need to modify the interface as follows:

```
template <int STEP, typename T>
class receipt_t : receipt_t<STEP-1, T>
{
   friend class T;

   receipt_t() {}                          // note: private
};

template <typename T>
class receipt_t<0, T>
{
   friend class T;

   receipt_t() {}                          // note: private
};

class a_better_algor
{
public:
   typedef receipt_t<0, a_better_algor> init_ok_t;
   typedef receipt_t<1, a_better_algor> iterate_ok_t;

   init_ok_t initialize();

   iterate_ok_t iterate(init_ok_t);

   bool stop(iterate_ok_t) const;

   double get_result(iterate_ok_t) const;
};
```

With the necessary evil of a template friendship declaration (which is non-standard yet), the idea should be clear: since the user cannot forge receipts, she must store the return value of initialize and pa[ss] it to iterate. Finally, to get the result, it's necessary to prove that at least one iteration was performed:[24]

```
a_better_algor A;
a_better_algor::init_ok_t RECEIPT1 = A.initialize();

while (true)
{
   a_better_algor::iterate_ok_t RECEIPT2 = a.iterate(RECEIPT1);
   if (a.stop(RECEIPT2))
      return a.get_result(RECEIPT2);
}
```

---

[24]A receipt system based on *types* does not deal with *instances*. For example, you could have two algors and unlock th[e] second with receipts from the first. This can be mitigated (at runtime!) by adding a state to the receipt. For example, y[ou] may want to store a pointer to the algor in the receipt itself and add assertions in the algor to enforce that the pointer i[n] the receipt is indeed equal to "this".

Note The code:

```
emplate <typename T>
lass ...

      friend class T;
```

not standard in classic C++ because the statement could be nonsensical when T is a native type (say, int).
owever, it's accepted by some compilers as an extension. In C++0x, it's legal, but the syntax is:

```
riend T;
```

a workaround, some (but not all) classic C++ compilers accept this. The rationale for this workaround is at it introduces an additional indirection, which allows the compiler to treat T as an "indirect" type, not as a mplate parameter.

```
emplate <typename T>
lass ...

struct nested_t { typedef T type; };
friend class nested_t::type;
```

.5. Algebraic Requirements

5.1. Less and NaN

jects of generic type T are often assumed *LessThanComparable.*

This means that either T::operator< is defined, or an instance of a binary predicate "less" is given as an ra argument.[25]

An algorithm should avoid mixing different comparison operators, such as operator<= and operator>, ause they could be inconsistent. The best solution is to replace them with operator< (or with the binary dicate "less").

a rule of thumb, if T is such that there's a single way to decide if A<B, because the comparison is trivial or fixed, then should supply T::operator< (e.g., T = RomanNumber). Conversely, if there's more than one feasible comparison, should not implement operator< and pass the right functional every time, to make your intentions explicit , T = Employee). These functionals may be defined inside T.

`X<Y`	`(assumed valid)`
`X>Y`	`Y<X`
`X≤Y`	`!(Y<X)`
`X≥Y`	`!(X<Y)`
`X==Y`	`!(X<Y) && !(Y<X)`
`X!=Y`	`(X<Y) || (Y<X)`

It's questionable if `operator==` should be assumed valid or replaced with the *equivalence test*. In fact, two calls to `operator<` may be significantly slower (as in `std::string`). However, in some cases, with additional hypotheses, one of the tests may be omitted. For example, if a range is sorted, a test with iterators `*i == *(i+k)` can be replaced by `!less(*i, *(i+k))`.

A NaN (Not-a-Number) is an instance of T that causes any comparison operator to "fail". In other words if at least one of `x` and `y` is NaN, then `x OP y` returns false if OP is <,>,<=,>=,== and returns true if OP is !=. In fact, a NaN can be detected by this simple test:

```
template <typename T>
bool is_nan(const T& x)
{
   return x != x;
}
```

Types `double` and `float` have a native NaN.

If T has a NaN, it can create problems with sorting algorithms. Two elements are equivalent if neither is less than the other,[26] so a NaN is equivalent to any other element. If you write, for example:

```
std::map<double, int> m;
// insert elements...
m[std::numeric_limits<double>::quiet_NaN()] = 7;
```

you are effectively overwriting a random (that is, an implementation dependent) value with 7.

The right way to deal with ranges that may contain NaN is to partition them out before sorting, or modify the comparison operator, so for example they fall at the beginning of range:

```
template <typename T>
struct LessWithNAN
{
   bool operator()(const T& x, const T& y) const
   {
      if (is_nan(x))
         return !is_nan(y);
      else
         return x<y;
   }
};
```

[26]Alternatively, if both `x<y` and `y<x` are true, then the comparison operator is invalid.

.6. The Barton-Nackman Trick

nuth wrote that a *trick* is a clever idea that is used once and a *technique* is a trick that is used at least twice. he Barton-Nackman *technique*, also known as *restricted template expansion*, is a way to declare non-ember functions and operators inside a class, marking them as friends:

```
emplate <typename T>
lass X

ublic:

 friend int f(X<T> b)                          // global function #1
 {
    return 0;
 }

 friend bool operator==(X<T> a, X<T> b)        // global operator #2
 {
    return ...;
 }


double> x;
x);          // calls #1
== x;        // calls #2
```

The *non-member* function and operator shown here are *non-template* functions that are injected in the ope of X<T>, when the class is instantiated. In other words, they are found with ADL, so at least one of the guments must have type X<T>.

The main use of this technique is to declare global functions that take an inner class of a template class.

```
nplate <typename T>
ruct outer

 template <int N>
 struct inner {};
```

You cannot write a template that takes outer<T>::inner<N> for arbitrary T, because T is non-deducible. wever the Barton-Nackman trick will do:

```
plate <typename T>
uct outer

template <int N>
struct inner
{
   friend int f(inner<N>)
   { return N; }
};
```

Regardless of the fact that f is not a template, you can manipulate the template parameters at will:

```
template <typename T>
struct outer
{
   template <int N>
   struct inner
   {
      friend inner<N+1> operator++(inner<N>)
      { return inner<N+1>(); }
   };
};

outer<double>::inner<0> I1;
++I1; // returns outer<double>::inner<1>
```

You can also write template functions in the same way, but *all parameters should be deducible* because ADL does not find functions with explicit template parameters. The following code is correct:

```
template <typename T>
struct outer
{
   template <int N>
   struct inner
   {
      inner(void*) {}

      template <typename X>
      friend inner<N+1> combine(inner<N>, X x)
      { return inner<N+1>(&x); }
   };
};

outer<double>::inner<0> I;
combine(I, 0);
```

Instead, the following example works only when outer is in the global scope, but not if it's enclosed in a namespace:

```
template <typename T>
struct outer
{
   template <typename S>
   struct inner
   {
      template <typename X>
      friend inner<X> my_cast(inner<S>)
      { return inner<X>(); }
   };
};
```

```
uter<double>::inner<int> I;
uter<double>::inner<float> F = my_cast<float>(I);
```

The only workaround for having a functional my_cast as shown here would be a static interface, with
1e base class at namespace level, but the required machinery is non-negligible:

```
/ note: global scope

emplate <typename T, typename S>
truct inner_interface

;

amespace XYZ

  template <typename T>
  struct outer
  {
     template <typename S>
     struct inner : inner_interface<T, S>
     {
        inner(int = 0) {}
     };
  };

 note: global scope

nplate <typename X, typename T, typename S>
oename XYZ::outer<T>::template inner<X>
 my_cast(const inner_interface<T,S>& x)

 // cast x to outer<T>::inner<S> if necessary
 return 0;

 main()

XYZ::outer<double>::inner<int> I;
my_cast<float>(I);
```

Obviously, my_cast could be simply a template member function of inner, but this may force clients to introduce a template keyword between the dot and the function name:

```
template <typename S>
struct inner
{
   template <typename X>
   inner<X> my_cast() const
   { return inner<X>(); }
};

outer<double>::inner<int> I;
outer<double>::inner<float> F = I.my_cast<float>();    // Ok.

template <typename T>
void f(outer<T>& o)
{
   o.get_inner().my_cast<float>();
   // error: should be
   // o.get_inner().template my_cast<float>()
}

//...
```

CHAPTER 7

Code Generators

This chapter deals with templates that generate code—partly static, partly executed at runtime. Suppose yo have to perform a simple comparison of powers:

```
int x = ...;
if (3⁴ < x⁵ < 4⁷)
```

Clearly, you would like to have static constants for 3^4 and 4^7 and a corresponding runtime powering algorithm to obtain x^5. However, a call to `std::pow(x, 5)` may be suboptimal, since 5 is a compile-time constant that might possibly be "embedded" in the call.

One of the goals of TMP is in fact to make the maximum information available to the compiler, so that can take advantage of it.

7.1. Static Code Generators

Iteration can be used in a purely static context; recall the repeated squaring algorithm from Chapter 3:

```
#define MXT_M_SQ(a)          ((a)*(a))

template <size_t X, size_t Y>
struct static_raise;

template <size_t X> struct static_raise<X,2>
{ static const size_t value = X*X; };

template <size_t X> struct static_raise<X,1>
{ static const size_t value = X; };

template <size_t X> struct static_raise<X,0>
{ static const size_t value = 1; };

template <size_t X, size_t Y>
struct static_raise
{
   static const size_t v0 = static_raise<X, Y/2>::value;
   static const size_t value = ((Y % 2) ? X : 1U) * MXT_M_SQ(v0);
};

double data[static_raise<3, 4>::value]; // an array with 81 numbers
```

static_raise does not generate any code, only a compile-time result (namely, a numeric constant).

The same algorithm is now used to implement *static code generation*. Static recursion generates a *function* for any specified value of the exponent.

Assume that 1 is a valid scalar.

```
emplate <typename scalar_t, size_t N>
truct static_pow

 static inline scalar_t apply(const scalar_t& x)
 {
   return ((N % 2) ? x : 1) *
    static_pow<scalar_t,2>::apply(static_pow<scalar_t,N/2>::apply(x));
 }
;

mplate <typename scalar_t>
ruct static_pow<scalar_t, 2>

static inline scalar_t apply(const scalar_t& x)
{ return x*x; }


mplate <typename scalar_t>
ruct static_pow<scalar_t, 1>

static inline scalar_t apply(const scalar_t& x)
{ return x; }


nplate <typename scalar_t>
cuct static_pow<scalar_t, 0>

static inline scalar_t apply(const scalar_t& x)
 return 1; }


e_t x = 3;
e_t n = static_pow<size_t, 4>::apply(x);    // yields 81
```

Here, template recursion does not produce a compile-time result, but a compile-time algorithm; in fact, tic_pow is a *code generator template*.

Note also that you can avoid multiplication by 1, which is implied by the ternary operator:

```
template <typename scalar_t, size_t N>
struct static_pow
{
  static inline scalar_t apply(const scalar_t& x, selector<false>)
  {
    return static_pow<2>::apply(static_pow<N/2>::apply(x));
  }
  static inline scalar_t apply(const scalar_t& x, selector<true>)
  {
    return x*apply(x, selector<false>());
  }

  static inline scalar_t apply(const scalar_t& x)
  {
    return apply(x, selector<(N % 2)>());
  }
};
```

In particular, this code generator is *strongly typed*. The user must specify the argument type in advance. This is not necessary for the algorithm to work properly. In fact, a weaker version that deduces its argument is fine too:

```
template <size_t N>
struct static_pow
{
   template <typename scalar_t>
      static inline scalar_t apply(const scalar_t& x)
   { ... }
};

template <>
struct static_pow<2>
{
   template <typename scalar_t>
   static inline scalar_t apply(const scalar_t& x) { return x*x; }
};

// ...
```

The invocation of strongly typed templates is more verbose, since the user explicitly writes a type that could be deduced:

```
size_t x = 3;
size_t n1 = static_pow<size_t, 4>::apply(x);    // verbose
size_t n2 = static_pow<4>::apply(x);            // nicer
```

However, it sometimes pays to be explicit. A cast on the argument is quite different from a cast of the esult, because the code generator will produce an entirely new function:

```
ouble x1 = static_pow<double, 4>::apply(10000000); // correct
ouble x2 = static_pow<4>::apply(10000000); // wrong (it overflows)

ouble x3 = static_pow<4>::apply(10000000.0); // correct again
```

Usually it's possible to code both a strong and a weak code generator at the same time by borrowing a ick from groups. You move the weak generator into a partial specialization, which is recalled by the general mplate.

```
ruct deduce



mplate <size_t N, typename scalar_t = deduce>
ruct static_pow;

mplate <>
ruct static_pow<2, deduce>

 template <typename scalar_t>
 static inline scalar_t apply(const scalar_t& x)
 { ... }


nplate <size_t N>
ruct static_pow<N, deduce>

 template <typename scalar_t>
 static inline scalar_t apply(const scalar_t& x)
 { ... }


primary template comes last

plate <size_t N, typename scalar_t>
uct static_pow

static inline scalar_t apply(const scalar_t& x)
{
   return static_pow<N>::apply(x);
}
```

A strict argument check is actually performed only by the primary template, which immediately s the deduce specialization. The order of declarations matters: `static_pow<N, deduce>` will likely use `tic_pow<2, deduce>`, so the latter must precede the former in the source file.

7.2. Double checked Stop

Compile-time recursion is usually obtained by having a template call "itself" with a different set of template parameters. Actually, there's no recursion at all, since a change in template parameters generates a different entity. What you get is static "loop unrolling".

The advantage of static recursion is that explicitly unrolled code is easier to optimize.

The following snippets perform a vector-sum of two arrays of known length:

```
template <size_t N, typename T>
void vector_sum_LOOP(T* a, const T* b, const T* c)
{
   for (int i=0; i<N; ++i)
      a[i] = b[i] + c[i];
}

template <size_t N, typename T>
void vector_sum_EXPLICIT(T* a, const T* b, const T* c)
{
   a[0] = b[0] + c[0];
   a[1] = b[1] + c[1];
   // ...
   // assume that it's possible to generate exactly N of these lines
   // ...
   a[N-1] = b[N-1] + c[N-1];
}
```

The explicitly unrolled version will be faster for small N, because modern processors can execute a few arithmetic/floating point operations in parallel. Even without specific optimizations from the compiler, the processor will perform the sums, say, four at a time.[1]

However, for large N, the code would exceed the size of the processor cache, so the first version will be faster from some point on.

The ideal solution in fact is a mixture of both:

```
static const int THRESHOLD = /* platform-dependent */;

template <size_t N, typename T>
void vector_sum(T* a, const T* b, const T* c)
{
   if (N>THRESHOLD)
   {
      int i=0;
      for (; (i+4)<N; i+=4)                // the constant 4 and...
      {
         a[i+0] = b[i+0] + c[i+0];         //
         a[i+1] = b[i+1] + c[i+1];         // ...the number of lines in this block
         a[i+2] = b[i+2] + c[i+2];         // are platform-dependent
         a[i+3] = b[i+3] + c[i+3];         //
      }
```

[1]Usually, this requires the additional assumption that a, b, and c point to unrelated areas of memory, but modern compilers will try to understand if these optimizations can be safely applied.

```
        for (; i<N; ++i)                          // residual loop
        {
            a[i] = b[i] + c[i];
        }
    }
    else
    {
        vector_sum_EXPLICIT<N>(a, b, c);
    }
```

This implementation has a problem anyway. Suppose THRESHOLD is 1000. When the compiler stantiates, say, vector_sum<1000,double>, it wastes time generating 1,000 lines that will never be called:

```
 (true)

 // ...

se

 a[0] = b[0] + c[0];
 a[1] = b[1] + c[1];
 // ...
 a[999] = b[999] + c[999];
```

To fix this issue, you add a *double check*:

```
se

vector_sum_EXPLICIT<(N>THRESHOLD ? 1 : N)>(a, b, c);
```

The double check is not simply an optimization. Static recursion can yield an *unlimited* number of lines, ume again you have an array of length N and need to fill it with consecutive integers. You hope to be able to te a function template integrize whose call produces native machine code that is logically equivalent to:

```
data[0] = 0;
data[1] = 1;
// ...
data[N-1] = N-1;
```

But you guess that when N is very large, due to the effect of processor caches, the unrolled loop will erate a huge amount of bytes, whose mass will eventually slow down the execution.[2]

---

s is commonly called code bloat.

So you use integrize to select a compile-time strategy or a runtime strategy:

```
template<typename T, int N>
void integrize(T (&data)[N])
{
   if (N<STATIC_LOWER_BOUND)
      integrize_helper<N>(data);
   else
      for (size_t i=0; i<N; ++i)
         data[i] = i;
}
```

First, start with an incorrect function:

```
template <int N, typename T>
void integrize_helper(T* const data)
{
   data[N-1] = N-1;
   integrize_helper<N-1>(data);
}
```

The recursion has no limit, so it will never compile successfully.
You might be tempted to make the following improvement:

```
template <int N, typename T>
void integrize_helper (T* const data)
{
   data[N-1] = N-1;
   if (N>1)
      integrize_helper<N-1>(data);
}
```

This version still doesn't work, since the compiler will produce a sequence of calls with unlimited depth. From some point on, the condition `if (N>1)` is always false, but it doesn't matter—such code woul be pruned by the optimizer, but the compiler will complain and stop much earlier!

```
data[2-1] = 2-1;              // here N=2
if (true)                     // 2>1?
{                             // integrize_helper<2-1>
   data[1-1] = 1-1;           // here N=1
   if (false)                 // 1>1?
   {                          // integrize_helper<1-1>
      data[0-1] = 0-1;        // here N=0
      if (false)              // 0>1?
      {
         //...
      }
   }
}
```

In other words, the compiler sees that `integrize_helper<1>` depends on `integrize_helper<0>`, hence ne unlimited recursion (at compile time).

The *double checked stop* idiom is again the solution:

```
emplate <int N, typename T>
oid integrize_helper(T* const data)

  data[N-1] = N-1;
  if (N>1)
     integrize_helper<(N>1) ? N-1 : 1>(data);
```

Note the extra parentheses around `N>1` (otherwise, the `>` between `N` and `1` will be parsed as the angle acket that closes the template).

Thanks to the double check, the compiler will expand code like this:

```
ta[2-1] = 2-1;               // here N=2
 (true)                      // 2>0?
                             // integrize_helper<2-1>
 data[1-1] = 1-1;            // here N=1
 if (1>1)
    call integrize_helper<1> again
```

The expansion is finite, since `integrize_helper<1>` mentions only itself (which is a well-defined entity, t a new one) and the recursion stops. Of course, `integrize_helper<1>` will never call itself at runtime. The timizer will streamline the `if(true)` branches and remove the last `if(false)`.

In general, the double checked stop idiom prescribes to stop a recursion, mentioning a template that s been already instantiated (instead of a new one) and preventing its execution at the same time.

Finally, you again apply the idiom as an optimization against code bloat:

```
nplate<typename T, int N>
.d integrize(T (&data)[N])

 if (N<STATIC_LOWER_BOUND)
    integrize_helper<(N<STATIC_LOWER_BOUND) ? N : 1>(data);
 else
    for (size_t i=0; i<N; ++i)
       data[i] = i;
```

7.3. Static and Dynamic Hashing

Sometimes it's possible to share an algorithm between a static and runtime implementation via kernel macros. The following example shows how to hash a string statically.

Assume as usual that a hash is an integer stored in a size_t and that you have a macro. Taking x, the old hash and a new character called c, here are some possibilities:

```
#define MXT_HASH(x, c)  ((x) << 1) ^ (c)
#define MXT_HASH(x, c)  (x) + ((x) << 5) + (c)
#define MXT_HASH(x, c)  ((x) << 6) ^ ((x) & ((~size_t(0)) << 26)) ^ (c)
```

■ **Note** The hashing macros require that c be a positive number. You could replace c with (c-CHAR_MIN), but this would make the hash platform-dependent. Where char is signed, 'a'-CHAR_MIN equals 97-(-128) = 225 and where char is unsigned, the same expression yields 97-0 = 97.

Furthermore, the same text in a std::string and in a std::wstring should not return two different hash codes.

Given that you disregard what happens for non-ASCII characters, an elegant workaround is to cast char c to unsigned char.

Constants should not be hard-coded, but rather generated at compile time.

You could replace the classic code

```
const char* text = ...;
if (strcmp(text, "FIRST")==0)
{
   // ...
}
else if (strcmp(text, "SECOND")==0)
{
   // ...
}
else if (strcmp(text, "THIRD")==0)
{
   // ...
}
```

ith something like this:

```
onst char* text = ...;
witch (dynamic_hash(text))

  case static_hash<'F','I','R','S','T'>::value:
     // ...
     break;

  case static_hash<'S','E','C','O','N','D'>::value:
     // ...
     break;
```

- Hashing will save a lot of string comparisons, even if it could produce false positives.[3]
- If `static_hash` produces duplicate values, the switch won't compile, so it will never produce false negatives (that is, the words "`FIRST`", "`SECOND`", and so on will always be matched without ambiguities).

The static algorithm uses template rotation and a very neat implementation:

```
mplate

 char C0=0, char C1=0, char C2=0, char C3=0, ..., char C23=0,
 size_t HASH = 0

ruct static_hash
static_hash<C1,C2...,C23,0, MXT_HASH(HASH, static_cast<unsigned char>(C0))>



nplate <size_t HASH>
ruct static_hash<0,0,0,0,...,0, HASH>
static_value<size_t, HASH>
```

The only degree of freedom in `dynamic_hash` is the function signature.
Here's a fairly general one, with some plain old vanilla C tricks:

```
::pair<size_t, const char*> dynamic_hash(const char* text,
                                         const char* separ = 0,
                                         const char* end = 0)

size_t h = 0;
const char* const end1 = separ ? text+strcspn(text, separ) : end;
const char* const end2 = (end && end<end1) ? end : end1;
```

re are 26^N sequences of N letters, and "only" say 2^{64} different hash values, so for `N>14`, no hash can be injective; ever a good hashing algorithm will "scatter" conflicts, so strings having the same hash will be *really* different.

```
    while (end2 ? text<end2 : (*text != 0))
    {
        const size_t c = static_cast<unsigned char>(*(text++));
        h = MXT_HASH(h, c);
    }
    return std::make_pair(h, text);
}

int main()
{
    const char* text = "hello, dynamic hash";
    dynamic_hash(text);                     // hash all string, up to char(0)
    dynamic_hash(text, ";,");               // hash up to any of the separators
    dynamic_hash(text, ";,", text+10); // up to separator, at most 10 chars
}
```

I chose to return a composite result, the hash value and the updated "iterator".

7.3.1. A Function Set for Characters

The selection of the correct function set can be done either by a deduced template parameter (as seen in string_traits in Section **4.2.1**) or by an environment template parameter.

A natural example is the problem of a character set: some string-conversion functions can be accelerated, given that some set of characters, say {'0', '1'... '9'}, is contiguous. If c belongs to the set, you can convert c to integer via a simple subtraction c - '0', but if the digit character set is arbitrarily scattered, a more complex implementation is needed.

You scan sets of characters with template rotation:

```
namespace charset {
template
<
    typename char_t,
    char_t C0,
    char_t C1 = 0,
    char_t C2 = 0,
    // ...
    char_t C9 = 0
>
struct is_contiguous
{
    static const bool value = (C0+1==C1) &&
        is_contiguous<char_t,C1,C2,C3,C4,C5,C6,C7,C8,C9>::value;
};

template <char C0>
struct is_contiguous<char,C0>
{
    static const bool value = true;
};
```

```
emplate <wchar_t C0>
truct is_contiguous<wchar_t,C0>

  static const bool value = true;
;
```

Next, the result of a static test can be saved in a global traits structure:

```
truct ascii

 static const bool value_lowerc =
   charset::is_contiguous<char,
     'a','b','c','d','e','f','g','h','i','j'>::value
   &&
   charset::is_contiguous<char,
     'j','k','l','m','n','o','p','q','r','s'>::value
   &&
   charset::is_contiguous<char,
     's','t','u','v','w','x','y','z'>::value;

static const bool value_upperc =
  charset::is_contiguous<char,
    'A','B','C','D','E','F','G','H','I','J'>::value
  &&
  charset::is_contiguous<char,
    'J','K','L','M','N','O','P','Q','R','S'>::value
  &&
  charset::is_contiguous<char,
    'S','T','U','V','W','X','Y','Z'>::value;

static const bool value_09 =
  charset::is_contiguous<char,
    '0','1','2','3','4','5','6','7','8','9'>::value;

static const bool value = value_09 && value_lowerc && value_upperc;
```

Suppose for the moment that `ascii::value` is true. You can write a function set to deal with the
cial case:

```
plate <typename T, T lower, T upper>
ine bool is_between(const T c)

return !(c<lower) && !(upper<c);


uct ascii_traits

typedef char char_type;
```

```
    static inline bool isupper(const char_type c)
    {
        return is_between<char,'A','Z'>(c);
    }

    static inline bool islower(const char_type c)
    {
        return is_between<char,'a','z'>(c);
    }

    static inline bool isalpha(const char_type c)
    {
        return islower(c) || isupper(c);
    }

    static inline bool isdigit(const char_type c)
    {
        return is_between<char,'0','9'>(c);
    }

    //...

    static inline char tolower(const char c)
    {
        return isupper(c) ? c-'A'+'a' : c;
    }

    static inline char toupper(const char c)
    {
        return islower(c) ? c-'a'+'A' : c;
    }
};
```

In a different implementation, you use std::locale:

```
template <typename char_t>
struct stdchar_traits
{
    typedef char_t char_type;

    static inline bool isupper(const char_t c)
    {
        return std::isupper(c, locale());
    }

    static inline bool islower(const char_t c)
    {
        return std::islower(c, locale());
    }
```

```
static inline bool isalpha(const char_t c)
{
   return std::isalpha(c, locale());
}

static inline bool isdigit(const char_t c)
{
   return std::isdigit(c, locale());
}

...

static inline char_t tolower(const char_t c)
{
   return std::tolower(c, std::locale());
}

static inline char_t toupper(const char_t c)
{
   return std::toupper(c, std::locale());
}
```

And eventually combine these types:

```
ruct standard {};
ruct fast {};

nplate <typename char_t, typename charset_t = fast>
ruct char_traits : stdchar_traits<char_t>


nplate <>
uct char_traits<char, fast>
ypeif<ascii::value, ascii_traits, stdchar_traits<char> >::type
```

The environment parameter `charset_t` is by default set to `fast`. If it's possible in the current platform, `fast` set is preferred; otherwise, the standard set is used.[4]

---

an exercise, the reader might generalize the idea to wchar_t, which in this implementation always picks the e-based function set.

7.3.2. Changing Case

This section lists some utilities used to change the case of characters. First, it introduces some tags. Note tha "case_sensitive" is treated as a "no conversion" label.[5]

```
struct case_sensitive {};
struct upper_case {};
struct lower_case {};
```

This example exploits the fact that char_traits offers a leveraged interface to mutate characters at runtime (the example is limited to char). The classic part of the work is a collection of functors.

```
template <typename mutation_t, typename traits_t = char_traits<char> >
struct change_case;

template <typename traits_t>
struct change_case<case_sensitive, traits_t>
{
   typedef typename traits_t::char_type char_type;

   char_type operator()(const char_type c) const
   {
      return c;
   }
};

template <typename traits_t>
struct change_case<lower_case, traits_t>
{
   typedef typename traits_t::char_type char_type;

   char_type operator()(const char_type c) const
   {
      return traits_t::tolower(c);
   }
};

template <typename traits_t>
struct change_case<upper_case, traits_t>
{
   typedef typename traits_t::char_type char_type;

   char_type operator()(const char_type c) const
   {
      return traits_t::toupper(c);
   }
};
```

[5]The motivation will be evident when you see an application to string hashing, later in the paragraph.

```
nt main()

  std::string s = "this is a lower case string";
  std::transform(s.begin(), s.end(), s.begin(), change_case<upper_case>());
```

Now you move to the analogous conversion at compile time.

```
emplate <typename case_t, char C, bool FAST = ascii::value>
truct static_change_case;
```

FAST is a hidden parameter; regardless of its value, a case-sensitive conversion should do nothing:

```
emplate <char C, bool FAST>
ruct static_change_case<case_sensitive, C, FAST>

 static const char value = C;
```

If FAST is true, the transformation is trivial. If FAST is false, unfortunately, every character that can
ange case needs its own specialization. Macros will save a lot of typing here.

```
mplate <char C>
ruct static_change_case<lower_case, C, true>

 static const char value = ((C>='A' && C<='Z') ? C-'A'+'a' : C);

mplate <char C>
ruct static_change_case<upper_case, C, true>

 static const char value = ((C>='a' && C<='z') ? C-'a'+'A' : C);

plate <char C>
uct static_change_case<lower_case, C, false>

static const char value = C;      // a generic char has no case

plate <char C>
uct static_change_case<upper_case, C, false>

static const char value = C;      // a generic char has no case

fine mxt_STATIC_CASE_GENERIC(C_LO, C_UP)                            \
                                                                     \
plate <> struct static_change_case<lower_case, C_UP, false>          \
tatic const char value = C_LO; };                                    \
                                                                     \
late <> struct static_change_case<upper_case, C_LO, false>           \
```

```
{ static const char value = C_UP; }

mxt_STATIC_CASE_GENERIC('a', 'A');
mxt_STATIC_CASE_GENERIC('b', 'B');
...
mxt_STATIC_CASE_GENERIC('z', 'Z');

#undef mxt_STATIC_CASE_GENERIC
```

This has an immediate application to both static_hash and dynamic_hash.

As usual, the macro is merely for convenience. Note that a non-deduced template parameter is introduced in the dynamic hash.

```
#define mxt_FIRST_CHAR(c)          \
     static_cast<unsigned char>(static_change_case<case_t, C>::value)

template
<
  typename case_t,
  char C0=0, char C1=0, char C2=0, char C3=0, ..., char C23=0,
  size_t HASH = 0
>
struct static_hash
: static_hash<case_t,C1,C2,...,C23,0, MXT_HASH(HASH, mxt_FIRST_CHAR(C0))>
{
};

template <typename case_t, size_t HASH>
struct static_hash<case_t,0,0,0,0,...,0, HASH>
: static_value<size_t, HASH>
{
};

template <typename case_t>
inline ... dynamic_hash(const char* text, ...)
{
  const change_case<case_t> CHANGE;
  size_t h = 0;
  const char* const end1 = (separ ? text+strcspn(text, separ) : end);
  const char* const end2 = (end && end<end1) ? end : end1;

  while (end2 ? text<end2 : (*text != 0))
  {
    const size_t c = static_cast<unsigned char>(CHANGE(*(text++)));
    h = MXT_HASH(h, c);
  }
  return std::make_pair(h, text);
}
```

Such a modified algorithm will alter the case of a string *inside the computation* of the hash value, so an upper case hash" is effectively a case-insensitive value:

```
witch (dynamic_hash<upper_case>(text).first)

 case static_hash<'F','I','R','S','T'>::value:
   // will match "First", "FIRST", "first", "fiRST"...
   break;
```

.3.3. Mimesis Techniques

nis section rewrites the dynamic_hash using mimesis techniques. In the new prototype, end is not optional, you have to provide more overloads to get a flexible syntax. As for the original C version:

```
mplate <typename case_t, typename iterator_t, typename end_t>
d::pair<size_t, iterator_t>
dynamic_hash(iterator_t begin, const end_t end, size_t h = 0)

typedef typename std::iterator_traits<iterator_t>::value_type char_t;
const change_case< case_t, char_traits<char_t> > CHANGE;

while (end != begin)
{
  const size_t c = static_cast<unsigned char>(CHANGE(*(begin++)));
  h = MXT_HASH(h, c);
}
return std::make_pair(h, begin);


nplate <typename case_t, typename iterator_t>
line std::pair<size_t, iterator_t>
dynamic_hash(iterator_t begin, size_t h = 0)

eturn dynamic_hash(begin, c_string_end<iterator_t>(), h);
```

You can plug in some useful mimesis-like objects[6]:

```
plate <typename char_t, char_t CLOSE_TAG>
uct stop_at

emplate <typename iterator_t>
nline bool operator!=(const iterator_t i) const

 return (*i != 0) && (*i != CLOSE_TAG);
```

---

re's no need for a complete mimesis implementation: a cast operator is not needed.

```
size_t h = dynamic_hash<case_insensitive>(text, stop_at<char, ';'>()).first;

template <bool (*funct)(const char), bool NEGATE>
struct apply_f
{
  template <typename iterator_t>
  inline bool operator!=(const iterator_t i) const
  {
    return funct(*i) ^ NEGATE;
  }
};

typedef apply_f<char_traits<char>::isspace, true> end_of_word;
typedef apply_f<char_traits<char>::isalpha, false> all_alpha;
```

end_of_word stops at the first space, and all_alpha stops at the first non-alphabetical character.

7.3.4. Ambiguous Overloads

The evolution of the dynamic_hash has led to adding more template parameters and more overloads. You need to be careful not to cause compilation problems because of *ambiguous overload* resolution.

The exact overload resolution rules are described in Appendix B of [2], but a rough summary is described here.

When the compiler meets a function call, it must pick, from the set of all functions with the same name, the most specialized set that matches the given arguments. It must emit an error if no such function exists or if the best match is ambiguous.

If you have several function templates named F, you denote them as F[1], F[2], and so on.[7] You say that F[1] is more specialized than F[2] if F[2] can be used wherever F[1] is used, with an exact argument match, but not vice versa.

For example:

```
template <typename T1, typename T2>
void F(T1 a, T2 b); // this is F[1]

template <typename T>
void F(T a, T b); // this is F[2]

template <typename T>
void F(T a, int b); // this is F[3]
```

The second template, F[2], is more specialized than F[1], because the call F(X,X) can refer to either one, but only F[2] matches F(X,Y) exactly. Similarly, F[3] is more specialized than F[1].

[7] This syntax will be used only in this section, where there's no possibility of confusion.

However, this is a partial ordering criterion. If no function is more specialized than the other(s), the ompiler will abort, reporting an ambiguous overload. In fact, in the previous example, `F[2]` and `F[3]` are ot comparable. `F[3]` will not match exactly `F(X,X)` and `F[2]` will not match exactly `F(X, int)`.[8]

```
nt z = 2;
(z, z);        // error: could be F[2] with T=int or F[3] with T=int
```

Informally, an easy unambiguous special case is total replacement. If a template parameter is ompletely replaced by fixed types or previous template parameters, the resulting function is more ecialized than the original. Take `F[1]`, replace every occurrence of `T2` with `T1`, and obtain `F[2]`; replace `T2` ith `int` and obtain `F[3]`.

A library writer usually provides a set of overloads, where one or more elements are function templates. ne of the problems, often underestimated or ignored, is to decide in advance if the set is *well-ordered*. well-ordered set will never generate ambiguity errors.

The combination of default arguments and templates often makes deduction very hard.

```
mplate <typename case_t, typename iterator_t, typename end_t>
..] dynamic_hash(iterator_t begin, const end_t end,
                 size_t crc = 0);  // dynamic_hash[1]

mplate <typename case_t, typename iterator_t>
..] dynamic_hash(iterator_t begin, size_t crc = 0);    // dynamic_hash[2]
```

To determine if this set is well-ordered, you need only to consider the case of a call with two arguments, d it's evident that the total replacement condition holds (replace `end_t` with `size_t`).

However, note that `dynamic_hash(T, int)` will invoke `dynamic_hash[1]`:

```
namic_hash(text, 123);   // invokes (1) [with end_t = int]
```

A user-friendly library will try to avoid ambiguities, first by using additional types:

```
ruct hash_type

 size_t value;

 hash_type() : value(0) {}
 explicit hash_type(const size_t c) : value(c) {}

plate <typename case_t, typename iterator_t, typename end_t>
.] dynamic_hash(iterator_t begin, end_t end, hash_type h = hash_type());

plate <typename case_t, typename iterator_t>
.] dynamic_hash(iterator_t begin, hash_type h = hash_type());
```

---

ther common error is the argument crossover. Suppose a class `C` has two template parameters `T1` and `T2`. If you partially ialize `C<T1,Y>` and `C<X,T2>` for some fixed `X` and `Y`, `C<X,Y>` is ambiguous, so it must be explicitly specialized too.

While this does not change the way the compiler picks functions, it will make the error more evident to the user, because now dynamic_hash(text, 123) will not even compile.

```
dynamic_hash(text, hash_type(123));         // this instead is correct
```

A radical change instead is obtained by wrapping the original return type in a typename only_if<[[condition]], ...>::type clause (See Section 4.3.3).

```
template <typename T1, typename T2>
struct different : selector<true>
{};

template <typename T>
struct different<T, T> : selector<false>
{};

template <typename case_t, typename iterator_t, typename end_t>
typename only_if<different<end_t, hash_type>::value, [...]>::type
  dynamic_hash(iterator_t begin, const end_t end, hash_type h = hash_type());
```

Suppose that you add the C version back in (denoted as dynamic_hash[3]):

```
template <typename case_t>
[...] dynamic_hash(const char* text, const char* const separator = 0, const char* const end
= 0, size_t h = 0)
```

This function, as is, can generate an ambiguous call. dynamic_hash(const char*) matches either dynamic_hash[2] (with iterator_t = const char*) or dynamic_hash[3]. The error depends on both functions being templates. Because case_t: had dynamic_hash[3] was a classic function, it would have been picked with higher priority.

To avoid the problem, remove the default arguments to separator and end.

7.3.5. Algorithm I/O

You can let dynamic_hash return a pair that contains the updated iterator position and the hash value.

Often the user will need to store the result just to split it:

```
std:pair<size_t, const char*> p = dynamic_hash(text);
text = p.second;
switch (p.first)
{
   //...
}
```

This can be verbose, especially if the iterator has a long type.[9]

C++11 gave a new meaning to the keyword auto exactly for this purpose:

```
uto p = dynamic_hash(text);
```

But observe that auto cannot refer to a part of an object. The following line is illegal:

```
td::pair<auto, const char*> p = dynamic_hash(text);
```

You could take an iterator by reference and update it, but this is not a fair solution, as it forces the caller duplicate the iterator if you want to save the original value.

Instead, you modify the return type. It will be an object conceptually similar to a pair, with the option to erwrite a reference with the result:

```
emplate <typename iterator_t>
ruct dynamic_hash_result

  size_t value;
  iterator_t end;

  dynamic_hash_result(const size_t v, const iterator_t i)
     : value(v), end(i)
  {
  }

  dynamic_hash_result& operator>>(iterator_t& i)
  {
     i = end;
     return *this;
  }
```

You change the return statement in the dynamic_hash functions accordingly (namely, replace d::make_pair(...) with dynamic_hash_result(...)).

The final function call is indeed compact. It updates text and returns the hash at the same time. ditionally, the .value suffix reminds you of static_hash<>::value. Of course, more variations are ssible.[10]

```
tch ((dynamic_hash(text) >> text).value)

case static_hash<'a','b','c'>::value:
//...
```

---

problem actually falls under the opaque type principle. If the return type of a function is "complex," you should er publish a convenient typedef to the users or allow them to use the object by ignoring its type (refer to Chapter 9 nore details).

follows from the opaque type principle, it's not necessary to document what the exact return type is, just state that rks like a std::pair with an extra operator>>. In principle, it would be reasonable to add a conversion operator dynamic_hash_result to std::pair<size_t,iterator_t>.

7.3.6. Mimesis Interface

Mimesis objects are lightweight and conceptually similar to functors, but their expressivity is close to a scalar. Since they are indeed instantiated, let's investigate the possibility of combining them with operators:

```
size_t h = dynamic_hash<case_insensitive>(text,
           stop_at<char, ';'>() || stop_at<char, ','>()).value;
```

This is a good task for a static interface[11]:

```
template <typename static_type>
class hash_end_type
{
public:
   const static_type& true_this() const
   {
      return static_cast<const static_type&>(*this);
   }

   template <typename iterator_t>
   inline bool operator!=(const iterator_t i) const
   {
      return true_this() != i;
   }
};

// note the CRTP

template <bool (*funct)(const char), bool NEGATE>
struct apply_f : public hash_end_type< apply_f<funct, NEGATE> >
{
   template <typename iterator_t>
   inline bool operator!=(const iterator_t i) const
   {
      return funct(*i) ^ NEGATE;
   }
};


// note again the CRTP
template <typename char_t, char_t CLOSE_TAG>
struct stop_at : public hash_end_type< stop_at<char_t, CLOSE_TAG> >
{
   template <typename iterator_t>
   inline bool operator!=(const iterator_t i) const
   {
      return (*i != CLOSE_TAG);
   }
};
```

[11]Since there's a single function in the class, this example does not derive from `static_interface` but replicates the co

Having all objects inherit the same interface, you can define "combo type" and logic operators:

```
truct logic_AND {};
truct logic_OR {};

emplate <typename T1, typename T2, typename LOGICAL_OP>
lass hash_end_type_combo
 public hash_end_type< hash_end_type_combo<T1, T2, LOGICAL_OP> >

  T1 t1_;
  T2 t2_;

blic:
  hash_end_type_combo(const T1& t1, const T2& t2)
  : t1_(t1), t2_(t2)
  {
  }

  template <typename iterator_t>
  inline bool operator!=(const iterator_t i) const
  {
     return combine(i, LOGICAL_OP());
  }

ivate:
  template <typename iterator_t>
     bool combine(const iterator_t i, logic_AND) const
  {
     return (t1_ != i) && (t2_ != i);
  }

  template <typename iterator_t>
  bool combine(const iterator_t i, logic_OR) const
  {
     return (t1_ != i) || (t2_ != i);
  }

plate <typename K1, typename K2>
ine hash_end_type_combo<K1, K2, logic_AND>
perator&& (const hash_end_type<K1>& k1, const hash_end_type<K2>& k2)

eturn hash_end_type_combo<K1, K2, logic_AND>(k1.true_this(), k2.true_this());

plate <typename K1, typename K2>
ine hash_end_type_combo<K1, K2, logic_OR>
perator|| (const hash_end_type<K1>& k1, const hash_end_type<K2>& k2)

eturn hash_end_type_combo<K1, K2, logic_OR>(k1.true_this(), k2.true_this());
```

Note the counterintuitive use of the operation tag. You may be tempted to replace logic_AND with an "active tag," such as std::logical_and<bool>, drop combine entirely, and just use the tag as a function call to produce the result:

```
template <typename iterator_t>
inline bool operator!=(const iterator_t i) const
{
   return LOGICAL_OP()(t1_ != i, t2_ != i);
}
```

This is *incorrect*, as it would blow short-circuit (when you express, say, A && B as F(A,B), all the arguments must be evaluated before calling F).

```
size_t h = dynamic_hash<case_insensitive>(text,
      stop_at<char,';'>() || stop_at<char,','>() || stop_at<char,0>()).value;
```

Note also that the check for null char is removed in stop_at. It now has to be added explicitly, but it's performed only once.

This syntax is an example of a *lambda expression*, which is the main topic of Section 9.2.

7.4. Nth Minimum

This section gives a step-by-step example of a simple recursive compile-time function that involves a data structure.

You write a container called nth_min<T, N>. An instance of this container receives values of type T, one at a time,[12] via an insert member function, and it can be asked for the smallest N elements met so far.

For a reason to be discussed later, let's impose the extra requirement that the container should not allocate its workspace from dynamic memory.

```
template <typename scalar_t, size_t N>
class nth_min
{
   scalar_t data_[N];

public:
   void insert(const scalar_t& x)
   {
      update(data_, x);
   }

   const scalar_t& operator[](const size_t i) const
   {
      return data_[i];
   }
};
```

[12]This is an *online* problem. In *offline* problems, all the input values are given at the same time. There's a data structure by David Eppstein (see http://www.ics.uci.edu/~eppstein/pubs/kbest.html) that solves the online problem using memory proportional to N and exhibits amortized constant-time operations. This example focuses on how to improve a naive implementation, not on creating an efficient algorithm.

The following paragraphs produce a suitable update function.[13]

```
emplate <typename scalar_t, int N>
nline void update(scalar_t (&data)[N], const scalar_t& x)

 // now N is known, start iterations here
```

First, you need to visualize the algorithm in recursive form. Assume as the induction hypothesis that ata_ contains the N smallest values met so far, in ascending order.

```
if (x ≥ data_[N-1])
      // x is not in the N minima
      discard x and return;
Else
      // here x < data_[N-1], so
      // data_[N-1] will be replaced either by x or by data_[N-2]
      if (x ≥ data_[N-2])
            data_[N-1] = x and return;
      Else
            data_[N-1] = data_[N-2];
            if (x ≥ data_[N-3])
                  data_[N-2] = x and return;
            Else
                  data_[N-2] = data_[N-3];
                  ...
```

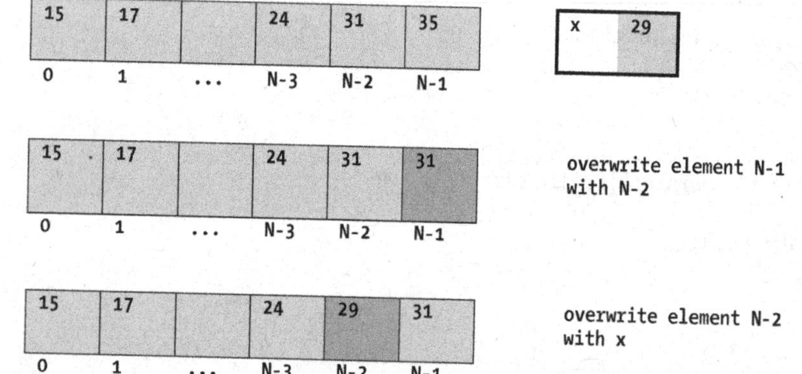

re, update and its auxiliary subroutines are global functions. This just makes the illustration easier, because it allows to focus on one feature at a time. You can safely declare all these functions as private static members of the container.

Now observe that "discard x" is equivalent to "write x in the non-existent position N". You factor out the write operation using a custom selector:

```
template <int N>
struct nth
{
};

template <typename scalar_t, int N, int SIZE>
void write(scalar_t (&data)[SIZE], const scalar_t& x, nth<N>)
{
   data[N] = x;
}

template <typename scalar_t, int SIZE>
void write(scalar_t (&data)[SIZE], const scalar_t& x, nth<SIZE>)
{
}
```

The second overload uses the dimension of the array. So `write(data,x,nth<I>())` actually means "write x in the Ith position of array data, if possible; otherwise, do nothing".

This small abstraction permits you to extend the same recursive pattern to the whole algorithm:

```
if (x ≥ data_[N-1])
        // x is not in the N minima
        data_[N] = x and return;
else
        if (x ≥ data_[N-2])
                data_[N-1] = x and return;
        else
        ...
```

```
template <typename scalar_t, int N, int SIZE>
void iterate(scalar_t (&data)[SIZE], const scalar_t& x, nth<N>)
{
   if (x < data[N])
   {
      data[N] = data[N-1];
      iterate(data, x, nth<N-1>());
   }
   else
   {
      write(data, x, nth<N+1>());        // write x at position N+1
   }
}
```

Next, you have to write an iteration terminator, and you can begin identifying values of template arameters that make the rest of the code meaningless. When `N==0`, `data[N-1]` is for sure not well-formed, o you specialize/overload the case where `N` is `0`. In fact, if you have to track down only the smallest element f the sequence, there's no shift involved:

```
emplate <typename scalar_t, int SIZE>
oid iterate(scalar_t (&data)[SIZE], const scalar_t& x, nth<0>)

  // here N=0, after this point, stop iterations
  // if x is less than minimum, keep x, else discard it

  if (x < data[0])
     data[0] = x;
  else
     write(data, x, nth<1>());
```

The else branch cannot be omitted, but if `SIZE` is 1, the optimizing compiler will wipe it out. Finally, the recursion starts backwards on the last element of the array, so you pass `N-1`:

```
mplate <typename scalar_t, int N>
id update(scalar_t (&data)[N], const scalar_t& x)

 iterate(data, x, nth<N-1>());
```

What's not elegant in this implementation is that `iterate<0>` contains duplicated code from `erate<N>`. The most elegant solution would end with an empty function.

Another generalization is needed. All `write` operations involve either a shift `data[K] = data[K-1]` or insertion `data[K] = x`, respecting array bounds. Can a single function template represent both?

Yes, if you are able to identify `x` with an element of data and specify only the index of the element to k:

```
nplate <typename scalar_t, int N, int SIZE, int J>
.d write(scalar_t (&data)[SIZE], const scalar_t& x, nth<N>, nth<J>)

data[N] = data[J];


plate <typename scalar_t, int SIZE, int J>
d write(scalar_t (&data)[SIZE], const scalar_t& x, nth<SIZE>, nth<J>)
```

If you compare the instructions `data[K] = data[K-1]` and `data[0] = x` from the implementation, you that `x` is naturally identified with `data[-1]`.

So you add two more specializations:

```
template <typename scalar_t, int N, int SIZE>
void write(scalar_t (&data)[SIZE], const scalar_t& x, nth<N>, nth<-1>)
{
   data[N] = x;
}

template <typename scalar_t, int SIZE>
void write(scalar_t (&data)[SIZE], const scalar_t& x, nth<SIZE>, nth<-1>)
{
}
```

To sum up, `write(data, x, N, J)` is a complicated way to say `data[N] = data[J]`; `N` and `J` are selectors, not integers. As usual, the function deduces the length of the array, so out-of-bounds accesses become no-ops.

```
template <typename scalar_t, int N, int SIZE>
void iterate(scalar_t (&data)[SIZE], const scalar_t& x, nth<N>)
{
   if (x < data[N])
   {
      write(data, x, nth<N>(), nth<N-1>());
      iterate(data, x, nth<N-1>());
   }
   else
   {
      write(data, x, nth<N+1>(), nth<-1>());    // line #1
   }
}

template <typename scalar_t, int SIZE>
void iterate(scalar_t (&data)[SIZE], const scalar_t& x, nth<-1>)
{
}
```

When `N=0` in the code, `write` translates to `data[0] = x`, as required, and iteration -1 is empty.

Note that you pay the price of generality in line 1, which is rather unclear at first sight, since you have explicitly use `nth<-1>` to access `x`.

If `N` is large, the fastest algorithm would possibly store objects in a large chunk of memory and sort them when necessary, doing all the work at runtime. In the worst case, if `K` is the number of items insertec execution time is proportional to `K.N` for the static version, but for small values of `N` and simple POD types (that is, when `operator<` and assignment do not have significant overhead), the static version will usually perform faster, due to its compactness and absence of hidden constants.[14]

[14]It seems that this kind of "greedy compact style" for small values of `N` gets most benefit from an aggressive optimiz compiler. A rudimentary stress test with 10.000.000 insertions and `N<32` showed a very large runtime difference (30–40%) between a "normal" and an "extreme" release build. Greedy algorithms and compact code take advantage technological factors, such as processor caches.

Finally, you can replace the write function call, whose hidden meaning is an assignment, with a real ssignment. Just use a proxy:

```
truct null_reference

  template <typename scalar_t>
  null_reference& operator= (const scalar_t&)
  {
     return *this;
  }


mplate <int K>
ruct nth

 template <typename scalar_t, int SIZE>
 static scalar_t& element(scalar_t (&data)[SIZE], const scalar_t& x)
 {
    return data[K];
 }

 template <typename scalar_t>
 static null_reference element(scalar_t (&data)[K], const scalar_t& x)
 {
    return null_reference();
 }


nplate <>
ruct nth<0>

template <typename scalar_t, int SIZE>
static scalar_t& element(scalar_t (&data)[SIZE], const scalar_t& x)
{
   return data[0];
}


plate <>
uct nth<-1>

template <typename scalar_t, int SIZE>
static const scalar_t& element(scalar_t (&data)[SIZE], const scalar_t& x)
{
   return x;
}
```

```
struct nth_min
{
   template <typename scalar_t, int SIZE>
   static void update(scalar_t (&data)[SIZE], const scalar_t& x)
   {
      iterate(data, x, nth<SIZE-1>());
   }

private:
   template <typename scalar_t, int N, int SIZE>
   static void iterate(scalar_t (&data)[SIZE], const scalar_t& x, nth<N>)
   {
      if (x < data[N])
      {
         nth<N>::element(data, x) = nth<N-1>::element(data, x);
         iterate(data, x, nth<N-1>());
      }
      else
      {
         nth<N+1>::element(data, x) = nth<-1>::element(data, x);
      }
   }

   template <typename scalar_t, int SIZE>
   static void iterate(scalar_t (&data)[SIZE], const scalar_t& x, nth<-1>)
   {
   }
};
```

7.5. The Template Factory Pattern

Templates are good at making compile-time decisions, but all programs need to take runtime decisions.

The *factory pattern* solves the runtime decision problem via polymorphism. An isolated function, call the *factory*, embeds all the logic and returns a pointer to a dynamically-created object, which drives the program flow with its virtual member function calls:

```
class abstract_task
{
   public:
      virtual void do_it() = 0;

      virtual ~abstract_task()
      {
      }
};
```

```
lass first_task : public abstract_task

  public:
     first_task(/* parameters */)
     {
        // ...
     }

     virtual void do_it()
     {
        // ...
     }
;

um task_type

 FIRST_TASK, SECOND_TASK, THIRD_TASK


stract_task* factory(task_type t)

 switch (t)
 {
    case FIRST_TASK:   return new first_task(...);
    case SECOND_TASK:  return new second_task(...);
    case THIRD_TASK:   return new third_task(...);
    default:           return 0;
 }


t main()

 task_type t = ask_user();
 abstract_task* a = factory(t);
 a->do_it();

 delete a;
 return 0;
```

Note that the only switch...case construct, that is, the link between the user choice and the program v, is hidden inside the factory.

As expected, templates have no exact equivalent, but the following pattern is definitely similar:

```
plate <typename TASK_T>
d do_the_work(TASK_T task)

task.loadParameters(...);
task.run();
task.writeResult(...);
```

```
enum task_type
{
   FIRST_TASK, SECOND_TASK, THIRD_TASK
};

void factory(task_type t)
{
   first_task t1;
   second_task t2;
   third_task t3;

   switch (t)
   {
      case FIRST_TASK:   do_the_work(t1); break;
      case SECOND_TASK:  do_the_work(t2); break;
      case THIRD_TASK:   do_the_work(t3); break;
      default:           throw some_exception();
   }
}
```

The function do_the_work is an example of *static polymorphism*. The usage of an object determines its interface and vice versa. Every static type for which the syntax is valid is automatically usable.

This approach offers the advantage of a unified workflow. There's a single function to debug and maintain, Obviously, having three overloads of do_the_work would minimize this benefit.

Here's another example—a function that takes an array and computes either the sum or the product of all elements.

```
enum compute_type { SUM, MULTIPLY };

double do_the_work(compute_type t, const double* data, size_t length)
{
   switch (t)
   {
   case SUM:
     return std::accumulate(data,data+length,0.0);

   case MULTIPLY:
     return std::accumulate(data,data+length,1.0,std::multiplies<double>());

   default:
     throw some_exception();
   }
}
```

You want to rework the code so that it takes numbers from a given text file and performs the requested operation on all elements, and all computations should be performed with a user-supplied precision.

This requires a *multi-layer template factory*. Roughly speaking, you have N function templates. The Kth unction has N-K arguments and K template parameters and it uses a switch block to branch execution to ne of the possible (K+1)th functions.

```
num result_type { SUM, MULTIPLY };
num data_type { FLOAT, DOUBLE };

emplate <typename T>
 factory_LAYER3(result_type t, const std::vector<T>& data)

 switch (t)
 {
 case SUM:
   return std::accumulate(data.begin(),data.end(),T(0));

case MULTIPLY:
  return std::accumulate(data.begin(),data.end(),T(1),std::multiplies<T>());

default:
  throw some_exception();
}


mplate <typename T>
factory_LAYER2(result_type t, std::istream& i)

 std::vector<T> data;
 std::copy(std::istream_iterator<T>(i), std::istream_iterator<T>(),
           std::back_inserter(data));
 return factory_LAYER3(t, data);


ble ML_factory(result_type t, data_type d, const char* filename)

std::ifstream i(filename);

switch (d)
{
   case FLOAT:
      return factory_LAYER2<float>(t, i);
   case DOUBLE:
      return factory_LAYER2<double>(t, i);
   default:
      throw some_exception();
}
```

The hardest design problem in template factories is usually *the type of the result*. Here the code silently exploits the fact that all functions return a result convertible to double.

7.6. Automatic Enumeration of Types

It's possible to exploit the `__LINE__` macro to create an easily extensible collection of types that can be accessed as an enumeration.

Consider the following prototype—you can trivially map an integer index into a selector:

```
template <int N>
struct single_value : selector<false>
{
};

template <>
struct single_value<7> : selector<true>        // user supplied case #1
{
};

template <>
struct single_value<13> : selector<true>       // user supplied case #2
{
};

// ...

template <>
struct single_value<128>          // terminator, equivalent to max size;
{                                 // it will be useful shortly
};
```

With greater generality we can write:

```
template <>
struct single_value<7> : MyType1          // user supplied case #1
{
};

template <>
struct single_value<13> : MyType2         // user supplied case #2
{
};
```

In fact, `single_value` is a metafunction that maps a range of integers, say [0...127] for simplicity, on types, which always returns `selector<false>`, except 7 → `MyType1` and 13 → `MyType2`.

Assume again that `MyType` is just `selector<true>`.

Now you will see a template class, `enum_hunter`, that maps *consecutive indices* to the user-supplied cases, so that `enum_hunter<1>` is[15] `single_value<7>`, `enum_hunter<2>` is `single_value<13>`, and so on.

[15]*is* means *derives from*.

The key idea is as follows:

- Since a default implementation is given, any `single_value<N>` exists.
- User-supplied specializations have their member `::value == true`.
- `enum_hunter<N>` will inspect all `single_value<J>`, starting at `J==0`, until it finds the Nth user-supplied value.
- `enum_hunter<N>` is actually `enum_hunter<N,0>`.
- `enum_hunter<N,J>` inspects `single_value<J>::value`. If it's false, it inherits from `enum_hunter<N,J+1>`. Otherwise, it inherits from `enum_hunter<N-1,J+1>` (except when `N-1` would be zero, where you pick `<0,J>` because the final result is precisely `single_value<J>`).
- When `N` reaches `0`, you are done. You met exactly `N` user-supplied values. If the initial `N` is too large, `J` will reach the terminator before `N` drops to `0`, and since the terminator is an empty class, the compiler will complain.

All this yields a surprisingly compact implementation (for the moment, ignore the fact that everything is rd-coded):

```
mplate <int N, int J=0>
ruct enum_hunter
enum_hunter<N-single_value<J>::value, J+1-(N == single_value<J>::value)>



nplate <int J>
ruct enum_hunter<0, J> : single_value<J>



nplate <>
uct enum_hunter<0, 0> : single_value<0>
```

This skeleton technique can lead to a couple of different applications—the simplest is to build a sparse npile-time *array* between arbitrary (but small) integers and types:

```
fine MXT_ADD_ENUMERATION(N, TYPE)  \
template <> struct single_value<N> : public TYPE, selector<true> {}

uct Mapped1

tatic double do_it() { return 3.14; }


uct Mapped2

atic double do_it() { return 6.28; }
```

```
MXT_ADD_ENUMERATION(7, Mapped1);
MXT_ADD_ENUMERATION(13, Mapped2);

double xx1 = enum_hunter<1>::do_it();  // == 3.14
double xx2 = enum_hunter<2>::do_it();  // == 6.28
```

Polishing up the macros, you parameterize the name of enum_hunter as ENUM and rename single_value as ENUM##_case.

```
#define MXT_BEGIN_ENUMERATION(ENUM)                                        \
                                                                           \
template <int N> struct ENUM##_case : static_value<int, 0> {};             \
                                                                           \
template <int N, int J=0> struct ENUM                                      \
: ENUM<N-ENUM##_case<J>::value, J+1-(N == ENUM##_case<J>::value)> {};      \
                                                                           \
template <int N> struct ENUM<0, N> : ENUM##_case<N> {};                    \
                                                                           \
template <> struct ENUM<0, 0> : ENUM##_case<0> {}

struct empty_class {};

#define MXT_END_ENUMERATION(ENUM, K) \
 template <> struct ENUM##_case<K> : {}

// we explicitly add a member "value" without using derivation.
// this allows TYPE itself to be selector<true>

#define MXT_ADD_ENUMERATION(ENUM, TYPE, K)      \
 template <> struct ENUM##_case<K> : TYPE       \
 { static const int value = 1; }
```

When using the macros, every directive in the sequence between begin/end will be added automatically using line numbers as a progressive index. Two directives on the same line won't compile, since you cannot specialize a class template twice.

```
MXT_BEGIN_ENUMERATION(MyTypeEnum);

MXT_ADD_ENUMERATION(MyTypeEnum, Mapped1, 7);   // this gets index 1
MXT_ADD_ENUMERATION(MyTypeEnum, Mapped2, 13);  // this gets index 2

MXT_END_ENUMERATION(MyTypeEnum, 128);
```

So MyTypeEnum<1> is Mapped1, MyTypeEnum<2> is Mapped2, but MyTypeEnum_case<...> is still available to the code. Observe that 7 and 13 in the example may not be needed, if you plan to use the enumeration via contiguous indices. However, you need to provide unique and ascending values. So you can just pass __LINE__ as parameter K.

Another application of type enumeration is that, unlike classic enums, several headers can add their own values. So you can "distribute" a function between different files.

Suppose you want to gather the list of files included in a cpp and you don't want each header to access a lobal variable:

```
include "H1.hpp"
include "H2.hpp"
include "H3.hpp"

nt main(int argc, const char* argv[])

  std::vector<std::string> global_list;
  // here initialize global_list
```

A rough solution could be as follows:

```
' flag_init.hpp

lefine MXT_INIT_LIST

 equivalent to BEGIN_ENUMERATION
mplate <int N> struct flag_init

 static void run(std::vector<std::string>& v)
 {
 }


mplate <int N>
id run_flag_init(std::vector<std::string>& v, static_value<int, N>)

 flag_init<N>::run(v);
 run_flag_init(v, static_value<int, N+1>());


 magic constant, terminator
.ine void run_flag_init(std::vector<std::string>& v, static_value<int, 64>)



 H1.hpp

def MXT_INIT_LIST

equivalent to ADD_ENUMERATION
pick a random number < 64

plate < > struct flag_init<7>

static void run(std::vector<std::string>& v)
{
   v.push_back("hello, I am " __FILE__);
}
```

```
#endif

// the rest of H1.hpp, then write similarly H2 and H3

// main.cpp

#include "flag_init.hpp"

#include "H1.hpp"
#include "H2.hpp"
#include "H3.hpp"

int main(int argc, const char* argv[])
{
   std::vector<std::string> global_list_of_flags;
   run_flag_init(global_list_of_flags);
}
```

7.7. If-Less Code

Sometimes program logic can be embedded in "smart objects" that know what to do, thus eliminating the need for `if`/`switch` blocks.

7.7.1. Smart Constants

As an example, suppose you need to code a suitable `print` function for a date class:

```
class date
{
   public:
      int day() const;
      int month() const;
      int year() const;
};

enum dateformat_t
{
   YYYYMMDD,
   YYMMDD,
   DDMMYYYY,
   // many more...
};

void print(date d, dateformat_t f)
{
   switch (f)
   {
      case YYYYMMDD:
         // Very verbose...
   }
}
```

Instead, you can write branch-free code. As usual, TMP techniques take advantage of storing nformation in places where it's not evident that meaningful data can be stored!

Suppose the format constants like YYYYMMDD are actually numbers with six decimal digits in the form f1 e1 f2 e2 f3 e3], where fi is the index of the "date field to print" (say, 0=year, 1=month and 2=day) nd ei is the width as a number of digits.

For example, 041222 would be "year with four digits (04), month with two digits (12), and day with two igits (22)," or simply YYYY-MM-DD. This would enable you to write:

```
onst int pow10[] = { 1, 10, 100, 1000, 10000, ... };
onst int data[3] = { d.year(), d.month(), d.day() };
onst char* sep[] = { "-", "-", "" );

or (int i=0; i<3; ++i)
 std::cout << std::setw(e[i]) << (data[f[i]] % pow10[e[i]]) << sep[i];
```

Generating such constants is easy:

```
um { Y, M, D };

mplate <unsigned F, unsigned W = 2>
ruct datefield : static_value<unsigned, F*10 + (W % 10)>



mplate <typename T1, typename T2 = void, typename T3 = void>
ruct dateformat

 static const unsigned pow10 = 100 * dateformat<T2,T3>::pow10;
 static const unsigned value = pow10 * T1::value + dateformat<T2,T3>::value;


nplate < >
ruct dateformat<void, void, void>

 static const unsigned value = 0;
 static const unsigned pow10 = 1;


m

YYYYMMDD = dateformat<datefield<Y,4>, datefield<M>, datefield<D> >::value,
  DDMMYY = dateformat<datefield<D>, datefield<M>, datefield<Y> >::value,
  YYYYMM = dateformat<datefield<Y,4>, datefield<M> >::value,

// ...
```

For simplicity, this implementation uses rotation on three parameters only.[16]

The print function follows:

```
void print(date d, dateformat_t f)
{
   const unsigned pow10[] = { 1, 10, 100, 1000, 10000, ... };
   const int data[3] = { d.year(), d.month(), d.day() };

   for (unsigned int fc = f; fc != 0; fc /= 100)
   {
      unsigned w = fc % 10;
      unsigned j = (fc % 100) / 10;

      std::cout << std::setw(w) << (data[j] % pow10[w]);
   }
}
```

7.7.2. Converting Enum to String

Similarly to what you did in the previous paragraph, you can encode a short string inside the value of an enumeration. The C++ standard guarantees that an enum is represented by a large unsigned integer, if any of the values are large. In practice, you can assume the enum will be a 64-bit integer. Since $2^{64} > 40^{12}$, you can store a string of length 12 as an integer in base 40, where A=1, B=2, and so on.

First you define the "alphabet":

```
template <char C> struct char2int;
template <size_t N> struct int2char;

#define C2I(C, I)  \
  template <> struct char2int<C> { static const size_t value = I; }

#define I2C(C, I)  \
  template <> struct int2char<I> { static const char value = C; }

#define TRANSLATE1(C1, N) \
  C2I(C1, N); I2C(C1, N)

#define TRANSLATE2(C1, C2, N) \
  C2I(C1, N); C2I(C2, N); I2C(C1, N)

TRANSLATE2('a', 'A', 1); // convert both 'A' and 'a' to 1, and 1 to 'a'
TRANSLATE2('b', 'B', 2);
// ...
TRANSLATE2('z', 'Z', 26);
```

[16] So you cannot generate patterns like YYYYMMDDYY.

```
RANSLATE1('0', 27);
RANSLATE1('1', 28);
/ ...
RANSLATE1('9', 36);
RANSLATE1('_', 37);

tatic const size_t SSTRING_BASE = 40;

emplate <size_t N, bool TEST = (N<SSTRING_BASE)>
truct verify_num

tatic const size_t value = N;
;

emplate <size_t N>
ruct verify_num<N, false>

 this will not compile if a number >= 40 is used by mistake


mplate <char C1, char C2 = 0, ..., char C12 = 0>
ruct static_string

static const size_t aux
              = verify_num< char2int<C1>::value >::value;
static const size_t value
              = aux + static_string<C2,...,C12>::value * SSTRING_BASE;


nplate <>
ruct static_string<0>

static const size_t value = 0;



plate <size_t VALUE>
::string unpack(static_value<size_t, VALUE>)

td::string result(1, char(int2char<VALUE % SSTRING_BASE>::value));
eturn result + unpack(static_value<size_t, VALUE/SSTRING_BASE>());


::string unpack(static_value<size_t, 0>)

td::string result;
eturn result;
```

```
#define MXT_ENUM_DECODER(TYPE)                    \
template <TYPE VALUE>                             \
std::string decode()                              \
{ return unpack(static_value<size_t, VALUE>()); }
```

Note that you separate the generic code from the "implementation". Now you define an enum:

```
enum MyEnum
{
  first = static_string<'f','i','r','s','t'>::value,
  verylong = static_string<'v','e','r','y','l','o','n','g'>::value
};

MXT_ENUM_DECODER(MyEnum); // Write this to get a "decode" function

std::cout << decode<first>(); // prints "first"
```

For simplicity, this example implements static decoding (that is, the decoded enum value is known at compile time). However, the same operation can be performed at runtime.[17]

In general this technique is effective when the actual value of the enum is not meaningful to the program.

7.7.3. Self-Modifying Function Tables

Consider a trivial example of a circular container, where elements are "pushed back" (at the moment, pretend anything is public):

```
template <typename T, size_t N>
struct circular_array
{
   T data_[N];
   size_t pos_;

   circular_array()
      : data_(), pos_(0)
   {
   }

   void push_back(const T& x)
   {
      data_[pos_] = x;
      if (++pos_ == N)
         pos_ = 0;
   }
};
```

You can convert push_back into a sort of self-modifying function, similar to trampolines (see Section 5.3. You will use a function pointer initialized with a suitable function template.

---

[17]Hint: Use a const array of char of length SSTRING_BASE and initialize it with { 0, int2char<1>::value, int2char<2>::value, ... }.

```
emplate <typename T, size_t N>
truct circular_array

  T data_[N];

  typedef void (*push_back_t) (circular_array<T, N>& a, const T& x);
  push_back_t pb_;

  template <size_t K>
  struct update_element_at
  {
     static void apply(circular_array<T, N>& a, const T& x)
     {
        a.data_[K] = x;
        a.pb_ = &update_element_at<(K+1) % N>::apply;
     }
  };

  circular_array()
     : data_(), pb_(&update_element_at<0>::apply)
  {
  }

  void push_back(const T& x)
  {
     pb_(*this, x);
  }
```

The key point of this pattern is that you have a collection of functions where all elements know the ion that follows, and so they can update a pointer with this information.

Updating the function pointer is not mandatory. A function may select itself as the next candidate. ppose you change the container policy so as to keep the first N-1 elements and then constantly overwrite last:

```
((K+1)<N)
a.pb_ = &update_element_at<K+1>::apply;
```

Self-modifying functions are usually elegant, but slightly less efficient than a classic switch, mostly :ause of technology factors such as caches or program flow predictors.

Applications include data structures whose behavior during initialization is different (a "warm-up" se) until a minimum number of elements have been inserted.

■ **Note** *ICF*, identical code folding, is a widespread optimization technique applied by compilers. Put simply, the linker will try to find "duplicate functions" and generate binary code only once. For example, `vector<int*>` and `vector<double*>` will probably generate identical code, so they can be merged.

While this reduces the size of the binary, it has the side effect that equality of function pointers may not work as expected. If `F` and `G` are identical (suppose they have an empty body), it's possible that `F != G` in a debug build and `F == G` in an ICF-optimized build.

Be careful when writing a self-modifying function that relies on equality/inequality of function pointers (obviously, comparisons with `NULL` pointers work fine).

CHAPTER 8

Functors

This chapter focuses on several techniques that help when writing (or when not writing) functors.

Most STL algorithms require compile-time function objects and this usually requires some manual coding:

```
struct Person
{
   unsigned int age;
   std::string home_address;

   double salary() const;
};

std::vector<Person> data;
std::sort(data.begin(), data.end(), /* by age */ );
std::partition(data.begin(), data.end(), /* by salary */ );
```

If you can modify Person, sometimes an elegant and quick solution is to write a public static member function and a member functor. This simultaneously attains the maximum efficiency and control, as your code has access to private members:

```
struct Person
{
private:
   unsigned int age;

public:
   static bool less_by_age(const Person& a, const Person& b)
   {
      return a.age < b.age;
   }

   struct BY_AGE
   {
      bool operator()(const Person& a, const Person& b) const
      {
         return Person::less_by_age(a, b);
      }
   };
};
```

```
td::vector<Person> data;
td::sort(data.begin(), data.end(), Person::less_by_age); // suboptimal
td::sort(data.begin(), data.end(), Person::BY_AGE());    // good
```

A static member function has access to private data. However it will be much harder for the compiler to nline the comparison, so a functor is usually better.

You can even factor out some code that converts the former to the latter:

```
emplate <typename T, bool (*LESS)(const T&, const T&)>
truct less_compare_t

  typedef T first_argument_type;
  typedef T second_argument_type;
  typedef bool result_type;

  bool operator()(const T& x, const T& y) const
  {
     return LESS(x, y);
  }


ruct Person

ivate:
 unsigned int age;

blic:
 static bool less_by_age(const Person& a, const Person& b)
 {
    return a.age < b.age;
 }

 typedef less_compare_t<Person, Person::less_by_age> BY_AGE;
```

The name of the function/functor is chosen to make the expression *clear at the point of instantiation*, : at the point of definition.

Note that non-generic functors (whose arguments have a fixed type) are usually members of the class.

It's generally fair to assume that a functor can be freely copied and passed by value. If a functor needs ny data members, you had better collect them in a separate structure and store only a reference. The er of the functor will be responsible for keeping the extra information alive:

```
uct information_needed_to_sort_elements

// ...


ss my_less

const information_needed_to_sort_elements& ref_;
```

```
public:

   explicit functor(const information_needed_to_sort_elements& ref)
   : ref_(ref)
   {
   }

   bool operator()(const Person& p1, const Person& P2) const
   { ... }
};

int main()
{
   information_needed_to_sort_elements i;
   // build a suitable container data...
   std::sort(data.begin(), data.end(), my_less(i));
}
```

STL algorithms do not provide any guarantee concerning the number of copies of function objects.

Another interesting feature is that a functor static type is irrelevant, because it's always deduced. If the functor is returned from a function, it will be used immediately (see Section 4.3.4); if it's passed to a functio template, it will bind to an argument that accepts anything.

This allows clients to generate anonymous instances of complex function objects at the call site:

```
i = std::find_if(begin, end, std::bind2nd(std::less<double>(), 3.14));

// the exact type of the functor is irrelevant
// since find_if has an argument that binds to anything:

// template <typename I, typename F>
// I find_if(I begin, I end, F func)
```

■ **Note** C++0x includes support for creation of lambda objects.

It is a new syntax that can pass anonymous "pieces of code" in curly brackets as if they were functors. This mitigates the problem of name pollution. In other words, it's not necessary to give a name to an entity that is reused.

See Section 12.4 for more details.

8.1. Strong and Weak Functors

ome functors are strongly typed. This means that the user fixes the argument of the function call when etermining the template arguments. All standard functionals are strongly typed.

```
emplate <typename T>
truct less

  bool operator()(const T& lhs, const T& rhs) const
  {
     return lhs < rhs;
  }
;

:d::sort(data.begin(), data.end(), less<Person>());
```

Alternatively, you can have a weak functor that accepts arguments with more freedom[1]:

```
:ruct weak_less

 template <typename T>
 bool operator()(const T& lhs, const T& rhs) const
 {
    return lhs < rhs;
 }

d::sort(data.begin(), data.end(), weak_less());
```

A strongly typed functor statically blocks all types that are incompatible with T, but since this is limited the interface, it can actually share the implementation with a weak functor:

```
nplate <typename T>
:uct less : private weak_less

bool operator()(const T& lhs, const T& rhs) const
{
   return static_cast<const weak_less&>(*this)(lhs, rhs);
}
```

---

se functors have been voted into C++14 with a slightly different terminology; they are called "transparent". e knowledge of the author, this book was the first place where the idea appeared publicly. For all the details, ttp://www.open-std.org/jtc1/sc22/wg21/docs/papers/2012/n3421.htm.

8.2. Functor Composition Tools

The STL offers facilities to compose functors and values. For example, std::bind2nd turns a binary operation and an operand into a unary function. Often, you'll need tools that perform the reverse.

The prefix by in by age is actually the composition of a binary relation with an accessor. age extracts the age from a person and by compares two ages. Here's a minimal implementation that abstracts this composition concept.

```
template <typename functor_t>
class by_t
{
   functor_t f_;

public:
   by_t(functor_t f)
   : f_(f)
   {}

   template <typename argument_t>
   bool operator()(const argument_t& a, const argument_t& b) const
   {
      return f_(a) < f_(b);
   }
};

template <typename functor_t>
inline by_t<functor_t> by(const functor_t& f)
{
   return f;
}

// see Section 1.1.4

template <typename R, typename A>
inline by_t<R (*)(A)> by(R (*f)(A))
{
   return f;
}

struct age_t
{
   unsigned int operator()(const Person& p) const
   {
      return p.age;
   }

   age_t(int = 0)
   {
   }
};
```

```
tatic const age_t AGE = 0[2];

nt main()

 std::vector<Person> data;
 std::sort(data.begin(), data.end(), by(AGE));
```

by is a functor composition tool. Since it does not impose any requirement on `functor_t`, it will accept ıitable static member functions, which are convenient if `Person::age` is private:

```
:ruct Person

:ivate:
  unsigned int age;

blic:
  static int AGE(const Person& p)
  {
     return p.age;
  }

d::sort(data.begin(), data.end(), by(Person::AGE));      // ok!
```

A functor/accessor may be given powerful *lambda* semantics.

Here is another preview of Section 9.2. In pseudo-intuitive notation, `comparator(A, S)` is a predicate ıt returns `true` on object `O` if `A(O)` is "less" than `S`. "less" is a generic binary predicate.

```
nplate

 typename scalar_t,
 typename accessor_t,
 template <typename T> class less_t

ıss comparator

 scalar_t x_;
 accessor_t a_;

lic:
 comparator(scalar_t x, accessor_t a = accessor_t())
 : x_(x), a_(a)
 {
 }
```

:e most functors are stateless, and so are not affected by initialization problems, global constants can be created in er files.

```
    template <typename argument_t>
    bool operator()(const argument_t& obj) const
    {
        less_t<scalar_t> less_;
        return less_(a_(obj), x_);
    }
};
```

Using a template-template parameter instead of a normal binary predicate saves you from typing scalar_t twice and makes an anonymous instance quite clear to read:

```
comparator<double, SALARY, std::greater>(3.0)
```

Another minor point is the class layout: x_ is declared before a_, because a_ will often be stateless and therefore a small object. x_ might have stronger alignment constraints.

Now you can add operators to the functor and promote it to a lambda predicate[3]:

```
struct age_t
{
  int operator()(const Person& a) const
  {
     return a.age;
  }

  template <typename T>
  comparator<T,age_t,std::less> operator<(const T& x) const
  {
     return comparator<T,age_t,std::less>(x, *this);
  }

  template <typename T>
  comparator<T,age_t,std::equal_to> operator==(const T& x) const
  {
     return comparator<T,age_t,std::equal_to>(x, *this);
  }
};

std::partition(data.begin(), data.end(), Person::AGE < 35);
std::partition(data.begin(), data.end(), Person::AGE == 18);
```

[3]As a rule, for expressiveness, it's best to write a fully-qualified Person::AGE rather than just AGE, so you must assume that there's a static constant of type age_t inside Person. This also allows age_t to be friend of Person. You can also consider Person::AGE() where AGE is either a member typedef for age_t or a static member function that returns a default instance of age_t.

With a little effort, you can add more syntactic tricks to the chaining operator:

```
onst selector<true> INCREASING;
onst selector<false> DECREASING;

emplate <typename T>
ool oriented_less(const T& x, const T& y, selector<true>)

  return x<y;


emplate <typename T>
ool oriented_less(const T& x, const T& y, selector<false>)

  return y<x;

```

oriented_less can flip operator< and simulate operator>.

```
mplate <typename functor_t, bool ASCENDING = true>
ass by_t

 functor_t f_;

blic:
 by_t(functor_t f) : f_(f) {}

 template <typename argument_t>
 bool operator()(const argument_t& a, const argument_t& b) const
 {
    return oriented_less(f_(a), f_(b), selector<ASCENDING>());
 }

 // inversion operators:

 by_t<functor_t, true> operator+() const
 {
    return f_;
 }

 by_t<functor_t, false> operator-() const
 {
    return f_;
 }
```

And finally, there's another by helper function:

```
template <bool DIRECTION, typename functor_t>
by_t<functor_t, DIRECTION> by(selector<DIRECTION>, const functor_t& v)
{
   return by_t<functor_t, DIRECTION>(v);
}
```

All this allows writing:

```
std::sort(data.begin(), data.end(), +by(Person::AGE));
std::sort(data.begin(), data.end(), -by(Person::AGE));
std::sort(data.begin(), data.end(), by(DECREASING, Person::AGE));
```

■ **Note** I chose `operator+` and `operator-` because by deals with numeric properties; the logical inversion of a unary predicate is better expressed with `operator!`

Also, lines #2 and #3 are identical. It's only a matter of style to pick the clearest.

The last improvement to `by_t` is to perform strict type checking in `operator()`.

The function call operator accepts almost anything, so more type checking will trap errors arising from code that compiles merely by chance:

```
std::vector<Animal> data;
std::sort(data.begin(), data.end(), by(Person::AGE));
```

A convenient approach is to exploit cooperation from the functor. If `functor_t` has a member `argument_type` it also will be the argument of a strong `operator()`. Otherwise, you use the weak function call operator.

As usual, you hide the decision in a template parameter and provide two partial specializations. First, some traits:

```
template <typename T>
struct argument_type_of
{
   typedef typename T::argument_type type;
};

template <typename A, typename R>
struct argument_type_of<R (*)(A)>
{
   typedef A type;
};

template <typename A, typename R>
struct argument_type_of<R (*)(const A&)>
{
   typedef A type;
};
```

```
.emplate <typename T>
truct has_argument_type
 selector<[[ true if T::argument_type exists4 ]]>

;

emplate <typename A, typename R>
truct has_argument_type<R (*)(A) >
 selector<true>

;

/ ...
```

The first specialization performs strict type checking.

```
mplate

typename functor_t,
bool ASCENDING = true,
bool STRICT_CHECK = has_argument_type<functor_t>::value

ruct by_t;

mplate <typename functor_t, bool ASCENDING>
ruct by_t<functor_t, ASCENDING, true>

// ...

typedef typename argument_type_of<functor_t>::type argument_type;

// note: strong argument type
bool operator()(const argument_type& a, const argument_type& b) const
{
 return oriented_less(f_(a), f_(b), selector<ASCENDING>());
}


plate <typename functor_t, bool ASCENDING>
uct by_t<functor_t, ASCENDING, false>

/ ...

/ note: weak argument type. This will accept anything
emplate <typename argument_t>
ool operator()(const argument_t& a, const argument_t& b) const

 return oriented_less(f_(a), f_(b), selector<ASCENDING>());
```

ails are described in Section 4.2.1.

To minimize code duplication, you factor out the function call operator in a template base and use a static_cast, as in CRTP:

```
template <typename functor_t, bool ASCENDING = true>
struct by_t;

template <typename functor_t, bool ASCENDING, bool STRICT_CHECK>
struct by_base_t;

template <typename functor_t, bool ASCENDING>
struct by_base_t<functor_t, ASCENDING, true>
{
  const functor_t& f() const
  {
    typedef by_t<functor_t, ASCENDING> real_type;
    return static_cast<const real_type&>(*this).f_;
  }

  typedef typename argument_type_of<functor_t>::type argument_type;

  bool operator()(const argument_type& a, const argument_type& b) const
  {
    return oriented_less(f()(a), f()(b), selector<ASCENDING>());
  }
};

template <typename functor_t, bool ASCENDING>
struct by_base_t<functor_t, ASCENDING, false>
{
  const functor_t& f() const
  {
    typedef by_t<functor_t, ASCENDING> real_type;
    return static_cast<const real_type&>(*this).f_;
  }

  template <typename argument_t>
  bool operator()(const argument_t& a, const argument_t& b) const
  {
    return oriented_less(f()(a), f()(b), selector<ASCENDING>());
  }
};

template <typename functor_t, bool ASCENDING = true>
struct by_t
: by_base_t<functor_t,ASCENDING,has_argument_type<functor_t>::value>
{
    // ...
};
```

3.3. Inner Template Functors

unctor wrappers may be used as interface-leveraging tools.

Syntactically, you take advantage of the fact that inner class templates know template parameters of the uter class.

.3.1. Conversion of Functions to Functors

ssume for simplicity that you have a collection of functions with a similar signature `T f(T, T, ..., T)`, here the number of arguments varies. Suppose further that the list of functions to be executed will be known runtime, so you need a base class with a virtual call whose unique signature could be `(const T*, size_t)`.[5]

Let's look for an automatic way of performing the conversion:

```
emplate <typename T>
truct base

 virtual T eval(const T*, size_t) const = 0;

 virtual ~base() {}
```

Given a function, say `double F(double,double)`, you could embed it in a functor, but you would have deduce T and F simultaneously:

```
mplate <typename T, T (*F)(T,T)>
ruct functor : public base<T>

  // ...
```

Actually, you need T before F, so you can build a class template on T only, and after that an inner nplate class:

```
nplate <typename T>
ruct outer

 template <T (*F)(T,T)>
 struct inner : public base<T>
 {
```

First you identify `outer<T>`, then you build `inner`:

```
plate <typename T>
uct function_call_traits

template <T (*F)()>
struct eval_0 : public base<T>
```

careful reader will notice that the following example does pass the length of the array, even if it is always ignored.

```
{
   virtual T eval(const T* , size_t) const { return F(); }
};

template <T (*F)(T)>
struct eval_1 : public base<T>
{
   virtual T eval(const T* x, size_t) const { return F(x[0]);   }
};

template <T (*F)(T, T)>
struct eval_2 : public base<T>
{
   virtual T eval(const T* x, size_t) const { return F(x[0], x[1]); }
};

// ...

template <T (*F)()>
eval_0<F>* get_ptr() const
{
   return new eval_0<F>;
}

template <T (*F)(T)>
eval_1<F>* get_ptr() const
{
   return new eval_1<F>;
}

template <T (*F)(T, T)>
eval_2<F>* get_ptr() const
{
   return new eval_2<F>;
}

   // ...
};

template <typename T>
inline function_call_traits<T> get_function_call(T (*F)())
{
   return function_call_traits<T>();
}

template <typename T>
inline function_call_traits<T> get_function_call(T (*F)(T))
{
   return function_call_traits<T>();
}
```

```
.emplate <typename T>
nline function_call_traits<T> get_function_call(T (*F)(T, T))

  return function_call_traits<T>();

/ ...

define MXT_FUNCTION_CALL_PTR(F)        get_function_call(F).get_ptr<F>()
```

Note that:

- F is used twice, first as a pointer, then as a template argument.
- The get_ptr functions are not static, bizarre as it may look, this is an example of a traits class that's actually meant to be instantiated (but used anonymously).

```
uble add0()

 return 6.28;

uble add1(double x)

 return x+3.14;

uble add2(double x, double y)

 return x+y;

: main()

 double x[5] = {1,2,3,4,5};

 base<double>* f[3] =
 {
    MXT_FUNCTION_CALL_PTR(add0),
    MXT_FUNCTION_CALL_PTR(add1),
    MXT_FUNCTION_CALL_PTR(add2)
 };

 for (int i=0; i<3; ++i)
    std::cout << f[i]->eval(x, 5);

// normal destruction code has been omitted for brevity
```

The previous example executes add0(), add1(x[0]), and add2(x[0], x[1]) via calls to the
.e interface.

8.3.2. Conversion of Members to Functors

The very same technique seen in the previous section can transform pointers into functors.[6]

In C++, simple structures with no access restrictions are often used to transport small pieces of data. Ideally, you'll want to maintain this simplicity and be able to write code with no overhead:

```
struct Person
{
   unsigned int age;
   double salary() const;
};

std::vector<Person> data;

// warning: pseudo-C++
std::sort(data.begin(), data.end(), by(Person::age));
std::sort(data.begin(), data.end(), by(Person::salary));
```

Because you can use a pointer-to-member as a template argument, it's not too hard to write an auxiliary wrapper that can help. Unfortunately, the instantiation is too verbose to be useful.

```
template <typename from_t, typename to_t, to_t from_t::* POINTER>
struct data_member
{
   const to_t& operator()(const from_t& x) const
   {
      return x.*POINTER;
   }
};

template <typename from_t, typename to_t, to_t (from_t::*POINTER)() const>
struct property_member
{
   to_t operator()(const from_t& x) const
   {
      return (x.*POINTER)();
   }
};

struct TEST
{
   int A;
   int B() const { return -A; }
};

TEST data[3] = {2,1,3};
```

[6]The analogous STL structures instead merely *embed* a pointer in a functor.

```
'/ very verbose...
td::sort(data, data+3, by(data_member<TEST, int, &TEST::A>()));
td::sort(data, data+3, by(property_member<TEST, int, &TEST::B>()));
```

However, it's not possible to write a generic class pointer as the only template parameter:

```
emplate <typename A, typename B, B A::*POINTER>
truct wrapper<POINTER>                                  // illegal: not C++
```

You have to resort again to a nested class template:

```
emplate <typename from_t, typename to_t>
truct wrapper

  template <to_t from_t::*POINTER>                      // legal!
  struct dataptr_t
  {
     const to_t& operator()(const from_t& x) const
     {
        return x.*POINTER;
     }
  };

  template <to_t from_t::*POINTER>
  dataptr_t<POINTER> get() const
  {
     return dataptr_t<POINTER>();
  }


nplate <typename from_t, typename to_t>
apper<from_t, to_t> get_wrapper(to_t from_t::* pointer)

 return wrapper<from_t, to_t>();
```

The example includes a function that takes the pointer to perform the first deduction, and again you 'e to supply the same pointer twice, once at runtime (whose *value* is basically ignored, but whose *type* is ᵉd for deduction) and once at compile-time:

```
fine MEMBER(PTR)    get_wrapper(PTR).get<PTR>()
```

- `get_wrapper` deduces arguments `T1` and `T2` automatically from PTR, so `get_wrapper(PTR)` will return `wrapper<T1, T2>`.
- Then you ask this wrapper to instantiate its member function `get` again on PTR, which returns the right object.

If PTR has type `int TEST::*`, the macro will produce a functor of type `dataptr_t<PTR>` (technically, `pper<TEST, int>:: dataptr_t<PTR>`).

However, any other overload will do. Here's an extended version:

```
template <typename from_t, typename to_t>
struct wrapper
{
   template <to_t from_t::* POINTER>
   struct dataptr_t
   {
      // optional:
      // typedef from_t argument_type;

      const to_t& operator()(const from_t& x) const
      {
         return x.*POINTER;
      }
   };

   template <to_t (from_t::*POINTER)() const>
   struct propptr_t
   {
      // optional:
      // typedef from_t argument_type;

      to_t operator()(const from_t& x) const
      {
         return (x.*POINTER)();
      }
   };

   template <to_t from_t::* POINTER>
   dataptr_t<POINTER> get() const
   {
      return dataptr_t<POINTER>();
   }

   template <to_t (from_t::*POINTER)() const>
   propptr_t<POINTER> get() const
   {
      return propptr_t<POINTER>();
   }
};

template <typename from_t, typename to_t>
wrapper<from_t, to_t> get_wrapper(to_t from_t::* pointer)
{
   return wrapper<from_t, to_t>();
}
```

```
emplate <typename from_t, typename to_t>
rapper<from_t, to_t> get_wrapper(to_t (from_t::*pointer)() const)

  return wrapper<from_t, to_t>();


define mxt_create_accessor(PTR)   get_wrapper(PTR).get<PTR>()

truct TEST

  int A;
  int B() const { return -A; }
;

:ST data[3] = {2,1,3};

.d::sort(data, data+3, by(mxt_create_accessor(&TEST::A)));
.d::sort(data, data+3, by(mxt_create_accessor(&TEST::B)));
```

As usual, if the name of the class contains a comma (such as `std::map<int, float>`), you need to 'pedef it before calling the macro.

---

e & is not strictly necessary. It's possible to redefine the macro as `get_wrapper(PTR).get<&PTR>()` in order invoke it on the plain qualified name.

cording to the Standard, the macro does not work inside templates as written. An additional `template` yword is necessary for the compiler to deduce correctly what `get` is, so the best option is to define a second acro named (say)

```
t_create_accessor_template

t_wrapper(PTR).template get<&PTR>()
```

This version needs to be used whenever PTR depends on a template parameter that has impact on the line ere the macro expands. On the other hand, it is forbidden whenever PTR does not depend on anything else.[7]

3.3. More on the Double Wrapper Technique

he previous paragraph, you saw a macro that looks like this one:

```
fine MEMBER(PTR)   get_wrapper(PTR).get<PTR>()
```

The argument PTR is used twice—the first time as an argument of a template function, which ignores its ıe but uses only its type and returns an "intermediate functor"; the second time as a template parameter ıe functor itself, which produces the final object that you need.

ıe compilers, including VC, won't notice the difference; however, GCC does care.

Let's revise this technique, to face an apparently unrelated problem.[8] In classic C++, enumeration values decay automatically to integers. This may cause bugs:

```
enum A { XA = 1 };
enum B { XB = 1 };

int main()
{
    A a = XA;
    B b = XB;
    a == b; // compiles and returns true, even if enums are unrelated
}
```

Let's introduce a simple helper functor: an object of type enum_const is a static value that compares exactly equal to one value from the same (non-anonymous) enumeration, but it cannot be compared to an integer or to a different type.

```
template <typename T, T VALUE>
struct enum_const
{
    bool operator==(T that) const
    {
        return VALUE == that;
    }

    // Barton-Nackman, see section 6.6
    friend inline bool operator==(T lhs, enum_const<T, VALUE> rhs)
    {
        return rhs == lhs;
    }
};

template <typename T>
struct enum_const_helper
{
    template <T VALUE>
    enum_const<T, VALUE> get() const
    {
        return enum_const<T, VALUE>();
    }
};

template <typename T>
inline enum_const_helper<T> wrap(T)
{
    return enum_const_helper<T>();
}
```

[8]This paragraph is intended exclusively as a teaching example, not as a solution for production code. In practice, this issue would be solved by promoting a compiler warning to an error, or by using modern C++ strongly-typed enumerati However, it's instructive as an example of how a (meta) programmer can bend the C++ syntax to solve small problems

So you can write code like:

```
#define enum_static_const(X) wrap(X).get<X>()

int main()

   A a = XA;
   B b = XB;
   a == b;                                // ok
   b == enum_static_const(XA);            // error
   enum_static_const(XB) == a;            // error
```

```
error: invalid operands to binary expression ('int' and 'enum_const<A, (A)1U>')
    b == enum_static_const(XA); // fails
    ~ ^  ~~~~~~~~~~~~~~~~~~~~~~
note: candidate template ignored: deduced conflicting types for parameter 'T' ('B' vs. 'A')
inline bool operator==(T lhs, enum_const<T, VALUE> rhs)
            ^

error: invalid operands to binary expression ('enum_const<B, (B)1U>' and 'int')
    enum_static_const(XB) == a; // fails
    ~~~~~~~~~~~~~~~~~~~~~ ^  ~
note: candidate function not viable: no known conversion from 'A' to 'B' for 1st argument;
    bool operator==(T that) const
```

The macro as written works, but it needs X to be a compile-time constant:

```
#define enum_static_const(X) wrap(X).get<X>()
```

Let's look for a workaround. The first question is, can wrap detect if X is a constant or a variable? It can partially—a variable can bind to a reference.[9]

```
template <typename T>
inline enum_const_helper<T> wrap(T, ...)

   return enum_const_helper<T>();


template <typename T>
inline enum_var_helper<T> wrap(T& x, int)

   return enum_var_helper<T>(x);
```

---

[9]If X has type const A, wrap will deduce T=const A and pick the second overload, if you carefully implement enum_var_helper.

Note the additional argument to wrap. Suppose X is a variable and you write wrap(X); both wrap(T&) and wrap(T) are valid matches, so the overload resolution is ambiguous. On the other hand, the expression wrap(X, 0) will prefer to match (T&, int) when possible, because 0 has exactly type int (which is better than ellipsis). So the macro becomes:

```
#define enum_static_const(X) wrap(X, 0).get<X>()
```

The second question is, if X is a variable, can you give a meaning to get<X>()? Again, let's introduce a dummy argument of type int:

```
template <typename T>
struct enum_const_helper
{
    template <T VALUE>
    enum_const<T, VALUE> get(int) const
    {
        return enum_const<T, VALUE>();
    }
};
```

And here's the final version of the macro:

```
#define enum_static_const(X) wrap(X, 0).get<X>(0)
```

Now the syntax is different: get may be a member object and get<X>(0) is actually (get.operator<(X)).operator>(0). This is valid, since the object returned by wrap has no dependency on other template parameters.

Here's the missing piece of code:

```
template <typename T>
struct enum_var
{
    const T value_;

    explicit enum_var(T val)
    : value_(val) {}

    bool operator==(T that) const
    {
        return value_ == that;
    }

        // Barton-Nackman again
    friend inline bool operator==(T lhs, enum_var<T> rhs)
    {
        return rhs == lhs;
    }
```

```
    enum_var operator<(T) const   // dummy operator<
    {   return *this;   }

    enum_var operator>(int) const // dummy operator>
    {   return *this;   }
;

emplate <typename T>
truct enum_var_helper

   enum_var<T> get;                  // surprise: data member called get

   enum_var_helper(T& x)
   : get(x) {}


um_static_const(XB) == b;       // picks enum_const<B,1>::operator==(b)
um_static_const(b) == XB;       // picks enum_var<B>(b).operator==(XB)
```

.4. Accumulation

accumulator is a functor that performs a logical "pass" over a sequence of elements and is updated via erator+= or operator+. This is implemented in the STL algorithm `std::accumulate`.

```
mplate <typename iterator_t, typename accumulator_t>
cumulator_t accumulate(iterator_t b, iterator_t e, accumulator_t x)

 while (b != e)
    x = x + *(b++);

 return x;
```

If x is `value_type(0)`, this actually produces the sum over the range.

Accumulators can be classified as *online* or *offline*. Offline objects may accumulate only once over a ge, and no more values can be added. On the other hand, online objects can accumulate disjoint ranges. ordinary sum is an online accumulation process, because the new total depends only on the previous al and the new values. An exact percentile would be an offline process, because the P-th percentile over disjoint ranges depends on *all* the values at once.[10])

The first step in a generalization is to accumulate `F(*i)`, not necessarily `*i`.[11]

```
plate <typename T>
uct identity

T operator()(T x) const { return x; }
```

---

ere are online accumulators that *estimate* percentiles with good accuracy, though.

u might want to look back at Chapter 5 again.

```
template <typename iter_t, typename accumulator_t, typename accessor_t>
accumulator_t accumulate(iter_t b, iter_t e, accumulator_t x, accessor_t F)
{
   while (b != e)
      x = x + F(*(b++));

   return x;
}

template <typename iter_t, typename accumulator_t>
accumulator_t accumulate(iterator_t b, iterator_t e, accumulator_t x)
{
   return accumulate(b, e, x,
            identity<typename std::iterator_traits<iter_t>::reference>());
}
```

With TMP it's possible to build multi-layered accumulators on the fly:

- Recognize a set of similar operations that will get a performance boost from being performed simultaneously, rather than sequentially.[12]
- Define a reasonable syntax for instantiating an unnamed multiple accumulator.
- Define a reasonable syntax for extracting the results.

8.4.1. A Step-by-Step Implementation

The rest of the section will write a suitable function named collect that will make it possible to write the following:

```
// collect F(*i) for each i in the range
// and produce sum, gcd and max

std::accumulate(begin, end, collect(F)*SUM*GCD*MAX)
```

You'll take advantage of the fact that std::accumulate returns the accumulator to dump the desired results, either one or many at a time:

```
int data[7] = { ... };
int S = std::accumulate(data, data+7, collect(identity<int>())*SUM).result(SUM);

int sum, gcd, max;
std::accumulate(begin, end, collect(F)*SUM*GCD*MAX)
               .result(SUM >>sum, GCD >>gcd, MAX >>max);
```

[12]For example, the maxmin algorithm has a complexity 25% lower than computing max and min in two steps.

Let's restart from the beginning.

First, you identify the elementary operations and assign a code to each:

```
num

  op_void,    // null-operation
  op_gcd,
  op_max,
  op_min,
  op_sum
;
```

Again, you'll use template rotation. The main object contains the list of operations; it executes the first, en rotates the list and dispatches execution. T is the accessor.

```
emplate <typename T, int O1 = op_void, int O2 = op_void,..., int On = op_void>
.ass accumulate_t

 typedef accumulate_t<T, O2, O3, ..., On > next_t;     // rotation

 static const int OP_COUNT = 1+next_t::OP_COUNT;

 scalar_t data_[OP_COUNT];

 static void apply(/* ... */)
 {
    // perform operation O1 and store result in data_[0]
    // then...

    next_t::apply(...);
 }
```

Then you implement the binary operations (some code is omitted for brevity):

```
nplate <int N>
:uct op_t;

plate <>
uct op_t<op_void>

vate:
explicit op_t(int = 0) {}


plate <>
uct op_t<op_sum>

explicit op_t(int = 0) {}
```

```
    template <typename scalar_t>
    scalar_t operator()(const scalar_t a, const scalar_t b) const
    {
        return a+b;
    }
};
```

You create some global constant objects; the explicit constructor has exactly this purpose.

```
const op_t< op_gcd > GCD(0);
const op_t< op_sum > SUM(0);
const op_t< op_max > MAX(0);
const op_t< op_min > MIN(0);
```

Note that nobody can construct op_t<op_void>.

Since you can perform exactly four different operations, you put four as the limit of template parameters

```
template
<
  typename accessor_t,
  int O1 = op_void, int O2 = op_void, int O3 = op_void, int O4 = op_void
>
class accumulate_t
{
    typedef typename accessor_t::value_type scalar_t;

    typedef accumulate_t<accessor_t,O2,O3,O4> next_t;

    template <typename T, int I1, int I2, int I3, int I4>
        friend class accumulate_t;

    static const int OP_COUNT = 1 + next_t::OP_COUNT;

    scalar_t data_[OP_COUNT];
    size_t count_;
    accessor_t accessor_;
```

Every object is constructed via an instance of the accessor:

```
public:
    accumulate_t(const accessor_t& v = accessor_t())
    : accessor_(v), count_(0), data_()
    {
    }

    // more below...
};
```

You have an array of results named data_. The i-th operation will store its result in data_[i].

The recursive computation part is indeed simple. There's a public operator+= that calls a private static nember function:

```
emplate <typename object_t>
ccumulate_t& operator+=(const object_t& t)

  apply(data_, accessor_(t), count_);    // <-- static
  return *this;
```

nd a global operator+:

```
emplate <typename accessor_t, int N1, ..., int N4, typename scalar_t>
:cumulate_t<accessor_t,N1,N2,N3,N4>
 operator+(accumulate_t<accessor_t,N1,N2,N3,N4> s, const scalar_t x)

  return s += x;
```

accessor_(t) yields the value to be accumulated over the memory cell *data. If count is 0, which eans that the cell is "empty," just write the value. Otherwise, invoke the first binary operation that merges the evious cell value and the new one. Then, advance the pointer to the next cell and forward the call to next_t:

```
atic void apply(scalar_t* const data, const scalar_t x, size_t& count)

*data = (count>0) ? op_t<01>()(*data, x) : x;
next_t::apply(data+1, x, count);
```

The recursion is stopped when all operations are op_void. At this point, you update the counter.

```
nplate <typename accessor_t>
ass accumulate_t <accessor_t, op_void, op_void, op_void, op_void>

/* ... */

static const int OP_COUNT = 0;

tatic void apply(scalar_t* const, const scalar_t, size_t& count)

 ++count;
```

You need another static recursion to retrieve the result:

```
vate:
template <int N>
static scalar_t get(const scalar_t* const data, op_t<N>)
{
   return 01==N ? data[0] : next_t::get(data+1, op_t<N>());
}
```

```
public:
   template <int N>
   scalar_t result(op_t<N>) const
   {
      return get(data_, op_t<N>());
   }
```

The recursion stopper is not expected to be invoked. However, it's necessary because `next_t::get` is mentioned (and thus, fully compiled anyway). It will be executed only if one asks for `result(op_t<K>)` for an object of type `accumulate_t<K1...Kn>` and `K` is not in the list.

In this case, you can induce any suitable runtime error:

```
template <typename accessor_t>
class accumulate_t <accessor_t, op_void, op_void, op_void, op_void>
{
private:
   template <int N>
   static scalar_t get(const scalar_t* const, op_t<N>)
   {
      // if you prefer,
      // throw std::runtime_error("invalid result request");
      return std::numeric_limits<scalar_t>::quiet_NaN();
   }

public:
   /* nothing here */
};
```

Since `SUM` is a global constant of the right type, you are eventually going to call `std::accumulate(begin,end,[...]).result(SUM)`.

At this point, you can write code that computes the result and code that retrieves the result, but you're still missing the accumulator factory. As frequently happens for all objects based on template rotation, you give the user a helper function that initially produces an "empty accumulator" (namely, `accumulate_t<T>`, or more precisely, `accumulate_t<T, 0, 0, ... ,0>`) and this empty object can be combined repeatedly with one or more `op_t`. In other words: there's an operator that combines `accumulate_t<T>` and an operation `N1`, performing a static "push-front" and returning `accumulate_t<T, N1>`.

If you pick `operator*` (binary multiplication) for chaining, the function looks like this:

```
template <int N, int N1, ... int Nk>
accumulate_t<T, N, N1, N2,..,Nk-1> operator*(accumulate_t<T, N1,..,Nk-1, Nk>, op_t<N>)
```

This chaining operator will contain a static assertion to ensure that the "dropped term" `Nk` is `op_void`.

Here's the global helper function:

```
template <typename accessor_t>
inline accumulate_t<accessor_t> collect(const accessor_t& v)
{
   return v;
}
```

Finally, here is a listing of the whole class, side by side with the recursion stopping specialization:

```
emplate

ypename accessor_t,
nt O1 = op_void, int O2 = op_void,
nt O3 = op_void, int O4 = op_void

lass
:cumulate_t

/pedef typename accessor_t::value_type
:alar_t;
:mplate <typename T, int I1, int I2,
t I3, int I4>
'iend class accumulate_t;

pedef
cumulate_t<accessor_t,O2,O3,O4,op_void>
xt_t;
atic const int OP_COUNT = 1+next_t::OP_
UNT;
alar_t data_[OP_COUNT];
ze_t count_;
:essor_t accessor_;
atic void apply(scalar_t* const data,
ıst scalar_t x, size_t& count)

ta = (count>0) ? op_t<O1>()(*data, x) :

t_t::apply(data+1, x, count);

plate <int N>
tic scalar_t get(const scalar_t* const
a, op_t<N>)

urn O1==N ?
a[0] : next_t::get(data+1, op_t<N>());
```

```
template
<
typename accessor_t

>
class
accumulate_t<accessor_t,op_void,...,op_void>
{

typedef typename accessor_t::value_type
scalar_t;
template <typename T, int I1, int I2, int
I3, int I4>
friend class accumulate_t;

static const int OP_COUNT = 0;

accessor_t accessor_;
static void apply(scalar_t* const,
const scalar_t, size_t& count)
{
++count;
}

template <int N>
static scalar_t get(const scalar_t* const,
op_t<N> )
{
assert(false);
return 0;
}
```

```
public:
accumulate_t(const accessor_t& v =
accessor_t())
: accessor_(v), count_(0), data_()
{
}
template <int N>
accumulate_t<accessor_t,N,O1,O2,O3>
operator* (op_t<N>) const
{
MXT_ASSERT(O4 == op_void);
return accessor_;
}
template <typename object_t>
accumulate_t& operator+=(const object_t& t)
{
apply(data_, accessor_(t), count_);
return *this;
}
template <int N>
scalar_t result(op_t<N>) const
{
return get(data_, op_t<N>());
}
size_t size() const
{
return count_;
}
};
```

```
public:
accumulate_t(const accessor_t& v =
accessor_t())
: accessor_(v)
{
}
template <int N>
accumulate_t<accessor_t, N>
operator* (op_t<N>) const
{

return accessor_;
}

template <typename object_t>
accumulate_t& operator+=(const object_t& t)
{

return *this;
}
};
```

The last feature provides the ability to retrieve more results at one time. This is extremely important, since it avoids storing the result of the accumulation.

You simply introduce an operator that binds a reference to each op_t (this example uses operator>> since it resembles an arrow). Another possible choice is operator<=, since <= can be seen as ←) and build a reference wrapper of unique type. From this temporary, an overloaded accumulator::result will extract both operands and perform the assignment.

```
RESULT1 r1;
RESULT2 r2;
accumulator.result(SUM >> r1, MAX >> r2);
```

The implementation is as follows:

```
emplate <typename scalar_t, int N>
truct op_result_t

  scalar_t& value;

  op_result_t(scalar_t& x)
  : value(x)
  {
  }
;

emplate <typename scalar_t, int N>
nline op_result_t<scalar_t, N> operator>> (const op_t<N>, scalar_t& x)

  return op_result_t<scalar_t, N>(x);
```

Then you add these methods to the general template (the macro is for brevity only):

```
efine ARG(J)    const op_result_t<scalar_t, N##J> o##J
 ARG(1) expands to "const op_result_t<scalar_t, N1> o1"

 template <int N1>
 const accumulate_t& result(ARG(1)) const
 {
    o1.value = result(op_t<N1>());
    return *this;
 }

 template <int N1, int N2>
 const accumulate_t& result(ARG(1), ARG(2)) const
 {
    result(o2);
    return result(o1);
 }

 template <int N1, int N2, int N3>
 const accumulate_t& result(ARG(1), ARG(2), ARG(3)) const
 {
    result(o3);
    return result(o1, o2);
 }

template <int N1, int N2, int N3, int N4>
const accumulate_t& result(ARG(1), ARG(2), ARG(3), ARG(4)) const
{
   result(o4);
   return result(o1, o2, o3);
}

def ARG
```

The expression MAX>>x silently returns op_result_t<[[type of x]],op_max>(x).

If x does not have the same type as the accumulated results, it will not compile.

A couple of extra enhancements will save some typing. Instead of having many result, you just add the first one and chain the subsequent calls via operator().[13]

```
template <int N1>
const accumulate_t& result(const op_result_t<scalar_t,N1> o1) const
{
  o1.value = result(op_t<N1>());
  return *this;
}

template <int N1>
const accumulate_t& operator()(const op_result_t<scalar_t,N1> o1) const
{
  return result(o1);
}
```

So instead of:

```
int q_sum, q_gcd, q_max;
std::accumulate(...).result(SUM >> q_sum, GCD >> q_gcd, MAX >> q_max);
```

the new syntax is:

```
std::accumulate(...).result(SUM >> q_sum)(GCD >> q_gcd)(MAX >> q_max);
```

or even:

```
std::accumulate(...)(SUM >> q_sum)(GCD >> q_gcd)(MAX >> q_max);
```

Second, you add an overload that returns the first result for functions that accumulate a single quantity

```
  scalar_t result() const
  {
     // MXT_ASSERT(O2 == op_void);
     return result(op_t<O1>());
  }

// now .result(SUM) is equivalent to .result()
int S = std::accumulate(data, data+7, collect(...)*SUM).result();
```

[13]More on this in Section 9.3.

8.5. Drivers

A well-written algorithm avoids unnecessary multiplication of code. To rewrite an existing algorithm for greater generality, you have to remove some "fixed" logic from it and plug it in again through a template parameter, usually a functor:

```
emplate <typename iterator_t>
oid sort(iterator_t begin, iterator_t end)

  for (...)
  {
     // ...
     if (a<b) // operator< is a good candidate for becoming a functor
     {}
  }
```

So you rewrite this as:

```
mplate <typename iterator_t, typename less_t>
id sort(iterator_t begin, iterator_t end, less_t less)

 for (...)
 {
    // now we ask the functor to "plug" its code in the algorithm
    if (less(a,b))
    {}
 }
```

A *driver* is an object that can guide an algorithm along the way.

The main difference between a functor and a driver is that the former has a general-purpose function- e interface (at least, `operator()`), which is open to user customization. On the other hand, a driver is a low el object with a verbose interface, and it's not meant to be customized (except for its name, it might not n be documented, as if it were a tag type). The framework itself will provide a small fixed set of drivers.

Consider the following example. You need an `sq` function that optionally logs the result on `std::cerr`. cause you cannot enforce such a constraint if you receive a generic logger object, you switch to drivers d then provide some:

```
uct dont_log_at_all

bool may_I_log() const    { return false;    }


uct log_everything

bool may_I_log() const   { return true; }
```

```
struct log_ask_once
{
   bool may_I_log() const
   {
      static bool RESULT = AskUsingMessageBox("Should I log?", MSG_YN);
      return RESULT;
   }
};

template <typename scalar_t, typename driver_t>
inline scalar_t sq(const scalar_t& x, driver_t driver)
{
   const scalar_t result = (x*x);
   if (driver.may_I_log())
      std::cerr << result << std::endl;
   return result;
}

template <typename scalar_t>
inline scalar_t sq(const scalar_t& x)
{
   return sq(x, dont_log_at_all());
}
```

Note that `driver_t::may_I_log()` contains neither code about squaring, nor about logging. It just makes a decision, driving the flow of the algorithm.

The big advantage of drivers is to reduce debugging time, since the main algorithm is a single function. Usually drivers have minimal runtime impact. However nothing prevents a driver from performing long and complex computations.

As a rule, you always invoke drivers through instances. An interface such as

```
template <typename driver_t>
void explore(maze_t& maze, driver_t driver)
{
   while (!driver.may_I_stop())
   { ... }
}
```

is more general than its stateless counterpart[14]:

```
template <typename driver_t>
void explore(maze_t& maze)
{
   while (driver_t::may_I_stop())
   { ... }
}
```

[14] Traits would be somehow equivalent to stateless drivers.

A driver is somehow analogous to the "public non-virtual / protected virtual" classic C++ idiom see Section 6.3). The key similarity is that the structure of the algorithm is fixed. The user is expected to ustomize only specific parts, which run only when the infrastructure needs them to.[15]

3.6. Algors

.n *algor*, or algorithmic functor, is an object that embeds an algorithm, or simply an algorithm with state.

The standard C++ library provides an `<algorithm>` header, which includes only functions. So it's natural identify function and algorithms, but it need not be the case.

The algor object implements a simple function-like interface—typically `operator()`—for the execution f the algorithm, but its state grants faster repeated executions.

The simplest case where an algor is useful is buffered memory allocation. `std::stable_sort` may equire the allocation of a temporary buffer that's necessarily released when the function returns. Usually is is not an issue, since time spent in (a single) memory allocation is dominated by the execution of the gorithm itself. A small input will cause a small memory request, which is "fast" (operating systems tend favor small allocations). A large input will cause a "slow" memory request, but this extra time will be noticed, since the algorithm will need much more time to run.

However, there are situations where a single buffer would suffice for many requests. When stable-rting many vectors of similar length, you can save allocation/deallocation time if you maintain the buffer an object:

```
mplate <typename T>
ass stable_sort_algor

 buffer_type buffer_;

blic:
 template <RandomAccessIterator>
 void operator()(RandomAccessIterator begin, RandomAccessIterator end)
 {
    // ensure that buffer_ is large enough
    // if not, reallocate
    // then perform the stable sort
 }

 ~stable_sort_algor()
 {
    // release buffer_
 }
```

To sum up, the simplest algor is just a sort of functor with state (in the last case, a temporary buffer), but ors may have a richer interface that goes beyond functors.

---

e also http://www.gotw.ca/publications/mill18.htm.

As a rule, algors are not copied or assigned. They are constructed and reused (say, in a loop) or used as unnamed temporaries for a single execution. You therefore don't need to worry about efficiency, only about safety. If buffer_type cannot be safely copied (if it's a pointer), you explicitly disable all the dangerous member functions, making them private or public do-nothing operations. If buffer_type is a value type (for example, vector<T>), you let the compiler generate safe, possibly inefficient, operators.

Another useful kind of algor is a *self-accumulator* that holds multiple results at once. There's no buffer involved (see Section 8.4).

```
template <typename T>
class accumulator
{
   T max_;
   T min_;
   T sum_;
   // ...

public:
   accumulator()
   : sum_(0) // ...
   {
   }

   template <typename iterator_t>
   accumulator<T>& operator()(iterator_t begin, iterator_t end)
   {
      for (;begin != end; ++begin)
      {
         sum_ += *begin;
         // ...
      }
      return *this;
   }

   T max() const { return max_; }
   T min() const { return min_; }
   T sum() const { return sum_; }
   // ...
};

int main()
{
   double data[] = {3,4,5 };

   // single invocation
   double SUM = accumulator<double>()(data, data+3).sum();

   // multiple results are needed
   accumulator<double> A;
   A(data, data+3);
   std::cout << "Range: " << A.max()-A.min();
}
```

An *interactive algor* has an interface that allows the caller to run the algorithm step-by-step. Suppose for xample you have to compute the square root to some level of precision:

```
emplate <typename scalar_t>
lass interactive_square_root

  scalar_t x_;
  scalar_t y_;
  scalar_t error_;

ublic:
  interactive_square_root(scalar_t x)
  : x_(x)
  {
     iterate();
  }

  void iterate()
  {
     // precondition:
     // y_ is some kind of approximate solution for y2=x
     // error_ is |y2-x|

     // now compute a better approximation
  }

  scalar_t error() const
  {
     return error_;
  }

  operator scalar_t() const
  {
     return y_;
  }
```

It's the user who drives the algorithm:

```
 main()

interactive_square_root<double> ISR(3.14);
while (ISR.error()>0.00001)
{
   ISR.iterate();
}
double result = ISR;
```

An algor of this kind usually takes all its parameters from the constructor.

A common use-case is an algorithm that produces *a set of solutions*. After execution, a member function permits the user to "visit" all the solutions in some order.[16] These algors might do all the work in the constructor:

```
template <typename string_t>
class search_a_substring
{
   const string_t& text_;
   std::vector<size_t> position_;

public:
   search_a_substring(const string_t& TEXT, const string_t& PATTERN)
   : text_(TEXT)
   {
      // search immediately every occurrence of PATTERN in TEXT
      // store all the positions in position_
   }

   bool no_match() const { return position_.empty(); }

   // the simplest visitation technique
   // is... exposing iterators

   typedef std::vector<size_t>::const_iterator position_iterator;

   position_iterator begin() const
   {
      return position_.begin();
   }

   position_iterator end() const
   {
      return position_.end();
   }
};
```

In the case of substring matching, the iterator will likely visit the matches from the first to the last. In a numerical minimization problem, the solutions may be N points where the function has the minimum value found so far.

[16]This has some similarity with the way `std::regex` works.

A more complex visitor-accepting interface could accept two *output* iterators, where the algor would write its solutions. You could build a "custom view" on the solutions according to the iterator `value_type`. For example, an algor that internally computes pairs (`Xj`, `Yj`) may emit just the first component or the entire pair (a simplified example follows):

```
lass numerical_minimizer

   std::function<double (double)> F;
   std::vector<double> X_;  // all the points where F has minima

ublic:

   // ...

   template <typename out_t>
   out_t visit(out_t beg, out_t end) const
   {
      typedef typename std::iterator_traits<out_t>::value_type> val_t;

      int i=0;
      while (beg != end)
         *beg++ = build_result(i++, instance_of<val_t>());

      return beg;
   }

ivate:

   template <typename T>
   double build_result(int i, instance_of<T>) const
   {
      return X_[i];
   }

   using std::pair;

   template <typename T>
   pair<double,double> build_result(int i, instance_of<pair<T,T>>) const
   {
      return std::make_pair(X_[i], F(X_[i]));
   }
```

8.7. Forwarding and Reference Wrappers

It's a common idiom for a class template to hold a member of a generic type, to which the class dispatches execution.

```
template <typename T>
class test
{
   T functor_;

public:
   typename T::value_type operator()(double x) const
   {
      return functor_(x);    // call forward
   }
};
```

Since the exact type of the member is not known, you may have to implement several overloads of `test::operator()`. Since this is a template, this is not a problem, because what's actually needed will be instantiated and the rest is ignored.

```
template <typename T>
class test
{
   T functor_;

public:
   /* we don't know how many arguments functor_ needs */

   template <typename T1>
   typename T::value_type operator()(T1 x) const
   {
      return functor_(x);       // call forwarding
   }

   template <typename T1, typename T2>
   typename T::value_type operator()(T1 x, T2 y) const
   {
      return functor_(x, y);    // call forwarding
   }

   // more...
};
```

Invoking the wrong overload (that is, supplying too many or unsupported arguments) will cause a ompiler error. However, note that arguments are forwarded by value, so you can modify the prototypes:

```
emplate <typename T1>
ypename T::value_type operator()(const T1& x) const

  return functor_(x);        // call forwarding
```

But if T requires an argument by non-const reference, the code will not compile.

To understand the severity of the problem, consider a slightly different example, where you *construct* a ıember with an unspecified number of parameters.

The STL guidelines suggest writing a single constructor for class test, which takes (possibly) a :eviously constructed object of type T:

```
est(const T& data = T())
 member_(data)
```

This strategy is not always possible. In particular, T might have an inaccessible copy constructor or it ay be a non-const reference.

In fact, let's forget the STL style for a moment and adapt the same idiom of operator() as shown previously.

```
mplate <typename T>
ass bad_test

 T member_;

blic:
 template <typename X1>
 bad_test(X1 arg1)
 : member_(arg1)
 {
 }

 template <typename X1, typename X2>
 bad_test(X1 arg1, X2 arg2)
 : member_(arg1, arg2)
 {
 }
```

As written, bad_test<T&> compiles, but a subtle bug arises[17]:

```
 main(int argc, char* argv[])

double x = 3.14;
```

e example is written as if all members were public.

```
    bad_test<double&> urgh(x);          // unfortunately, it compiles
    urgh.member_ = 6.28;                // bang!

    int i = 0;
    assert(x == 6.28);                  // assertion failed!

    // ...
}
```

The constructor of urgh is instantiated on type double, not double&, so urgh.member_ refers to a temporary location in the stack of its constructor (namely, the storage space taken by arg1), whose content is a temporary copy of x.

So you modify bad_test to forward arguments by const reference. At least, good_test<double&> will not compile (const double& cannot be converted to double&).

```
template <typename T>
class good_test
{
   T member_;

public:
   template <typename X1>
   good_test(const X1& arg1)
   : member_(arg1)
   {
   }
};
```

However, an additional wrapping layer can solve both problems:

```
template <typename T>
class reference_wrapper
{
   T& ref_;

public:
   explicit reference_wrapper(T& r)
      : ref_(r)
   {
   }

   operator T& () const
   {
      return ref_;
   }

   T* operator& () const
   {
      return &ref_;
   }
};
```

```
emplate <typename T>
nline reference_wrapper<T> by_ref(T& x)

  return reference_wrapper<T>(x);

nt main()

 double x = 3.14;

 good_test<double> y0(x);  // ok: x is copied into y0.member_

 good_test<double&> y1(x); // compiler error!
 y1.member_ = 6.28;         // would be dangerous, but does not compile

 good_test<double&> y2(by_ref(x));

 y2.member_ = 6.28;         // ok, now x == 6.28
```

Using by_ref, the good_test<double&> constructor is instantiated on argument nst reference_wrapper<double&>&, which is then converted to double&.

Note Once again, the argument-forwarding problem is solved in C++0x with R-value references.

CHAPTER 9

The Opaque Type Principle

Template type names can be too complex for the user to use directly, as they may be verbose or they may require very complex syntax. So you should either publish a convenient typedef or allow users to ignore their type altogether.

Plain C is full of opaque types.

In C, a file stream is handled via a pointer to an unknown FILE structure that resides in system memory (the C runtime pre-allocates a small number of these structures). To retrieve the current position in an open file, you call fgetpos(FILE*, fpos_t), passing the file pointer and another opaque type that acts as a bookmark. You can't know or modify the current position but can restore it via a call to fsetpos(FILE*, fpos_t). From the user perspective, an instance of fpos_t is completely opaque. Since only the name is known, the type has no interface except for the default constructor, copy constructor, and assignment.

In the opaque type principle, opaqueness is related only to the *type name*, not to the interface. In other words, the object has an unspecified type and a known interface—it may be an iterator or a functor.

Being the "difficult to write" type, you don't want to store the object but should instead use it immediately, on the creation site.

9.1. Polymorphic Results

Suppose a function performs a computation that produces several results at a time.

You can pack all of them in a polymorphic result and allow the user to select what's needed.

Let's take a simplified example:

```
template <typename iterator_t >
[[???]] average(iterator_t beg, iterator_t end)
{
   typename std::iterator_traits<iterator_t>::value_type total = 0;
   total = std::accumulate(beg, end, total);
   size_t count = std::distance(beg, end);

   return total/count;
}
```

A fixed return type will destroy the partial results, which could be useful. So you can delay the aggregation of the sub-items and change the code like this:

```
template <typename T, typename I>
class opaque_average_result_t
{
```

```
  T total_;
  I count_;

ublic:
  opaque_average_result_t(T total, I count)
  : total_(total), count_(count)
  {
  }

  // default result is the average

  operator T () const
  {
     return total_/count_;
  }

  T get_total() const
  {
     return total_;
  }

  I get_count() const
  {
     return count_;
  }

mplate <typename VALUE_TYPE, typename iterator_t >
aque_average_result_t<VALUE_TYPE, size_t> average(iterator_t beg, iterator_t end)

 VALUE_TYPE total = 0;
 total = std::accumulate(beg, end, total);
 size_t count = std::distance(beg, end);

 return opaque_average_result_t<VALUE_TYPE, size_t>(total, count);
```

Now the client can use the original algorithm in many more ways:

```
::vector<double> v;
ble avg = average<double>(v.begin(), v.end());
ble sum = average<double>(v.begin(), v.end()).get_total();
```

Since the return type is opaque, it's not convenient to store the result, but it's easy to pass it to a function plate, if needed:[1]

```
?> x = average<double>(v.begin(), v.end());
```

also Section 12.3.

```
template <typename T>
void receive(T res, double& avg, double& sum)
{
   avg = res;
   sum = res.get_total();
}

std::vector<double> v;
double avg, sum;
receive(average<double>(v.begin(), v.end()), avg, sum);
```

9.2. Classic Lambda Expressions

Lambda expressions are opaque function objects created on the call site. They combine some elementary pieces with meaningful operators. The resulting functor will later replay the operator sequence on its arguments. For example, given two suitable objects of type “lambda variables” X and Y, then (X+Y)*(X-Y) will be a functor that takes two arguments and returns their sum multiplied by their difference.

It’s a good exercise to build a simplified implementation and understand the underlying template techniques. These have been proposed originally by Todd Veldhuizen in his seminal article, “Expression Templates”.

You can write code like this: cos(X+2.0) is an expression that returns a functor whose operator() computes cos(x+2.0) given a double x.

```
lambda_reference<const double> X;

std::find_if(..., X<5.0 && X>3.14);
std::transform(..., cos(X+2.0));

lambda_reference<double> Y;

std::for_each(..., Y+=3.14);

lambda_reference<const double, 0> ARG1;
lambda_reference<const double, 1> ARG2;

std::sort(..., (ARG1<ARG2));
```

You can make the following assumptions. Some will be removed later and some will hopefully become clearer as you proceed:

- For clarity, T will be a friendly scalar type, double or float, so all the operators are well-defined.
- A lambda expression will receive at most K=4 arguments, *all* of which are the same type T&. In particular:
    - lambda_reference<double> and lambda_reference<const double> are different, the latter being a “lambda-const reference to double”.
    - An expression must contain references to objects of the same type.

- For simplicity, all constants initially have type T and X+2 is considered invalid syntax, because X refers to a double and 2 is an int. Therefore, you have to write X+2.0 (you will learn how to remove this limitation later in this chapter).
- We explicitly try to write functions that look similar, so they easily can be generated with preprocessor macros, even when they are not listed here.

.2.1. Elementary Lambda Objects

et's rewrite the fundamental definition here: a lambda object is a functor that is generated with a special ntax (namely, assembling some placeholders with operators). The effect of the functor is to replay the ame operators on its actual arguments. For example, if X is one such placeholder, then the expression X+2 roduces a functor that takes one argument and returns its argument plus 2.

First, you define an *empty* static interface. Observe that T is not used at the moment, but you will shortly alize why it's necessary.

```
mplate <typename true_t, typename T>
ass lambda

otected:
 ~lambda()
 {
 }

blic:
 const true_t& true_this() const
 {
    return static_cast<const true_t&>(*this);
 }
```

The first (trivial) object is a lambda-constant. That's a functor that returns its constant result, whatever arguments. Since in particular it's a lambda expression, you derive this from the interface:

```
nplate <typename T>
ss lambda_const : public lambda<lambda_const<T>, T>

typedef const T& R;

T c_;

lic:
typedef T result_type;

lambda_const(R c)
: c_(c)
{
}
```

```
    result_type operator()(R  = T(), R  = T(), R  = T(), R  = T()) const
    {
        return c_;
    }
};
```

Note that a lambda-constant can take zero or more arguments, but it is a function object, so the invocation must use some form of `operator()`.

The second object is `lambda_reference<T, N>`, defined as a functor that takes at least `N` arguments of type `T&` and returns the `N`th. The choice of accepting `T&` as an argument implies that `lambda_reference<T>` won't work on a literal:

```
lambda_reference<double> X1;
lambda_reference<const double> Y1;

X1(3.14);    // error: needs double&
Y1(3.14);    // ok: takes and returns const double&
```

The selection of a variable is not trivial. As usual, argument rotation is the preferred technique. Furthermore, since a reference is cheap, this example introduces a technique known as the *duplication of the arguments* in order to reduce the number of overloads. The last argument of `operator()` is "cloned" so it always passes four items.

```
template <typename T, size_t N = 0>
class lambda_reference: public lambda<lambda_reference<T, N>, T>
{
    static T& apply_k(static_value<size_t,0>, T& x1, T&, T&, T&)
    {
        return x1;
    }

    template <size_t K>
    static T& apply_k(static_value<size_t,K>, T& x1, T& x2, T& x3, T& x4)
    {
        return apply_k(static_value<size_t,K-1>(), x2, x3, x4, x1);
    }

public:
    typedef T& result_type;

    result_type operator()(T& x1, T& x2, T& x3, T& x4) const
    {
        MXT_STATIC_ASSERT(N<4);
        return apply_k(static_value<size_t,N>(), x1, x2, x3, x4);
    }

    result_type operator()(T& x1, T& x2, T& x3) const
    {
        MXT_STATIC_ASSERT(N<3);
        return apply_k(static_value<size_t,N>(), x1, x2, x3, x3);
    }
```

```
  result_type operator()(T& x1, T& x2) const
  {
    MXT_STATIC_ASSERT(N<2);
    return apply_k(static_value<size_t,N>(), x1, x2, x2, x2);
  }

  result_type operator()(T& x1) const
  {
    MXT_STATIC_ASSERT(N<1);
    return apply_k(static_value<size_t,N>(), x1, x1, x1, x1);
  }
;
```

.2.2. Lambda Functions and Operators

unary function F applied to a lambda expression is a functor that returns F applied to the result of the mbda.[2]

Thanks to the static interface, the implementation can treat *any* lambda expression at once. Also, lambda<X, T> can be stored in an object of type X (and the copy is cheap).

```
mplate <typename F, typename X, typename T>
ass lambda_unary : public lambda<lambda_unary<F,X,T>, T>

  X x_;
  F f_;

blic:
  lambda_unary(const lambda<X,T>& that)
  : x_(that.true_this())
  {
  }

  typedef typename F::result_type result_type;

  result_type operator()() const
  {
    return f_(x_());
  }

  result_type operator()(T& x1) const
  {
    return f_(x_(x1));
  }

  result_type operator()(T& x1, T& x2) const
  {
    return f_(x_(x1, x2));
  }
```

ymbols, (F(λ))(x) := F(λ(x)), where x may be a tuple.

```
   result_type operator()(T& x1, T& x2, T& x3) const
   {
      return f_(x_(x1, x2, x3));
   }

   // ...
};
```

The previous code builds a functor f_, whose operator() is called, but you also need to plug in global/static member functions. Thus, a small adapter is needed:

```
template <typename T, T (*F)(T)>
struct unary_f_wrapper
{
   typedef T result_type;

   T operator()(const T& x) const { return F(x); }
};
```

Next, you collect all global functions in the traits class:

```
template <typename T>
struct unary_f_library
{
   static T L_abs(T x) { return abs(x); }
   static T L_cos(T x) { return cos(x); }
   // ...
};
```

And eventually you start defining functions on lambda objects:

```
#define LAMBDA_ABS_TYPE       \
   lambda_unary<unary_f_wrapper<T, &unary_f_library<T>::L_abs>, X, T>

template <typename X, typename T>
LAMBDA_ABS_TYPE abs(const lambda<X, T>& x)
{
   return LAMBDA_ABS_TYPE(x);
}

#define LAMBDA_COS_TYPE       \
   lambda_unary<unary_f_wrapper<T, &unary_f_library<T>::L_cos>, X, T>

template <typename X, typename T>
LAMBDA_COS_TYPE cos(const lambda<X, T>& x)
{
   return LAMBDA_COS_TYPE(x);
}

...
```

This scheme applies also to unary operators, simply using a different functor.

```
emplate <typename T>
truct lambda_unary_minus

 typedef T result_type;
 result_type operator()(const T& x) const { return -x; }
;

define LAMBDA_U_MINUS_TYPE   lambda_unary<lambda_unary_minus<T>, X, T>

emplate <typename X, typename T>
AMBDA_U_MINUS_TYPE operator-(const lambda<X, T>& x)

  return LAMBDA_U_MINUS_TYPE(x);
```

The more features you add, the more complex the return types become, but these are completely dden from the user.

A binary operation, say +, can be defined similarly: (`lambda<X1,T> + lambda<X2,T>`) is a functor at distributes its arguments to both its addends.[3] So, analogous to the unary case, you will define a ecific object to deal with the binary operators, namely `lambda_binary<X1, F, X2, T>`. In particular *ixed* binary operations, such as `lambda<X1,T> + T`, are a special case, handled with a promotion of T to `mbda_const<T>`.

```
mplate <typename X1, typename F, typename X2, typename T>
ass lambda_binary : public lambda< lambda_binary<X1,F,X2,T>, T >

 X1 x1_;
 X2 x2_;
 F f_;

olic:
 lambda_binary(const lambda<X1,T>& x1, const lambda<X2,T>& x2)
 : x1_(x1.true_this()), x2_(x2.true_this())
 {
 }

 typedef typename F::result_type result_type;

 result_type operator()() const
 {
    return f_(x1_(), x2_());
 }

 result_type operator()(T& x1) const
 {
    return f_(x1_(x1), x2_(x1));
 }
```

---

ymbols again, $(\lambda 1+\lambda 2)(x) := \lambda 1(x)+\lambda 2(x)$, where x may be a tuple.

```
    result_type operator()(T& x1, T& x2) const
    {
       return f_(x1_(x1, x2), x2_(x1, x2));
    }

    result_type operator()(T& x1, T& x2, T& x3) const
    {
       return f_(x1_(x1, x2, x3), x2_(x1, x2, x3));
    }

    // ...
};
```

■ In this implementation, logical operators will not use short circuit. If T were int, the lambda object X>0 && (1/X)<5 will crash on a division by zero, while the analogous C++ statement returns false.

Arithmetic operators like + can be written as f_(x1_(...), x2_(...)) as previously, but this is incorrect for && and ||, whose workflow is more complex:

```
b1 := x1_(...);
if (f_(b1, true) == f_(b1, false))
        return f_(b1, true);
else
        return f_(b1, x2_(...))
```

In the discussion that follows, somewhat sacrificing correctness for clarity, we treat all operators as normal binary predicates, and we leave writing partial specializations of lambda_binary for logical operators from the pseudo-code above as an exercise.

Now you define "concrete" binary functions:

```
template <typename T, T (*f)(T, T)>
struct binary_f_wrapper
{
   typedef T result_type;
   T operator()(const T& x, const T& y) const { return f(x,y); }
};

template <typename T>
struct binary_f_library
{
   static T L_atan2(T x, T y) { return atan2(x, y); }
   // ...
};

#define ATAN2_T(X1, X2)                                              \
  lambda_binary<X1,                                                  \
                binary_f_wrapper<T, &binary_f_library<T>::L_atan2>, \
                X2, T>
```

```
.emplate <typename X1, typename X2, typename T>
.TAN2_T(X1, X2) atan2(const lambda<X1,T>& L, const lambda<X2,T>& R)

  return ATAN2_T(X1, X2) (L, R);


emplate <typename X1, typename T>
TAN2_T(X1, lambda_const<T>) atan2(const lambda<X1,T>& L, const T& R)

  return atan2(L, lambda_const<T>(R));


emplate <typename T, typename X2>
TAN2_T(lambda_const<T>, X2) atan2(const T& L, const lambda<X2,T>& R)

  return atan2(lambda_const<T>(L), R);
```

Finally, you need another extension. There are three types of operators

- Binary predicates, with signature bool `F(const T&, const T&)`
- Binary operators, with signature T `F(const T&, const T&)`
- Assignments, with signature T& `F(T&, const T&)`

This translates to the following C++ code:

```
um lambda_tag

 LAMBDA_LOGIC_TAG,
 LAMBDA_ASSIGNMENT_TAG,
 LAMBDA_OPERATOR_TAG


nplate <typename T, lambda_tag TAG>
:uct lambda_result_traits;

nplate <typename T>
:uct lambda_result_traits<T, LAMBDA_ASSIGNMENT_TAG>

 typedef T& result_type;
 typedef T& first_argument_type;
 typedef const T& second_argument_type;


plate <typename T>
uct lambda_result_traits<T, LAMBDA_OPERATOR_TAG>

typedef T result_type;
typedef const T& first_argument_type;
typedef const T& second_argument_type;
```

```
template <typename T>
struct lambda_result_traits<T, LAMBDA_LOGIC_TAG>
{
   typedef bool result_type;
   typedef const T& first_argument_type;
   typedef const T& second_argument_type;
};
```

So you can write:

```
template <typename T>
struct lambda_less
{
   typedef lambda_result_traits<T, LAMBDA_LOGIC_TAG> traits_t;

   typedef typename traits_t::result_type result_type;
   typedef typename traits_t::first_argument_type arg1_t;
   typedef typename traits_t::second_argument_type arg2_t;

   result_type operator()(arg1_t x, arg2_t y) const
   {
      return x < y;
   }
};

template <typename T>
struct lambda_plus
{
   typedef lambda_result_traits<T, LAMBDA_OPERATOR_TAG> traits_t;

   typedef typename traits_t::result_type result_type;
   typedef typename traits_t::first_argument_type arg1_t;
   typedef typename traits_t::second_argument_type arg2_t;

   result_type operator()(arg1_t x, arg2_t y) const
   {
      return x + y;
   }
};

template <typename T>
struct lambda_plus_eq
{
   typedef lambda_result_traits<T, LAMBDA_ASSIGNMENT_TAG> traits_t;

   typedef typename traits_t::result_type result_type;
   typedef typename traits_t::first_argument_type arg1_t;
   typedef typename traits_t::second_argument_type arg2_t;
```

```
result_type operator()(arg1_t x, arg2_t y) const
{
   return x += y;
}
```

These objects have minimal differences.

Logical and standard operators are identical to any other binary function, except the return type mpare with atan2). Here is the implementation of lambda's operator<:[4]

```
efine LSS_T(X1,X2)        lambda_binary<X1, lambda_less<T>, X2, T>

nplate <typename X1, typename X2, typename T>
_T(X1,X2) operator<(const lambda<X1,T>& L, const lambda<X2,T>& R)

return LSS_T(X1, X2) (L, R);


plate <typename X1, typename T>
_T(X1, lambda_const<T>) operator<(const lambda<X1,T>& L, const T& R)

return L < lambda_const<T>(R);


plate <typename T, typename X2>
_T(lambda_const<T>, X2) operator<(const T& L, const lambda<X2,T>& R)

return lambda_const<T>(L) < R;
```

The assignment operators do not allow the third overload, which would correspond to a lambda ression such as (2.0 += X), a somewhat suspicious C++ statement:

```
fine PEQ_T(X1,X2)     lambda_binary<X1, lambda_plus_eq<T>, X2, T>

plate <typename X1, typename X2, typename T>
_T(X1,X2) operator+=(const lambda<X1,T>& L, const lambda<X2,T>& R)

return PEQ_T(X1,X2) (L,R);


plate <typename X1, typename T>
_T(X1,lambda_const<T>) operator+=(const lambda<X1,T>& L, const T&R)

return L += lambda_const<T>(R);
```

---

don't explicitly list the code for operator+, which is almost identical, but we will use it freely in the rest of the section.

Here is a sample that uses all the previous code:

```
lambda_reference<double, 0> VX1;
lambda_reference<double, 1> VX2;

double data[] = {5,6,4,2,-1};
std::sort(data, data+5, (VX1<VX2));

std::for_each(data,data+5, VX1 += 3.14);
std::transform(data,data+5, data, VX1 + 3.14);
std::transform(data,data+5, data, 1.0 + VX1);

std::for_each(data,data+5, VX1 += cos(VX1));
```

Here's a sample that deliberately produces an error, which is still human-readable:

```
const double cdata[] = {5,6,4,2,-1};
// add 3.14 to all the elements of a constant array...
std::for_each(cdata, cdata+5, VX1 += 3.14);

error C2664: 'double &lambda_binary<X1,F,X2,T>::operator ()(T &) const' :
cannot convert parameter 1 from 'const double' to 'double &'
          with
          [
                    X1=lambda_reference<double,0>,
                    F=lambda_plus_eq<double>,
                    X2=lambda_const<double>,
                    T=double
          ]
          Conversion loses qualifiers

          see reference to function template instantiation being compiled
          '_Fn1 std::for_each<const double*,lambda_binary<X1,F,X2,T>>(_InIt,_InIt,_Fn1)

          with
          [
      _Fn1=lambda_binary<lambda_reference<double,0x00>,lambda_plus_eq<double>,lambda_
      const<double>,double>,
                              X1=lambda_reference<double,0>,
                              F=lambda_plus_eq<double>,
                              X2=lambda_const<double>,
                              T=double,
                              _InIt=const double *
          ]
```

You would expect the following code to work correctly; instead, it does not compile. The error log may be long and noisy, but it all leads to operator+. The precise error has been isolated here:

```
double data[] = {5,6,4,2,-1};
const double cdata[] = {5,6,4,2,-1};
```

```
ambda_reference<const double> C1;

td::transform(cdata,cdata+5, data, C1 + 1.0);

rror: 'lambda_binary<X1,lambda_plus<T>,lambda_const<T>,T> operator +(const lambda<true_t,T>
,const T &)' :

emplate parameter 'T' is ambiguous
    could be 'double'
    or    'const double'
```

This issue is equivalent to:

```
emplate <typename T>
truct A



mplate <typename T>
id F(A<T>, T)



const double> x;
uble i=0;

x, i);    // error: ambiguous call.
          // deduce T=const double from x, but T=double from i
```

This is where type traits come in. You take the parameter T only from the lambda expression and let the e of the constant be dependent. More precisely all mixed operators with an argument of type const T& uld be changed to accept typename lambda_constant_arg<T>::type.

```
plate <typename T>
uct lambda_constant_arg

typedef const T& type;


plate <typename T>
uct lambda_constant_arg<const T>

typedef const T& type;
```

The C++ Standard specifies that if a parameter can be deduced from one of the arguments, it's deduced then substituted in the remaining ones. If the result is feasible, then the deduction is accepted as valid, n particular in a signature like this:

```
plate <typename T>
d F(A<T> x, typename lambda_constant_arg<T>::type i);
```

the only context where T is deducible is the type of x, so ambiguities cannot occur any more. In particular, it's now possible to add constants of any type convertible to T:

```
std::transform(cdata, cdata+5, data, C1 + 1);
// don't need to write C1 + 1.0
```

Note finally that these lambda expressions are not too rigorous about the number of arguments. The only explicit check occurs as a static assertion in lambda_reference.[5]

```
lambda_reference<const double, 0> C1;
lambda_reference<const double, 1> C2;

double t1 = ((C1<C2)+(-C1))(3.14);                // error: C2 requires 2 args
double t2 = ((C1<C2)+(-C1))(3.14, 6.28);          // ok
double t3 = ((C1<C2)+(-C1))(3.14, 6.28, 22/7); // ok, "22/7" ignored
```

9.2.3. Refinements

Note that unary and binary operations do contain a copy of the functor representing the operation, but the functor is always default-constructed. You can add a wrapper that embeds any user functor in a lambda expression. Just modify the constructor as follows:

```
public:
   lambda_unary(const lambda<X,T>& that, F f = F())
   : x_(that.true_this()), f_(f)
   {
   }
```

This example uses this feature immediately to create a *functor* that takes a functor-on-T and returns a functor-on-lambda:

```
int main()
{
   MyFunctor F;
   lambda_reference<double> X;

   std::transform(data, data+n, data, lambda_wrap[F](3*X+14)); // = F(3*X+14)
}
```

lambda_wrap is a global instance of lambda_wrap_t<void> whose operator[] absorbs a suitable user functor. The choice of [] instead of () gives extra visual clarity, since it avoids confusion with function arguments.

```
template <typename F = void>
class lambda_wrap_t
{
   F f_;
```

[5]This can be fixed, by storing a static constant named min_number_of_arguments in every lambda implementation. Atomic lambdas, such as lambda_reference, will define it directly and derived lambdas will take the maximum from their nested types. Finally, this constant may be used for static assertions. We leave this as an exercise.

```
ublic:
  lambda_wrap_t(F f)
  : f_(f)
  {
  }

  template <typename X, typename T>
  lambda_unary<F, X, T> operator()(const lambda<X, T>& x) const
  {
     return lambda_unary<F, X, T>(x, f_);
  }
;

emplate <>
lass lambda_wrap_t<void>

iblic:
 lambda_wrap_t(int = 0)
 {
 }

 template <typename F>
 lambda_wrap_t<F> operator[](F f) const
 {
    return f;
 }


nst lambda_wrap_t<void> lambda_wrap = 0;
```

This is used as in:

```
ruct MyF

typedef double result_type;

result_type operator()(const double& x) const
{
   return 7*x - 2;
}


bda_reference<double> V;
::for_each(begin, end, lambda_wrap[MyF()](V+2));    // will execute MyF(V+2)
```

The same technique can be extended even further to implement the ternary operator (which cannot be rloaded) and the hypothetical syntax could be:

```
[CONDITION].then_[X1].else_[X2]
```

The dot that links the statements together shows clearly that the return type of `if_[C]` is an object se member `then_` has another `operator[]`, and so on.

9.2.4. Argument and Result Deduction

Loosely speaking, a composite lambda object `G:=F(λ)` takes an argument `x` and returns `F(λ(x))`. The *argument type* of `G` is the argument type of λ and the *result type* of `G` is the result type of `F`.

Up to now, we avoided the problem of defining these types, because they were either fixed or explicitly given.

- The scalar type `T` in the lambda interface acts as the argument of its `operator()`. Whenever a function is applied to `lambda<X,T>`, `T` is borrowed and plugged in the result, which is say `lambda<Y,T>`.
- The return type of lambda's `operator()` instead may vary, so it's published as `result_type`. For example, `lambda_unary<F,X,T>` takes `T& x` from the outside and returns whatever `F` gives back from the call `F(X(x))`. `F` may return a reference to `T` or `bool`.

In the process, however, silent casts from `bool` to `T` may occur.

For example, the function object `abs(C1<C2)` takes two arguments of type `double`. It feeds them to `less` which in turn returns `bool`, but this is promoted again to `double` before entering `abs`.

In general, this is the desired behavior:

```
(C1<C2);                // returns bool
((C1<C2)+2);            // operator+ will promote "bool" to "double"
```

`operator&&` can be implemented as a clone of `operator<`; however, `&&` would take two `T`s, not two `bool`s. In simple cases, this will just work, but in general you'll need more flexibility.

```
(C1<C2) && (C2>C1); // operator&& will promote two bools to double, then return bool
```

You should prescribe only the arguments of `lambda_reference` and let every lambda object *borrow both arguments and results* correctly. `lambda_reference` is in fact the only user-visible object and its type parameter is sufficient to determine the whole functor.

This change also allows you to remove `T` from the lambda interface:[6]

```
template <typename X>
class lambda
{
protected:
   ~lambda()
   {
   }

public:
   const X& true_this() const
   {
      return static_cast<const X&>(*this);
   }
};
```

[6]The rest of the chapter assumes that all the code presented up to now has been updated.

```
emplate <typename T, size_t N = 0>
lass lambda_reference : public lambda< lambda_reference<T, N> >

ublic:
  typedef T& result_type;
  typedef T& argument_type;

  result_type operator()(argument_type x1) const
  {
     MXT_STATIC_ASSERT(N<1);
     return apply_k(static_value<size_t, N>(), x1, x1, x1, x1);
  }

  // ...
;
```

You are going to replace the usage of T in every “wrapping” lambda class with a (meta)function of the sult_type of the inner object:

```
mplate <typename F, typename X>
ass lambda_unary : public lambda< lambda_unary<F,X> >

 X x_;
 F f_;

blic:
 typedef typename F::result_type result_type;
 typedef typename X::argument_type argument_type;

 // ...
```

However, while T is a plain type (maybe const qualified, but never a reference), argument_type will en be a reference. So you need a metafunction to remove any qualifier:

```
plate <typename T>
uct plain

typedef T type;


plate <typename T>
uct plain<T&> : plain<T>



plate <typename T>
uct plain<const T> : plain<T>
```

```
template <typename T>
class lambda_const : public lambda< lambda_const<T> >
{
   typedef typename plain<T>::type P;
   P c_;

public:
   typedef P result_type;
   typedef const P& argument_type;

   // ...
};
```

The nasty issue lies in the binary operators, where you have two lambdas, X1 and X2.

Whose argument_type should you borrow? It's easy to see that *both types* must be inspected, because some deduction must be performed.

For example, if X is a lambda non-const reference, it needs T&. A lambda-constant needs const T&. The expression (X+1.0) is a functor that takes an argument and passes it to both a lambda reference and a lambda-constant, so this should be T&. In general, you need a commutative metafunction that is able to "deduce" a feasible common argument type.

```
template <typename X1, typename F, typename X2>
class lambda_binary : public lambda< lambda_binary<X1,F,X2> >
{
   X1 x1_;
   X2 x2_;
   F f_;

public:
   typedef typename F::result_type result_type;
   typedef typename
      deduce_argument<typename X1::argument_type, typename X2::argument_type>::type
      argument_type;

   // ...
};
```

The problem of combining two arbitrary functionals is even deeper. First, the elimination of T makes all the return types more complex. For example, now the lambda_plus object will have to take care of the addition not of two Ts, but of *any* two different results coming from any different lambdas:

```
// before
lambda_binary<X1, lambda_plus<T>, X2, T>

// after
lambda_binary<X1, lambda_plus<typename X1::result_type, typename X2::result_type>, X2>
```

Furthermore, the *return type* of "a generic addition" is not known:[7]

[7]On the other hand, assignment and logical operators have a deducible return type. The former returns its first argument (a non-const reference); the latter returns bool. The new keyword decltype of C++0x would allow deducing this type automatically.

```
.emplate <typename T1, typename T2>
.truct lambda_plus

  typedef const typename plain<T1>::type& arg1_t;     // not a problem
  typedef const typename plain<T2>::type& arg2_t;     // not a problem

  typedef [[???]] result_type;

  result_type operator()(arg1_t x, arg2_t y) const
  {
     return x + y;
  }
;
```

So you need another metafunction "deduce result" that takes `arg1_t` and `arg2_t` and gives back a suitable type. Luckily, this issue is solvable by TMP techniques under reasonable assumptions, because you have only few degrees of freedom. Involved types are `T` (deduced from `lambda_reference` and unique in the whole mplate expression), `T&`, `const T&`, and `bool`.

.2.5. Deducing Argument Type

u'll now look for a metafunction `F` that deduces the common argument type. `F` should satisfy:

- Symmetry: `F<T1,T2> := F<T2,T1>`
- The strongest requirement prevails: `F<T&, ...> = T&`
- `const T&` and `T` have the same behavior: `F<const T&, ...> = F<T, ...>`

Meta-arguments of `F` are argument types of other lambda objects:

```
typename X1::argument_type, typename X2::argument_type>
```

Eventually it suffices that `F` returns either `T&` or `const T&`. The simplest implementation is to reduce th arguments to references. If they have the same underlying type, you should pick the strongest; erwise, the compiler will give an error:

```
nplate <typename T>
:uct as_reference

typedef const T& type;


plate <typename T>
uct as_reference<T&>

typedef T& type;


plate <typename T>
uct as_reference<const T&> : as_reference<T>
```

```
template <typename T1, typename T2>
struct deduce_argument
: deduce_argument<typename as_reference<T1>::type, typename as_reference<T2>::type>
{
};

template <typename T>
struct deduce_argument<T&, T&>
{
   typedef T& type;
};

template <typename T>
struct deduce_argument<T&, const T&>
{
   typedef T& type;
};

template <typename T>
struct deduce_argument<const T&, T&>
{
   typedef T& type;
};
```

Observe that the specialization `deduce_argument<T&, T&>` will be used also when `T` is a `const` type.

9.2.6. Deducing Result Type

You can use a similar methodology to write code that deduces the result type. Namely, you will break down the list of cases you want to cover and implement additional metafunctions as needed. First, notice that the expected result of a function call is *never* a reference, so you must start ensuring that at the call location no references are passed:

```
template <typename T1, typename T2>
struct lambda_plus
{
   typedef const typename plain<T1>::type& arg1_t;
   typedef const typename plain<T2>::type& arg2_t;

   typedef
      typename deduce_result<typename plain<T1>::type, typename plain<T2>::type>::type
      result_type;

   result_type operator()(arg1_t x, arg2_t y) const
   {
      return x + y;
   }
};
```

This time you need four specializations:

```
emplate <typename T1, typename T2>
truct deduce_result;

emplate <typename T>
truct deduce_result<T, bool>

  typedef T type;
;

emplate <typename T>
truct deduce_result<bool, T>

  typedef T type;
;

mplate <typename T>
ruct deduce_result<T, T>

  typedef T type;

mplate <>
ruct deduce_result<bool, bool>

  typedef bool type;
```

The last specialization is necessary; otherwise, `<bool, bool>` would match *any* of the three (with `bool`), so it would be ambiguous.

2.7. Static Cast

e limitations of a result/argument deduction may lead to some inconsistency. While a classic addition `l+bool` has type `int`, the addition of Boolean lambda objects returns `bool`:

```
bda_reference<const double,0> C1;
bda_reference<const double,1> C2;

C1<C2) + (C2<C1))(x, y);      // it returns bool
```

Both `(C1<C2)` and `(C2<C1)` have "function signature" `bool (const double&, const double&)` and so `bda_plus` will be instantiated on `<bool, bool>`. By hypothesis, when arguments are equal, `uce_result<X, X>` gives `X`.

The only way to solve similar issues is a lambda-cast operator. Luckily, it's easy to reproduce the syntax `tatic_cast` using a non-deducible template parameter:

```
plate <typename T1, typename T2>
uct lambda_cast_t
```

```
    typedef T2 result_type;

    result_type operator()(const T1& x) const
    {
        return x;
    }
};

#define LAMBDA_CAST_T(T,X)   \
    lambda_unary<lambda_cast_t<typename X::result_type, T>, X>

template <typename T, typename X>
LAMBDA_CAST_T(T,X) lambda_cast(const lambda<X>& x)
{
    return x;
}

(lambda_cast<double>(C1<C2)+lambda_cast<double>(C1<C2))(3.14, 6.28);
// now returns 2.0
```

9.2.8. Arrays

Todd Veldhuizen pioneered the application of "template expressions" to fast operation on arrays, in order t minimize the use of temporaries.[8]

```
valarray<double> A1 = ...;
valarray<double> A2 = ...;

valarray<double> A3 = 7*A1-4*A2+1;
```

Naive operators will, in general, produce more "copies" of the objects than necessary. The subexpression `7*A1` will return a temporary array, where each element is seven times the corresponding entry in `A1`; `4*A2` will return another temporary, and so on.

Instead, you can use a lambda-like expression:

```
template <typename X, typename T>
class valarray_interface
{
    // X is the true valarray and T is the scalar
    // ...

    public:
    // interface to get the i-th component

    T get(size_t i) const
    {
        return true_this().get(i);
    }
```

[8]The name `valarray` is used on purpose, to remark that these techniques fit `std::valarray`.

```
   size_t size() const
   {
      return true_this().size();
   }

   operator valarray<T>() const
   {
      valarray<T> result(size());
      for (size_t i=0; i<size(); ++i)
         result[i] = get(i);

      return result;
   }
;
```

The interface can be cast to a real valarray. This cast triggers the creation of *one* temporary object, hich is filled componentwise (which is the most efficient way).

The product valarray<T> * T returns a valarray_binary_op< valarray<T>, std::multiplies<T>, :alar_wrapper<T>, and T>. This object contains a const reference to the original valarray.

```
emplate <typename VA1, typename F, typename VA2, typename T>
.ass valarray_binary_op
 public valarray_interface< valarray_binary_op<VA1,F,VA2,T> >

  const VA1& va1_;
  const VA2& va2_;
  F op_;

blic:
  // ...

  T get(size_t i) const
  {
     return op_(va1_.get(i), va2_.get(i));
  }
```

The key optimization for successfully using expression templates with complex objects, such as arrays, arefully using const references:

```
st VA1& va1_;
st VA2& va2_;
```

onst reference is generally fine, since it binds to temporaries, but it will not prevent the referenced object n dying.

example, (A*7)+B will produce one temporary (A*7), and another object that has a const reference to it, a const reference to B. Since A*7 is alive "just in that line of code", if one could store the expression and uate it later, it would crash the program.

may actually want to use traits to determine a suitable storage type. If VA1 is valarray<T>, then it's venient to use const VA1&. If VA1 is simply a scalar, const VA1 is safer.

To sum up, the line

```
valarray<double> A3 = A1*7;
```

will magically trigger the componentwise evaluation of the template expression on the right, using either a cast operator in the interface, or—even better—a dedicated template constructor/assignment in `valarray<T>`.[9]

The cast operator is not easy to remove. Since `A1*7` is expected to be a `valarray`, it might even be used as a `valarray`, say writing `(A1*7)[3]` or even `(A1*7).resize(n)`. This implies that `valarray` and `valarray_interface` should be very similar, when feasible.

Another advantage of the static interface approach is that many different objects can behave as a fake `valarray`. As an equivalent of `lambda_const`, you can let a scalar `c` act as the array `[c, c, ..., c]`:

```
template <typename T>
class scalar_wrapper
: public valarray_interface< scalar_wrapper<T> >
{
   T c_;
   size_t size_;

public:
   scalar_wrapper(T c, size_t size)
   : c_(c), size_(size)
   {
   }

   T get(size_t i) const
   {
      return c_;
   }
};
```

9.3. Creative Syntax

This section is devoted to exploiting template syntax tricks, such as operator overloads, to express concept that differ from the standard meaning.

Some operators convey a natural associativity; the simplest examples are sequences connected with +, <<, and comma:

```
std:string s = "hello";
std:string r = s + ' ' + "world" + '!';

std::ofstrean o("hello.txt");
o << s << ' ' << "world" << '!';

int a = 1,2,3,4,5,6,7;
```

[9]In other words, a constructor that takes `const valarray_interface<X,T>&`. The details should follow easily and are l to the reader. The cast operator is required if operators return a type that you cannot modify directly (such as `std::stri`

The user expects these operators to be able to form chains of arbitrary length. Additionally, operator[] ınd operator() can sometimes have a similar meaning; in particular, the former should be used when the ength of the chain is *fixed*:

```
rray a;
[2];                    // ok: the user expects a single subscript

atrix m;
[2][3];                 // ok: a matrix is expected to have 2 coordinates

omeObject x;
[2][3][1][4][5]; // bad style, here the meaning is obscure

ensor<double,5> t;
[2][3][1][4][5]; // good style: the user intuitively expects 5 "dimensions"
```

You can exploit this syntax by writing operators that consume the first argument and return *something* at can handle the remaining chain. Consider the line:

```
d::cout << a << b << c;
```

This expression has the form: F(F(F(cout, a), b), c), so F(cout, a) should return an object X ch that there exists an overload of F that accepts X and b, and so on. In the simplest case, F(cout, a) just turns cout.

You are now going to cover this argument in full detail.

3.1. Argument Chains with () and []

metimes operator() is used to form chains, starting from a function object.

Let's analyze some hypothetical code:

```
uble f(int, double, char, const char*);

uble r1 = bind_to(f)(argument<2>('p')) (37, 3.14, "hello");
          ^^^^^^^^^^^^^^^^^^^^^^^^^^^^^^
 produces a new function:

 double f1(int a, double b, const char* c)
 { return f(a, b, 'p', c);

ble r2
  bind_to(f)(argument<0>(17))(argument<2>('p')) (3.14, "hello");
 ^^^^^^^^^^^^^^^^^^^^^^^^^^^^^^^^^^^^^^^^^^^^^^^^^
produces a new function:
double f2(double b, const char* c)
{ return f(17, b, 'p', c);
```

Given that `f` is a function taking `N` arguments, you can guess the following facts:

- `bind_to(f)` returns an object with two different `operator()`.
- The first form takes an expression whose syntax is `argument<K>(x)` and returns a functor that fixes `x` as the `K`th argument of `f`. This first form can be invoked repeatedly to fix several arguments in the same statement.
- The second `operator()` takes all the remaining arguments at a time and evaluates the function.

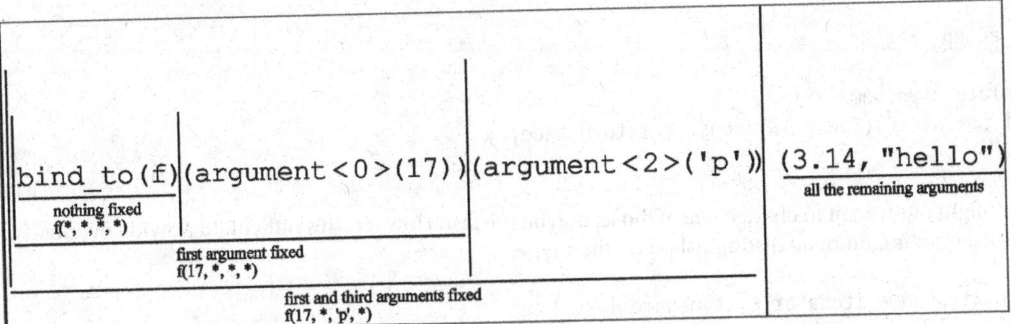

Another paradigmatic example is a function that needs several objects (usually functors or accessors, but there's no formal requirement), which you don't want to mix with the other arguments, because either:

- There are too many: `F(..., x1, x2, x3, x4...)`.
- They cannot be sorted by "decreasing probability of having the default value changed" and the caller may have to put arbitrary values in unspecified positions. `F(..., X1 x1 = X1(), X2 x2 = X2()...)` may need to be invoked as `F(..., X1(), X2(), ..., x7, X8(), ...)`.
- Each object is associated with a distinct template parameter, say `X1, X2...`, so a function call with two arguments swapped by mistake will likely compile.[10]

To illustrate the situation, let's pick an algorithm that needs *three* objects: a less-comparator, a unary predicate, and a logger:

```
template <typename iterator_t, typename less_t, typename pred_t, typename logger_t>
void MyFunc(iterator_t b, iterator_t e, less_t less, pred_t p, logger_t& out)
{
   std::sort(b, e, less);
   iterator_t i = std::find_if(b, e, p);
   if (i != e)
      out << *i;
}
```

[10]See "price" and "quality" in the knapsack examples in Section 6.2.1.

However, all these arguments would have a default type, namely `std::ostream` as logger (and `td::cout` as a default value for out) and the following two types:

```
truct basic_comparator

  template <typename T>
  bool operator()(const T& lhs, const T& rhs) const
  { return lhs < rhs; }
;

truct accept_first

  template <typename T>
  bool operator()(const T&) const { return true; }
;
```

You might often want to change *one* of those, maybe the last. However, it's difficult to provide overloads, ecause arguments cannot be distinguished on their type:

```
mplate <typename iterator_t, typename less_t >
id MyFunc(iterator_t b, iterator_t e, less_t less)
 ... }

mplate <typename iterator_t, typename logger_t>
id MyFunc(iterator_t b, iterator_t e, logger_t& out)
 ... }
 ambiguous: these functions will generate errors, if given a named variable as 3rd
gument
```

So you use the *argument pack* technique. First, you tag the arguments.

```
um { LESS, UNARY_P, LOGGER };

nplate <size_t CODE, typename T = void>
ruct argument

 T arg;

 argument(const T& that)
 : arg(that)
 {
 }


plate <size_t CODE>
uct argument<CODE, void>

argument(int = 0)
{
}
```

```
   template <typename T>
   argument<CODE, T> operator=(const T& that) const
   {
      return that;
   }

   argument<CODE, std::ostream&> operator=(std::ostream& that) const
   {
      return that;
   }
};
```

Then you provide named global constants:

```
const argument<LESS> comparator = 0;
const argument<UNARY_P> acceptance = 0;
const argument<LOGGER> logger = 0;

template <typename T1, typename T2, typename T3>
struct argument_pack
{
   T1 first;
   T2 second;
   T3 third;

   argument_pack(int = 0)
   {
   }

   argument_pack(T1 a1, T2 a2, T3 a3)
   : first(a1), second(a2), third(a3)
   {
   }
```

argument_pack::operator[] takes an argument<N,T> and replaces its Nth template argument with T:

```
      template <typename T>
      argument_pack<T, T2, T3> operator[](const argument<0, T>& x) const
      {
            return argument_pack<T, T2, T3>(x.arg, second, third);
      }

      template <typename T>
      argument_pack<T1, T, T3> operator[](const argument<1, T>& x) const
      {
         return argument_pack<T1, T, T3>(first, x.arg, third);
      }
```

```
        template <typename T>
        argument_pack<T1, T2, T> operator[](const argument<2, T>& x) const
        {
                return argument_pack<T1, T2, T>(first, second, x.arg);
        }
;
```

This code introduces a global constant named where and overloads the original function twice
regardless of the actual number of parameters):

```
ypedef argument_pack<basic_comparator, accept_first, std::ostream&> pack_t;

/ note: a global variable called "where"
tatic const pack_t where(basic_comparator(), accept_first(), std::cout);

emplate <typename iterator_t, typename T1, typename T2, typename T3>
oid MyFunc(iterator_t b, iterator_t e, const argument_pack<T1,T2,T3> a)

  return MyFunc(b, e, a.first, a.second, a.third);


emplate <typename iterator_t >
oid MyFunc(iterator_t b, iterator_t e)

  return MyFunc(b, e, where);
```

So now it's possible to write:

```
Func(v.begin(), v.end(), where[logger=std::clog]);
Func(v.begin(), v.end(), where[logger=std::cerr][comparator=greater<int>()]);
```

logger is a constant of type argument<2,void>, which gets upgraded to argument<2,std::ostream&>.
is instance replaces the third template parameter of pack_t with std::ostream& and the value of
ck_t::third with a reference to std::cerr.

Observe that the code shown in this section is not generic, but it's strongly tied to the specific function
. However, complex functions that require argument packs should generally be just a few per project.

4. The Growing Object Concept

's start with an example. String sum has an expected cost of a memory reallocation[11]:

```
plate <typename T>
::string operator+(std::string s, const T& x)

// estimate the length of x when converted to string;
// ensure s.capacity() is large enough;
```

te that s is passed by value. According to the NVRO (Named Value Return Optimization), if there is only one return
ment and the result is a named variable, the compiler can usually elide the copy, directly constructing the result on the
r's stack.

```
    // append a representation of x to the end of s;
    return s;
}
```

If there are multiple sums on the same line, evidently, the compiler knows the sequence of arguments:

```
std::string s = "hello";
std::string r = s + ' ' + "world!";

// repeated invocation of operator+ with arguments: char, const char*
// may cause multiple memory allocations
```

So you will want to:

- Collect all the arguments at once and sum their lengths
- Execute a single memory allocation
- Traverse the sequence of arguments again and concatenate them

The *growing object* is a pattern that allows traversing a C++ expression before execution. The idea of the technique is to inject in the expression a proxy with special operators that "absorb" all the subsequent arguments.

The *proxy* is a temporary agglomerate object whose operators make it "grow" including references to their arguments. Finally, when growth is complete, the object can process *all* arguments at once and transform them into the desired result.

Thus in the previous example, `s+' '` is not a string, but a proxy that contains a reference to `s` and a char. This object grows when `"world"` is added, so `s+' '+"world"` contains also a `const char*`.

Informally, a growing object is implemented as a pair containing the previous state of the object and some new tiny data (say, a reference). Additionally, there are three possible variants of "pair":

- A class with two members: a reference to the previous growing object and a tiny object
- A class with two members: a copy of the previous growing object and a tiny object
- A class that derives from the previous growing object, with a tiny object as the only member

In pseudo-template notation, the three different models can be written:

```
template <...>
class G1<N>
{
    const G1<N-1>& prev_;
    T& data_;
};

template <...>
class G2<N>
{
    G2<N-1> prev_;
    T& data_;
};
```

```
template <...>
class G3<N> : public G3<N-1>
{
   T& data_;
};
```

The first is the fastest to build, because augmenting a temporary object G1 with new data involves no copy, but the lifetime of G1 is the shortest possible. The other types have similar complexity, since their construction involves copying Gj<N-1> anyway, but they slightly differ in the natural behavior.

The great advantage of G1 is that both constructors and destructors run exactly once and in order. Instead, to create a G2<N>, you must produce two copies of G2<N-1>, three copies of G2<N-2>..., K+1 copies of G2<N-K>..., and so on.

This is especially important because you might need G<N> to run some code *when the growth is complete* and the destructor of G<N> would be one of the options.

Any of these Gj contains references, so for example no growing object can be *thrown*.

Furthermore, there are some known recursive patterns in computing the result:

- *Inward link*: G<N> either computes the result directly, or it delegates G<N-1>, passing information "inward":

```
private:

      result do_it_myself()
      {
            // ...
      }

      result do_it(arguments)
      {
            if (condition)
                  return do_it_myself();
            else
                  return prev_.do_it(arguments);
      }

public:
      result do_it()
      {
            return do_it(default);
      }
```

- *Outward link*: G<N> asks recursively for a result from G<N-1> and post-processes it.

```
result do_it()
{
      result temp = prev_.do_it();
      return modify(temp);
}
```

- *Direct access*: G<N> computes J and asks G<J> for a result. This pattern has a different implementation for inheritance-based growing objects.

```
template <...>
class G1<N>
{
      result do_it_myself(static_value<int, 0>)
      {
            // really do it
      }

      template <int K>
      result do_it_myself(static_value<int, K>)
      {
            return prev_.do_it_myself(static_value<int, K-1>());
      }

public:
      result do_it()
      {
            static const int J = [...];
            return do_it_myself(static_value<int, J>());
      }
};

template <...>
class G3<N> : G3<N-1>
{
      result do_it_myself()
      {
            // ...
      }

public:
      result do_it()
      {
            static const int J = ...;
            return static_cast<growing<J>&>(*this).do_it_myself();
      }
};
```

9.4.1. String Concatenation

You implement the first growing object with a sequence of *agglomerates* (see Section 3.6.8).

Since objects involved in a single statement live at least until the end of the expression, you can think an agglomeration of const references. The expression (string+T1)+T2 should not return a string, but rath a structure containing references to the arguments (or copies, if they are small).[12]

---

[12]See Section 9.2.8.

```
emplate <typename T1, typename T2>
lass agglomerate;

emplate <typename T>
gglomerate<string, const T&> operator+(const string&, const T&);
```
[13]

```
emplate <typename T1, typename T2, typename T>
gglomerate<agglomerate<T1, T2>, const T&>
  operator+(const agglomerate<T1, T2>, const T&);
```

So the sum in the prototype example below would return `agglomerate< agglomerate<string, char>, onst char*>`:

```
td::string s = "hello";
td::string r = s + ' ' + "world!";
```

Eventually, all the work is done by a cast operator, which converts `agglomerate` to `string`:

- Sum the lengths of `this->first` and `this->second` (`first` is another `agglomerate` or a string, so both have a `size()` function; `second` is a reference to the new argument).
- Allocate a string of the right size.
- Append all the objects to the end of the string, knowing that internally no reallocation will occur.

Note that the agglomerates are built in reverse order, with respect to arguments; that is, the object that ecutes the conversion holds the last argument. So, it has to dump its `agglomerate` member *before* its gument member.

```
 using namespace std;

nplate <typename T, bool SMALL = (sizeof(T)<=sizeof(void*))>
ruct storage_traits;

nplate <typename T>
uct storage_traits<T, true>

 typedef const T type;


plate <typename T>
uct storage_traits<T, false>

typedef const T& type;


assume that T1 is string or another agglomerate
and T2 is one of: char, const char*, std::string
```

---

e example is obviously fictitious, as you cannot really add the operator to `std::string`.

```
template <typename T1, typename T2>
class agglomerate
{
   T1 first;
   typename storage_traits<T2>::type second;

   void write(string& result) const
   {
      // member selection based on the type of 'first'
      write(result, &first);
   }

   template <typename T>
   void write(string& result, const T*) const
   {
      // if we get here, T is an agglomerate, so write recursively:
      // mind the order of functions

      first.write(result);
      result += this->second;
   }

   void write(string& result, const string*) const
   {
      // recursion terminator:
      // 'first' is a string, the head of the chain of arguments

      result = first;
   }

   size_t size()
   {
      return first.size() + estimate_length(this->second);
   }

   static size_t estimate_length(char)
   {
      return 1;
   }

   static size_t estimate_length(const char* const x)
   {
      return strlen(x);
   }

   static size_t estimate_length(const string& s)
   {
      return s.size();
   }

public:
   operator string() const
```

```
  {
     string result;
     result.reserve(size());
     write(result);
     return result;        // NVRO
  }
;
```

The first enhancement allows accumulating information in a *single pass* through the chain:

```
oid write(string& result, size_t length = 0) const

 write(result, &first, length + estimate_length(this->second));


emplate <typename T>
oid write(string& result, const T*, size_t length) const

 first.write(result, length);
 result += this->second;


id write(string& result, const string*, size_t length) const

 result.reserve(length);
 result = first;


erator string() const

 string result;
 write(result);
 return result;


:d::string s = "hello";
:d::string r = s + ' ' + "world!";
```

---

n classic C++, each call to `string::operator+` returns a different temporary object, which is simply copied. the initial example produces two intermediate strings: namely t1="hello" and t2="`hello world!`". Since h temporary involves a copy, this has quadratic complexity.

h C++0x language extensions, `std::string` is a moveable object. In other words, its operators will ect when an argument is a temporary object and allow you to steal or reuse its resources. So the vious code might actually call two different sum operators. The first produces a temporary anyway ause you are not allowed to steal from local variable 's'); the second detects the temporary and reuses nemory.

Conceptually, the implementation could look like this:

```
string operator+(const string& s, char c)
{
        string result(s);
        return result += c;
}

string operator+(string&& tmp, const char* c)
{
        string result;
        result.swap(tmp);
        return result += c;
}
```

Where the notation string&& denotes a reference to temporary. Even more simply:

```
string operator+(string s, char c)
{
        return s += c;
}

string operator+(string&& tmp, const char* c)
{
        return tmp += c;
}
```

In other words, C++0x string sum is conceptually similar to:[14]

```
std::string s = "hello";
std::string r = s;
r += ' ';
r += "world!";
```

But a growing object performs even better, being equivalent to:

```
std::string s = "hello";
std::string r;
r.reserve(s.size()+1+strlen("world!");
r += s;
r += ' ';
r += "world!";
```

So C++0x extensions alone will not achieve a better performance than a growing object.

[14]See also Scott Meyers, "Effective Modern C++," Item 29: "Assume that move operations are not present, not cheap, ar not used."

).4.2. Mutable Growing Objects

\ growing object may be used to provide enhanced assertions:[15]

```
td::string s1, s2;
..
MART_ASSERT(s1.empty() && s2.empty())(s1)(s2);

ssertion failed in matrix.cpp: 879412:
xpression: 's1.empty() && s2.empty()'
alues: s1 = "Wake up, Neo"
       s2 = "It's time to reload."
```

This code may be implemented with a plain chainable `operator()`:

```
lass console_assert

 std::ostream& out_;

blic:
 console_assert(const char*, std::ostream& out);

 console_assert& operator()(const std::string& s) const
 {
    out_ << "Value = " << s << std::endl;
    return *this;
 }

 console_assert& operator()(int i) const;
 console_assert& operator()(double x) const;
 // ...


:fine SMART_ASSERT(expr) \
   if (expr) {} else console_assert(#expr, std::cerr)
```

This macro starts an argument chain using `operator()`, and since it's not a growing object, *arguments* *st be used immediately*. But you could have a more intricate "lazy" approach:[16]

```
plate <typename T1, typename T2>
ss console_assert

const T1& ref_;
const T2& next_;
mutable bool run_;
```

: the article on assertions by Alexandrescu and Torjo, which is also the source of the first sample in this paragraph: .
: extra clarity, we omitted the information collection phase (the estimation of the string length) from this example. In
std::ostream does not need to be managed.

```
public:
   console_assert(const T1& r, const T2& n)
   : ref_(r), next_(n), run_(false)
   {}

   std::ostream& print() const
   {
      std::ostream& out = next_.print();
      out << "Value = " << ref_ << std::endl;
      run_ = true;
      return out;
   }

   template <typename X>
   console_assert<X, console_assert<T1, T2> >
      operator()(const X& x) const
   {
      return console_assert<X, console_assert<T1, T2> >(x, *this);
   }

   ~console_assert()
   {
      if (!run_)
         print();
   }
};

template < >
class console_assert<void, void>
{
   std::ostream& out_;

public:
   console_assert(const char* msg, std::ostream& out)
   : out_(out << "Assertion failed: " << msg << std::endl)
   {
   }

   std::ostream& print() const
   {
      return out_;
   }

   template <typename X>
   console_assert<X, console_assert<void, void> >
      operator()(const X& x) const
   {
      return console_assert<X, console_assert<void, void> >(x, *this);
   }
};
```

```
#define SMART_ASSERT(expr) \
    if (expr) {} else console_assert<void, void>(#expr, std::cerr)
```

The previous sample shows that it's possible to modify the growing object from inside, stealing or passing resources through the members.

In particular, a step-by-step code expansion yields the following:

```
SMART_ASSERT(s1.empty() && s2.empty())(s1)(s2);

if (s1.empty() && s2.empty())
   {}
else
   console_assert<void, void>("s1.empty() && s2.empty()", std::cerr)(s1)(s2);
// ^^^^^^^^^^^^^^^^^^^^^^^^^^^^^^^^^^^^^^^^^^^^^^^^^^^^^^^^^^^^^^^^^^^^^^^^^^^^^^^
// constructor of console_assert<void, void>
```

If assertion is false, three nested temporaries are created:

```
)      console_assert<void,void>
-      console_assert<string,console_assert<void,void>>
       console_assert<string,console_assert<string,console_assert<void,void>>>
```

- T2 is created and immediately destroyed. Since run_ is false, it invokes print.
- print calls next_.print.
    - T0 passes its stream to T1.
    - T1 prints its message, sets run_=true, and passes the stream up to T2.
- T2 prints its message and dies.
- T1 is destroyed, but since run_ is true, it stays silent.
- T0 is destroyed.

A specialization such as console_assert<void,void> is called the *chain starter*. Its interface might be nificantly different from the general template.

The interface of the growing object usually does not depend on the number of arguments that were ed together.[17]

4.3. More Growing Objects

neralizing the pattern, given a type container C, you implement a generic agglomerate chain<traits, C>. only public constructor lies in the chain starter and the user can sum any chain and an argument.

---

is is not obvious at all. In the last example of Section 9.3, we considered an agglomerate, namely bind_to(f) gument)...(argument), whose syntax depends on the length of the chain. In fact, binding one argument of four yields actor that takes 4-1=3 free arguments, and so on.

For simplicity, the decision about how to store arguments in the chain (by copy or by reference) is given by a global policy:[18]

```
template <typename T>
struct storage_traits
{
   typedef const T& type;
};

template <typename T>
struct storage_traits<T*>
{
   typedef T* type;
};

template <typename T>
struct storage_traits<const T*>
{
   typedef const T* type;
};

template <>
struct storage_traits<char>
{
   typedef char type;
};
```

During the "agglomeration," a chain of length N+1 is generated by a chain of length N and a new argument. The new chain stores both and combines some new piece of information (for example, it sums the estimated length of the old chain with the expected length of the new argument).

Eventually, this piece of information is sent to a "target object," which then receives all the arguments some order.

Since all these actions are parametric, you can combine them in a traits class:

- `update` collects information from arguments, one at a time.
- `dispatch` sends the cumulative information to the target object.
- `transmit` sends actual arguments to the target object.

```
struct chain_traits
{
   static const bool FORWARD = true;

   struct information_type
   {
      // ...
   };

   typedef information_type& reference;
```

[18]This allows you to present simplified code. You can easily add a storage policy as a template parameter.

```
    typedef ... target_type;

    template <typename ARGUMENT_T>
    static void update(const ARGUMENT_T&, information_type&);

    static void dispatch(target_type&, const information_type&);

    template <typename ARGUMENT_T>
    static void transmit(target_type&, const ARGUMENT_T&);
;
```

Update will be called automatically during object growth; dispatch and transmit will be called lazily if ıe chain is cast to or injected in a target_type.

First you implement the empty chain.

Analogous to the stream reference in Section 9.4.2 above, this class will store just the common ıformation. Additional layers of the growing object will refer to it using traits::reference.

```
:mplate <typename traits_t, typename C = empty>
.ass chain;

:mplate <typename traits_t>
ass chain<traits_t, empty>

  template <typename ANY1, typename ANY2>
  friend class chain;

  typedef typename traits_t::information_type information_type;
  typedef typename traits_t::target_type target_type;

  information_type info_;

  void dump(target_type&) const
  {
  }

lic:
  explicit chain(const information_type& i = information_type())
  : info_(i)
  {
  }

fine PLUS_T  \
      chain<traits_t, typename push_front<empty, T>::type>

template <typename T>
PLUS_T operator+(const T& x) const
{
   return PLUS_T(x, *this);
}
```

```
    const chain& operator >> (target_type& x) const
    {
        x = target_type();
        return *this;
    }

    operator target_type() const
    {
        return target_type();
    }
};
```

A nonempty chain instead contains:

- A data member of type `front<C>`, stored as a `storage_traits<local_t>::type`.
- A chain of type `chain<pop_front<C>>`, *stored by const reference*. Since C is nonempty, you can safely `pop_front` it.
- A reference to the information object. Storage of `information_type` is traits-dependent. It may be a copy (when `traits_t::reference` and `traits_t::information_type` are the same) or a true reference.

The private constructor invoked by `operator+` first copies the information carried by the tail chain, then it updates it with the new argument.

```
template <typename traits_t, typename C>
class chain
{
    template <typename ANY1, typename ANY2>
    friend class chain;

    typedef typename traits_t::target_type target_type;
    typedef typename front<C>::type local_t;
    typedef chain<traits_t, typename pop_front<C>::type> tail_t;

    typename storage_traits<local_t>::type obj_;
    typename traits_t::reference info_;
    const tail_t& tail_;

    void dump(target_type& x) const
    {
        tail_.dump(x);
        traits_t::transmit(x, obj_);
    }

    chain(const local_t& x, const tail_t& t)
    : obj_(x), tail_(t), info_(t.info_)
    {
        traits_t::update(x, info_);
    }
```

```
public:
   template <typename T>
   chain<traits_t,typename push_front<C,T>::type> operator+(const T& x) const
   {
      typedef
         chain<traits_t, typename push_front<C, T>::type> result_t;
      return result_t(x, *this);
   }

   const chain& operator >> (target_type& x) const
   {
      traits_t::dispatch(x, info_);
      dump(x);
      return *this;
   }

   operator target_type() const
   {
      target_type x;
      *this >> x;
      return x;
   }
```

The private dump member function is responsible for transmitting recursively all arguments to the target. Note that you can make the traversal parametric and reverse it with a simple Boolean:

```
id dump(target_type& x) const

if (traits_t::FORWARD)
{
   tail_.dump(x);
   traits_t::transmit(x, obj_);
}
else
{
   traits_t::transmit(x, obj_);
   tail_.dump(x);
```

Finally, you show an outline of the traits class for string concatenation:

```
uct string_chain_traits

static const bool FORWARD = true;

typedef size_t information_type;
typedef size_t reference;

typedef std::string target_type;
```

```
   template <typename ARGUMENT_T>
   static void update(const ARGUMENT_T& x, information_type& s)
   {
      s += estimate_length(x);
   }

   static void dispatch(target_type& x, const information_type s)
   {
      x.reserve(x.size()+s);
   }

   template <typename ARGUMENT_T>
   static void transmit(target_type& x, const ARGUMENT_T& y)
   {
      x += y;
   }
};

typedef chain<string_chain_traits> begin_chain;

std::string q = "lo ";
std::string s = (begin_chain() + "hel" + q + 'w' + "orld!");
```

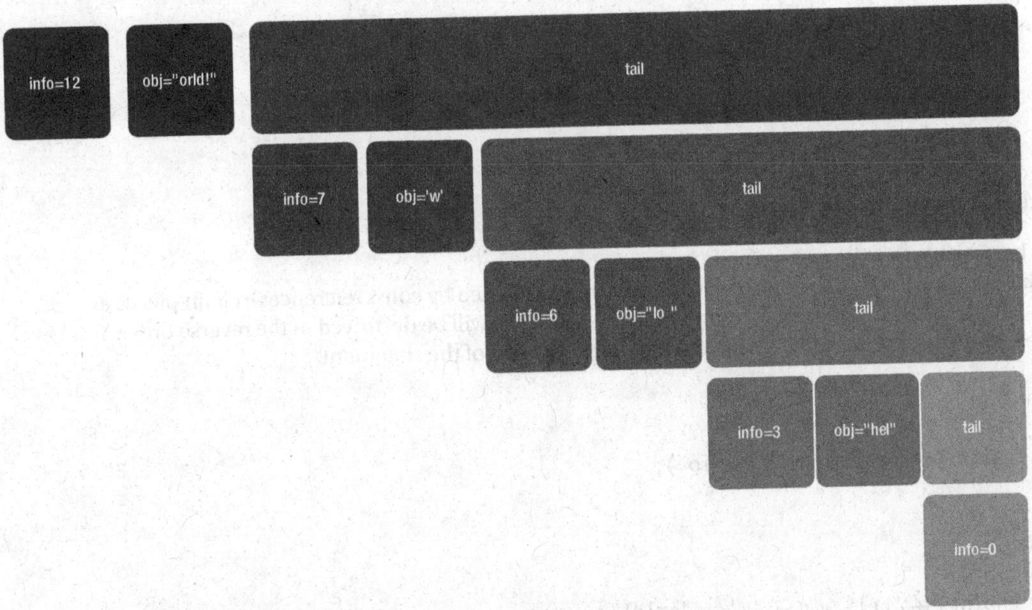

***Figure 9-1.** Chain diagram. Objects are constructed from bottom to top*

- Since you are not allowed to modify `std::string`, you have to start the chain explicitly with a default-constructed object.
- Code that runs only once before a chain starts can be put in `information_type` constructor. Then you can begin the chain with `begin_chain(argument)`.
- The *storage policy* is a place where custom code may be transparently plugged in to perform conversions. For example, to speed up the int-to-string conversion, you could write:

```
emplate <>
truct storage_traits<int>

  class type
  {
     char data_[2+sizeof(int)*5/2];[19]

  public:
     type(const int i)
     {
        // perform the conversion here
        _itoa(i, data_, 10);
     }

     operator const char* () const
     {
        return data_;
     }
 };
```

4.4. Chain Destruction

nay be possible to write custom code in the *chain destructor*.

Since you have only one copy of each chain (they are linked by const references), chain pieces are ıstructed in order from the first argument to the last. They will be destroyed in the reverse order. You have opportunity to execute some finalization action at the end of the statement.

```
~chain()
{
   traits_t::finalize(obj_, info_);
}

::string s;
::string q = "lo ";
gin_chain() + "hel" + q + 'w' + "orld!") >> s;
```

is an integer of type `int_t`, the number of digits in base 10 for n is `ceil(log10(n+1))`. Assuming that a byte contains t bits and that `sizeof(int_t)` is even, the largest integer is `256^sizeof(int_t)-1`. When you put this in place of n, ll obtain a maximum number of `ceil(log10(256)*sizeof(int_t)) ~ (5/2)*sizeof(int_t)` digits. You would 1 for sign and 1 for the terminator.

Then the leftmost object will append "hello world!" to s with at most a single reallocation. Finally, the destructors will run finalize in reverse order (from left to right).

If chains are stored by value, the order of destruction is fixed (first the object, then its members). But there will be multiple copies of each sub-chain (namely, all the temporaries returned by operator+). Evidently, if C1 holds a copy of C0 and C2 holds a copy of C1, there are three copies of C0 and so, without some additional work, you will not know which sub-chain is being destroyed.

9.4.5. Variations of the Growing Object

If you have to add growing objects to a read-only class (as std::string should be), instead of inserting manually a chain starter, you can:

- Replace the chain starter with a global function that processes the first argument (this is equivalent to promoting the empty chain's operator+ to a function).
- Switch to operator() for concatenation (this makes the bracket syntax uniform).

```
template <typename traits_t, typename T>
chain<traits_t,typename push_front<empty,T>::type> concatenate(const T& x)
{
   typedef chain<traits_t, typename push_front<empty, T>::type> result_t;
   return result_t(x, chain<traits_t>());
}

std::string s = concatenate("hello")(' ')("world");
```

Another variation involves the extraction of the result. Sometimes the cast operator is not desirable. You may decide to replace both = and + with the stream insertion syntax, so you'd write:

```
std::string s;
s << begin_chain() << "hello" << ' ' << "world";
```

This is feasible, but it requires some trick to break the associativity, because the language rules will make the compiler execute:

```
(s << begin_chain()) << "hello" << ' ' << "world";
^^^^^^^^^^^^^^^^^^^^
```

While you would prefer:

```
s << (begin_chain() << "hello" << ' ' << "world");
     ^^^^^^^^^^^^^^^^^^^^^^^^^^^^^^^^^^^^^^^^^^^^
```

In the old approach, the result was the last piece of information; now it's the first. So you have to modify the chain and carry it around. You store a pointer to the result in the empty chain so that it can be read only once. The unusual operator<< fills this pointer and then returns its *second* argument, not the first; this is the associativity-breaker.

This section shows only briefly the differences from the previous implementation:

```
template <typename traits_t, typename C = empty>
class chain;
```

```
template <typename traits_t>
class chain<traits_t, empty>

   // ...
   mutable target_type* result_;

public:
   // ...

   const chain& bind_to(target_type& x) const
   {
      result_ = &x;
      return *this;
   }

   target_type* release_target() const
   {
      target_type* const t = result_;
      result_ = 0;
      return t;
   }


mplate <typename traits_t>
nst chain<traits_t>& operator<<(typename traits_t::target_type& x,
                                const chain<traits_t>& c)

 return c.bind_to(&x);


mplate <typename traits_t, typename C>
ass chain

// ...

target_type* release_target() const
{
 return tail_.release_target();


lic:
emplate <typename T>
hain<traits_t, typename push_front<C,T>::type> operator<<(const T& x) const

 typedef chain<traits_t, typename push_front<C, T>::type> result_t;
 return result_t(x, *this);


chain()
```

```
    if (target_type* t = release_target())
      dump(*t);
  }
};
```

The last object in the chain will be destroyed first, and it will be the only one to succeed in release_target.

9.5. Streams

As introduced in the previous section, the stream insertion syntax is one of the most uniform, so it's visually clear yet flexible and open to customizations.

9.5.1. Custom Manipulators and Stream Insertion

Say you want to print a bitstring (see Section 5.2.3) in the C++ way, via stream insertion.

A bitstring implements many static interfaces at the same time.

```
class bitstring
: public pseudo_array<bitstring, bit_tag>
, public pseudo_array<bitstring, nibble_tag>
, public pseudo_array<bitstring, byte_tag>
{ ... };
```

How do you decide which of the interfaces should send its data to the stream? In other words, how can you elegantly select between bit-wise, byte-wise, and nibble-wise printing?

Recall that a manipulator is an object that flows in the stream, takes the stream object, and modifies its state:[20]

```
using namespace std;

ostream& flush(ostream& o)
{
   // flush the stream, then...
   return o;
}

// a manipulator is a function pointer that takes and returns a stream by reference
typedef ostream& (*manip_t)(ostream&);

ostream& operator<<(ostream& o, manip_t manip)
{
   manip(o);
   return o;
}

cout << flush << "Hello World!";
```

[20]See Section 1.4.7 on manipulators.

Note that, while some objects modify the state of the stream permanently, in general the effect of a nanipulator insertion is lost after the next insertion. In the previous code, cout will need reflushing after the nsertion of the string.

However, nothing prevents the manipulator from returning an entirely different stream. Being part of a ubexpression, the original stream is surely alive, so it can be wrapped in a shell that intercepts any further all to operator<<.

```
lass autoflush_t

  ostream& ref;

ublic:
  autoflush_t(ostream& r)
  : ref(r)
  {}

  template <typename T>
  autoflush_t& operator<<(const T& x)
  {
     ref << x << flush;
     return *this;
  }

  operator ostream& () const
  {
     return ref;
  }


toflush_t* autoflush() { return 0; }

line autoflush_t operator<<(ostream& out, autoflush_t* (*)())

 return autoflush_t(out);


t << autoflush << "Hello" << ' ' << "World";
```

All insertions after autoflush are actually calls to autoflush_t::operator<<, not to std::ostream.
Note also that the code generates a unique signature for the manipulator with the proxy itself.

A *stream proxy* need not be persistent. It may implement its own special insertion and a generic erator that "unwraps" the stream again if the next object is not what's expected.

Suppose you have a special formatter for double:

```
ss proxy

ostream& os_;

lic:
explicit proxy(ostream& os)
: os_(os)
```

```
   {
   }

   ostream& operator<<(const double x) const
   {
      // do the actual work here, finally clear the effect of the
      // manipulator, unwrapping the stream
      return os_;
   }

   // the default insertion simply reveals the enclosed stream

   template <typename T>
   ostream& operator<<(const T& x) const
   {
      return os_ << x;
   }
};

proxy* special_numeric() { return 0; }

inline proxy operator<<(ostream& os, proxy* (*)())
{
   return proxy(os);
}

cout
   << special_numeric << 3.14      // ok, will format a double
   << special_numeric << "hello"; // ok, the manipulator has no effect
```

If instead the template operator<< is omitted, a double will be *required* after the manipulator. To sum up, by altering the return type of operator<<, you can write manipulators that:

- Affect only the next insertion, as long as an instance of X is inserted; otherwise, they are ignored.
- Affect only the next insertion and require the insertion of X immediately thereafter; otherwise, there's a compiler error.
- Affect all the next insertions until the end of the subexpression.
- Affect all the next insertions until X is inserted:

```
template <typename any_t>
proxy_dumper& operator<<(const any_t& x) const
{
   os_ << x;
   return *this;
}
```

This is exactly the solution you need for bitstring; treating the static interface type tags as manipulators. Insertion returns a template proxy that formats the next bitstring according to the (statically known) type tag, using a suitable function from the static interface itself.

```
using std::ostream;

template <typename digit_t>
class bistring_stream_proxy

   ostream& os_;

public:
   bistring_stream_proxy(ostream& os)
   : os_(os)
   {
   }

   ostream& operator<<(const pseudo_array<bitstring, digit_t>& b) const
   {
      b.dump(os_);
      return os_;
   }

   template <typename any_t>
   ostream& operator<<(const any_t& x) const
   {
      return os_ << x;
   }

inline bistring_stream_proxy<bit_t> operator<<(ostream& o, bit_t)

   return bistring_stream_proxy<bit_t>(o);

inline bistring_stream_proxy<octet_t> operator<<(ostream& o, octet_t)

   return bistring_stream_proxy<octet_t>(o);

inline bistring_stream_proxy<nibble_t> operator<<(ostream& o, nibble_t)

   return bistring_stream_proxy<nibble_t>(o);
```

9.5.2. Range Insertion with a Growing Object

Another exercise is the insertion of a range into a stream. You need a custom item to start a chain:

```
cout << range << begin << end;
```

The first proxy (returned by `std::cout << range`) takes an iterator and grows (see the previous section). The insertion of a second iterator of the same kind triggers the full dump:

```
template <typename iterator_t = void*>
class range_t
{
   std::ostream& ref_;
   iterator_t begin_;

public:
   explicit range_t(std::ostream& ref)
   : ref_(ref), begin_()
   {
   }

   range_t(range_t<> r, iterator_t i)
      : ref_(r.ref_), begin_(i)
   {
   }

   std::ostream& operator<<(iterator_t end)
   {
      while (begin_ != end)
         ref_ << *(begin_++);

      return ref_;
   }

   std::ostream& operator<<(size_t count)
   {
      while (count--)
         ref_ << *(begin_++);

      return ref_;
   }
};

range_t<>* range() { return 0; }

inline range_t<> operator<<(std::ostream& os, range<>* (*)())
{
   return range_t<>(os);
}

template <typename iterator_t>
inline range_t<iterator_t> operator<<(range_t<> r, iterator_t begin)
{
   return range_t<iterator_t>(r, begin);
}
```

The range proxy accepts a range represented either by `[begin...end)` or by `[begin, N)`. In theory, it's ossible to specialize even more:

```
emplate <typename iterator_t = void*>
lass range_t

rivate:
 // ...

 void insert(iterator_t end, std::random_access_iterator_tag)
 {
    // faster algorithm here
 }

ublic:
 // ...

 std::ostream& operator<<(iterator_t end)
 {
    insert(end, typename iterator_traits<iterator_t>::iterator_category());
    return ref_;
 }
```

.6. Comma Chains

e comma operator is sometimes overloaded together with assignment to get some form of lazy/iterative tialization. This mimics the common C array initialization syntax:

```
t data[] = { 1,2,3 };

 equivalent to:
 data[0] = 1; data[1] = 2; data[2] = 3
```

Because of standard associativity rules, regardless of its meaning, an expression like this:

```
 x, y, z;
```

ompiled as

```
A = x), y), z);
```

ere each comma is actually a binary operator, so actually

```
.operator=(x)).operator,(y)).operator,(z)
```

Note the difference between this syntax and the *growing object*. The latter associates all the items on the t side of assignment, left to right:

```
((x+y)+z);
```

Here, you have the opportunity to modify A iteratively, because the part of the expression containing A is the first to be evaluated:

- Define a proxy object `P<A>`, which contains a reference to A.
- Define `P<A>::operator` so that it takes an argument x. It combines A and x and returns `*this` (which is the proxy itself).
- Define `A::operator=(x)` as `return P<A>(*this),x`.

Suppose you have a wrapper for a C array:

```
template <typename T, size_t N>
struct array
{
   T data[N];
};
```

Being a `struct` with public members, such an object can be initialized with the curly bracket syntax:

```
array<double, 4> a = { 1,2,3,4 };
```

However, you cannot do the same on an existing object:[21]

```
array<double, 4> a = { 1,2,3,4 };

// ok, but now assign {5,6,7,8} to a...

const array<double, 4> b = { 5,6,7,8 };
a = b;

// is there anything better?
```

Let the assignment return a proxy with a special comma operator:

```
template <typename T, size_t N>
struct array
{
   T data[N];

private:
   template <size_t J>
   class array_initializer
   {
      array<T, N>* const pointer_;

      friend struct array<T, N>;
```

[21]C++0x language extensions allow you to initialize some objects (including `std::array`) with a list in curly brackets. For more details, refer to `http://en.cppreference.com/w/cpp/utility/initializer_list`.

```
    template <size_t K>
    friend class array_initializer;

    array_initializer(array<T, N>* const p, const T& x)
    : pointer_(p)
    {
       MXT_ASSERT(J<N);
       pointer_->data[J] = x;
    }
```

The proxy, being the result of operator=, is conceptually equivalent to a reference, so it's quite natural o forbid copy and assignment by declaring a member const (as in this case) or reference.

For convenience, the proxy is an inner class of array and its constructor is private; array itself and all roxies are friends. Note that the constructor performs a (safe) assignment.

The proxy has a public comma operator that constructs another proxy, moving the index to the ext position. Since the user expects the expression A = x to return a reference to A, you can also add a onversion operator:

```
class array_initializer
{
   // ...
public:
   array_initializer<J+1> operator, (const T& x)
   {
      return array_initializer<J+1>(pointer_, x);
   }

   operator array<T, N>& ()
   {
      return *pointer_;
   }

}; // end of nested class
```

Finally, the array assignment just constructs the first proxy:

```
lic:
array_initializer<0> operator=(const T& x)
{
   return array_initializer<0>(this, x);
}
```

Note that the fragment:

```
ay<int,4> A;
 15,25,35,45;
```

ughly equivalent to:

```
(A = 15),25),35),45);
```

where, as mentioned, each comma is an operator. This expression, after `array::operator=`, expands at compile time to:

```
(((array_initializer<0>(A, 15), 25), 35), 45);
```

The construction of `array_initializer<0>` sets `A[0]=15`, then the `array_initializer` comma operator constructs another initializer that assigns `A[1]`, and so on.

To build a temporary `array_initializer<I>`, you have to store a `const` pointer in a temporary on the stack, so the whole process is somehow equivalent to:

```
array<int,4>* const P1 = &A;
P1->data[0] = 15;
array<int,4>* const P2 = P1;
P2->data[1] = 25;
array<int,4>* const P3 = P2;
P3->data[2] = 35;
array<int,4>* const P4 = P3;
P4->data[3] = 45;
```

If the compiler can propagate the information that all assignments involve `A`, the code is equivalent to a hand-written initialization. All `const` modifiers are simply hints for the compiler to make its analysis easier.

Comma chains often exploit another language property: destruction of temporary proxy objects. In general, the problem can be formulated as: *how can a proxy know if it is the last one?*

In the previous example, you might like:

```
array<int,4> A;
A = 15,25;                  // equivalent to {15,25,0,0}
```

but also

```
array<int,4> A;
A = 15;                     // equivalent to {15,15,15,15} not to {15,0,0,0}
```

The expression compiles as `array_initializer<0>(&A,15).operator,(25)`; this returns `array_initializer<1>(&A,25)`.

The only way a proxy can transmit information to the next is via the comma operator. The object can keep track of invocation and its destructor can execute the corresponding action:

```
template <size_t J>
class array_initializer
{
   array<T, N>* pointer_; // <-- non-const

public:
   array_initializer(array<T, N>* const p, const T& x)
   : pointer_(p)
   {
      MXT_ASSERT(J<N);
      p->data[J] = x;
   }
```

```
array_initializer<J+1> operator, (const T& x)
{
   array<T, N>* const p = pointer_;
   pointer_ = 0; // <-- prevent method re-execution
   return array_initializer<J+1>(p, x);
}

~array_initializer()
{
   // if operator, has not been invoked
   // then this is the last proxy in chain

   if (pointer_)
   {
      if (J == 0)
         std::fill_n(pointer_->data+1, N-1, pointer_->data[0]);
      else
         std::fill_n(pointer_->data+(J+1), N-(J+1), T());
   }
}
```

Altering the semantics of destructors, in general, is risky. Here, however, you can assume that these
jects should not be stored or duplicated, and the implementation enforces that so that (non-malicious)
ers cannot artificially prolong the life of these proxies.[22]

- Put the proxy in a private section of array, so its name is inaccessible to the user.
- Declare all dangerous operators as non-const, so if a proxy is passed to a function by const reference, they cannot be invoked. A non-const reference must refer to a non-temporary variable, which is unlikely.
- Forbid copy construction.

While it is possible to perform an illegal operation, it *really* requires malicious code:

```
nplate <typename T>
tamper(const T& x)

T& r = const_cast<T&>(x);
r, 6.28;

return r;


ay<double, 10> A;
ay<double, 10> B = tamper(A = 3.14);
```

ception safety may be a dependent issue. If the destructor of a proxy performs non-trivial work, it could throw.

- The argument of tamper is const T&, which can bind to any temporary. Thus it defeats the name-hiding protection.
- const_cast removes the const protection and makes the comma operator callable.
- r.operator,(6.28) as a side effect sets r.pointer_ = 0.
- The returned reference is still alive when the compiler is going to construct B, but the conversion operator dereferences the null pointer.

Observe that a function like tamper looks harmless and may compile for every T.

9.7. Simulating an Infix

Let's analyze the following fragment:

```
double pi = compute_PI();
assert(pi IS_ABOUT 3.14);
```

We will not solve the problem of comparing floats, but this paragraph will give you an idea of simulating new infixes. If an expression contains operators of different priority, you can take control of the right part before you execute the left part (or vice versa). For example, IS_ABOUT may be a macro that expands to:

```
assert(pi == SOMETHING() + 3.14);
```

SOMETHING::operator+ runs first, so you immediately capture 3.14. Then a suitable operator== takes care of the left side.

Here's some code that will do:

```
template <typename float_t>
class about_t
{
   float_t value_;

public:
   about_t(const float_t value)
   : value_(value)
   {
   }

   bool operator==(const float_t x) const
   {
      const float_t delta = std::abs(value_ - x);
      return delta < std::numeric_limits<float_t>::epsilon();
   }
};

template <typename float_t>
inline bool operator==(const float_t x, const about_t<float_t> a)
{
   return a == x;
}
```

```
struct about_creator_t

   template <typename float_t>
   inline about_t<float_t> operator+(const float_t f) const
   {
      return about_t<float_t>(f);
   }
;

define IS_ABOUT             == about_creator_t() +
```

Obviously, the role of + and == can be reversed, so as to read the left side first.

Note also that if all these objects belong to a namespace, the macro should qualify `about_creator_t` fully.

The curious reader may wish to investigate the following algorithm, which is given without explanations.

wo numbers X and Y are given.

---

1. If `X==Y` return true.
2. Check trivial cases when one or both numbers are infinite or NAN and return accordingly.
3. Pick epsilon from `std::numeric_limits`.
4. Let `D := |X-Y|`.
5. Let `R := max(|X|,|Y|)`.
6. Return `R<epsilon OR D<(R*epsilon)`.

A variant of the algorithm also tests `D<epsilon`.

PART 3

#include <prerequisites>
#include <techniques>
#include <applications>

CHAPTER 10

Refactoring

Templates can be considered a generalization of ordinary classes and functions. Often a preexisting function or class, which is already tested, is promoted to a template, because of new software requirements; this will often save debugging time.

However, be careful before adding template parameters that correspond to implementation details, because they are going to be part of the type. Objects that do not differ significantly may not be interoperable. Consider again the example from Section 1.4.9, which is a container that violates this rule:

```
template <typename T, size_t INITIAL_CAPACITY = 0>
class special_vector;
```

It makes sense to have operators test equality on any two `special_vector<double>`, regardless of their initial capacity.

In general, all member functions that are orthogonal to extra template parameters either need to be promoted to templates or be moved to a base class.[1]

In fact, two implementations are possible:

- A template function `special_vector<T,N>::operator==` that takes `const special_vector<T,K>&` for any `K`:

```
template <typename T, size_t N>
class special_vector
{
public:

   template <size_t K>
   bool operator==(const special_vector<T, K>&);

   // ...
};
```

[1]A similar debate was raised about STL allocators. The notion of "equality of two containers of the same kind" obviously requires the element sequences to be equal, but it's unclear whether this is also sufficient.

- `special_vector<T,N>` inherits from a public `special_vector_base<T>`. This base class has a protected destructor and `operator==(const special_vector_base<T>&)`:

```
emplate <typename T>
lass special_vector_base

ublic:

ool operator==(const special_vector_base<T>&);

  // ...
;

emplate <typename T, size_t N>
lass special_vector : public special_vector_base<T>

  // ...
;
```

The latter example allows more flexibility. The base class should not be directly used, but you can pose wrappers as smart pointers/references, to allow arbitrary collections of special vectors (having the me T) without risking accidental deletion. To illustrate this, suppose you were to change the code slightly follows:

```
mplate <typename T>
ass pointer_to_special_vector;

mplate <typename T, size_t N>
ass special_vector : private special_vector_base<T>

 // thanks to private inheritance,
 // only the friend class will be able to cast special_vector to
 // its base class
 friend class pointer_to_special_vector<T>;


plate <typename T>
ss pointer_to_special_vector        // <-- visible to users

special_vector_base<T>* ptr_;       // <-- wrapped type

lic:

template <size_t K>
pointer_to_special_vector(special_vector<T,K>* b = 0)
: ptr_(b)
{}
```

```
    // fictitious code...

    T at(size_t i) const { return (*ptr_)[i]; }
};

int main()
{
    std::list< pointer_to_special_vector<double> > lp;

    special_vector<double, 10> sv1;
    special_vector<double, 20> sv2;

    lp.push_back(&sv1);
    lp.push_back(&sv2);          // ok, even if sv1 and sv2 have different static types
}
```

10.1. Backward Compatibility

A typical refactoring problem consists of modifying an existing routine so that any caller can choose either the original behavior or a variation.

To begin with a rather trivial example, assume you want to (optionally) log the square of each number, and you don't want to duplicate the code. So, you can modify the classic function template sq:

```
template <typename scalar_t>
inline scalar_t sq(const scalar_t& x)
{
   return x*x;
}

template <typename scalar_t, typename logger_t>
inline scalar_t sq(const scalar_t& x, logger_t logger)
{
   // we shall find an implementation for this...
}

struct log_to_cout
{
   template <typename scalar_t>
   void operator()(scalar_t x, scalar_t xsq) const
   {
      std::cout << "the square of " << x << " is " << xsq;
   }
};

double x = sq(3.14);                      // not logged
double y = sq(6.28, log_to_cout());       // logged
```

The user will turn on the log, passing a custom functor to the two-argument version of `sq`. But there are lifferent ways to implement the new function over the old one:

- *Encapsulation*: Make a call to `sq(scalar_t)` inside `sq(scalar_t, logger_t)`. This solution's implementation risk is minimal.

```
emplate <typename scalar_t>
nline scalar_t sq(const scalar_t& x)

 return x*x;


emplate <typename scalar_t, typename logger_t>
nline scalar_t sq(const scalar_t& x, logger_t logger)

 const scalar_t result = sq(x);
 logger(x, result);
 return result;
```

- *Interface adaptation*: Transform `sq(scalar_t)` so as to secretly call `sq(scalar_t, logger_t)` with a no-op logger. This is the most flexible solution.[2]

```
ruct dont_log_at_all

 template <typename scalar_t>
 void operator()(scalar_t, scalar_t) const
 {
 }


nplate <typename scalar_t, typename logger_t>
line scalar_t sq(const scalar_t& x, logger_t logger)

const scalar_t result = x*x; // the computation is performed here
logger(x, result);
return result;


nplate <typename scalar_t>
ine scalar_t sq(const scalar_t& x)

return sq(x, dont_log_at_all());
```

ile encapsulation conveys to the user a "sense of overhead," interface adaptation suggests that the new `sq` is much
r and can be used freely.

- *Kernel macros*: Work when the core of the algorithm is extremely simple and needs to be shared between static and dynamic code.

```
#define MXT_M_SQ(x)   ((x)*(x))

template <typename scalar_t>
inline scalar_t sq(const scalar_t& x)
{
   return MXT_M_SQ(x);
}

template <typename int_t, int_t VALUE>
struct static_sq
{
   static const int_t result = MXT_M_SQ(VALUE);
};
```

■ **Note** The use of kernel macros will be superseded by the C++0x keyword `constexpr`.

The square/logging example is trivial, but code duplication is regrettably common. In many STL implementations, `std::sort` is written twice:

```
template <typename RandomAccessIter>
void sort(RandomAccessIter __first, RandomAccessIter __last);

template <class RandomAccessIter, typename Compare>
void sort(RandomAccessIter __first, RandomAccessIter __last, Compare less);
```

Using interface adaptation, the first version is a special case of the second:

```
struct weak_less_compare
{
   template <typename T1, typename T2>
   bool operator()(const T1& lhs, const T2& rhs) const
   {
      return lhs < rhs;
   }
};

template <typename RandomAccessIter>
void sort(RandomAccessIter __first, RandomAccessIter __last)
{
   return sort(__first, __last, weak_less_compare());
}
```

10.2. Refactoring Strategies

This section considers an example problem and exposes some different techniques.

10.2.1. Refactoring with Interfaces

A preexisting private_ptr class holds the result of a malloc in a void* and frees the memory block in the destructor:

```
class private_ptr

  void* mem_;

public:

  ~private_ptr() { free(mem_); }

  private_ptr() : mem_(0)
  { }

  explicit private_ptr(size_t size) : mem_(malloc(size))
  { }

  void* c_ptr() { return mem_; }

  //...
```

Now you need to extend the class so that it can hold a pointer, either to a malloc block or to a new object type T.

Since private_ptr is responsible for the allocation, you could just introduce a private interface with table virtual functions, create a single derived (template) class, and let private_ptr make the right calls:

```
class private_ptr_interface

public:
 virtual void* c_ptr() = 0;
 virtual ~private_ptr_interface() = 0;


template <typename T>
class private_ptr_object : public private_ptr_interface

 T member_;

public:
 private_ptr_object(const T& x)
 : member_(x)
 {
 }
```

```
    virtual void* c_ptr()
    {
        return &member_;
    }

    virtual ~private_ptr_object()
    {
    }
};

template < >
class private_ptr_object<void*> : public private_ptr_interface
{
    void* member_;

public:
    private_ptr_object(void* x)
    : member_(x)
    {
    }

    virtual void* c_ptr()
    {
        return member_;
    }

    virtual ~private_ptr_object()
    {
        free(member_);
    }
};

class private_ptr
{
    private_ptr_interface* mem_;

public:
    ~private_ptr()
    {
        delete mem_;
    }

    private_ptr()
    : mem_(0)
    {
    }
```

```
   explicit private_ptr(size_t size)
   : mem_(new private_ptr_object<void*>(malloc(size)))
   {
   }

   template <typename T>
   explicit private_ptr(const T& x)
   : mem_(new private_ptr_object<T>(x))
   {
   }

   void* c_ptr()
   {
      return mem_->c_ptr();
   }

   //...
;
```

Note that virtual function calls are invisible outside `private_ptr`.[3]

0.2.2. Refactoring with Trampolines

e former approach uses two allocations to store a `void*`: one for the memory block and one for the xiliary `private_ptr_object`. Trampolines can do better:

```
mplate <typename T>
ruct private_ptr_traits

 static void del(void* ptr)
 {
    delete static_cast<T*>(ptr);
 }


nplate <typename T>
uct private_ptr_traits<T []>

static void del(void* ptr)
{
   delete [] static_cast<T*>(ptr);
}
```

ther words, callers of the code do not have to worry about inheritance. They can pass any T and the class will wrap it tly and automatically. This idea was developed further in a talk by Sean Parent and is freely downloadable from this `http://channel9.msdn.com/Events/GoingNative/2013/Inheritance-Is-The-Base-Class-of-Evil`.

```
template < >
struct private_ptr_traits<void*>
{
   static void del(void* ptr)
   {
      free(ptr);
   }
};

template < >
struct private_ptr_traits<void>
{
   static void del(void*)
   {
   }
};

class private_ptr
{
   typedef void (*delete_t)(void*);

   delete_t del_;
   void* mem_;

public:
   ~private_ptr()
   {
      del_(mem_);
   }

   private_ptr()
   : mem_(0), del_(&private_ptr_traits<void>::del)
   {
   }

   explicit private_ptr(size_t size)
   {
      mem_ = malloc(size);
      del_ = &private_ptr_traits<void*>::del;
   }

   template <typename T>
   explicit private_ptr(const T& x)
   {
      mem_ = new T(x);
      del_ = &private_ptr_traits<T>::del;
   }
```

```
template <typename T>
explicit private_ptr(const T* x, size_t n)
{
    mem_ = x;
    del_ = &private_ptr_traits<T []>::del;
}

void* c_ptr()
{
    return mem_;
}

//...
;
```

0.2.3. Refactoring with Accessors

ppose you have algorithms that process a sequence of simple objects:

```
ruct stock_price

 double price;
 time_t date;


mplate <typename iterator_t>
uble computePriceIncrease(iterator_t begin, iterator_t end)

 return ((end-1)->price - begin->price)
       / std::difftime(begin->date, (end-1)->date) * (24*60*60);
```

Refactoring may be needed to allow you to process data from two independent containers:

```
d::vector<double> prices;
d::vector<time_t> dates;

problem: we cannot call computePriceIncrease
```

You have several choices for the new algorithm I/O:

- Assume that iterators point to pair, where first is price and second is date (in other words, write end->first - begin->first...). This in general is a poor style choice, as discussed previously.
- Mention explicitly begin->price and begin->date (as shown previously). The algorithm does not depend on the iterator, but the underlying type is constrained to the interface of stock_price.
- Pass two disjoint ranges. The complexity of this solution may vary.

```
template <typename I1, typename I2>
double computePriceIncrease(I1 price_begin, I1 price_end, I2 date_begin, I2 date_end)
{
   // the code must be robust and handle ranges of different length, etc.
}
```

- Pass one range and two accessors.

```
template <typename I, typename price_t, typename date_t>
double computePriceIncrease(I begin, I end, price_t PRICE, date_t DATE)
{
   double p = PRICE(*begin);
   time_t t = DATE(*begin);
   //...
}

struct price_accessor
{
   double operator()(const stock_price& x) const
   {
      return x.price;
   }
};

struct date_accessor
{
   time_t operator()(const stock_price& x) const
   {
      return x.date;
   }
};

computePriceIncrease(begin, end, price_accessor(), date_accessor());
```

Note that you can trick accessors into looking elsewhere, for example, in a member variable:

```
struct price_accessor_ex
{
   const std::vector<double>& v_;

   double operator()(const int x) const
   {
      return v_[x];
   }
};
```

```
struct date_accessor_ex
{
   const std::vector<time_t>& v_;

   time_t operator()(const int x) const
   {
      return v_[x];
   }
;

nt main()

  std::vector<double> prices;
  std::vector<time_t> dates;

  // ...

  assert(prices.size() == dates.size());

  std::vector<int> index(prices.size());
  for (int i=0; i<prices.size(); ++i)
     index[i] = i;

  price_accessor_ex PRICE = { prices };
  date_accessor_ex DATE = { dates };

  computePriceIncrease(index.begin(), index.end(), PRICE, DATE);
```

Accessors may carry around references to an external container, so they pick an element deduced from e actual argument. In some special cases, you can use pointers to avoid creating a container of indices. is approach, however, should be used with extreme care.

```
 warning: this code is fragile:
 changing a reference to a copy may introduce subtle bugs

ruct price_accessor_ex

 double operator()(const double& x) const
 {
    return x;
 }


uct date_accessor_ex

const double* first_price_;
size_t length_;
const time_t* first_date_;
```

```
time_t operator()(const double& x) const
  {
    if ((&x >= first_price_) && (&x < first_price_+length_))
      return first_date_[&x - first_price_];
    else
      throw std::runtime_error("invalid reference");
  }
};

int main()
{
   price_accessor_ex PRICE;
   date_accessor_ex DATE = { &prices.front(), prices.size(), &dates.front() };

   computePriceIncrease(prices.begin(), prices.end(), PRICE, DATE);
}
```

The algorithm takes a reference to a price and deduces the corresponding date accordingly.

10.3. Placeholders

Every C++ object can execute some actions. Empty objects, such as `instance_of`, can execute meta-actions such as declare their type and "bind" their type to a template parameter or to a specific function overload.

Sometimes the job of TMP is to *prevent* work from being done, by replacing an object with a similar empty object and an action with a corresponding meta-action.

Type `P<T>` is called a *placeholder for* `T` if `P<T>` is a class whose public interface satisfies the same pre- and post-conditions as `T`, but has the least possible runtime cost. In the most favorable case, it does nothing at all.

10.3.1. Switch-Off

The switch-off is an algorithm-refactoring technique that allows you to selectively "turn off" some features without rewriting or duplicating functions. The name comes from the paradigmatic situation where a function takes an object by reference, which is "triggered" during execution, and eventually returns an independent result, which is a by-product of the execution. The object may be a container that receives information during the execution or a synchronization object.

```
void say_hello_world_in(std::ostream& out)
{
   out << "hello world";
}

double read_from_database(mutex& s)
{
  // acquire the mutex, return a value from the DB, and release the mutex
}
```

A quick and elegant way to get a different result with minimal code rework is to supply a hollow object with a reduced interface and that, in particular, does not need any dynamic storage. Step by step:

- Rename the original function and promote the parameter to a template type:

```
emplate <typename T>
oid basic_say_hello_world_in(T& o)
```

- Add an overload that restores the original behavior:

```
nline void say_hello_world_in(std::stream& o)

  return basic_say_hello_world_in(o);
```

- Finally, provide an object that "neutralizes" most of the effort:

```
truct null_ostream

  template <typename T>
  null_ostream& operator<<(const T&)
  {
     return *this;
  }


line void say_hello_world_in()

  null_stream ns;
  basic_say_hello_world_in(ns);
```

The switch-off idiom requires exact knowledge of the (subset of the) object's interface used in the ain algorithm.

When you're designing a custom container, it may occasionally be useful to add an extra template rameter to enable a *hollow-mode*. You take the original class and promote it to a template:

```
class spinlock
{
typedef void* ptr_t;
typedef volatile ptr_t vptr_t;
public:
spinlock(vptr_t*const);
bool try_acquire();
bool acquire();
// ...
};
```

→

```
template <bool SWITCH_ON = true>
class spinlock;

template < >
class spinlock<true>
{
typedef void* ptr_t;
typedef volatile ptr_t vptr_t;
public:
spinlock(vptr_t* const);
bool try_acquire();
bool acquire();
// ...
};

template < >
class spinlock<false>
{
// hollow implementation
spinlock(void*)
{}
bool try_acquire()
{ return true; }
bool acquire()
{ return true; }
//...
};
```

Had the class been a template, you would need to add one more Boolean parameter.

Of course, the crucial point of the duplication of the interface is the set of cautious, but meaningful, default answers of the hollow class, provided that such duplication is possible (see below for a counter-example). This also allows you to identify the minimal interface for an object to be considered "valid". The interface of an object is defined by its usage.

Finally, you can restrict the program to spinlocks (which may be "on" or "off"):

```
template <typename ..., bool IS_LOCKING_REQURED>
void run_simulation(..., spinlock<IS_LOCKING_REQURED>& spin)
{
   if (spin.acquire())
   {
      //...
   }
}
```

Or to objects of an unspecified type, whose interface is implicitly assumed compatible with `spinlock`:

```
template <typename ..., typename lock_t>
void run_simulation(..., lock_t& lock)

   if (lock.acquire())
   {
      //...
   }
```

Either choice is valid, but there are situations where one is preferred (see Section 5.2 for more details).

Another application is *twin reduction*. There are algorithms that manipulate one or two items at time and execute the same actions simultaneously on both. To avoid duplication, you want a single nplementation of the algorithm that accepts one or two arguments.

Prototype examples are sorting two "synchronized" arrays and matrix row reduction. This algorithm, ue to Gauss, performs a sequence of elementary operations on a matrix `M` and turns it into a diagonal r triangular) form. If the same operations are applied in parallel on an identity matrix, it also obtains the verse of `M`.[4]

So you can write a general-purpose function that *always takes two* matrices of different static type and eats them as identical:

```
mplate <typename matrix1_t, typename matrix2_t>
id row_reduction(matrix1_t& matr, matrix2_t& twin)

 // ...

  for (size_t k=i+1; k<ncols && pivot!=0; ++k)
  {
     matr(j, k) -= pivot*matr(i, k);
     twin(j, k) -= pivot*twin(i, k);
  }

 // ...
```

Assume that you already have a matrix class:[5]

```
nplate <typename scalar_t>
ss matrix

lic:
typedef scalar_t value_type;

size_t rows() const;
size_t cols() const;
```

---

on-mathematically inclined reader may want to consider an analogous case: software that executes a series of ons and at the same time records a list of "undo" steps.

interface of a data structure is frequently remodeled for ease of algorithms. This lesson was one of the milestones e STL design.

```
    void swap_rows(const size_t i, const size_t j);

    value_type& operator()(size_t i, size_t j);
    value_type operator()(size_t i, size_t j) const;
};
```

It's not possible to extend it following the hollow-mode idiom, because there's no satisfactory default answer for functions returning a reference:[6]

```
template <typename scalar_t, bool NO_STORAGE = false>
class matrix;

template <typename scalar_t>
class matrix<scalar_t, false>
{
    /* put the usual implementation here */
};

template <typename scalar_t>
class matrix<scalar_t, true>
{
public:
    value_type& operator()(size_t i, size_t j)
    {
        return /* what? */
    }
    //...
};
```

So you drop the reference entirely and move down one level. You neutralize both the container and the contained object. The twin matrix is a container defined on a *ghost scalar*; a class whose operators do nothing:

```
template <typename T>
struct ghost
{
    // all operators return *this

    ghost& operator-=(ghost)
    {
        return *this;
    }

    //...
};
```

[6]As a rule, hollow containers own no memory. You could object that here you could use a single scalar_t data mem and return a reference to the same object for any pair of indices, but this strategy would consume a lot of CPU runtim overwriting the same memory location for no purpose.

```
template <typename T>
inline ghost operator*(T, ghost g) { return g; }

emplate <typename T>
nline ghost operator*(ghost g, T) { return g; }

emplate <typename scalar_t>
lass matrix<scalar_t, true>

   size_t r_;
   size_t c_;

ublic:
   typedef ghost<scalar_t> value_type;

   size_t rows() const { return r_; }
   size_t cols() const { return c_; }

   void swap_rows(const size_t, const size_t) {}

   value_type operator()(size_t i, size_t j)
   {
      return value_type();
   }

   const value_type operator()(size_t i, size_t j) const
   {
      return value_type();
   }
```

`ghost<T>` will be a stateless class such that every operation is a no-op. In particular, the line `in(j, k) -= pivot*twin(i, k)` translates into a sequence of do-nothing function calls.
Some more detail on this point is needed.

.3.2. The Ghost

ere are no truly satisfactory ways to write ghost scalars. Most implementations are semi-correct but they have nasty side effects:

- Ghosts are likely to haunt your namespaces if they are not properly constrained. Since their interfaces should support virtually all C++ operators, you will probably need to write some global operators, and you want to be sure these will appear only when necessary.
- The main purpose of ghosts is to prevent work from being done. If `G` is a ghost, then `G*3+7` should compile and do nothing. It's very easy to obtain an implementation that compiles, but erroneously does some work— say, because `G` is converted to integer `0`.

A ghost should be a class template that mimics its template parameter T and it resides in a different namespace. You can assume for simplicity that T is a built-in numeric type, so you can implement all possible operators.

```
template <typename T>
struct ghost
{
   ghost(T)  {}
   ghost()   {}
   //...
};
```

For coherence, comparison operators return a result compatible with the fact that ghost is monostate (all ghosts are equivalent), so operator< is always false and operator== is always true.

As a rule, most arithmetic operators can be defined with suitable macros:[7]

```
#define mxt_GHOST_ASSIGNMENT(OP)                                      \
      ghost& operator OP##= (const ghost) { return *this; }

#define mxt_GHOST_UNARY(OP)                                           \
      ghost operator OP() const { return *this; }

#define mxt_GHOST_INCREMENT(OP)                                       \
      ghost& operator OP () { return *this; }                         \
      const ghost operator OP (int) { return *this; }

template <typename T>
struct ghost
{
   ghost(const T&){}
   ghost()   {}

   mxt_GHOST_INCREMENT(++);    // defines pre- and post-increment
   mxt_GHOST_INCREMENT(--);

   mxt_GHOST_ASSIGNMENT(+);    // defines operator+=
   mxt_GHOST_ASSIGNMENT(-);
   // ...

   mxt_GHOST_UNARY(+);
   mxt_GHOST_UNARY(-);
   //...
};
```

[7]Mind the use of token concatenation ##. You might be tempted to write `operator ## OP` to join operator and +, but is illegal, because in C++, operator and + are two different tokens. On the other hand, ## is required between + and = to generate `operator +=`, so you need to write `operator OP ## =`.

For the arithmetic/comparison operators, you need to investigate these possibilities:

1. Member operators with argument `ghost<T>`.
2. Member operators with argument `T`.
3. `Template` member operators with argument `const X&`, where `X` is an independent template parameter.
4. Nonmember operators, such as

```
emplate <typename T>
host<T> operator+(ghost<T>, ghost<T>)          // variant #1

emplate <typename T>
host<T> operator+(T, ghost<T>)                 // variant #2

emplate <typename T1, typename T2>
???> operator+(ghost<T1>, ghost<T2>)           // variant #3

emplate <typename T1, typename T2>
???> operator+(T1, ghost<T2>)                  // variant #4
```

Each choice has some problems.

1. Member operators will perform argument promotion on the right side, but *template global operators* require a perfect match for argument deduction.[8] With member operators `ghost<T>::operator+(ghost<T>) const`, any sum of the form `ghost<T> + X` will succeed whenever it's possible to build a temporary `ghost<T>` from `X` (since a ghost constructor is not explicit). However, `X + ghost<T>` will not compile.
2. The problem is mostly evident when `T` is a numeric type (say, `double`) and `X` is a literal zero. A member `operator+` will take care of `ghost<double> + 0`, since 0 `(int)` → 0.0 `(double)` → `ghost<double>`, but `0 + ghost<double>` must be handled by a global operator whose signature cannot be too strict, as 0 is not a double.
3. This implies that in this case, only variant #4 is feasible, because no other operator would match exactly `(int, ghost<double>)`.
4. However, you want operators to match as many types as possible, but not more. While you should be able to write `int + ghost<double>`, you don't want to accept *anything*.

```
st<double> g;

 0;                // should work
 g;                // should work

::cout + g;        // should not work!
 std::cout;        // should not work!
```

As a rule, the global operator should delegate the execution to a member function:

```
template <typename T1, typename T2>
inline ghost<T2> operator+ (T1 x, const ghost<T2> y)
{
   return y + x;
}
```

`y + x` is indeed a call to any member `operator+`, so you can pass the responsibility for accepting T1 as argument to the ghost's own interface (the compiler will try any overloaded `operator+`).

A conversion operator is necessary to make assignments legal:

```
operator T() const
{
   return T();
}

ghost<double> g = 3.14;
double x = g;        // error: cannot convert from ghost to double
```

Conversely, with the conversion operator and a bad implementation of operators, innocuous code will suddenly become ambiguous:

```
ghost<double> g;
g + 3.14;
```

For example, there may be an ambiguity between:

- Promotion of `3.14` to `ghost<double>`, followed by `ghost<double>::operator+(ghost<double>)`.
- Conversion of g to `double`, followed by an ordinary sum.

Since both paths have equal rank, the compiler will give up.

In different situations, the conversion will be unexpectedly called:

```
ghost<double> g = 3.14;
double x = 3*g + 7;
```

This code should be translated by the compiler into this sequence:

```
double x = (double)(operator*(3, g).operator+(ghost<double>(7)));
```

If the global `operator*` cannot be called for any reason (say, it expects `double, ghost<double>`, so it won't match), the code is still valid, but it silently executes something different:

```
double x = 3*(double)(g) + 7;
```

---

[8]The user-defined constructor that converts T to `ghost<T>` is considered only after template argument deduction. Note that the constructor here is not even `explicit`. See [2], Section B.2.

This costs two floating-point operations at runtime, so it defeats the ghost purpose.[9] Summing up, in the best implementation:

- The ghost constructor is strongly typed, so it needs one argument convertible to T.
- You need both member and non-member operators:
  - Member operators that will accept any argument (any type X) and will check X with a static assertion (using the constructor itself).
  - Non-member operators that will blindly delegate anything to member functions.

What's described here is an implementation without making use of macros. Anyway, functions enerated by the same preprocessor directive have been grouped:

```
define mxt_GHOST_GUARD(x)        sizeof(ghost<T>(x))

emplate <typename T>
truct ghost

  ghost(const T&) {}

  ghost() {}

  operator T() const
  {
     return T();
  }

  ghost& operator++ () { return *this; }
  const ghost operator++ (int) { return *this; }

  ghost& operator-- () { return *this; }
  const ghost operator-- (int) { return *this; }

  template <typename X> ghost& operator+= (const X& x)
  { mxt_GHOST_GUARD(x); return *this; }

  template <typename X> ghost& operator-= (const X& x)
  { mxt_GHOST_GUARD(x); return *this; }

  template <typename X> ghost operator+ (const X& x) const
  { mxt_GHOST_GUARD(x); return *this; }

  template <typename X> ghost operator- (const X& x) const
  { mxt_GHOST_GUARD(x); return *this; }

  template <typename X> bool operator== (const X& x) const
  { mxt_GHOST_GUARD(x); return true; }
```

---

t: always leave a breakpoint in the conversion operator.

```
    template <typename X> bool operator!= (const X& x) const
    { mxt_GHOST_GUARD(x); return false; }

    ghost operator+() const { return *this; }

    ghost operator-() const { return *this; }
};

template <typename X, typename Y>
ghost<Y> operator+ (const X& x, const ghost<Y> y) { return y + x; }

template <typename X, typename Y>
ghost<Y> operator- (const X& x, const ghost<Y> y) { return -(y - x); }

template <typename X, typename Y>
bool operator== (const X& x, const ghost<Y> y) { return y == x; }

template <typename X, typename Y>
bool operator!= (const X& x, const ghost<Y> y) { return y != x; }
```

CHAPTER 11

Debugging Templates

As TMP code induces the compiler to perform calculations, it's virtually impossible to follow it step by step. However, there are some techniques that can help. This chapter in fact contains a mix of pieces of advice an debugging strategies.

11.1. Identify Types

Modern debuggers will always show the exact type of variables when the program is stopped. Moreover, a lot o information about types is visible in the call stack, where (member) functions usually are displayed with their full list of template arguments. However, you'll often need to inspect intermediate results and return types.

The following function helps:

```
template <typename T>
void identify(T, const char* msg = 0)
{
   std::cout << (msg ? msg : "") << typeid(T).name() << std::endl;
}
```

Remember that type_info::name gives no guarantees about the readability of the returned string.[1] Using a free function to return void makes it easy to switch between debug and optimized builds, as the co can simply use a preprocessor directive to replace the function, say, with an empty macro. However, this approach does not work when you need to identify a class member, such as when you're debugging lambd expressions. (See Section 9.2). You may want to check if the return type has been correctly deduced; the be solution is to add a small, public data member:

```
template <typename X1, typename F, typename X2>
class lambda_binary : public lambda< lambda_binary<X1,F,X2> >
{
   // ...

   typedef typename
   deduce_argument
```

[1]See http://en.cppreference.com/w/cpp/types/type_info/name.

```
    <
        typename X1::argument_type,
        typename X2::argument_type
    >::type
    argument_type;

#ifdef MXT_DEBUG
    instance_of<result_type> RESULT_;
#endif

    result_type operator()(argument_type x1, argument_type x2) const
    {
        identify(RESULT_);
        return f_(x1_(x1, x2), x2_(x1, x2));
    }
};
```

Adding a data member is especially useful because interactive debuggers allow you to inspect objects in memory and display their exact type.

In general, whenever a metafunction compiles but gives the wrong results, add members of type instance_of and static_value to inspect the intermediate steps of the computation, then create a *local instance* of the metafunction on the stack.

```
template <size_t N>
struct fibonacci
{
    static const size_t value = fibonacci<N-1>::value + fibonacci<N-2>::value;

    static_value<size_t, value> value_;
    fibonacci<N-1> prev1_;
    fibonacci<N-2> prev2_;
};

int main()
{
    fibonacci<12> F;
}
```

Then look at F in the debugger. You can inspect the constants from their type.[2]

11.1.1. Trapping Types

Sometimes in large projects, an erroneous pattern is detected. When this happens, you need to list all the code lines where the bad pattern is used. You can use templates to create *function traps* that do not compile and inject them in the error pattern, so that the compiler log will point to all the lines you are looking for.

---

[2] Additionally, there exist interactive meta-debuggers. Meta-debuggers use their own compiler under the hood, so their output might differ from what is observed in the actual binary, but they are extremely valuable when investigating a metafunction that does *not* compile. One can be found here: http://metashell.readthedocs.org/en/latest/

Suppose for a moment that you discover that a `std::string` is passed to `printf` and you suspect this happens several times in the project.

```
std::string name = "John Wayne";
printf("Hello %s", name);   // should be: name.c_str()

class Foo{};
printf("I am %s", Foo());
```

Brute-force iteration through all occurrences of `printf` would take too much time, so you can instead add some trap code in a common included file. Note that you have to write a static assertion that is always false, but depends on an unspecified parameter `T`. In the following code, `MXT_ASSERT` is a static assertion:

```
template <typename T>
void validate(T, void*)
{
}

template <typename T>
void validate(T, std::string*)
{
   MXT_ASSERT(sizeof(T)==0); // if this triggers, someone is passing
                             // std::string to printf!
}

template <typename T>
void validate(T x)
{
   validate(x, &x);
}

template <typename T1>
void printf_trap(const char* s, T1 a)
{
   validate(a);
}

template <typename T1, typename T2>
void printf_trap(const char* s, T1 a, T2 b)
{
   validate(b);
   printf_trap(s, a);
}

template <typename T1, typename T2, typename T3>
void printf_trap(const char* s, T1 a, T2 b, T3 c)
{
   validate(c);
   printf_trap(s, a, b);
}

// ...

#define printf printf_trap
```

This trap code will cause a compiler error every time a string is passed to `printf`.

It's important to be able to mention `std::string` (in `validate`), so the previous file must include `string>`. But if you are testing a user class, this might not be feasible (including project headers that might :ause loops), so you simply replace the explicit validation test with a generic SFINAE static assertion:

```
emplate <typename T>
oid validate(T, void*)

 MXT_ASSERT(!is_class<T>::value); // don't pass classes to printf;
```

1.1.2. Incomplete Types

lass templates might not require that T be a complete type. This requirement is usually not explicit, and it epends on the internal template implementation details.

STL containers, such as vector, list, and set, can be implemented so as to accept incomplete types, ecause they allocate storage dynamically. A necessary and sufficient condition to decide if T may be complete is to put in a class a container of itself.

```
:ruct S1

  double x;
  std::vector<S1> v;


ruct S2

 double x;
 std::list<S2> l;
```

In particular, an *allocator* should not assume that T is complete; otherwise, it might be incompatible th standard containers.

A static assertion is easily obtained by just asking the compiler the size of a type:

```
nplate <typename T>
ruct must_be_complete

 static const size_t value = sizeof(T);


uct S3

double x;
must_be_complete<S3> m;


t.cpp: error C2027: use of undefined type 'S3'
```

This technique is used to implement *safe deletion*. A pointer to an incomplete type may be deleted, but this causes undefined behavior (in the best case, T's destructor won't be executed).

```
template <typename T>
void safe_delete(T* p)
{
   typedef T must_be_complete;
   sizeof(must_be_complete);
   delete x;
}
```

Determining if a template will get a complete type as an argument may not be easy.

Standard allocators have a rebind member that allows any allocator<T> to create allocator<X>, and different implementations will take advantage of the feature to construct their own private data structures. A container, say std::list<T>, may need allocator<node<T>> and *this* class may be incomplete.

```
template <typename T>
class allocator
{
   typedef T* pointer;

   template <typename other_t>
   struct rebind
   {
      typedef allocator<other_t> other;
   };

   // ...
};

template <typename T, typename allocator_t>
struct list
{
   struct node;
   friend struct node;

   typedef typename allocator_t::template rebind<node>::other::pointer node_pointer;
   // the line above uses allocator<node> when node is still incomplete

   struct node
   {
      node(node_pointer ptr)
      {
      }
   };

   // ...
};
```

To compile the node constructor, node_pointer is needed. So the compiler looks at allocator ::rebind<node>::other, which is in fact allocator<node>.

Suppose you now have an efficient class that manages memory blocks of fixed length N:

```
template <size_t N>
class pool;
```

To wrap it correctly in a generic stateless allocator, you may be tempted to write:

```
emplate <typename T>
lass pool_allocator

  static pool<sizeof(T)>& get_storage();

  // ...
;
```

But in this case, the presence of sizeof(T) at class level requires T to be complete. Instead, you switch a lazy instantiation scheme with a template member function:

```
emplate <typename T>
lass pool_allocator

  template <typename X>
  static pool<sizeof(X)>& get_storage()
  {
     static pool<sizeof(X)>* p = new pool<sizeof(X)>;
     return *p;
  }

  // ...

  void deallocate(pointer ptr, size_type)
  {
     get_storage<T>().release(ptr);
  }
```

Now, at class level, sizeof(T) is never mentioned.

■ **Note** As mentioned in Section 10.14 of [7], there's a difference between stack and heap allocation:

```
static T& get1()
{
   static T x;
   return x;
}

static T& get2()
{
   static T& x = *new T;
   return x;
}
```

The former will destroy x at some unspecified moment at the end of the program, while the latter never destroys x.

So, if T::~T() releases a resource, say a mutex, the first version is the right one. However, if the destructor of another global object invokes get1(), it might be that x has already been destroyed (a problem known as "static initialization order fiasco").

11.1.3. Tag Global Variables

A non-type template parameter can be an arbitrary pointer to an object having an external linkage. The limitation is that this pointer cannot be dereferenced at compile time:

```
template <int* P>
struct arg
{
   arg()
   {
      myMember = *P; // dereference at runtime
   }

   int myMember;
};

extern int I;
int I = 9;
arg<&I> A;
```

It would be illegal instead to write:

```
template <int* P>
struct arg : static_value<int, *P> // dereference at compile time
```

You can use pointers to associate some metadata to global constants:

```
'/ metadata.hpp

emplate <typename T, T* global>
truct metadata

 static const char* name;
;

define DECLARE_CPP_GLOBAL(TYPE, NAME)                                   \
  TYPE NAME;                                                            \
  template <> const char* metadata<TYPE, &NAME>::name = #NAME

/ main.cpp

include "metadata.hpp"

ECLARE_CPP_GLOBAL(double, xyz);

t main()

  printf(metadata<double, &xyz>::name);  // prints "xyz"
```

1.2. Integer Computing

is section quickly reviews some problems that static integer computations may cause.

.2.1. Signed and Unsigned Types

mmon issues may arise from the differences between `T(-1)`, `-T(1)`, `T()-1`, and `~T()` when `T` is an integer type.

- If `T` is unsigned and large, they are all identical.
- If `T` is signed, the first three are identical.
- If `T` is unsigned and small, the second and third expressions may give unexpected results.

Let's borrow a function from the implementation of `is_signed_integer` (see Section 4.3.2).

```
plate <typename T>
tic selector<(T(0) > T(-1))> decide_signed(static_value<T, 0>*);
```

Replace `T(-1)` with `-T(1)` and suddenly two regression tests fail. (But which ones?)

```
l t01 = (!is_signed_integer<unsigned char>::value);
l t02 = (!is_signed_integer<unsigned int>::value);
l t03 = (!is_signed_integer<unsigned long long>::value);
l t04 = (!is_signed_integer<unsigned long>::value);
l t05 = (!is_signed_integer<unsigned short>::value);
```

```
bool t11 = (is_signed_integer<char>::value);
bool t12 = (is_signed_integer<int>::value);
bool t13 = (is_signed_integer<long long>::value);
bool t14 = (is_signed_integer<long>::value);
bool t15 = (is_signed_integer<short>::value);
```

The reason for failure is that the "unary minus" operator promotes small unsigned integers to `int`, so `-T(1)` is `int` and the whole comparison is shifted into the `int` domain, where `0 > -1` is true. To see this, execute the following:

```
unsigned short u = 1;
identify(-u);
```

11.2.2. References to Numeric Constants

As a rule, don't pass static constants to functions directly:

```
struct MyStruct
{
   static const int value = 314;
}

int main()
{
   double myarray[MyStruct::value];
   std::fill_n(myarray, MyStruct::value, 3.14); // not recommended
}
```

If `fill_n` takes the second argument by `const` reference, this code may fail *linking*. Taking the address of the constant requires the constant to be redeclared in the `.cpp` file (as is the case for any other static member). In TMP, this is rarely the case.

As a cheap workaround, you can build a temporary integer and initialize it with the constant:

```
// not guaranteed by the standard, but usually ok
std::fill_n(myarray, int(MyStruct::value), 3.14);
```

For extreme portability, especially for enumerations and `bool`, you can build a function on the fly:

```
template <bool B> struct converter;

template <> struct converter<true>
{ static bool get() { return true;  } };

template <> struct converter<false>
{ static bool get() { return false; } };

// instead of: DoSomethingIf(MyStruct::value);
DoSomethingIf(converter<MyStruct::value>::get());
```

11.3. Common Workarounds

11.3.1. Debugging SFINAE

A common "cut and paste" error is the addition of a useless non-deducible template parameter to a unction. Sometimes, the compiler will complain, but if the function is overloaded, the SFINAE principle will ilently exclude it from overload resolution, which will generally lead to subtle errors:

```
emplate <typename X, size_t N>
tatic YES<[condition on X]> test(X*);

tatic NO test(...);
```

In this fragment, N cannot be deduced, thus the second test function will always be selected.

1.3.2. Trampolines

ompiler limitations may affect trampolines. In classic C++, local classes have some limitations (they cannot nd to template parameters). They may cause spurious compiler and linker errors:

```
emplate <typename T>
ruct MyStruct

  template <typename X>
  void doSomething(const X& m)
  {
     struct local
     {
        static T* myFunc(const void* p)
        {
           // compilers may have problems here using template parameter X
        }
     };

     // call local::myFunc(&m);
  }
```

The workaround is to move most of template code outside of the local class:

```
plate <typename T>
uct MyStruct

template <typename X>
static T* MyFunc(const X& m)
{
   // do the work here
}
```

```
  template <typename X>
  void DoSomething(const X& m)
  {
     struct local
     {
        static T* MyFunc(const void* p)
        {
           // put nothing here, just a cast
           return MyStruct<T>::MyFunc(*static_cast<const X*>(p));
        }
     };

     // ...
  }
};
```

11.3.3. Compiler Bugs

Compiler bugs are rare, but they do occur, especially within template metaprogramming. They usually produce obscure diagnostics.[3]

```
error C2365: 'function-parameter' : redefinition; previous definition was a 'template parameter'. see declaration of 'function-parameter'
```

Compilers get confused by templates when:

- They cannot deduce that an expression is a type.
- They don't perform automatic conversion correctly, or in the right order, so they emit incorrect diagnostics.
- Some language keywords may not work correctly in a static context.

Here is an example of this last statement. `sizeof` will usually complain if an expression is invalid. Here is what happens when you try to dereference a `double`:

```
int main()
{
   sizeof(**static_cast<double*>(0));
}

error: illegal indirection
```

[3]Note that all the examples in this section rely on bugs of a specific version of some popular C++ compilers (which we don't mention), so hopefully, they won't be reproducible. However, they are good examples of what could go wrong.

The same test may fail to trigger SFINAE correctly. The following code used to print "Hello" with an old ersion of a popular compiler:[4]

```
emplate <size_t N>
truct dummy

;

emplate <typename X>
ummy<sizeof(**static_cast<X*>(0))>* test(X*)

  printf("Hello");
  return 0;


har test(...)

  return 0;


t main()

  double x;
  test(&x);
```

The next example is due to implicit conversions:

```
uble a[1];
uble b[1];
uble (&c)[1] = true ? a : b;

ror: 'initializing' : cannot convert from 'double *' to 'double (&)[1]'
      A reference that is not to 'const' cannot be bound to a non-lvalue
```

Thus you can see that the compiler is erroneously converting the array to pointer in the ternary erator. However, the *bug might not trigger* inside a template function:

```
nplate <typename T>
d f()

T a;
T b;
T& c = true ? a : b;


ouble [1]>();
```

---

ltype may suffer from similar issues.

Ensuring *portability* is a non-trivial development effort. An informal definition of portability is, "code that works in multiple platforms, potentially adapting to the platform itself (with preprocessor directives, and so on)". Code that is *standard conformant* will work everywhere, without changes (given a bug-free compiler). In practice, portability is a combination of both standard conformant code and code that works around some specific compiler limitations/bugs. Some compilers have subtle non-standard behavior; they may have extensions (for example, they may silently allow creating variable-length arrays on the stack), they may tolerate minor syntax errors (such as `this->` or the use of `::template`), and even some ambiguities (for example, static casts of objects with multiple bases). However, aiming for standard conformance is extremely important, because it guarantees that if a piece of (metaprogramming) code works, it will continue working even with future versions of the same compiler.

If code that looks correct does not compile, it may help to:

- Simplify a complex type introducing extra `typedef`s or vice versa.
- Promote a function to template or vice versa.
- Test a different compiler if the code cannot be changed further.

CHAPTER 12

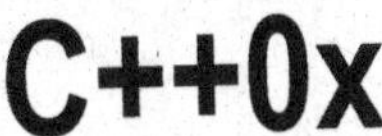

C++0x

"I note that every C++0x feature has been implemented by someone somewhere."

Bjarne Stroustru

We conventionally call "classic C++" the language in its final revision in 2003, as opposed to "modern C++" (also informally known as C++0x), introduced in 2011 and subsequently refined in 2014. The set of changes was huge, but the new rules in general were written to ease TMP and make the code less verbose. Additionally, compilers come with a new arsenal of standard classes, containers, language tools (like `std::bind`), and traits that expose meta-information previously known only to the compiler.[1]

The simplest example is the metafunction `std::has_trivial_destructor<T>`.

It's not possible to detect if a type has a trivial destructor by language only. The best default implementation in classic C++ would be "return `false` unless `T` is a native type".[2]

This chapter briefly scratches the surface of a huge topic, so don't consider this chapter a complete reference. Some of the descriptions are slightly simplified, for the benefit of extra clarity.

12.1. Type Traits

Compilers already offer a complete set of metafunctions:

```
#include <type_traits>
```

This will bring some metafunctions in namespace `std` or `std::tr1` (depending on the compiler and t standard library).[3]

---

[1]As the situation is evolving quickly, refer to online documentation. It's not easy to find a comparison table that is simultaneously complete and up-to-date, but at the time of this writing, good references are `http://wiki.apache.or stdcxx/C++0xCompilerSupport` and `http://cpprocks.com/c11-compiler-support-shootout-visual-studio- gcc-clang-intel/`.

[2]As a rule, however, it's acceptable for metafunctions to return a "suboptimal" value. If a class destructor is known to be trivial, then the code may be optimized. A drastic assumption like "no destructor is trivial" will probably make the program slower, but it shouldn't make it wrong.

[3]They are described in the freely downloadable "Draft Technical Report on C++ Library Extensions" (`http://www.open-std.org/jtc1/sc22/wg21/docs/papers/2005/n1836.pdf`).

In particular, some metafunctions that were described in this book are present in C++0x, with a different ıame. Some examples are listed in the following table.[4]

his Book	C++0x Equivalent
tatic_value	std::integral constant
nly_if	std::enable_if
ypeif	std::conditional
as_conversion	std::is_convertible

2.2. Decltype

milarly to sizeof, decltype resolves to the type of the C++ expression given in brackets (without valuating it at runtime), and you can put it wherever a type is required:

```
t a;
uble b;

cltype(a+b) x = 0;        // x is double
```

decltype can have a positive impact on SFINAE. The following metafunction detects correctly a swap ember function, testing the expression x.swap(x), where x is a non-constant reference to X.

Since swap usually returns void, you use pointer-to-decltype for types that pass the test, and a n-pointer class for the rest. Then you cast this to yes/no as usual:

```
efine REF_TO_X   (*static_cast<X*>(0))

ruct dummy {};

nplate <typename T>
ruct has_swap

 template <typename X>
 static decltype(REF_TO_X.swap(REF_TO_X))* test(X*);

 static dummy test(...);

 template <typename X>
 static yes_type cast(X*);

 static no_type cast(dummy);

 static const bool value = sizeof( cast(test((T*)0)) )==sizeof(yes_type);
```

st of metafunctions that ship with C++11-compliant compilers can be found here: ://en.cppreference.com/w/cpp/header/type_traits.

Additionally, the C++11 header <utility> adds a new function equivalent to the macro REF_TO_X.

In a SFINAE-expression, you may mention a member function call (the previous example reads "the result of REF_TO_X.swap(REF_TO_X)"), so you need an instance of T. However, you cannot simply call a constructor, say as T(), because T may not have a public default constructor. A workaround is to produce a fake reference, such as REF_TO_X, as the expression is not evaluated anyway. But in C++11 you can just use the expression std::declval<T>(). This is safer because, as opposed to macros, it will work only in an unevaluated context.

12.3. Auto

The keyword auto has a new meaning since C++11. It is used to declare a local variable that needs to be initialized immediately. The initialization object is used to deduce the actual type of the variable, exactly as it happens for template parameters:

```
auto i = 0;
```

The actual type of i is the same as the template deduced from the call f(0), where f would be (pseudo-code):

```
template <typename auto>
void f(auto i);
```

auto will always resolve to a value type. In fact, its intended use is to store results coming from a function, without explicitly mentioning their type (think auto i = myMap.begin()). If the user really wants a reference, auto can be explicitly qualified (as any template parameter):

```
const auto& i = cos(0.0);
```

auto will resolve to double, because that's what would happen when calling g(cos(0.0)), with

```
template <typename auto>
void g(const auto& i);
```

Remember that a generic template parameter will not match a reference:

```
int& get_ref();

template <typename T>
void f(T x);

f(get_ref());        // T = int, not reference-to-int
```

On the other hand, decltype returns the exact static type of an expression, as defined:[5]

```
int i = 0;
decltype(get_ref()) j = i;        // j is reference-to-int
```

[5]For a detailed explanation of the differences between auto and decltype, see [17].

decltype has a few rules for handling references:

- decltype(variable) or decltype(class member) result in the same declared type as the operand; if x is a double in current scope, decltype(x) is deduced to be double, not double&.
- decltype(function call) is the type of result returned by the function.[6]
- If none of the previous rules is true and if the expression is an lvalue of type T, the result is T&; otherwise, it's T.

In particular, some "bizarre-looking" expressions like decltype(*&x), decltype((x)), or ecltype(true ? x : x) will yield double& because none of the operands is a plain variable, so the third ule prevails.

12.4. Lambdas

ambda expressions ("lambdas" for short) provide a concise way to create function objects on the fly. hey are not a new language feature, but rather a new syntax:

```
(int i) { return i<7; }

(double x, double y) { return x>y; }
```

Each line represents an *instance* of an object of type "functor" (called *closure*) taking one or more guments and returning decltype(return statement). So you can pass this object to an algorithm:

```
d::partition(begin, end, [](int i) { return i<7; });

d::sort(begin, end, [](double x, double y) { return x>y; });
```

This is equivalent to the more verbose:

```
ruct LessThan7

 bool operator()(int i) const
 {
    return i<7;
 }


 main()

std::vector<int> v;
std::partition(v.begin(), v.end(), LessThan7());
```

---

compiler will find the appropriate function with the standard overload resolution rules, as if it were a normal call.

The obvious advantages are more clarity (the line that executes the partitioning becomes self-contained) and omission of irrelevant information (as you don't need to find a meaningful name for the functor, nor for its parameters).

The brackets [] are called *lambda introducers*, and they can be used to list local variables that you want "captured," which means added to the functor as members. In the example that follows, the closure gets a copy of N (the introducer [&N] would pass a reference).

```
int N = 7;

std::partition(v.begin(), v.end(), [N](int i) { return i<N; });
```

Again, this lambda is equivalent to the more verbose:

```
class LessThanN
{
 private:
   int N_;

 public:

   LessThanN(int N)
   : N_(N)
   {}

   bool operator()(int i) const
   {
      return i<N;
   }
};
```

There are some more syntax details. You can specify the return type explicitly after the argument list. This is indeed useful when you want to return a reference (by default, the return type is an rvalue).

```
[](int i) -> bool { ... }
```

Closures can be stored using auto:

```
auto F = [](double x, double y) { return cos(x*y); }
```

Finally, a lambda created inside a member function is allowed to capture this; the lambda function ca operator will be able to access anything that was available in the original context. In practice, the code of t lambda body works *as if* it were written directly in the place it's declared.

```
class MyClass
{
 private:
   int myMember_;
   void doIt() const { ... }
   void doMore() { ... }
```

```
public:

   int lambdizeMyself() const
   {
      auto L = [this]()
               {
                  doIt();              // ok: doIt is in scope
                  doMore();            // error: doMore is non-const
                  return myMember_;    // ok, private members can be read
               };

      return L();
   }
;
```

The following example (due to Stephan T. Lavavej) shows that lambdas can interact with template arameters. Here a lambda is used to perform the logical negation of an unspecified unary predicate.

```
emplate <typename T, typename Predicate>
oid keep_if(std::vector<T>& v, Predicate pred)

   auto notpred = [&pred](const T& t) { return !pred(t); };
   v.erase(remove_if(v.begin(), v.end(), notpred), v.end());
```

2.5. Initializers

a function has a long return type, you may be forced to write it twice—both in the function signature d when building the result. This redundancy is likely to cause maintenance and refactoring problems. onsider the following example from 9.4.2:

```
mplate <typename X>
nsole_assert<X, console_assert<T1, T2> > operator()(const X& x) const

 return console_assert<X, console_assert<T1, T2> >(x, *this);
```

In classic TMP, this is avoided with non-explicit single-argument constructors (when feasible):

```
plate <typename T1, typename T2>
ss console_assert

public:
   console_assert(int = 0) {}


plate <typename X>
sole_assert<X, console_assert<T1, T2> > operator()(const X& x) const

return 0;    // much simpler, but we cannot pass parameters...
```

In C++0x, a new language feature called *braced initializer list* allows you to build an object using curly brackets and (in some cases) to omit the type name:

```
std::pair<const char*, double> f()
{
   return { "hello", 3.14 };
}

template <typename X>
console_assert<X, console_assert<T1, T2> > operator()(const X& x) const
{
   return { x, *this };
}
```

The compiler will match the items in the initializer list against the arguments of all constructors and pick the best, according to the overload resolution rules.

12.6. Template Typedefs

C++0x extends the traditional `typedef` syntax with a new `using` statement:

```
typedef T MyType; // old syntax

using MyType = T; // new syntax
```

However, the new syntax is also valid with templates:

```
template <typename T>
using MyType = std::map<T, double>; // declares MyType<T>

MyType<string> m; // std::map<string, double>
```

12.7. Extern Template

12.7.1. Linking Templates

In classic C++, the compiler needs to see the entire body of the function/class template, to be able to generate template instantiations. The default behavior is to generate only member functions that are actu used in the translation unit, so roughly speaking, every .cpp file that uses a template class will produce a copy of the code in the corresponding binary object. Finally, the linker will collect all the binary objects an produce a single executable, usually identifying and removing duplicates correctly.

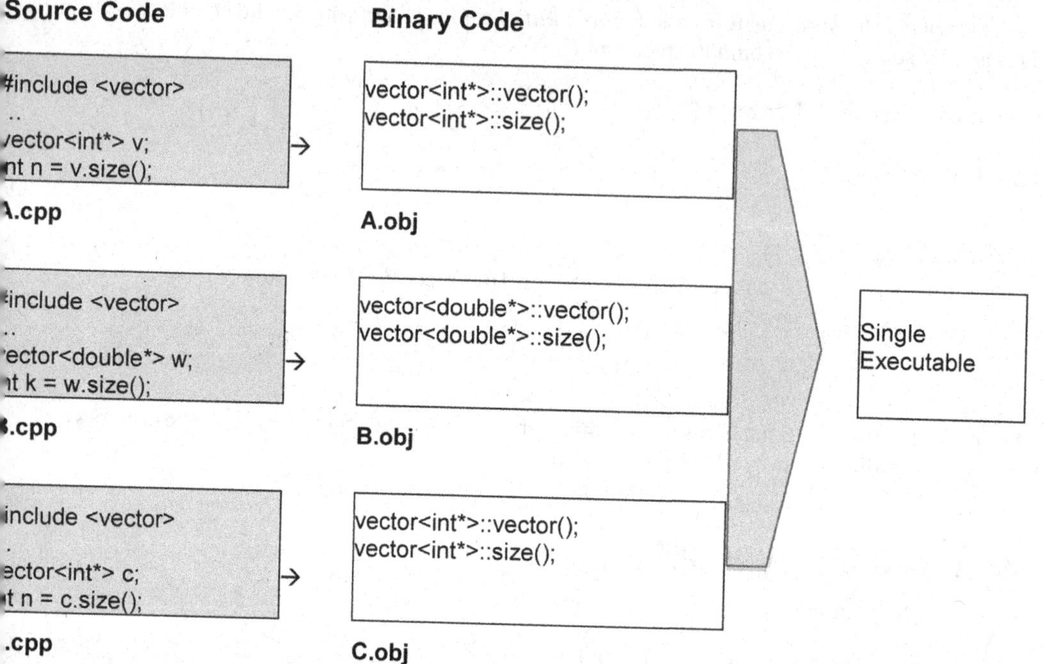
Source Code
Binary Code
#include <vector>
..
vector<int*> v;
nt n = v.size();
.cpp
vector<int*>::vector();
vector<int*>::size();
A.obj
include <vector>
..
ector<double*> w;
t k = w.size();
.cpp
vector<double*>::vector();
vector<double*>::size();
B.obj
Single
Executable
include <vector>
.
ector<int*> c;
t n = c.size();
.cpp
vector<int*>::vector();
vector<int*>::size();
C.obj

In ordinary code, symbols cannot be defined twice, but template-generated code is marked as e-duplicable," and the linker in the final step will remove both C++ duplicates (like `vector<int*>::size()`, hich was generated twice) and machine-code duplicates. It may detect that all `vector<T*>` produce the me assembly for every `T`, so the final executable will contain just *one* copy of each member function.

However, this happens because the vector header contains all the relevant code. Let's write a template ss as if it were a plain class (remember that as a rule, this is incorrect).

```
 xyz.h

nplate <typename T>
ass XYZ

 public:
    int size() const;

xyz.cpp

plate <typename T>
 XYZ<T>::size() const

return 7;
```

Now any translation unit that includes `xyz.h` (and links against `xyz.cpp`) will be able to compile correctly any code, including:

```
// main.cpp
#include <xyz.h>

int main()
{
   XYZ<int> x;
   return x.size();
}
```

However, the program won't link, because in the translation unit `main.cpp` the compiler does not see the relevant template bodies. On the other hand, `XYZ` can be fully used *inside* `xyz.cpp`:

```
// xyz.cpp

template <typename T>
int XYZ<T>::size() const
{
   return 7;
};

int f()
{
   XYZ<int> x;             // Ok.
   return x.size();        // Ok.
}
```

Now, as a side effect, the binary object `xyz.obj` will contain the binary code for the relevant member functions that are used (namely, the constructor `XYZ::XYZ()` and `XYZ::size`). This implies that `main.cpp` will now link correctly!

The compiler will verify that `main.cpp` is syntactically correct. Since it's unable to produce the code in-place, it will mark the symbols as "missing," but the linker will eventually find and borrow them from `xyz.cpp`.

Needless to say, this works because both files are using `XYZ<same type>` and the same member functions.

The standard offers a way to force instantiation of a template *and all its member functions,* in a translation unit. This is called *explicit instantiation.*

```
template class XYZ<int>;
```

Namespaces and functions can be used:

```
// assume that we included <vector>

template class std::vector<int>;

// assume that we included this template function:
// template <typename T>
// void f(T x)

template void f<int>(int x);
```

A possible use is to limit the set of types that the user can plug in to a template:

```
'/ xyz.cpp

:emplate <typename T>
.nt XYZ<T>::size() const

  return ...;
;

/ these are the only types that the user will be able to plug in
/ XYZ<T>. otherwise the program won't link.

emplate class XYZ<int>;
emplate class XYZ<double>;
emplate class XYZ<char>;
```

Now this translation unit will contain the binary code for all member functions of XYZ, so they can be orrectly "exported" to other units when assembling the final executable.

2.7.2. Extern Template

C++0x (and as an extension in many classic C++ compilers), it's possible to *prevent* the compiler from stantiating a template automatically and force a behavior like the one described in the last section.

```
.tern template class XYZ<int>;
```

This forces the template class to link like an ordinary class (so in particular, inlining is still possible), and nay save compilation time.

According to the C++ standard, this syntax prevents implicit instantiation, but *not* explicit instantiation. you can in principle put a single extern template declaration in an .hpp file (after the template code), and ingle explicit instantiation in a .cpp file.[7]

```
'/////////////////////////
 special_string.hpp

nplate <typename T>
ass special_string

 public:
   int size() const { ... }


ern template special_string<char>;
ern template special_string<wchar_t>;
```

---

er compilers need not respect this behavior when both directives are present, so some use of the preprocessor be required.

```
////////////////////////////////
// special_string.cpp

#include "special_string.hpp"

template special_string<char>;
template special_string<wchar_t>;
```

12.9. Variadic Templates

Since C++11, the list of template arguments can have a variable length:

```
template <typename... T>
struct typearray
{};

template <size_t... N>
struct list_of_int
{};

typearray<int> t1;                      // Ok.
typearray<int, double, float> t3;       // Also ok.
typearray<> t0;                         // An empty list also works.
```

The ellipsis (...) to the *left* of T declares that T can match a (possibly empty) list of parameters. T is indeed called a *template parameter pack*. On the other hand, an ellipsis to the *right* of an expression involving a parameter pack name expands it (put simply, it clones the expression for every type in the pack).

```
template <typename... T>
void doSomething(T... args)           // conceptually equivalent to:
                                      // T1 arg1, T2 arg2, ... , Tn argn
{
   typearray<T> e;                    // error: T is unexpanded

   typearray<T...> e;                 // ok, gives: <T1, ..., Tn>
   list_of_int<sizeof(T)...> l;       // ok, gives: <sizeof(T1), ..., sizeof(Tn)>
}
```

You can use pattern matching to "iterate" over a parameter pack:

```
void doSomething()                                  // will match 0 arguments
{
}

template <typename HEAD, typename... TAIL>
void doSomething(HEAD h, TAIL... tail)        // will match 1 or more arguments
{
   std::cout << h << std::endl;
   doSomething(tail...);
}
```

As an exercise, take a look at this metafunction `count<T, A...>`, which counts how many times
a type T appears in a pack A:

```
emplate <typename T, typename... A>
truct count;

emplate <typename T, typename... A>
truct count<T, T, A...>

   static const int value = 1 + count<T, A...>::value;
;

emplate <typename T, typename T2, typename... A>
truct count<T, T2, A...> : count<T, A...>
};

emplate <typename T>
truct count<T> : std::integral_constant<int, 0>
;
```

The ellipsis can trigger more than one expansion at the same time. Suppose for example that you want check that no type in a pack was repeated twice:

```
mplate <typename T, typename... A>
t assert()

  static_assert(count<T, A...>::value <= 1, "error");
  return 0;


mplate <typename... N>
id expand_all(N...)



nplate <typename... A>
id no_duplicates(A... a)

  expand_all(assert<A, A...>()...);  // double expansion
```

This double expansion will call:

```
and_all(assert<A1, (all A)>(), assert<A2, (all A)>(), ...)
```

`expand_all` gets any number of arguments of any type and ignores them entirely. This is necessary to ger the expansion of the parameter pack. In practice, all `assert<...>` functions will either fail to compile eturn 0, so `no_duplicates` will be easily inlined and produce almost no code.

APPENDIX A

Exercises

A.1. Exercises

In all the following problems, the reader should assume that a single writable file with some template code is given; more files can be added, and the rest of the project is read-only.

A.1.1. Extension

A function template is given:

```
template <typename T>
void f(T x)
{
    printf("hello T");
}
```

- Add another overload that is to be called for every class that derives from BASE and prints "hello BASE-or-derived"
- Ensure that your solution is robust. Change the return type of `f` to `int` and see if your solution still holds
- Ensure that your solution is robust. Add a plain function – say `int f(double x)` – in the same file and see if compilation fails
- Think of an alternative solution that minimizes the changes to the existing code.

A.1.2. Integer

The following code:

```
template <typename T>
uint32 f(T x) { ... }

// ...
printf("%x", f(a));
```

is emitting a warning: return type of `f` is incompatible with `%x`.

What kind of investigation would you perform?

A.1.3. Date Format

Following Section 7.7.1, implement a constant generator with an even more natural syntax, such as:

```
YYYYMMDD = dateformat<'Y','Y',Y','Y','M','M','D','D'>::value
```

or

```
YYYYMMDD = dateformat<'Y','Y',Y','Y','/','M','M','/','D','D'>::value
```

.1.4. Specialization

template class is given:

```
emplate <typename T>
lass X
 /* very long implementation... */ };
```

Modify X so that X<double> has precisely one additional data member (say, int) and one extra member unction. Perform minimal changes to existing code (so if the source file is under version control software, e differences are self-explanatory).

..1.5. Bit Counting

e code below:

```
 returns the number of bits of base

mplate <size_t BASE>
ruct nb

static const size_t value
   = nb<BASE % 8>::value
       + nb<(BASE/8) % 8>::value + nb<BASE/16>::value;

nplate <> struct nb<0> { static const size_t value = 0; };
nplate <> struct nb<1> { static const size_t value = 1; };
nplate <> struct nb<2> { static const size_t value = 1; };
nplate <> struct nb<3> { static const size_t value = 2; };
nplate <> struct nb<4> { static const size_t value = 1; };
nplate <> struct nb<5> { static const size_t value = 2; };
plate <> struct nb<6> { static const size_t value = 2; };
plate <> struct nb<7> { static const size_t value = 3; };
```

- Is completely correct and it shows a new technique not seen previously in this book (or in any other equivalent book)
- Has a trivial bug, but the technique is comparable to Section 3.6.6 and thereafter
- Has at least one nontrivial bug, which cannot be easily fixed

A.1.6. Prime Numbers

As an exercise for debugging techniques, we present an example of a non-trivial metafunction `is_prime<N>::value`.

The reader is expected to be able to understand the code, at least in principle, even if some of the algorithm details are not known.

```
#define mxt_EXPLICIT_VALUE(CLASS, TPAR, VALUE)      \
template <> struct CLASS<TPAR> { static const size_t value = VALUE; }

template <size_t N>
struct wheel_prime;

mxt_EXPLICIT_VALUE(wheel_prime, 0,  7);
mxt_EXPLICIT_VALUE(wheel_prime, 1, 11);
mxt_EXPLICIT_VALUE(wheel_prime, 2, 13);
mxt_EXPLICIT_VALUE(wheel_prime, 3, 17);
mxt_EXPLICIT_VALUE(wheel_prime, 4, 19);
mxt_EXPLICIT_VALUE(wheel_prime, 5, 23);
mxt_EXPLICIT_VALUE(wheel_prime, 6, 29);
mxt_EXPLICIT_VALUE(wheel_prime, 7, 31);

template <size_t A>
struct nth_tentative_prime
{
   static const size_t value
      = 30*((A-3)/8) + wheel_prime<(A-3) % 8>::value;
};

mxt_EXPLICIT_VALUE(nth_tentative_prime, 0, 2);
mxt_EXPLICIT_VALUE(nth_tentative_prime, 1, 3);
mxt_EXPLICIT_VALUE(nth_tentative_prime, 2, 5);

template
<
   size_t A,
   size_t N,
   size_t K = nth_tentative_prime<N>::value,
   size_t M = (A % K)
>
struct is_prime_helper
{
   static const bool EXIT = (A < MXT_M_SQ(K));
   static const size_t next_A = (EXIT ? 0 : A);
   static const size_t next_N = (EXIT ? 1 : N+1);
};

template <size_t A, size_t N, size_t K>
struct is_prime_helper<A, N, K, 0>
{
   static const size_t next_A = 0;
   static const size_t next_N = 0;
};
```

```
template <size_t A, size_t N = 0>
struct is_prime
: is_prime<is_prime_helper<A, N>::next_A,
           is_prime_helper<A, N>::next_N>


;

emplate <> struct is_prime<0,0> { static const bool value = false; };
emplate <> struct is_prime<0,1> { static const bool value = true;  };
emplate <> struct is_prime<1,0> { static const bool value = true;  };
emplate <> struct is_prime<2,0> { static const bool value = true;  };
```

.1.7. Typeinfo without RTTI

he typeinfo wrapper in Section 5.3.2 relies on the compiler to generate a runtime identifier for different pes. If this is not available, then a different implementation can be used (at least in some cases):

- Create a traits class `TI<T>` having a single static member function `T f()` that returns `T()`
- Use a `reinterpret_cast` and convert `&TI<T>::f` to `void (*)()`
- Use this latter pointer as index in a `std::map`
- Prove that this works (Hint: step #1 is necessary because of ICF, see page 354; for step #3, See Section 20.3.3 of the Standard)
- Note that pointer-based type identifiers work with static types, while `typeinfo` uses dynamic types, so this technique in general is weaker.

.1.8. Hints and Partial Solutions

e give a solution to Exercise #1, because of its practical importance.

Obviously overload alone doesn't work. We can select BASE but a DERIVED will prefer the template ction (with T=DERIVED it's an exact match).

```
mplate <typename T>
id f(T x)

 printf("hello T");


id f(BASE& x)

 printf("hello BASE");
```

Instead we introduce another layer:

```
plate <typename T>
d f(T x)

g(&x, &x);
```

```
template <typename T>
void g(T* p, void*)
{
   printf("hello T");
}

template <typename T>
void g(T* p, BASE*)
{
   printf("hello BASE-OR-DERIVED");
}
```

Conversion of T* to BASE* is preferred.

Note that the same technique solves also another problem; when invoking a member function on the argument, we can prevent virtual calls:

```
template <typename T>
void g(T* p, void*)
{
   printf("Not a BASE. No call was made.");
}

template <typename T>
void g(T* p, BASE* b)
{
   b->doit();    // always virtual, if BASE::doit is virtual
   p->doit();    // may be virtual or not
   p->T::doit(); // always non-virtual
}
```

Observe that in principle T may *hide* BASE::doit, so the second call won't be virtual:

```
class BASE
{
public:
   virtual void doit();
};

class D1 : public BASE
{
public:
   void doit(int i = 0);
};

class D2 : public D1
{
public:
   virtual void doit();
};
```

APPENDIX B

Bibliography

[1] Alexandrescu A., “Modern C++ Design”, Addison-Wesley

[2] Vandevoorde, D. and Josuttis, N., “C++ Templates: The Complete Guide”, Addison-Wesley

[3] Abrahams D. and Gurtovoy A., “C++ Template Metaprogramming”, Addison-Wesley

[4] Sutter H., “Exceptional C++ Style”, Addison-Wesley

[5] Wilson, “Imperfect C++”, Addison-Wesley

[6] Austern M., “Generic Programming and the STL”, Addison-Wesley

[7] Cline M., “C++ FAQ (lite)”, `http://www.cs.rit.edu/~mjh/docs/c++-faq/`

[8] Meyers S., “Effective STL”

[9] Coplien, J., “Curiously Recurring Template Patterns”, C++ Report, February 1995, pp. 24-27.

[10] Stroustrup, B., “Design and Evolution of C++”, Addison-Wesley, Reading, MA, 1993.

[11] Barton, J.J. and Nackman L.R., “Scientific and Engineering C++”, Addison-Wesley, Reading, MA, 1994.

[12] Veldhuizen, T. “Expression Templates”, C++ Report, June 1995, reprinted in *C++ Gems*, edited by Stanley Lippman.

[13] Myers Nathan C., “A New and Useful Template Technique: Traits”, C++ Report, June 1995, `http://www.cantrip.org/traits.html`

[14] C++ 0x (C++11) Final Committee Draft:

C++11 – ISO/IEC 14882:2011: `$60 from ansi.org`

[15] Meyers S., Effective Modern C++, O’Reilly 2014

[16] Meucci, A. “Risk and Asset Allocation”, Springer 2005

Index

A

Accessors, 486
Accumulation
  accessor, 397
  binary operations, 396
  collect fuction, 395
  elementary operations, 396
  global constant objects, 397
  global helper function, 399
  i-th operation, 397
  multi-layered accumulators, 395
  operator*, 399
  operator+, 398
  op_void, 398
  output, 401
  recursion-stopping specialization, 400
  runtime error, 399
  static recursion, 398
  template parameters, 397
  template rotation, 396
  types, 394
Agglomeration, 455
Algorithms
  accessors, 294
  algebraic requirements, 320
  algorithm I/O, 347
  Barton-Nackman trick, 322
  classification, 280
  *i returns, 276
  iterator (*see* Iterators)
  mimesis, 297
  properties, 293, 296
  range begin...end process, 301
  receipts, 317
  reordering algorithms, 275
  selective copying algorithms, 275
  set partition, 284
  swap-based/copy-based, 277
Angle brackets, 14
Argument pack technique, 442
Argument rotation, 419
Artistic Style (AStyle), 39–40

B

Barton-Nackman trick, 322
Base copy constructor, 16
Bit counting, 528
Bitstring, 463
Body level, 21
Boolean type, 69
Buffer_type algor, 407

C

C++0x
  auto, 517
  decltype, 516
  extern template, 524
  initializers, 520
  lambda expressions, 518
  linking templates, 521
  metafunctions, 516
  typedef syntax, 521
  variadic templates, 525
Chain destructor, 460
Chain starter, 454
Classic patterns
  action(range), 63
  action(value), 63
  boolean type, 69
  bool T::empty() const, 62
  default and
    value initialization, 71
  literal zero, 69
  manipulators, 63
  operators position, 66

Classic patterns (*cont.*)
ptrdiff_t, 57
secret inheritance, 67
size_t, 57
void T::clear(), 62
void T::property(X), 63
void T::swap(T&), 58
X T::base() const, 62
X T::get() const, 62
X T::property() const, 63
Class level, 21
Class template, 6
Code generators
double checked stop
arithmetic/floating point operations, 331
integrize template, 333
loop unrolling, 331
vector-sum, 331
enumeration types, 361
If-Less code (*see* If-Less code)
Nth Minimum, 351
static (*see* Static code generators)
static and dynamic hashing (*see* Static and dynamic hashing)
template factory pattern, 357
ode safety, 72
omma chains, 468
ompareAndSwap, 212
ompile-time polymorphism, 229
onversion functions, 384
-+ templates
angle brackets, 14
class template, 6
compiler error, 9
compile-time constants, 8
division by zero, 9
errors, 8
explicit specialization, 7
function template, 6
function types and function pointers, 16
integer literals, 10
integer operation, 9
metafunction, 7
non-standard language operators, 10
non-template base classes, 19
non-type parameters, 8, 10
parameter list, 6
position, 20
sizeof, 10
sq<double>, 7
static constants, 10
template
arguments, 7
member functions, 11
parameters, 7
typename, 11
type parameters, 8
types and non-types
integers and pointers, 6
universal constructors, 15
Curiously recurring template pattern (CRTP), 233, 383

D

Date format, 528
Debugging templates
compiler bugs, 511
integer computations
references to numeric constants, 509
signed and unsigned types, 508
portability, 513
SFINAE principle, 510
trampolines, 510
types
incomplete types, 504
tag global variables, 507
trapping types, 502
type_info::name, 501
Discriminated unions, 252
Drivers, 404

E

Enum conversion, 367
Exponential unrolling, 114
Extension, 527

F

fgetpos, 415
Forwarding/reference wrappers, 411
fsetpos, 415
Function pointers, 16
Function template, 6
Function types, 16
Functors, 47
accumulation (*see* Accumulation)
buffer_type algor, 407
composition tools
CRTP, 383
helper function, 381
lambda predicate, 379
person/age relationship, 378
template parameter, 381
template-template parameter, 379
drivers, 404
forwarding/reference wrappers, 411
inner template

conversion functions, 384
members conversion
(*see* Members conversion)
interactive algor, 408
self-accumulator algor, 407
static member function, 373
strong/weak, 376

G

get_ptr functions, 386

H

has_abs_method, 176
Heuristic algorithms, 115
Hints and partial solutions, 530

I, J, K

Identical code folding (ICF), 371
If-Less code
enum conversion, 367
self-modifying function, 369
smart constants, 365
Implicit promotion techniques, 221
Inline function, 76
Inner class templates, 33
Input iterator, 233
Integer, 527
Interactive algor, 408
Interfaces
code unification, 229
compile-time polymorphism, 229
copy constructor, 232
dereferenceable entity, 232
emptiness, 230
global functions, 230
input iterator and output iterator, 233
member functions, 230
minimal set of concepts, 232
object returned by operator, 233
static
ambiguous inheritance diagram, 244
base class, 237
BASE<T> object, 234
bitstring class, 243
clone_of metafunction, 241
common errors, 237
compile-time steps, 236
CRTP, 233
declaration, 241
derived class, 234
grouping ideas, 240
improved inheritance diagram, 245
macro, 241
member selection, 248
memberspace problem, 245
PrintSomeNumber function, 235
random algorithms, 242
reference-to-base, 235
static_cast, 233
summable<...> interface, 235
template, 242
"virtual" callback mechanism, 233
type hiding
*begin parameter, 250
boundary crossing with trampolines, 262
generic_t, 261
iterator handling, 250
metafunctions, 250
option_map container, 252, 255
option_parser container, 252, 258
parameterless options, 260
storing object, 251
trampolines, 253
typeinfo wrapper, 254
variant objects, 252
virtual function, 260
variant
opaque object, 264
parameter deletion with virtual calls, 265
with visitors, 266
wrapping
containers, 272
references, 230
Is_PRIME<N> value, 529–530
Iterators
definition, 275
identification, 286
iterator_t, 276
metafunction, 286
requirements, 283
set partition, 284
sort algorithm, 289
value type, 292
wrapping
const_iterators, 304
expander, 305
fake pairs, 311
iterator_expander, 305
multiplier_iterator, 304
operator->, 304
pair_iterator, 311

L

Lambda-constant, 418
Lambda expressions, 518
argument and result deduction, 431
arithmetic operators, 423
arrays, 437

Lambda expressions (*cont.*)
assignments, 424
binary operation, 422
binary operators, 424
binary predicates, 424
concrete binary functions, 423
cos(X+2.0), 417
deducing argument type, 434
deducing result type, 435
elementary lambda object, 418
enum lambda_tag, 424
error log, 427
global/static member functions, 421
lambda-const reference, 417
logical and standard operators, 426
refinements, 429
static cast, 436
unary function, 420
unary operators, 422
mbda_reference, 431
ambda semantics, 378
mbda_wrap, 429
ess and NaN, 320
teral zero, 69
ogger, 444

M

acro expansion rules, 90
embers conversion
enum_const, 391
get<X>(0), 393
nested class template, 388
pointer-to-member, 387
PTR, 388
wrap, 393
mberspace problem, 245
tafunctions, 50
mesis interface, 349
mesis techniques, 344
lti-layered accumulators, 395
lti-layer template factory, 360

N

nespace level, 21
n-inline member functions, 76
n-mutating function, 280
n-template base classes, 19
Minimum, 351

O

Opaque type principle
bitstring, 463
comma, 439
comma chains, 468
growing object concept
chain destruction, 460
chain_traits, 455
console_assert, 454
definition, 445
direct access, 447
inward link, 446
outward link, 446
proxy, 445
pseudo-template notation, 445
SMART_ASSERT, 452
string concatenation, 447
string sum, 444
variations, 461
infix simulation, 473
lambda expressions (*see* Lambda expressions)
operator(), 440
operator[], 443
polymorphic result, 415
range insertions, 466
operator(), 381
Output iterator, 233
Overload resolution
concept traits, 186
fake_incrementable, 222
function pointers
argument dominance, 226
erase, 223
swap, 224
groups
auxiliary functions, 175
clustered implementation, 174
companion global function template, 173
default template implementation, 174
definition, 173
"double-layer" template, 177
has_abs_method, 176
implicit argument promotion, 177
maths<double>, 178
non-template function, 176
operator%, 180
runtime decay, 181
single action, 173
template struct, 173
typedefs, 179

has_conversion<L,R>::L2R, 221
implicit promotion techniques, 221
merging traits
alternative blocks, 195
binary_relation_traits, 194, 197
code rearrangement, 194
derivation and hidden template parameter, 195
flags idiom, 196
"native" operators, 198
static_highest_bit<N>::value, 197
namespace, 223
platform-specific traits, 189
SFINAE
advantage, 200
A<int>, 199
limitations, 216
multiple decisions, 204
Only_If, 206
partial specializations, 220
pointer, 200
returned functors, 208
sizeof, 200
software updates, 212
workarounds, 215
string function
constant-time, 185
const char*, 186
semi-opaque interface, 184
std::string, 186
strlen, 183

■ P, Q

Partial specialization, 26
Placeholder, 489
Pointer paradox, 26
Pointer-to-function type, 16
Preprocessor
include guards, 85
macro expansion rules, 90
PrintSomeNumber function, 235
Push_back, 369

■ R

Refactoring
accessors, 486
compatibility
encapsulation, 480
interface adaptation, 480–481
kernel macros, 481
template sq, 479
ghost, 494
interfaces, 482
placeholder, 489
switch-off, 489
template parameters, 477
trampolines, 484
Reordering minmax algorithm, 282

■ S

Secret inheritance, 67
Self-accumulator algor, 407
SFINAE principle, 510
Skeleton technique, 362
Small object toolkit
hollow types
constraints, 96
instance_of, 93
selector, 94
static value, 95
static assertions
assert legal, 100
Boolean assertions, 98
overloaded operators, 103
pointers, 104
tagging techniques
function pointers, 110
inheritance, 116
overload mechanisms, 107
program compiles, 108
runtime argument, 106
similar signature, 106
static useless argument, 107
tag iteration, 113
tags type, 108
sorted_vector, 272, 274
Specialization, 528
sq function, 404
Static and dynamic hashing
algorithm I/O, 347
ambiguous overload, 345
changing case, 341
character set functions, 337
classic code, 335
macros, 335
mimesis interface, 349
mimesis techniques, 344
template rotation, 336
Static code generators
static_pow, 328
static_raise, 328
strongly typed template, 329
struct deduce, 330
Static interfaces
ambiguous inheritance diagram, 244
base class, 237
BASE<T> object, 234
bitstring class, 243
clone_of metafunction, 241

Static interfaces (*cont.*)
common errors, 237
compile-time steps, 236
CRTP, 233
declaration, 241
derived class, 234
grouping ideas, 240
improved inheritance diagram, 245
macro, 241
member selection, 248
memberspace problem, 245
PrintSomeNumber function, 235
random algorithms, 242
reference-to-base, 235
static_cast, 233
summable<...> interface, 235
template, 242
Static member function, 373
Static programming
compilation complexity
auxiliary class, 125
full recursion, 125
linear complexity, 123
low-complexity, 123
MXT_M_SQ, 124
template instances, 123
hidden template parameters
companion technique, 130
disambiguation, 136
primary template, 133
static recursion, 131
metaprogramming idioms
header files, 127
random elements, 127
static short circuit, 128
struct, 126
variables, 126
preprocessor, 121
traits (*see* Traits)
type containers
agglomerates, 160
arrays, 148
conversions, 164
depth, 152
empty/void, 149
find, 154
front and back, 153
metafunctors, 167
push and pop, 156
returning error, 151
template rotation, 158
typeat, 150
typelist, 149–150
typepair, 149
STL containers, 504
Strong/weak functors, 376
Style, 3
AStyle plugin, 39–40
comments, 41
elements, 39
generality, 48
macros
code appearance, 42
constexpr, 43
infix _M_, 42
integer functions, 42
intercepting, 46
lowercase prefix mxt, 42
macro directive, 43
MXT, 42
namespace directives, 42
metafunctions, 50
multidimensional_vector::empty, 41
namespaces and using declarations, 54
naming convention, 41
symbols, 46
template parameters, 49
Substitution failure is not an error (SFINAE)
advantage, 200
A<int>, 199
limitations, 216
multiple decisions, 204
Only_If, 206
partial specializations, 220
pointer, 200
returned functors, 208
sizeof, 200
software updates, 212
workarounds, 215
Switch-off, 489

T

Tamper, 473
Templates
argument deduction
automatic deduction, 28
built-in C++ cast operator, 24
cast and function template invocation, 24
class template, 28
disambiguation, 23
dummy argument, 28
function templates, 23, 27
non-deduced parameters, 28
non-deducible, 24
non-type arguments, 27
obscure error messages, 28
overload resolution, 29

pattern matching, 27
template-dependent, 24
C++ (*see* C++ templates)
class and typename, 25
classic patterns (*see* Classic patterns)
code safety, 72
compiler assumptions
argument names, 85
bugs, 81
catalog, 83
dirty code modifications, 82
empty destructor addition, 75
error messages, 79
inline function, 76
language features, 83
language-neutral idioms, 74–75
memory-helping tricks, 85
non-standard behavior, 83
standard-conforming compiler, 75
warning, default level, 82
function template, 3
global object, 4
inner class, 33
parameter, 381
position, 20
preprocessor (*see* Preprocessor)
purpose of TMP, 5
rotation, 156
self-adapting, 5
specialization
class templates, 25
compiler error, 31
forward declaration, 31
full specialization, 32
global function template, 22
namespace level, 22, 30
non-deducible types, 23
and overload, 21
partial specialization, 32
sq, 3, 5
squaring numeric type, 4
style conventions (*see* Style)
template name, 24
template-template parameters, 25, 379
transforming sequence, 4
type, 4
visual equivalence, 4
Tentative interface, 267
Traits
concept, 186
definition, 138
ios_char_traits, 139
largest unsigned integer, 140
merging
alternative blocks, 195
binary_relation_traits, 194, 197
code rearrangement, 194
derivation and hidden template parameter, 195
flags idiom, 196
"native" operators, 198
static_highest_bit<N>::value, 197
platform-specific, 189
streambuf template, 139
string function
constant-time, 185
const char*, 186
semi-opaque interface, 184
std::string, 186
strlen, 183
type dismantling, 147
type traits
argument_type, 146
assignable, 145
base class, 143
codes implementation, 142
const objects, 146
definition, 141
DER, 143
immutable, 145
inheritance, 143
intrusive const-ness, 146
operator=, 145
specializations, 144
static constants, 141
Trampolines, 253, 484
boundary crossing with, 262
virtual function, 260
typeinfo wrapper, 530
typename, 11

U

Universal assignments, 15
Universal constructors, 15
Universal copy constructors, 15
Using-namespace declarations, 54

V, W, X, Y, Z

Variadic templates, 525
Virtual function table pointer, 269
Virtual inheritance, 270